Flesh of the Gods

THE RITUAL USE OF HALLUCINOGENS

EDITED BY

PETER T. FURST

PRAEGER PUBLISHERS
New York · Washington

BOOKS THAT MATTER

Published in the United States of America in 1972
by Praeger Publishers, Inc.
111 Fourth Avenue, New York, N.Y. 10003

Third printing, 1974

© 1972 by Praeger Publishers, Inc.
Chapters 6 and 7 © 1972 by R. Gordon Wasson

Library of Congress Catalog Card Number: 78–143970

Printed in the United States of America

Contents

PETER T. FURST

Introduction

Any social phenomenon that achieves a certain significance warrants systematic and dispassionate scientific inquiry, in the hope that we may understand its norms or laws, minimize its potential hazards for individuals and society, and maximize its potential benefits. Hallucinogens—i.e., *nonaddictive* narcotics that apparently act on the mental processes in such a way as to induce temporary "altered states of consciousness," as distinct from the dangerous *addictive* narcotics such as heroin—are clearly such a phenomenon. Yet it is a fact of American life that legal restrictions imposed since the 1960's have seriously impeded legitimate scientific research on these substances while barely affecting uncontrolled experimentation beyond raising its social costs. To a great extent this is the consequence of emotional public reaction to the near-messianic claims made by some researchers for LSD as a kind of panacea, without sufficient attention to its possible risks, and to its ready assimilation as "instant chemical religion" by a youth subculture already alienated from the traditional values of their elders. Ironically, this same older generation itself continues to be firmly committed to the use of a staggering amount of legal, though hardly less potentially dangerous, stimulants and depressants. In any case, even if all the scientific data in the world had declared one or another hallucinogen to be safe within certain limits, it is unlikely that the reaction of the larger society to these "new" drugs would have been very different, for the reason that the mystical and introspective aspects of drug use run counter to certain long-accepted values of Western culture, especially its action- and achievement-oriented North American variant.

In the meantime, notwithstanding horror stories of broken chromosomes, stoned teenagers permanently blinded by staring into the sun,

and LSD-related death leaps from high places, it has become increasingly
clear that the effects of hallucinogens are subject to a wide variety of
extra-pharmacological variables that require rigorous scientific control.
Like any human artifact, these potent substances—whether synthesized
in the laboratory, like LSD, or collected from nature, like morning-glory
seeds (whose active principles are somewhat similar to LSD)—have
potential for good and evil. Which it is to be depends as much on who
uses them, in what contexts, for what purposes, and under what kinds
of control as it does on the substance itself.

These would not seem to be such revolutionary conclusions and indeed
should have been widely accepted had there been systematic study of
the numerous non-Western * cultural contexts in which hallucinogens
have been used for centuries. For, as Harvard botanist Richard Evans
Schultes points out in these pages, hallucinogens have been part and
parcel of man's cultural baggage for thousands of years; moreover, as
the other contributors to this volume document, hallucinogenic or psychoactive plants have been of great significance in the ideology and
religious practices of a wide variety of peoples the world over, and in
some traditional cultures continue to play such a role today. The native
peoples of the New World, especially those of Middle and South America,
alone utilized nearly a hundred different botanical species for their
psychoactive properties, not counting the scores of plants used for
the brewing of alcoholic beverages to induce ritual intoxication. Anthropologist Weston La Barre (whose approach to the origins of religion
is thoroughly naturalistic and strongly oriented toward the Freudian
view of man) attributes this phenomenon to a kind of cultural programming for personal ecstatic experience reaching back to the American
Indians' ideological roots in the shamanistic religion of the Upper
Paleolithic and Mesolithic hunting and gathering cultures of northeastern Asia. If La Barre is right—and the cumulative evidence tends to
support him—this would take the practice and, more important, its
philosophical underpinnings back at least fifteen or twenty thousand
years, an estimate that if anything may be too conservative.

Perhaps the discovery that certain substances found in nature help
man to move beyond his everyday experiences to "Otherworlds" and the
institutionalizing of these personal ecstatic experiences into an ideological
and ritual framework accepted by the group as a whole (i.e., religion,
but not necessarily an organized cult) goes back almost to the beginnings
of human culture. Shamanism as a universal *Ur*-religion, which eventually

* In the cultural, not the geographic sense—i.e., societies that, like those of the
Indians of the Western Hemisphere, neither belong to the Judeo-Christian religious
and ethical traditions nor trace the mainstream of their ideas to Greco-Roman or
northern European sources.

gave rise to various cults, including the great world religions, must reach deep into the Paleolithic—at least as far back as the oldest known deliberate interments of the dead by Neanderthal man, *ca.* 100,000 years ago, and perhaps hundreds of thousands of years earlier. The striking similarities between the basic premises and motifs of shamanism the world over suggest great antiquity as well as the universality of the creative unconscious of the human psyche.

Wherever shamanism is still encountered today, whether in Asia, Australia, Africa, or North and South America, the shaman functions fundamentally in much the same way and with similar techniques—as guardian of the psychic and ecological equilibrium of his group and its members, as intermediary between the seen and unseen worlds, as master of spirits, as supernatural curer, etc. He seeks to control the weather and to ensure the benevolence of ancestor spirits and deities. Where hunting continues to have importance (ideologically or economically), he ensures, by means of his special powers and his unique psychological capacity to transcend the human condition and pass freely back and forth through the different cosmological planes (as these are conceived in the particular world view of his group), the renewal of game animals and, indeed, of all nature.

I would not wish to give the impression that all scholars are agreed on the antiquity of the "psychedelic phenomenon" in shamanism. The well-known historian of religion Mircea Eliade, for one, has suggested that the use of narcotics and alcohol to trigger ecstatic trance states represents a relatively recent degeneration of shamanic technique and that only the "spontaneous" religious experience, without the use of chemicals, can be considered "pure" (Eliade, 1964:401). In fact, however, it is difficult to distinguish phenomenologically between so-called spontaneous religious experiences (often the result of extreme physiological or psychological stress) and those that are pharmacologically induced. In any event, the linguistic, archaeological, historical, and ethnographic evidence tends to support the view of some ethnobotanists and anthropologists, this writer included, that the widespread contemporary use of botanical hallucinogens, fermented beverages, and tobacco in New World shamanism does in fact have its remote origins in Old World Paleolithic and Mesolithic shamanism, and that the Paleo-Indian immigrants into North America came culturally predisposed toward a conscious exploration of their new environment for psychotropic plants. This view is supported by the fact that virtually all hallucinogenic plants are extremely bitter and unpleasant to the taste, if not actually nauseating, and that many species require complex pharmacological preparation in order to be effective, thus reducing the likelihood of chance discovery in the course of the everyday food quest.

If R. Gordon Wasson is right (and many scholars find his arguments
—not to be confused with John Allegro's fanciful assertions in *The
Sacred Mushroom and the Cross*—persuasive), on linguistic grounds alone
we can assume that the ritual use of the *Amanita muscaria,* or fly
agaric, mushroom must go back at least seven thousand years, eventually
spreading from Siberia to India. There it came to be immortalized
in the second millennium B.C. as the divine Soma of the Rig-Veda of the
ancient Indo-Europeans. There is reason to believe that the ambrosia
imbibed by the gods and heroes of Greek mythology was likewise a
decoction of *Amanita muscaria,* which gives the Mediterranean of the
first millennium B.C. something in common with Siberia, where travelers
and ethnographers in the nineteenth and early twentieth centuries
observed the ritual use of the sacred red-capped mushroom by shamans
of hunting and reindeer-herding tribes.

As for New World mushrooms, from archaeological, historical, and
ethnographic evidence we know that various species of psychotropic
fungi have been in uninterrupted use in Middle America for at least
three thousand years. It is also becoming evident that the ritual ingestion of hallucinogenic mushrooms—known to the Aztecs as *teonanacatl,*
or god's flesh—was far more widespread in ancient Mesoamerica than
is suggested by the limited distribution of archaeological mushroom
effigy stones in southeastern Mexico and Guatemala. There was also
apparently a shamanistic "mushroom cult" in western Mexico, where
mushroom representations dating to *ca.* A.D. 100–200, have been found,
and where a tradition of mushroom use among neighboring non-Huichol
people in the state of Jalisco still persists among the contemporary
Huichol. Recently also, two students of Michael D. Coe at Yale University, Allen Turner and Barbara Rich, discovered a present-day ritual
use of hallucinogenic mushrooms among the Chol-speaking Maya, who
live near the ancient Maya ceremonial center of Palenque, Chiapas
(M. D. Coe, personal communication). Surprisingly, in view of the many
decades of intensive Maya studies, this is the first report of ritual
ingestion of psychotropic fungi among any of the modern descendants
of the builders of one of the most advanced civilizations of ancient
America. Considering the persistence of other pre-Hispanic traditions
among Maya-speakers, the present-day custom may well have its origins
in Classic or Post-Classic Maya ritual; perhaps, as Coe suggests, the
artist-priests of Palenque itself found inspiration for their magnificent
creations in mushroom-induced supernatural visions.

For peyote there is evidence in the pre-Columbian funerary art of
western Mexico dating back almost two thousand years. The sacred
morning-glory, whose hallucinogenic seeds were known to the Aztecs as
ololiuqui, is not only represented in murals at and near Teotihuacán

(very prominently in the "Paradise of Tlaloc" mural at Tepantitla [A.D. 400–500?]), but appears on many painted pottery vessels of the Teotihuacán civilization (Furst, 1970). North of Mexico the Mescal or Red Bean cult, involving the seeds of the *Sophora secundiflora* shrub, may well be as old as six or seven thousand years, judging from archaeological evidence found in Texas caves. These same rock shelters also contain numerous esoteric polychrome paintings of considerable complexity, which Newcomb (1967:65–80) attributes to shamans who depicted their hallucinogenic trance experiences.

This interpretation of archaeological petroglyphs finds some support in analogous ethnographic data from South America, for Reichel-Dolmatoff (1967) reports that contemporary animal art on the rock faces of the Vaupés region of Colombia is the work of shamans in their supernatural trance encounters with the Master of Animals. In this connection, it is of interest that the same author demonstrates in the following pages a direct relationship between common South American Tukano art symbols and the psychedelic *yajé* experience. We do not, of course, know when *yajé* was discovered, but for another widespread South American custom, the inhaling of hallucinogenic snuff, we have evidence dating to 1800 B.C. in the form of a whalebone snuffing tablet and birdbone snuffing tube found by Junius Bird in the preceramic Peruvian coastal site of Huaca Prieta. *San Pedro (Trichocereus pachanoi),* a mescaline-containing cactus of the Cereus family whose ritualized use by contemporary Peruvian folk healers Douglas Sharon describes, is depicted on ceremonial and burial textiles of the Chavín culture of Peru, which flourished in the first millennium B.C. At least three thousand years before Americans were lighting up annually over 530 billion cigarettes, American Indians were using tobacco strictly for ritual purposes. As anthropologist Johannes Wilbert documents in this book, some Indian societies still use tobacco to achieve states of altered consciousness and ecstasy similar to those induced elsewhere with peyote, mushrooms, morning-glories, or, for that matter, LSD. It is not certain how long sub-Saharan African peoples have known the hallucinogenic *iboga* plant, whose contemporary role in Fang culture is described by anthropologist James W. Fernandez, but its use doubtless predates the first European mention of it in the nineteenth century.

What is new, then, is not the discovery of substances in nature that act powerfully on the mind and are capable of triggering visual, auditory, olfactory, and tactile sensations which the user experiences as supernatural phenomena belonging to the "Otherworld," the realm of spirits. As Schultes says, what is new is only their fascination for Western man and the medical, legal, and social consequences of their use by a considerable proportion of the population—by no means all of them under thirty. If I seem to be implying that when middle-class Americans of whatever age make pilgrimages to Oaxaca, Mexico, to partake of the mysterious powers of the sacred mushroom they are only doing what Mexican Indians have been doing for thousands of years, that is not my intention, nor is it the theme of this book. Undeniably, there are both external and internal aspects of hallucinogenic drug use in contemporary Western culture that recall elements of their use in traditional non-Western magico-religious contexts. Some of these similarities —"spontaneous ritualization" (see footnote, p. 229), for example, or the well-known custom of sharing, which reminds one of the institutionalized sharing of peyote among the Huichol—may be superficial. But the observations of the Czechoslovakian psychoanalyst Stanislav Grof, among others, are more significant. The work of Grof at the Psychiatric Research Center in Prague from 1960 to 1967 involved some fifty patients who underwent a total of 2500 individual LSD sessions in a project designed to study the possibility of the use of LSD for personality diagnostics and therapy of psychogenic disorders. In the course of these sessions patients reported religious experiences and phenomena that, according to Grof, resembled the basic tenets initially of the Judeo-Christian, and then increasingly of the Oriental religions (e.g., bloody sacrifice, suffering and agony leading to death, rebirth and some great good for mankind, cosmic union, eternal circulation of life, etc.) as well as some familiar elements from American Indian religions, particularly those of sacrifice for the ultimate good of man and the gods.* The best-known case here would be Aztec religion, but the theme of sacrifice from which flows a great good for mankind is a prominent feature in many other aboriginal New World religions (as, indeed, in Christianity). Reichel-Dolmatoff's account of the mythic origin of *yajé* in these pages is an example; another is the symbolic killing and dismemberment of the Deer-Peyote and the sharing of its "flesh" on the Huichol peyote hunt, described in my article.

To be sure, Grof's experimental drug therapy involved mature patients and rigorously controlled administrations of LSD "in the framework of psychoanalytically oriented psychotherapy" (Grof, 1970a:57), but ordinary users have reported similar experiences, a phenomenon that has inspired the extravagant claim that the LSD trip is a "religious pilgrimage." The observed connection between the psychedelic experience and religious ecstasy notwithstanding, there are fundamental differences

---

* Although Grof's subjects were generally well educated, they were not personally familiar—certainly not in any depth—with the content or symbols of those non-Western religions. Their common experiences are therefore of more than passing interest, not only for the origins of religion but for our understanding of the unconscious; Grof, for one, came to feel that the Prague study validated the Jungian approach more than it did the Freudian.

that set the traditional magico-religious use of hallucinogens apart. These have to do above all with a basic function of the psychedelic experience in non-Western cultures—to facilitate the integration of the individual into the total society and the values by which it lives, as opposed to the association of hallucinogens in Western cultures with alienation and rejection of the corrupted values of the parental generation. This aspect of the sacred hallucinogens emerges especially clearly from Reichel-Dolmatoff's essay: the Indian, by taking the hallucinogen, experiences first death and then rebirth "in a state of wisdom"—i.e., as a full-fledged member of his tribe. Having seen and experienced the supernaturals and the mythological events of tribal tradition with his own eyes and other senses in the yajé trance, "he is . . . convinced of the truth of his religious system."

This is precisely the purpose of the Huichol peyote quest: "Eat peyote," the officiating shaman urges his companions, "so that you will learn what it is to be Huichol." Be it mushrooms, yajé, peyote, tobacco, or *iboga,* the psychoactive plant in the traditional culture transports the user to a "land beyond," whose geography he already knows because he has heard it described innumerable times before; what he finds "on the other side" substantiates the validity of tradition—i.e., the values of the parental generation. He already has the answers, so that for him the psychedelic experience is in part, at least, a quest for their confirmation. It is the means to a known end, not, as for so many youthful devotees of the Western cult of psychedelia, an end in itself.

This, of course, goes to the heart of the matter—who uses drugs and for what purpose in Western as opposed to non-Western, or traditional, society. In *The Making of the Counter Culture* (1969), Theodore Roszak agrees that the psychedelic experience can bear "significant fruit when rooted in the soil of a mature and cultivated mind" (or, one might add, the mind of a young Indian who is a full and conscious participant in his ancestral culture). The danger, he argues, lies in the fact that the experience has been

> laid hold of by a generation of youngsters who are pathetically a-cultural and who often bring nothing to the experience but a vacuous yearning. They have, in adolescent rebellion, thrown off the corrupted culture of their elders and, along with that soiled bath water, the very body of the Western heritage—at best, in favor of exotic traditions they only marginally understand; at worst, in favor of an introspective chaos in which the seventeen or eighteen years of their unformed lives float like atoms in a void.

Roszak's indictment may be too sweeping—one cannot ignore the elements of a typical crisis cult in the psychedelic movement among the young, and certainly not all seventeen- and eighteen-year-olds, even among those who use drugs or smoke pot, are "pathetically a-cultural" or reject all of Western heritage (on the contrary, they tend to stress, at least theoretically, its "lost virtues")—but his message is valid: you get out of the drug experience only what you put into it. The "Otherworld" from which you seek illumination is, after all, only your own psyche. If hallucinogens such as LSD function as "very powerful unspecified amplifier(s) of mental processes" (Grof, 1970b), it follows that an intellectual void is not likely to be miraculously filled with instant wisdom, of either the Eastern or the Western kind, through the use of chemicals, no matter how pretty the images. And, as drug users know, the images are by no means always pretty.

Despite these fundamental differences, the role of hallucinogens in societies other than ours has considerable relevance to our own time and place. If nothing else, understanding the function and the social and physiological effects of the abundant sacred hallucinogenic pharmacopoeia among non-Western peoples may, on the one hand, help lower the level of public hysteria about real or fancied dangers in the use of hallucinogens and, on the other, make drug users themselves more aware of spurious versus genuine culture. Ideally, it may also help in the formulation of more realistic and intelligent drug legislation. The fact is that we still know far too little of this important area of the study of man. More than four centuries after Sahagún described mushroom and peyote ceremonies in Mexico, and after a century of anthropological field work among so-called primitive peoples, many of whom had a wide knowledge of psychoactive plants in their environment, we are only just beginning to consider the real cultural, psychological, historical, and pharmacological significance of these potent substances. But while the specialized scientific literature on the chemistry and physiological effects of hallucinogens has grown by leaps and bounds, with the exception of the North American Indian peyote cult (properly the Native American Church), relatively little attention has been paid to those societies that long ago institutionalized the psychedelic phenomenon—with ritual rather than legal controls—and that have employed hallucinogens for centuries without the dire social and individual consequences so often ascribed to sustained use of these narcotics. There is an obvious need, then, to illuminate the role of the cultural variable in the use of hallucinogens, the important and often decisive parts these drugs have played and continue to play in a variety of sociocultural contexts (especially in religious belief and ritual and the preservation of cultural independence and integrity), and the part they might have played historically in the remote origins of religion itself.

Appreciation of the influence of the cultural variable on the nature of psychedelic experiences is especially desirable because the characteristic fragmentation of scientific research into discrete categories limits the value of conclusions derived exclusively from laboratory experiments. For example, research that concentrates solely on a single, artificially isolated "active principle," such as mescaline from among the thirty-odd alkaloids identified in peyote, or THC from *Cannabis,* may lose significance in light of such phenomena as the little-understood interaction between various chemical constituents of living plants and, equally important, the interplay between psychopharmacological effects and the cultural context and culturally conditioned individual and communal expectations. The cultural factor becomes even more relevant in view of suspicions by some researchers that hallucinogens may act primarily as triggers for expected experiential phenomena, rather than actually themselves causing these phenomena. In a forthcoming book, Weil (1972), for example, suggests that the pharmacological action of these drugs may constitute a neutral effect that can be interpreted negatively or positively, depending on the social-psychological, idiosyncratic, or cultural situation. The ecstatic trance of a Huichol who feels himself to be in touch with the supernaturals, then, would be a particular culturally conditioned interpretation of a pharmacological stimulus that in a very different context—the surreptitious spiking of someone's food or drink with LSD, for instance—might be interpreted only as an especially violent form of food poisoning accompanied by mental disorientation.

This book, like the public lecture series at the University of California at Los Angeles in the spring of 1970 on which it is based, is intended to provide the psychedelic phenomenon with some of its essential cultural and historical dimensions. Without such a perspective, any conclusions—for or against—are incomplete and to some degree irrelevant. Of the ten papers included here, seven were first presented, in somewhat different form, in the lecture series and were subsequently expanded and refined for publication. These are the essays by William A. Emboden, James W. Fernandez, Weston La Barre, Richard Evans Schultes, and R. Gordon Wasson, as well as my own paper on peyote. The other three chapters, by Johannes Wilbert, Gerardo Reichel-Dolmatoff, and Douglas Sharon, were solicited from their authors because each presents new and unique material of significance to our understanding of the traditional cultural context of psychotropic substances.

In designing the original lecture series and, subsequently, this book, the editor was faced with two problems: (1) what may we legitimately include under the catch-all rubric "hallucinogen" without offending the sensibilities of botanists and pharmacologists? and (2) how can we avoid the appearance of overemphasizing one geographic or cultural region of the world—to wit, the Western Hemisphere? For example, is tobacco a hallucinogen? We know that American Indians, who for better or worse gave tobacco to the world, used it exclusively in their sacred and ritual enterprises and never just for recreation—at least not until the white man corrupted its original purpose. We also know that, as noted earlier, tobacco was widely employed by Indians to induce trance states akin to those triggered by the "true" hallucinogens, such as the psilocybe and fly agaric mushrooms, the *Banisteria* vine, or *iboga*. Some authorities suspect—and it may yet be confirmed pharmacologically—that tobacco, which belongs to the same botanical family as the hallucinogenic *Datura* (e.g., "Jimson weed"), does indeed contain "mind-altering" components, which may vary in significance from species to species. But what actually decided us in favor of its inclusion here was the fact that, despite hundreds of published references to ceremonial smoking and accounts of tobacco-induced trances from Columbus' time to the present, there was not one ethnographically reliable, in-depth examination of the tobacco-shaman complex, or any thorough treatment of its underlying mythology in an indigenous culture. In this respect Professor Wilbert's paper must be considered a real breakthrough.

As for *Cannabis*, it may not in any of its forms rank with peyote, yajé, mushrooms, or the various psychotropic snuffs as a traditional "vehicle of ecstasy," but its confirmed substitution for peyote in certain curing rituals of Mexican Indians alone would justify its treatment in these pages. Besides, an ethnobotanical and historical review of its cultural role through the ages cannot help but be useful in the contemporary debate over its merits or demerits as a "social drug." With respect to the apparently disproportionate attention paid to New World hallucinogens, the reason lies in the cultural reality: although, as Professor Schultes notes, the Old World probably contains no fewer hallucinogenic species than the New, it is a fact that the New World outstrips the Old by ten to one in the number actually employed by its human inhabitants.

I am indebted to Miss Lois E. Smith, Director, Department of Social Sciences, and Mr. Edwin C. Monsson, Coordinator, Special Programs, University Extension, UCLA, for having made the original lecture series possible; to the contributors for sharing their considerable knowledge with a wider audience than is usually reached by specialized scientific journals; to Michael B. Sullivan for his literate English translation of Professor Reichel-Dolmatoff's chapter from the original Spanish; to Audrey Zielonka for her diligent typing of the final manuscript; and to my wife, Dee, for her enthusiastic participation in field research among the Huichol and in the preparation of this volume. To all of them my appreciation and gratitude.

FLESH OF THE GODS

1

RICHARD EVANS SCHULTES

An Overview of Hallucinogens in the Western Hemisphere

> The savage in the jungle beneath a sheltering roof of leaves and the native of the storm-swept island secures through these drugs a greater intensity of life. . . . Various are the motives which induce civilized men to seek a transient sensation of pleasure. The potent influence of these substances leads us on the one hand into the darkest depths of human passion, ending in mental instability, physical misery and degeneration, and on the other to hours of ecstasy and happiness or a tranquil and meditative state of mind.
> —LEWIS LEWIN, 1964

> The use of hallucinogens has been described as one of the major advances of this century . . . they have had a massive impact upon psychiatry, and may produce marked changes in our society. The violent reaction for and against the hallucinogens suggests that even if these compounds are not universally understood and approved of, they will neither be forgotten nor neglected.
> —A. HOFFER and H. OSMOND, 1967

There can be little doubt that the second half of the twentieth century will be remembered as a time when "mind-altering," or hallucinogenic, substances came into increasing use, serious as well as frivolous, in sophisticated Western societies. Yet Western civilization's new-found ways of attaining the "mystic experience" by altering the chemical homeostasis of the body represents nothing new; for thousands of years, primitive societies the world over have used psychotomimetic plants for purposes of religious ritual, divination, or magic. Along with the current resurgence of interest in astrology, the occult, and extrasensory perception, this development in Western

3

society may be a temporary phenomenon, but it is nevertheless very real; here and there it recalls, at least superficially, the so-called primitive use of hallucinogenic substances. A knowledge of how primitive societies have employed these agents in their long experience with them may help us to understand their role in our own culture.

As is true in any fast-developing field of research, an extensive nomenclature has grown up for narcotics that are capable of inducing various kinds of hallucination. Lewin called them the *phantastica,* although he recognized that this term "does not cover all that I should wish to convey." These agents have also been referred to as *eidetics, hallucinogens, phantasticants, psychodelics, psychelytics, psychotica, psychoticents, psychogens, psychotomimetics, psychodysleptics,* and *schizogens.* The most widely used term in the United States is the etymologically unsound and biologically inaccurate word *psychodelic,* which, through popular usage, has now acquired secondary and tertiary meanings (e.g., "psychodelic music," "psychodelic colors," etc.). Although no single word is wholly satisfactory, I prefer the term *hallucinogen,* which applies, it seems to me, more widely and descriptively than most of the others.

Unlike psychotropic drugs that act normally only to calm or to stimulate (tranquilizers, caffeine, alcohol, etc.), the hallucinogens act on the central nervous system to bring about a dreamlike state, marked, as Hofmann has noted, by extreme alteration in the sphere of experience, in the perception of reality, changes even of space and time and in consciousness of self. They invariably induce a series of visual hallucinations, often in kaleidoscopic movement, usually in brilliant and rich colors, and frequently accompanied by auditory, tactile, olfactory, and gustatory hallucinations and a variety of concomitant sensations (synesthesia). Then there are other plants, put to special uses in primitive societies, that apparently induce only auditory hallucinations. One of the difficulties in delimiting these hallucinogens results from the often cloudy distinction in the terminology of psychologists between *hallucination* and *illusion.** In any event, I believe that Hofmann's definition of *psychotomimetic* aptly covers, for our general purposes, both *psychotomimetic* and *hallucinogen:*

a substance which produces changes in thought, perception and mood, occurring alone or in conjunction with each other, without causing major disturbances of the autonomic nervous system—i.e., clouding of consciousness or other serious disability. High doses generally elicit hallucinations. Disorientation, memory disturbance, hyperexcitation or stupor, and even narcosis

* From the point of view of the indigenous culture, such distinctions are of course meaningless, since the drug-induced experience is regarded as neither "hallucination" nor "illusion" but as another form of reality—indeed, often the ultimate reality.—ED.

occur only when excess dosages are administered and are, therefore, not characteristic.

The effects of many hallucinogens are so extraordinary that most of these plants early acquired an exalted place in primitive society, often becoming sacred and the object of direct worship. In almost all primitive cultures, sickness and death are believed to be due to interference from supernatural spheres. For this reason, the psychic effects of drugs are often far more important in primitive medical practice than the purely physical ones. Consequently, hallucinogens above all other plants are found to be closely connected with magic and sorcery in the treatment of disease and the struggle against death, and in related religious observances.

We now know that the divinity residing in these special plants is chemical in nature, but the ethnobotanist investigating the use of narcotics in primitive cultures must never lose sight of the native's interpretation of his "magical" or "sacred" plants. To ignore or deprecate his views may doom the most meticulously planned scientific inquiry to failure.*

Since most hallucinogens are of plant origin, the first approach to any study of these "mind-altering" substances must obviously be botanical. A sound understanding of their value and effectiveness, their toxicity or innocuousness, requires, first, evaluation of their botanical identity. Concomitantly, their chemical composition and physiological effects must be clarified before behavioral study can yield significant results.

To begin with, it should be noted that of the vast number of plant species—variously estimated at from 200,000 to 800,000—only a few have ever been utilized as hallucinogens. There are many more species with hallucinogenic properties than primitive societies have used to alter the mind. Some may not have been discovered by even the most thoroughly inquisitive man living in close association with his vegetal environment. Some may have proved too toxic for safe employment. Whatever the reason, it is interesting that, although psychoactive species are scattered widely throughout the plant kingdom, those species that are employed purposefully as hallucinogens appear to be concentrated among the fungi and the angiosperms, while the bacteria, algae, lichens, bryophytes, ferns,

* In this connection, John Harshberger, who first employed the term *ethnobotany*, wrote more than seventy years ago: "It is of importance . . . to seek out these primitive races and ascertain the plants which they have found available in their economic life, in order that perchance the valuable properties they have utilized in their wild life may fill some vacant niche in our own." Although a number of native "folk medicines" have been found to be highly effective and have been adopted by Western medicine, clearly much more remains to be done in this field.

and gymnosperms have been conspicuously poor or lacking in hallucinogenically utilized species.

Another interesting phenomenon is that for some reason the New World cultures have employed many more species of plants hallucinogenically than the Old World. The reason certainly cannot be botanical, for there is no evidence to suggest that the floras of the Eastern Hemisphere are poorer (or richer) in plants possessing hallucinogenic constituents than those of the Western half of the globe.

La Barre, in the concluding chapter of this volume, explains the interesting disparity between the two hemispheres on a cultural basis. The American Indians, he believes, basically preserved as their religion the shamanistic ideology of ancient hunting peoples, whose "epistemological touchstone for reality was direct psychic experience of the forces of nature." Substantial portions of this old shamanism survived even in societies that turned to sedentary agriculture and civilization. They sought to ensure this state of union with the natural and supernatural environment by means of psychotropic or hallucinogenic plants. In the Old World, on the other hand, the plants became progressively less important as the old shamanistic religion of the hunters became submerged and suppressed by new religious systems adapted to the demands of agricultural, feudal, and urban society, until today these formerly sacred substances are but dimly recognizable (for example, in fairy tales and folklore) as "psychedelic vehicles of divinity." That, at least in part, helps to explain the relative abundance of known botanical agents employed for ecstasy in the Americas.

Hallucinogenically active plant principles may be grouped roughly into two general sections: the *non-nitrogenous* and the *nitrogen-containing* constituents.

The nitrogen-containing compounds include the most important and the largest number of hallucinogenic agents. Most of them are alkaloids or related substances and the majority are biogenetically derived from the indolic amino acid tryptophane. They may be subdivided into several important groups: (1) β-carbolines, (2) ergolines, (3) indoles, (4) isoquinolines, (5) isoxazoles, (6) β-phenylethylamines, (7) quinolizidines, (8) tropanes, and (9) tryptamines.

The non-nitrogenous compounds are much fewer and play a lesser role, but they are the active principles in at least two well-known hallucinogens: dibenzopyrans and phenylpropenes. Other compounds, such as catechols and alcohols, may be responsible for hallucinogenic or similarly psychoactive effects in some minor and still poorly understood plants.

It must also be borne in mind that there are hallucinogenic plants utilized in primitive societies which have not yet been identified botanically and that there are others, botanically known, for which we have no knowledge concerning the chemical identity of the active principle.

The major New World hallucinogens may be discussed according to a botanical, chemical, ethnological, or geographical classification. For the present purpose, it may be most advantageous to group them together under plant families arranged in strict alphabetic order without consideration of their phylogenetic relationships.

AGARICACEAE (AGARIC FAMILY)

Conocybe, Panaeolus, Psilocybe, Stropharia

The Spanish conquerors of Mexico found the Indians practicing several religious cults in which deities were worshiped with the aid of hallucinogenic plants. One of the most important—and to the Spaniards perhaps the most loathsome—was the cult of *teonanacatl,* the Nahuatl name for mushrooms, meaning "flesh of the gods." There is no doubt that the mushrooms were used or about how they were employed, since the Spanish chroniclers railed against this pagan ritual vehemently and frequently. To the Indian mind, nothing that Christianity offered was comparable to this revered form of plant life, with its hallucinatory powers, so the mushrooms represented a great obstacle to the spread of the newly arrived European religion.

The mushroom cult appears to have deep roots in native tradition. Frescoes have been found in central Mexico dating back to *ca.* A.D. 300 with designs that seem to put mushroom worship in this part of Mesoamerica back at least that far. Much more ancient—at least as far back as 300–500 B.C.—are the remarkable archaeological artifacts now known as "mushroom stones" that have been unearthed in considerable numbers from Late Formative sites in highland Guatemala and southeastern Mexico. Some types may date even to 1000 B.C. These effigies comprise an upright stem with a manlike or animal face (often that of the jaguar), crowned with an umbrella-shaped top.

One of the first European reports of the sacred Mexican mushrooms —in the monumental *Historia de las cosas de Nueva España,* also known as the Florentine Codex, by Fray Bernardino de Sahagún, a Spanish cleric who wrote between 1547 and 1569—refers to *nanacatl* in several places. According to Sahagún, there are mushrooms "which are harmful and intoxicate like wine" so that those who eat them "see visions, feel a faintness of heart and are provoked to lust." The natives ate the mushrooms with honey, and when

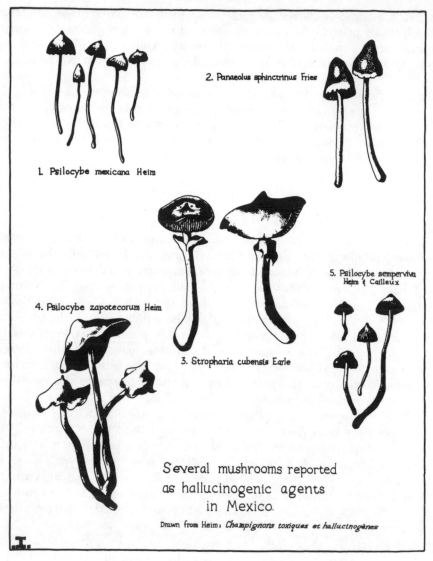

2. Panaeolus sphinctrinus Fries

1. Psilocybe mexicana Heim

5. Psilocybe semperviva Heim (Cailleux

4. Psilocybe zapotecorum Heim

3. Stropharia cubensis Earle

Several mushrooms reported as hallucinogenic agents in Mexico.

Drawn from Heim: *Champignons toxiques et hallucinogènes*

Fig. 1.

. . . they begin to be excited by them, start dancing, singing, weeping. Some do not want to eat but sit down . . . and see themselves dying in a vision; others see themselves being eaten by a wild beast, others imagine that they are capturing prisoners of war, that they are rich, that they possess many slaves, that they had committed adultery and were to have their heads crushed for the offense . . . and when the intoxication has passed, they talk over amongst themselves the visions which they have seen.

Several reports from the early years after the Conquest tell of the deep importance of the intoxicating mushrooms to Mexican religion and life. For example, these sacred fungi were served at the coronation feast of Moctezuma in 1502. That the use of the hallucinogenic mushrooms survived all attempts by the Spanish friars to suppress the indigenous cults is clear from the writings of such seventeenth-century clerics as Jacinto de la Serna, Hernando Ruíz de Alarcón, and others, who composed long treatises deploring the use of mushrooms and other hallucinogenic plants in pagan rites and "idolatries."

By far the most trustworthy early record of hallucinogenic mushrooms is that of Dr. Francisco Hernández (1651), physician to the King of Spain, who spent a number of years in the field studying the medicinal lore of the Mexican Indians. He wrote of three kinds of intoxicating mushrooms that were worshiped. Those known as *teyhuintli,* he reported, caused

> not death but a madness that on occasion is lasting, of which the symptom is a kind of uncontrolled laughter . . . these are deep yellow, acrid, and of a not displeasing freshness. There are others again which, without inducing laughter, bring before the eye all sorts of things, such as wars and the likeness of demons. Yet others there are not less desired by princes for their festivals and banquets, and these fetch a high price. With night-long vigils are they sought, awesome and terrifying. This kind is tawny and somewhat acrid.

Notwithstanding these very specific historical references, no mushrooms utilized as a hallucinogen in magico-religious rites were found and identified botanically in the first four centuries after the Conquest of Mexico. In 1915, Safford suggested that *teonanacatl* was actually not a mushroom at all but the peyote cactus. A dried mushroom and a dried peyote, the argument went, shriveled up and looked alike. It was presumed that the botanical knowledge of both Indians and Spanish chroniclers—including a medical doctor fully trained in botany—was deficient, and that the natives had misled the Spaniards.

This "identification" was widely accepted, despite several objections that *teonanacatl* was a dung-fungus still revered by the Indians of Oaxaca. Actual specimens associated with divinatory rites were collected in the late 1930's, first by Roberto Weitlaner and later by B. P. Reko and myself. These proved to be *Panaeolus sphinctrinus.* Another mushroom that I collected as hallucinogenic was later identified and reported as *Stropharia cubensis.* Both were found in use among the Mazatec of northeastern Oaxaca.

Later intensive studies by well-qualified teams of specialists, especially the Wassons, Heim, Singer, and Guzmán, have uncovered the use, mainly in Oaxaca, of a number of species of *Psilocybe, Conocybe,* and *Stropharia.* Species of *Psilocybe* and *Stropharia* are the most important, and the most significant of the many hallucinogenic species are apparently *Psilocybe mexicana, P. caerulescens* var. *mazatecorum, P. caerulescens* var. *nigripes, P. yungensis, P. mixaeensis, P. Hoogshagenii, P. aztecorum, P. muriercula,* and *Stropharia cubensis.* Recent investigators have failed to find *Panaeolus sphinctrinus* employed, but it must be remembered not only that different practitioners of the cult of the sacred mushroom have their own favorite species but that they tend to vary the species they use according to seasonal availability and the precise purpose for which the narcotic is to be taken.

Psilocybe mexicana is probably the most important species utilized hallucinogenically in Mexico. It is a small, tawny inhabitant of wet pastures. *Psilocybe aztecorum,* of lesser importance, is known by the Indians as "child of the waters." *Psilocybe zapotecorum,* found in marshy ground, is called "crown of thorn"; *P. caerulescens* var. *mazatecorum* is called "landslide" mushroom; and *P. caerulescens* var. *nigripes* has a native epithet meaning "mushroom of superior reason." The strongest species hallucinogenically appears to be *Stropharia cubensis.*

Field work has now established the hallucinogenic use of mushrooms in divinatory and other magico-religious ceremonies in at least nine tribes of modern Mexico, probably centered among the Mazatecs in northeastern Oaxaca. Among the Mazatecs, the mushroom ritual comprises an all-night ceremony with prayers and long repetitive chants incorporating ancient pagan and Christian elements. The shaman is often a woman. There is not infrequently an elaborate curing ritual during the ceremony.

The phytochemistry of the sacred mushrooms has been of extraordinary significance. A white crystalline substance, psilocybine, isolated from several species and proved to be highly active as a hallucinogen, is an acidic phosphoric acid ester of 4-hydroxydimethyltryptamine. An unstable derivative, psilocine, is usually also present in trace amounts. Allied to other naturally occurring organic compounds such as bufotenine and serotonine, psilocybine has greatly interested biochemists because it is the first compound of this curious structure that has been found in plant tissue. Psilocybine, a hydroxy indole alkylamine with a phosphoric acid radical, is probably biogenetically derived from tryptophane. Psilocybine has been isolated from a number of species of *Psilocybe* as well as from *Conocybe, Panaeolus,* and *Stropharia.* These constituents have also been found in several North American and European species of mushrooms that are not employed for narcotic purposes.

Aside from the hallucinogenic effects of the psilocybine-containing mushrooms of Mexico, the most obvious symptoms of the intoxication are muscular relaxation, flaccidity, and dilation of the pupil of the eye, followed by emotional disturbances such as extreme hilarity and difficulty in concentration. Auditory as well as visual hallucinations appear at this period, eventually followed by lassitude, mental and physical depression, and serious alteration of time perception. The subject, without a loss of consciousness, is rendered completely indifferent to his environment, which becomes unreal to him as his dreamlike state becomes real.

Early missionaries to Amazonian Peru reported a "tree fungus" as the source of an intoxicating beverage of the Yurimagua Indians. No evidence exists that mushrooms are employed hallucinogenically in South America at the present time, but *Psilocybe yungensis,* a species which is known to contain hallucinatory principles and which has been found in the region, has been suggested as the possible identification of this elusive narcotic.

CACTACEAE (CACTUS FAMILY)

Ariocarpus, Epithelantha, Lophophora, Neoraimondia, Pachycereus, Trichocereus

Since the Cactus family offers some of the most bizarre shapes and forms that evolution has produced in the plant kingdom, it is perhaps understandable that some of the species have become closely connected with native beliefs and ritual practices. But this interesting family contains in the tissues of a number of its species unusual psychoactive constituents even more attractive than outer form to medicinal, religious, and magical aspects of native culture. Undoubtedly the most important of these species is *Lophophora Williamsii,* the peyote cactus.*

Peyote was first fully described by Hernández (1651), who called it *Peyotl zacatecensis:*

> The root is nearly medium size, sending forth no branches or leaves above the ground, but with a certain woolliness adhering to it on account of which it could not be aptly figured by me. . . . It appears to have a sweetish and moderately hot taste. Ground up and applied to painful joints, it is said to give relief. . . . This root . . . causes those devouring it to foresee and predict things . . . or to discern who has stolen from them some utensil or anything else; and other things of like nature. . . . On which account, this root scarcely issues forth, as if it did not wish to harm those who discover it and eat it.

Sahagún, the first European to discuss peyote seriously, suggested that

* See Peter T. Furst, below.

the Toltecas and Chichimecas had employed it for many hundreds of years and that it was a "common food of the Chichimecas," who used it to give them courage to fight and enable them to transcend thirst, hunger, and fear; it was thought to protect them from all danger, and those who ingested it saw "visions either frightful or laughable."

Fig. 2. The first botanical illustration of peyote (*Lophophora Williamsii*), published as *Echinocactus Williamsii*. From *Botanical* Magazine, LXXIII (1847), t. 4296.

In spite of the virulence of early Spanish attempts to stamp out the pagan religion in which peyote figured so prominently, the sacred cactus ritual survived in more or less pure form in the more remote deserts and mountains, while elsewhere it came to be intertwined with Christian ritual and belief. So strongly entrenched in aboriginal thought was this sacred cactus that even certain Christianized Indians of Mexico held that a patron saint—El Santo Niño de Peyotl—used to appear among the plants on the hillsides, a belief that still survives in Mexican folklore. As early as 1591 a chronicler denounced peyote as "satanic trickery." All through the seventeenth century and into the eighteenth, ecclesiastical opposition raged furiously. An eighteenth-century description referred to the cactus as the "diabolic root." In 1720, peyote was prohibited throughout Mexico, and all Indians within reach of the law and church were forced to practice their rituals in secret. The ecclesiastics went so far as to incorporate in a religious manual of 1760 questions in the form of a catechism that equated the eating of peyote with cannibalism! Today the use of peyote by the Huichol, Cora, Tarahumara, and other Indians in their religious ceremonies is no longer illegal; indeed, peyote is freely available in Mexican herb markets as a valued medicinal plant.

The earliest undoubted record of the use of peyote in what is now the territory of the United States dates from 1760 in Texas. The cactus was certainly known to American Indians during the Civil War, but it did not come strongly to public attention until about 1880, when the Kiowa and Comanche tribes began actively to practice and spread a new kind of peyote ceremony, quite different from the peyote rituals of the tribes of northwestern Mexico.

The exact route of the introduction of the peyote religion* from Mexico into the United States is not known, and there may have been several routes at different periods. Raids into the Mescalero country may have been the principal method of acquainting Plains Indians with the plant and its cult. Slow and gradual diffusion northward almost certainly took place as well. At any rate, the cult was well established among the Kiowas and Comanches between 1880 and 1885 and was being spread with missionary zeal. By the late 1920's, the cult had been forced, by the strong hostility and outright untruthful propaganda of many organized Christian missionary groups, to incorporate itself into the Native American Church—a legally constituted religious sect due the protection and respect enjoyed by any other religious group. In 1920 there were some 13,300 adherents in about thirty tribes. At present, an estimated 250,000 Indians in tribes as far north as Saskatchewan, Canada, practice this religion, which advocates brotherly love, high moral principle, abstention from alcohol, and other admirable teachings.

There is still disagreement about the reasons peyote use spread so fast,

* *Cf.* La Barre, 1938, 1969; Aberle, 1966.

edging out other well-established Indian "nativistic" movements, such as the famous Ghost Dance.* According to Slotkin (1956) an anthropologist who himself became an adherent of the peyote church,

> The Peyote Religion was nativistic but not militant. Culturally, it permitted the Indians to achieve a cultural organization in which they took pride. Socially, it provided a supernatural means of accommodation to the existing domination-subordination relation. . . . The Peyote Religion's program of accommodation, as opposed to the Ghost Dance's program of opposition, was the basic reason for the former's success and the latter's failure.

The fact that it could induce visual hallucinations undoubtedly contributed to the rapid spread of peyote through the culture of the Plains region.† However, the awe and respect in which the Indians of Mexico and the United States have long held this cactus as supernatural medicine and stimulant—quite apart from its vision-inducing qualities—have probably not been sufficiently appreciated.

The tribes of northern Mexico have long ascribed divine origin to peyote. According to the Tarahumara, when Father Sun departed from earth to dwell on high, he left peyote behind to cure all man's ills and woes. Its medicinal powers were so great—and its psychoactive effects, of course, are to the Indians the epitome of "medicinal power"—that it was considered a vegetal incarnation of a deity. The legends of its effectiveness as a supernatural medicine have kept peyote from being used hedonistically as a narcotic and have helped to maintain its exalted role as a near-divinity—a place it holds to this day, even among highly acculturated Indian groups in the United States.

In the United States, the Kiowa-Comanche peyote ceremony established during the last century is still followed today, with minor alterations. It usually consists of an all-night meeting with the worshipers sitting in a circle around a peyote altar, led in prayer, chants, and meditation by a "road man." The meeting ends in the morning with a

---

* The Ghost Dance religion, which first arose in 1870 among the Indians of the Western Plains, and which ended in 1890 in the tragic massacre of 300 unarmed Sioux at Wounded Knee Creek, was based on the vision . . . that a great mass of mud and water would soon roll over the earth, destroying the white men and all their gear. The Indians should dance the old round dance and, as they danced, the flood would roll over them. When it was over, the earth would be green again, animals and plants would be as in the old days, and the ancestral dead would come back (Underhill, 1965). See also La Barre, *The Ghost Dance* (1970).—Ed.

† Among North American Indians, especially hunting and gathering tribes, not only shamans but also ordinary men had the capacity to experience visions and obtain the aid of supernatural spirits. This could be achieved only through a strenuous "vision quest," involving fasting, thirsting, purification, exposure—even self-mutilation and torture. "The result would be a trance or a vivid dream in which the visionary made contact with his future guardian spirit and perhaps even received some visible token to prove the fact" (Underhill, 1965).—Ed.

communal meal. This contrasts strongly with the ancient ritual still practiced in northern Mexico, usually a longer ceremony of which dancing is a major part.

North of Mexico, it is usually the dried, discoidal top or crown of the cactus—the "mescal button"—that is chewed and swallowed during the ceremony. In Mexico, the plants are still more or less ceremonially collected where they grow. In many parts of the United States, the Indian peyotists have to purchase the buttons, which, since they are well-nigh indestructible, can be shipped long distances and stored indefinitely.

Lophophora Williamsii represents a veritable factory of alkaloids. More than thirty alkaloids and their amine derivatives—many of them, to be sure, in minute concentrations—have been isolated from the plant. Although most, if not all, of them are in some way or other biodynamically active, their effects are not well understood. They belong mainly to the phenylethylamine and biogenetically related simple isoquinolines. The phenylethylamine mescaline is the vision-inducing alkaloid, and experimental psychology has found mescaline to be of extreme interest as a tool. Other alkaloids are undoubtedly responsible for the tactile, auditory, and occasionally other hallucinations of the peyote intoxication.

Peyote intoxication, among the most complex and variable effects of all hallucinogenic plants, is characterized by brilliantly colored visions in kaleidoscopic movement, often accompanied by auditory, gustatory, olfactory, and tactile hallucinations. Sensations of weightlessness, macroscopia, depersonalization, and alteration or loss of time perception are normally experienced.

There are very real differences between peyote intoxication and mescaline intoxication. Among aboriginal users, it is the fresh or dried head of the cactus, with its total alkaloid content, that is ingested; mescaline is ingested only experimentally and then produces the effects of but one of the alkaloids, without the physiological interaction of the others that are present in the crude plant material. As a consequence, descriptions of the visual hallucinations of mescaline found in such writings as those of Aldous Huxley should not be equated too closely with the visual effects experienced by Indian peyotists.

Doses vary greatly among Indian users, who may ingest anywhere from four mescal buttons to more than thirty. Peyote intoxication characteristically has two phases: a period of contentment and hypersensitivity followed by calm and muscular sluggishness, often accompanied by hypercerebrality and colored visions. Before visual hallucinations appear, usually within three hours after ingestion of the drug, the subject sees flashes of color across the field of vision, the depth and saturation of the colors (which always precede the visions) defying description.

There seems to be a sequence frequently followed in the visions: from geometric figures to familiar scenes and faces to unfamiliar scenes and faces and in some cases objects. The literature is rich in detailed descriptions of visual hallucinations from both peyote and mescaline intoxication, and they provide a wealth of data for psychological and psychiatric research.

Although the visual hallucinations are important in native peyote cults, peyote, as we have said, is revered in large part because of its usefulness as a "medicine." Its medicinal powers, in turn, derive from its ability, through the visions, to put a man into contact with the spirit world, from which, according to aboriginal belief, come illness and even death, and to which the medicine men turn for their diagnoses.

The magico-therapeutic powers of *Lophophora Williamsii* have such wide repute in Mexico that many plants have been confused with or related to it by vernacular terms. They are not all in the cactus family, although a number of cactus species in seven genera, popularly classed as peyotes, are related to *Lophophora* in folklore and folk medicine: *Ariocarpus, Astrophytum, Aztekium, Dolichothele, Obregonia, Pelecyphora,* and *Solisia.* They may have similar toxic effects, may superficially resemble *Lophophora,* or may be used together with *Lophophora.* Non-cactaceous plants similarly associated by name or folk use with *Lophophora* belong to genera in the Compositae, Orchidaceae, Solanaceae, Crassulaceae, and Leguminosae.

In this connection, it should be pointed out that in northern Mexico Indians have valued other cactus species, variously equating them with peyote. The Tarahumara, for example, esteem several of them very highly. According to Lumholtz (1902),

> . . . high mental qualities are ascribed especially to all species of *Mammillaria* and *Echinocactus,* small cacti, for which a regular cult is instituted. The Tarahumara designate several as *hikuli,* though the name belongs properly only to the kind most commonly used by them. These plants live for months after they have been rooted up, and the eating of them causes a state of ecstasy. They are, therefore, considered demi-gods who have to be treated with great reverence. . . . The principal kinds thus distinguished are known to science as *Lophophora Williamsii* and *Lophophora Williamsii* var. *Lewinii* . . . The Tarahumara speak of them as the superior hikuli *(hikuli wanamé)* or simply hikuli, they being hikuli *par excellence.* . . . Besides hikuli wanamé . . . the Tarahumara know and worship the following varieties: (i) Mulato *(Mammillaria micromeris)* [now known as *Epithelantha micromeris*]. This is believed to make the eyes large and clear to see sorcerers, to prolong life and to give speed to runners. (ii) *Rosparia.* This is only a more advanced vegetative stage of the preceding species—though it looks quite different, being white and spiny. . . . (iii) *Sunami (Mammillaria fissurata)* [now known as *Ariocarpus fissuratus*]. It is rare, but it is believed to be even

more powerful than wanamé and is used in the same way as the latter; the drink produced from it is also strongly intoxicating. Robbers are powerless to steal anything where Sunami calls soldiers to its aid. (iv) *Hikuli walula saeliami.* This is the greatest of all, and the name means "hikuli great authority." It is extremely rare among the Tarahumaras, . . . growing in clusters of from eight to twelve inches in diameter . . . with young ones around it. All these various species are considered good, as coming from Tata Dios and well disposed toward the people. But there are some kinds of hikuli believed to come from the Devil. One of these, with long white spines, is called *ocoyome.* It is very rarely used, and only for evil purposes. If anyone should happen to touch it with the foot, it would cause the offending leg to break.

Even in the modern Tarahumara culture, narcotic cacti play a role in festivals: hikuri, *Lophophora Williamsii;* peyote cimarrón, *Ariocarpus fissuratus;* and *Epithelantha micromeris.* All these species grow far from present-day Tarahumara country. Another cactus—čawé (*Pachycereus pecten-aboriginum*)—is still found in territory inhabited by the Tarahumara and is employed by them as a narcotic. Several of these Tarahumara narcotic cacti contain alkaloids capable of inducing visual hallucinations.

Certain species of the tall columnar cactus plants of the high and dry Andes in South America are likewise known to contain alkaloids, including, especially, mescaline. It is, therefore, not suprising that Peruvian Indians have discovered the vision-inducing properties of *Trichocereus* and prepare a hallucinogenic drink from *T. Pachanoi,* known locally as *San Pedro,** which mestizo *curanderos,* or curers, administer to their patients or ingest themselves for purposes of diagnosis, divination, and confrontation with the hostile spirits causing the illness. It also enters an intoxicating drink called *cimora,* which is said to contain extracts of another cactus, the tall, columnar *Neoraimonda macrostibas,* as well as *Isotoma longiflora* (Campanulaceae), *Pedilanthus titimoloides* (Euphorbiaceae), and a species of *Datura* (Solanaceae). Several of these admixtures are alkaloidal and may themselves contain hallucinogenic constituents.

CONVOLVULACEAE (MORNING-GLORY FAMILY)

Ipomoea, Rivea

One of the most important sacred hallucinogens among Mexican Indians at the time of the Conquest was *ololiuqui,* the small, round, lentil-like seed of a vine with cordate leaves known in the Nahuatl language as *coaxihuitl,* or "snake plant." Persecution by ecclesiastical

* See Dougles Sharon, below.

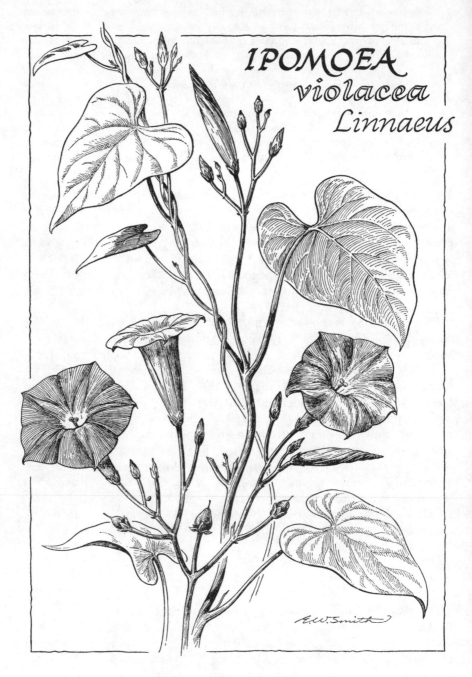

Fig. 3.

authorities drove it into the hinterlands, where its hallucinogenic use still persists. Still, although it represents one of the major Mexican divinatory plants to this day, it is perhaps one of the least well known; until recently, even its identity was in doubt.

Sahagún enumerated three plants called *ololiuqui*, one of which was an "herb called *coatl-xoxouhqui* (green snake plant), [which] bears a seed called ololiuqui." Another early account, dated 1629, reported that "when it is drunk, this seed deprives of his senses him who has taken it, for it is very powerful." Yet another reads that

> these seeds . . . are held in great veneration. . . . They place offerings to the seeds . . . in secret places so that the offerings cannot be found if a search be made. They also place these seeds among the idols of their ancestors. . . . They do not wish to offend ololiuqui with demonstrations before the judges [of the Inquisition] of the use of the seeds and with public destruction of the seed by burning.

The most reliable discussions of the hallucinogenic effects and uses of ololiuqui appear to be those of Hernández, who, after describing in great detail its many presumed medicinal virtues, stated that

> . . . when the priests wanted to commune with their gods and to receive messages from them, they ate this plant to induce a delirium. A thousand visions and satanic hallucinations appeared to them.

Christian persecution drove the native cult of ololiuqui into hiding, and corroboration of the identity of the plant waited for more than 400 years. All evidence from the literature and several early drawings, especially the excellent illustrations provided by Hernández, indicate that the plant must be a morning-glory.

In Mexico, the attribution of ololiuqui to the Convolvulaceae was rather generally accepted as early as 1854. Urbina identified it as *Ipomoea sidaefolia* (*Rivea corymbosa*) some seventy years ago. In 1919, B. P. Reko defined *ololuc* as the round lentil-like seed of *Rivea corymbosa* and, in 1934, published a historical review of the use of ololiuqui. Narcotic seeds which he sent to Safford were determined as representing this convolvulaceous species.

It was apparently Hartwich who, in 1911, first stated that ololiuqui might be a member of the Solanaceae, a suggestion supported by Safford in 1915, when he mistakenly identified ololiuqui as *Datura meteloides*. His identification, still widely accepted, was based on several arguments. Many Indian groups in Mexico use *Datura* as a hallucinogen, but, although this genus certainly was well provided with psychoactive compounds, no convolvulaceous genus was known to possess any principles affecting the central nervous system. The flowers of the morning-glories were tubular and superficially resembled those of *Datura*, and the Indians could easily have misled the early Spanish writers by substituting the former for the latter—at least that was the theory. Furthermore, the symptoms described for ololiuqui intoxication coincided well with those known for *Datura* intoxication. Underlying Safford's arguments was his belief that

> . . . a knowledge of botany has been attributed to the Aztecs which they were far from possessing. . . . The botanical knowledge of the early Spanish writers . . . was perhaps not much more extensive: their descriptions were so inadequate that, even to the present day, the chief narcotic of the Aztecs, *ololiuchqui,* which they all mention, remains unidentified.

Unjustified as was Safford's lack of faith in the botanical knowledge of the Aztecs and of such early writers as Hernández, it was probably very influential in his dismissal of the Convolvulaceae as a source of ololiuqui.

It was only in 1939 that unquestionably identifiable voucher specimens of *Rivea corymbosa* were collected. In northeastern Oaxaca, Reko and I encountered a cultivated plant in the dooryard of a Zapotec *curandero* who employed the seeds in his divinatory rituals. I reported these seeds from several other tribes of Oaxaca: Chinantecs, Mazatecs, Mixtecs, and sundry groups of Zapotecs. In 1941, I published a summary of what was then known of ololiuqui and *Rivea corymbosa*, and the identification of the ancient and modern hallucinogen appeared finally to have been clarified.

The notion that the Convolvulaceae as a family is devoid of intoxicating principles was dispelled in 1937, when Santesson reported psychoactive substances in the seeds of *Rivea corymbosa*. He was not able to investigate thoroughly the nature of the active constituent, but he suggested that it might be a glycoside linked with an alkaloid. His pharmacological experiments indicated that an extract induced in animals a "partial deadening of the mind, a kind of semi-narcosis."

There was little interest in *Rivea corymbosa* as a hallucinogen until 1955, when a psychiatrist, Humphrey Osmond, first described an intoxication from seeds of this morning-glory. Chemists immediately became interested, but no psychoactive constituents were isolated until Hofmann, discoverer of the most powerful hallucinogen known, lysergic acid diethylamide (LSD 25), announced to the unbelieving scientific world that the seeds contained lysergic acid derivatives. It was difficult to accept such a discovery at first, since this class of compounds—in fact, some of the very compounds that Hofmann attributed to this morning-glory—were known in the plant kingdom only from the entirely unrelated genus of lower fungi *Claviceps*, the ergot parasite of rye and other grasses. Chemotaxonomically, such an occurrence would be highly unlikely. Furthermore, it was early suspected that the spores of the fungus had invaded tissues of the morning-glory. Later chemical analyses and pathological studies of the morning-glory seeds, however, fully substantiated Hofmann's work.

The principal psychotomimetic compound is ergine or *d*-lysergic acid amide. There is an alkaloid of secondary importance, isoergine or *d*-isolysergic acid amide. Several other ergoline alkaloids are present but seem not to be psychoactive. According to Hofmann (1966), in tests which he and a laboratory assistant conducted on themselves, two milligrams of an indolic extract from the seeds of *Rivea corymbosa* sufficed to bring about "clear-cut psychic effects: a dream-like state resulted with drowsiness and alteration in the perception of objects and colors. This showed that the indole fraction of the *Rivea* extract contained the psychic active principle."

The classification and botanical nomenclature of the Convolvulaceae are confused. *Rivea corymbosa* has many synonyms. *Ipomoea sidaefolia* and *Turbina corymbosa* are frequently employed. Since *Rivea corymbosa* has become firmly established in the literature, however, it would seem wise to continue using it until a thorough study of this family of plants determines more clearly which binomial should be adopted.

A second vital step in the story of the sacred Mexican morning-glories was made in 1960, when MacDougall published his report of the hallucinogenic use of the seeds of *Ipomoea violacea* among the Zapotecs of Oaxaca. This species is sometimes known—especially in horticultural circles—as *Ipomoea tricolor*. Parsons first reported from Zapotecs of Mitla, Oaxaca, the use of *badoh negro*, and I originally thought that this was also referable to *Rivea corymbosa*. The seeds of the two species are quite different, however, although they are employed for the same purpose: *Rivea corymbosa* seeds are brown and round; those of *Ipomoea violacea* are black, long, and angular. Furthermore, it appeared that the seeds of the latter morning-glory were more potent than those of the former.

Chemical studies of *Ipomoea violacea* indeed confirm ethnobotanical suspicions about the potency of the seeds. *Ipomoea violacea* contains the same or similar psychoactive lysergic acid derivatives, but the psychotomimetic alkaloids are present in heavier concentrations.

Wasson has suggested that *Ipomoea violacea* may be the elusive Aztec narcotic mentioned in the chronicles as *tlitliltzin,* a Nahuatl term derived from the word for "black," with a reverential suffix. An early chronicler, for example, spoke of "ololiuqui, peyotl, and tlitliltzin," ascribing similar properties to them.

To sum up, then, until very recently—the 1950's—no intoxicating principles were known in the Morning-glory family. Now, thanks to preliminary phytochemical surveys, we realize that indole derivatives

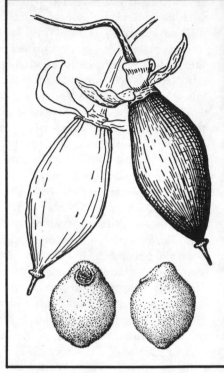

Fig. 4*a*.

Fig. 4*b*. Capsules and seeds
of *Rivea Corymbosa.*

are not uncommon in *Argyreia, Convolvulus, Ipomoea,* and *Sticto-cardia* and that they will probably be found elsewhere in the Convolvulaceae.

LABIATAE (MINT FAMILY)

Salvia

Until recently, no mints have been known to be employed as sacred hallucinogens in the New World, even though such use should not have come as a surprise. The family is rich in essential oils of complex composition, some components of which are thought to have psychoactive properties.

An interesting *Salvia* was reported as a hallucinogen of the Mazatec Indians of Oaxaca by Wasson in 1962. It was a new species, named *Salvia divinorum* because of its use by shamans and curers practicing divination. The plant has psychotomimetic effects that resemble those of the mushroom but are of shorter duration and not so striking. Kaleidoscopic movement and three-dimensional designs characterize the intoxication induced by the ingestion of the juice of sixty-eight leaves. To date, however, no hallucinogenic principle has been isolated.

The plant is familiar to all Mazatec Indians. Many, if not most, families grow a supply. The plants are vegetatively reproduced from a shoot inserted into wet ground. The natives usually choose isolated mountain ravines for planting it, far from daily occupations. *Salvia divinorum* does not often flower, and seeds are unknown—an indication

Fig. 5.

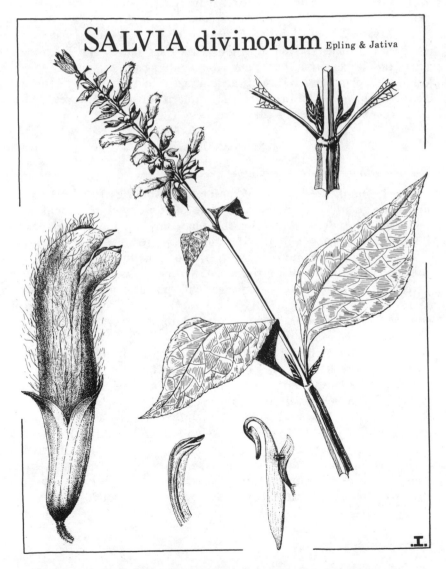

that it may possibly represent a cultigen of considerable age which perhaps no longer occurs in a wild state.

The Mazatecs call *Salvia divinorum hojas de la Pastora* ("leaves of the Shepherdess") or *hojas de Maria Pastora* ("leaves of Mary the Shepherdess") in Spanish, or *ska-Pastora* in Mazatec-Spanish.

Wasson has suggested that *Salvia divinorum* may represent an ancient Aztec narcotic known by the Nahuatl name *pipilzintzintli*. This species may also represent the "magic plant" reported by B. P. Reko in 1945, "whose leaves produce visions and which the Cuicatecs and Mazatecs call 'divination leaf'." Furthermore, it is probably the plant reported by Weitlaner as *yerba María*, collected only after the native medicine man kneels and prays to it, and employed in medical divination in northeastern Oaxaca.

In Oaxaca, *Salvia divinorum* seems to be utilized only when supplies of the mushrooms and morning-glory seeds are short. The Indians may chew the leaves fresh but more commonly crush them in a metate, dilute the plant materials in water, and strain the mixture. Formerly, according to native informants, the whole plant was employed, but the Mazatec now prefer only the leaves.

LEGUMINOSAE (PEA FAMILY)

Anadenanthera, Mimosa, Sophora

The Leguminosae are one of the most alkaloid-rich families of plants and consequently the potential source of a number of potent hallucinogens. Thus it is surprising that man has not found and bent to his magical uses more of the leguminous species.

One of the most famous of the New World hallucinogens is the snuff prepared from a tree of northern South America called *Anadenanthera peregrina* or *Piptadenia peregrina*. This potent snuff was so widely known in anthropological circles that until recently almost all narcotic snuffs of South America were attributed to this tree, even in regions where the species does not occur.

Probably the earliest report of snuff prepared from *Anadenanthera peregrina* dates from 1496, when Europeans first saw it in use among the Taino Indians of Hispaniola. Friar Ramón Pané, commissioned by Columbus "to collect all ceremonies and antiquities," wrote in detail concerning this drug and its place in Indian society. His reports were first published in 1511 in Martyr's compilations about the New World. "This *kohobba* powder," which Martyr described as "an intoxicating herb," "is so strong that those who take it lose consciousness; when the stupefying action begins to wane, the arms and legs become loose and the head droops." Taking it with a cane about a foot long, they "put one end in the nose and the other in the powder and . . . draw it into themselves through the nose." Its action was rapid, for "almost immediately, they believe they see the room turn upside-down and men walking with their heads downwards." The "sorcerer" took the drug with his patients, and it "intoxicates them so that they do not know what to do and . . . speak of many things incoherently," believing all the time that they are in communication with spirits.

Snuff from *Anadenanthera* is apparently no longer employed in the Antilles, where, of course, few aboriginal groups still exist. In 1916, Safford, noting the similarities between the current use of yopo snuff in the Orinoco and the reported effects of cohoba, identified the cohoba as *Anadenanthera peregrina*. Up to that time, there had been much confusion in the literature, and the snuff called *cohoba* was commonly

Fig. 6. *Anadenanthera perigrina*. Bôa Vista, Brazil.

considered to have been tobacco. Years earlier, however, in 1898, Uhle had concluded that "the extreme strength of the powder described by Petrus Martyr, exceeding that of tobacco, decides its different nature and its *Piptadenia* character."

The center of the use of *Anadenanthera* snuff is, and probably always has been, the Orinoco basin, where it is widely known as *yopo*. The West Indian tribes are generally thought to have been invaders from northern South America. If this is true, then the snuffing of *Anadenanthera* powder in the West Indies could be regarded as a culture trait imported from South America. *Anadenanthera peregrina* occurs wild— that is, free from any hint of present or past cultivation—only in South America.

An early report of yopo among the Otomac Indians of the Orinoco basin is found in Gumilla's famous *El Orinoco Ilustrado*, first published in 1741:

> They have another most evil habit of intoxicating themselves through the nostrils, with certain malignant powders which they call *yupa*, which quite takes away their reason, and furious, they grasp their weapons. . . . They prepare this powder from certain pods of the *yupa* . . . but the powder itself has the odor of strong tobacco. That which they add to it, through the ingenuity of the devil, is what causes the intoxication and fury . . . they put their shells [large snails] into the fire and burn them to quicklime . . . [which] they mix with the yupa . . . and after reducing the whole to the finest powder, there results a mixture of diabolic strength, so great that in touching this powder with the tip of the finger, the most confirmed devotee of snuff cannot accustom himself to it, for in simply putting his finger which touched the yupa near his nose he bursts forth into a whirlwind of sneezes. The Saliva Indians and other tribes . . . also use the yupa, but as they are gentle, benign, and timid, they do not become maddened like our Otomacs who . . . before a battle . . . would throw themselves into a frenzy with yupa, wound themselves, and, full of blood and rage, go forth to battle like rabid tigers.

A number of other missionary reports from the Orinoco area of Colombia and Venezuela reiterate the details offered by Gumilla. The earliest scientific report on this narcotic appears to be that of Alexander von Humboldt, who botanically identified the plant as *Acacia Niopo*, stating that the Maypure Indians of the Orinoco break the long pods of this tree, moisten them, and allow them to ferment; after the softened beans turn black, they are kneaded into small cakes with *Manihot* flour and lime from snail shells. These cakes are powdered when a supply of snuff is desired.

Like Gumilla, von Humboldt felt that the biodynamic activity of the snuff was attributable to the lime admixture. "It is not to be believed

that the niopo acacia pods are the chief cause of the stimulating effects
of the snuff used by the Otomac Indians. These effects are due to the
freshly calcined lime."

The earliest detailed scientific report is that given by the British
botanical explorer Richard Spruce, who encountered the drug in the
mid-nineteenth century among the Guahibo Indians of the Orinoco
basin of Colombia and Venezuela.

The literature concerning the snuffing of narcotic powders has become extraordinarily confused. There is no doubt that sundry wholly
unrelated plants enter into South American snuffs. Undoubtedly the
most important snuffing material was and still is tobacco, mainly from
Nicotiana tabacum, and snuffing may well be the most widespread
method of using it, especially in the wet, tropical lowlands areas. In
certain areas of the northwest Amazon—e.g., among Indians of the Reo
Miritiparaná of Colombia—coca-powder (*Erythroxylon Coca*) is snuffed.
Recent studies have shown the importance and widespread employment of intoxicating snuffs made from *Virola* bark. Yet the literature
—especially the anthropological—has exaggerated the importance and
distribution of the leguminous snuffs from *Anadenanthera.*

Many ascribe the sources of Amazon snuffs to various leguminous
trees, and the British botanist Bentham concluded that "all South
American trees . . . referred to as the source of narcotic snuffs were
probably one species and were identical with Linnaeus' *Mimosa peregrina.*"

It seems that one of the most extraordinarily mistaken generalizations
in ethnobotany—that all the intoxicating snuffs of the Amazon that were
not obviously tobacco must have been prepared from *Anadenanthera
peregrina*—has stemmed from Bentham's conclusion. Recent literature
and maps showing the distribution of snuffs made presumably from
Anadenanthera include the entire Orinoco basin and adjacent areas of
southern Venezuela to the east; westward across the northern Colombian
Andes; much of the Magdalena Valley; down the Andes through Colombia, Ecuador, Peru, and Bolivia; the coastal region of Peru; scattered
isolated areas in northern Argentina; and the central and western
Amazon Valley. One must remember that not one species—*Anadenanthera peregrina*—is involved but that there have been suggestions that
other species of this genus have entered the South American snuff-
making picture.

Anadenanthera peregrina, a beautiful, medium-sized tree with a thick,
corky bark and a graceful crown with dark green, acacia-like foliage, is
a species that occurs both naturally and cultivated in the open plains
or *llanos* region of the Orinoco basin of Colombia and Venezuela, in
savannahs and light forests of what was British Guiana, and in Brazil

in the open grasslands or *campos* of the Rio Branco region and locally in savannah-like areas in the lower Rio Madeira basin. If *Anadenanthera peregrina* occurs elsewhere in South America, it would have to be a rare tree or two brought in and cultivated by recently migrated Indian tribes.

Even within the local range of *Anadenanthera peregrina*, it is not safe to assume that all narcotic snuffs are referable to this genus or species. For example, a number of erroneous identifications of narcotic snuff have attributed powders prepared from *Virola* bark to *Anadenanthera peregrina*. One reason for this confusion may be the fact that in many parts of the Amazon—especially in the Rio Negro basin—the term *paricá*, which often does refer to leguminous trees, has been applied indiscriminately to narcotic snuff from *Anadenanthera* and *Virola*.

Until recently, there has been much uncertainty concerning the active hallucinogenic principles of *Anadenanthera peregrina*. At one time, it was felt that the central nervous activity produced by yopo-snuff was due mainly, if not wholly, to 5-hydroxy-N,N-dimethyltryptamine, or bufotenine.* Recent analyses of carefully authenticated and identified material, however, have shown that other tryptamine derivatives are present in the seeds of *Anadenanthera peregrina*: N,N-dimethyltryptamine, N-monomethyltryptamine, 5-methoxy-N, 5-methoxy-N-monomethyltryptamine, N,N-dimethyltryptamine-N-oxide, 5-hydroxy-N, N-dimethyltryptamine-N-oxide.

It was Safford who apparently first suggested that species of *Anadenanthera* other than *A. peregrina* may be the source of narcotic snuffs

---

* This hallucinogenic drug is present also in the skin of poisonous toads, e.g., *Bufo marinus*. Such toads have long played an important role in mythology and ritual art, not only in Mesoamerica (especially among the Maya) but in Central and South America, a circumstance that I suggested in a discussion at the International Congress of Americanists in Stuttgart, Germany, in 1968, might possibly be related to the hallucinogenic properties in toad and frog poisons. A number of South American tropical-forest tribes are known to use frog or toad poison to induce ecstatic trance states akin to those resulting from the various botanical hallucinogens; in these cases, however, the drug is introduced directly into the bloodstream through self-inflicted burns or wounds rather than ingested orally. M.D. Coe (personal communication) found large quantities of *Bufo* remains in the important Olmec ceremonial site of San Lorenzo, Veracruz (1200–900 B.C.); these might have served as food but it is equally possible that the Olmec used poisonous toads as additives or "fortifiers" for fermented ritual beverages. This practice, first reported after the Spanish Conquest from the Maya highlands by Thomas Gage in the early 1600's, survives to the present day among the Quiché-Maya of Guatemala (Robert M. Carmack, personal communication). It should be noted that the action of bufotenine on the human brain is not as yet well understood—for example, it appears, that unlike other hallucinogens, bufotenine does not fully penetrate the blood-brain barrier—nor is it known whether there might not be some special effects from the combination of alcohol and toad poison, with its relatively high content of serotonine (a substance also found in the human brain), as well as bufotenine, in the ritual beverages of Mesoamerica.—ED.

in South America. He identified the *vilca* or *huilca* of southern Peru and Bolivia and the *cébil* of northern Argentina with seeds of what he called *Piptadenia macrocarpa,* now referred to as *Anadenanthera colubrina* var. *Cebil.*

The term *vilca* in modern Peru sometimes refers to *Anadenanthera colubrina,* although this or similar names may signify a number of different plants in South America. An early report, dating from *ca.* 1571, stated that Inca "sorcerers" prophesied by contacting the devil through an intoxication induced by drinking *chicha* (maize beer) and an herb called vilca. Even earlier records mentioned a medicinal plant of this name, some of them emphasizing its laxative and emetic properties. The cébil snuff used in northern Argentina at the time of the arrival of the Spaniards appears to "have been *Anadenanthera*-derived," although the use of this genus "further south beyond its natural distribution is less likely. Yet there, further south, the Comechingon Indians took something called *Sebil* through the nose. . . , and the Huarpe Indians chewed a substance called *Cibil* for endurance."

However weak and circumstantial the evidence that vilca and cébil were prepared from *Anadenanthera,* there would seem to be no phytochemical reason why this could not be so. *Anadenanthera colubrina* has been shown by Altschul to be morphologically very closely related to *A. peregrina.* Furthermore, some of the same hallucinogenic tryptamines found in varying proportions in *Anadenanthera peregrina* have been located in material said to be referable to *A. colubrina.* It is obvious that extensive research must be done on South American hallucinogenic snuffs in general and on the use of *Anadenanthera* in particular before we can approach understanding.

In eastern Brazil another legume—*Mimosa hostilis*—forms the basis of the famous *ajuca* or *vinho de jurema,* a "miraculous drink" taken in ceremony among the Karirí, Pankarurú, Tusha, and Fulnio Indians of Pernambuco and Paraiba. The source of vinho de jurema was identified as recently as 1946 by Gonçalves de Lima.

The roots of this small tree or large shrub of the dry scrubby *caatingas* are prepared in a potently hallucinogenic beverage taken by priests, strong young men, warriors, and old women, who kneel with bowed heads to partake of it. The ceremony was formerly performed before battle, and all participants would then see

> . . . glorious visions of the spirit world, with flowers and birds. They might catch a glimpse of the clashing rocks that destroy souls of the dead journeying to their goal or see the Thunder Bird shooting lightning from a huge tuft on his head and producing claps of thunder by running about.

The jurema cult is ancient and formerly was practiced by many more tribes, including the Guegue, Acroa, Pimenteira, Atanaye, and others

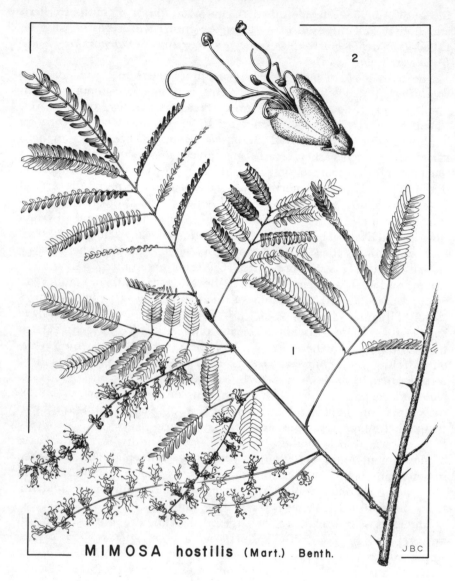

MIMOSA hostilis (Mart.) Benth.

Fig. 7.

now extinct. An early report dates from 1788; another from 1843. The latter asserted that jurema was taken in order to "pass the night navigating through the depths of slumber."

Several species of *Mimosa*—a genus closely related to *Anadenanthera* —may be involved, since they are generically referred to as jurema in northeastern Brazil. One of several kinds is *jurema prêta*, believed to be

Mimosa hostilis, but *jurema branca* may refer also to *M. verrucosa*, from the bark of which a stupefacient is said to be derived.

In 1946, an alkaloid named *nigerine* was reported from the roots of *Mimosa hostilis*, but later chemical studies have shown that this base is identical with N, N-dimethyltryptamine, the same constituent responsible for the hallucinogenic effects produced by *Anadenanthera* seeds.

Sophora secundiflora

One of the most interesting New World narcotics is the *mescal bean* or *red bean*, the seed of a small tree of the American Southwest and Mexico, known botanically as *Sophora secundiflora*. *S. secundiflora* is a beautiful shrub—today often planted as an ornamental—with leathery, glossy, evergreen leaflets and large clusters of violet or violet-blue flowers and woody pods containing usually three or four bright red beans.

These seeds formerly were basic to a vision-seeking cult. They contain the alkaloid cytisine, which is characteristic of a number of species of the family. Cytisine is capable in overdoses of causing nausea, convulsions, hallucinations, and even death from respiratory failure. A number of the other twenty-five species of *Sophora* contain cytisine or a related alkaloid, but no species other than *S. secundiflora* seems to have been employed for its narcotic properties.

The use of *Sophora secundiflora* goes back to archaeological times. The seeds have been found in sites dated before A.D. 1000, often with evidence that they were used ritualistically. From at least twelve sites in caves and rock shelters in southwestern Texas finds of Sophora beans have been recorded; their dating is uncertain, but radiocarbon dates for material from evidently related sites in northern Mexico range all the way from 7500 B.C. to A.D. 200. According to the archaeologist Campbell (1958), although the presence of mescal beans in cave and rock shelters, "even when included in containers holding utilitarian as well as non-utilitarian objects," does not necessarily prove the existence of a mescal-bean cult, there "is additional archaeological evidence which does suggest the presence of a prehistoric cult that may have involved the use of the mescal bean."

The Spanish explorer of the Texas coast, Cabeza de Vaca, mentioned mescal beans as an article of trade among the Indians in 1539. The Stephen Long Expedition in 1820 reported the Arapaho and Iowa using large red beans as a medicine and narcotic. A well-developed mescal-bean cult was known among the Apache, Comanche, Delaware, Iowa, Kansa, Omaha, Oto, Osage, Pawnee, Ponca, Tonkawa, and Wichita; other tribes of the central and northwestern Plains groups valued the bean as a medicine or fetish, although they apparently failed to develop a distinct cult surrounding its use. The cult has various names: Wichita

Dance, Deer Dance, Whistle Dance, Red Bean Dance, and Red Medicine Society. In all these ceremonies, the seeds were employed as an oracular or divinatory medicine for inducing visions in initiatory rites and as a ceremonial emetic and stimulant.

The many parallels and similarities between the peyote ceremony among the Plains tribes and the Red Bean Dance and their obvious southern origin, in Texas and northern Mexico, suggest that the much safer hallucinogen peyote more or less took the place of the dangerously toxic mescal bean. Even today, the "road man" or peyote leader in certain Plains tribes—Kiowa and Comanche, for example—wears as part of his ornamental dress a necklace of *Sophora secundiflora* beans and often has mescal beans sewn on his leggings.

It is reported that on occasion the Comanche, Oto, and Tonkawa tribes mixed peyote and the mescal bean in a narcotic drink. This mixture is of special interest pharmacologically, for it must have been extraordinarily potent. Ethnobotanically, it is of interest because it was apparently practiced in transitional periods between the dying out of the Red Bean Dance and the establishment of the peyote ceremony that later led to the Native American Church.

LYTHRACEAE

Heimia

The small lythraceous genus *Heimia*, with three poorly defined species occurring from the southern United States to Argentina, has provided one of the most interesting hallucinogens of the New World, yet little is known about its use. *Sinicuichi* (the Mexican name for *Heimia salicifolia*) does not induce visions but is a wholly auditory hallucinogen.

The leaves of this shrub, slightly wilted, are crushed in water, and the juice is set out to ferment in the sun. The resulting drink is slightly intoxicating, causing giddiness, a drowsy euphoria, a darkening of the surroundings, a shrinking of the world around, altered perception of time and space, forgetfulness, removal from a state of reality, and auditory hallucinations. Sounds appear to come from a great distance and are distorted.

The natives consider *sinicuichi* sacred and endowed with supernatural powers. It helps them, they assert, to recall vividly events of many years earlier, even to remember prenatal events.

Despite recent chemical studies of *Heimia salicifolia,* the total picture of *sinicuichi* intoxication is far from clear. Five quinolizidine alkaloids have been isolated, one of which—cryogenine—has been shown experimentally to mimic qualitatively and semiqualitatively the action of the total alkaloid extract of the plant.

MALPIGHIACEAE

Banisteriopsis, Tetrapteris

Thousands of South American Indians—in the western Amazon, the Orinoco, and on the slopes of the Pacific coast of Colombia and Ecuador —use an extraordinary hallucinogen elaborated basically from jungle

Fig. 8.

HEIMIA
salicifolia
Link & Otto

BANISTERIOPSIS *Caapi*

(Spruce ex Griseb.) Morton

Fig. 9.

lianas: *Banisteriopsis Caapi,** or the closely related *B. inebrians.* The narcotic drink prepared from the bark of either of these plants is variously known as *caapi, ayahuasca, yajé, natema,* or *pinde,* according to the area and group of Indians. In some regions—especially in the very westernmost part of its Amazon range—the bark is prepared in a cold-water infusion; in other localities, the bark or stems are subjected to long boiling. In parts of the Orinoco, the fresh bark may be chewed, and there are indications that it may also be taken in the form of a snuff.

There are herbarium collections of another species of *Banisteriopsis* —*B. muricata*—which, because of the vernacular name *ayahuasca* assigned to them by the collector, suggest that this species may also occasionally be employed as the source of the narcotic in eastern Peru.

This narcotic enters deeply into almost all aspects of the life of the peoples who take it to an extent reached by hardly any other hallucinogen. As *ayahuasca,* its Peruvian name, it is known as the "vine of the souls," and partakers often "experience" death and the separation of body and soul. To some Colombian Indians the drinking of this preparation represents a return to the maternal womb, the source of all creation; the partakers see all the gods, the first human beings and animals, and understand the establishment of their social order. Those who take yajé "die" only to be reborn in a state of greater wisdom. In the northwest Amazon, caapi serves the Indian for prophetic, divinatory, and other magic purposes and to fortify the bravery of male adolescents who must undergo the painful *yurupari* initiation ceremony.

The narcotic effects may be violent and with unpleasant aftereffects, especially when the drink is made by boiling the bark and most certainly when some other toxic plants enter the preparation as admixtures. Nausea and vomiting are almost always early characteristics of the effects of the drink. This is followed by a pleasant euphoria, then by visual hallucinations, initially tinged with blue or purple. Excessive doses bring on frighteningly nightmarish visions—often of jaguars and snakes—and a feeling of extremely reckless abandon, although consciousness is usually not lost nor is the use of the limbs unduly affected.

This bizarre intoxicant was discovered in 1851 by Richard Spruce, an English plant explorer on the upper Rio Negro of the Brazilian Amazon, where it was called caapi. Spruce identified the drug as a new species of the Malpighiaceae, and he named it *Banisteria Caapi.* Later studies have shown that it is more correctly called *Banisteriopsis Caapi.* Several years later, in the Ecuadorian Amazon, he encountered a narcotic drink locally known as ayahuasca and correctly surmised that it was the same plant he had described from the Rio Negro. At about the same time,

* See G. Reichel-Dolmatoff, below.

an Ecuadorian geographer wrote that ayahuasca was used among the Zaparos, Angateros, Mazanes, and other Indians of Amazonian Ecuador to foresee the future; discover the truth; help deliberations on war, attack, and defense; learn the source of malevolent magic; welcome visitors from other clans; and ascertain the faithfulness of their women.

Probably no other hallucinogenic preparation has been so fraught with confusion. Careless research and even active imaginations and outright guesswork have bedeviled studies of the malpighiaceous narcotics for a century. This confusion characterizes not only the anthropological reports about its use but also the botanical and chemical studies that have been published.

One of the most troublesome points of confusion concerns the identification of yajé as the apocynaceous vine *Prestonia amazonica (Haemadictyon amazonicum)* and the inference that yajé was a different narcotic from ayahuasca and caapi. Although this identification is very widely established in the literature, recent studies have conclusively shown that it is a serious error. These narcotic drinks have also been confused with *Datura* beverages among the Jívaros. Yajé has even been identified as a species of *Aristolochia*. The malpighiaceous vine *Mascagnia psilophylla* var. *antifebrilis* has been reported as the basic plant employed, but this identification appears to be an error.

Perhaps the greatest uncertainty concerns the identification of the admixtures utilized locally in the preparation of ayahuasca, caapi, or yajé. That many different plants are added to the basic drink made from the bark of *Banisteriopsis Caapi* or *B. inebrians* is well recognized. The exact identity of few is known, however. Much ethnobotanical field work remains to be done, especially in the Amazon, on this problem. It is complicated because many of the admixtures are very localized, restricted in some instances even to a single shaman.

The Sionas of Colombia add what is probably *Datura suaveolens* to their yajé drink to strengthen its effects. Their neighbors, the Inganos of Mocoa, are said to employ *Alternanthera Lehmannii* for the same purpose. In parts of the Vaupés of Colombia, a few leaves of the apocynaceous *Malouetia Tamaquarina* are sometimes added to caapi. Tobacco may occasionally constitute one of the additives. It is reported that the Tukanos of the boundary region between Brazil and Colombia employ five vines as admixtures with caapi, but they are known only by native names. A species of the solanaceous *Brunsfelsia*—probably *B. bonadora*—itself hallucinogenic, is used as an additive in Ecuador and unquestionably also in adjacent parts of Colombia.

Undoubtedly, the most interesting plants added are a species of *Psychotria* and *Banisteriopsis Rusbyana*. The reason for the extraordinary significance of these two plants will be clear when the chemistry of the narcotic preparations has been considered.

The chemistry of the narcotic species of *Banisteriopsis* has probably been more extensively studied than their botany. Nonetheless, failure to

Fig. 10.

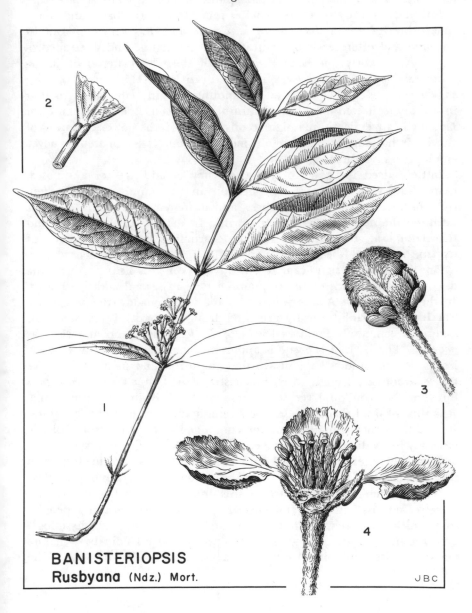

BANISTERIOPSIS
Rusbyana (Ndz.) Mort.

JBC

insist, until recently, upon strictly vouchered material for analysis has been the chief cause of the chaotic state of our understanding.

The earliest chemical studies made were carried out probably on *Banisteriopsis Caapi*. A number of alkaloids were described under names such as *telepathine, yageine, banisterine*; all of them eventually were identified as harmine, an alkaloid long known and isolated from Syrian rue (*Peganum Harmala*), an Asiatic plant of the Zygophyllaceae. More recent and carefully vouchered studies indicate that the bark (and sometimes the leaves) of *Banisteriopsis Caapi* and *B. inebrians* contain harmine and often lesser concentrations of harmaline and d-tetrahydroharmine. Recently, pieces of the stems of the type material of *Banisteriopsis Caapi*, collected by Spruce in Brazil over 115 years ago, have shown the presence of harmine in amounts roughly equivalent to that in freshly collected material! Harmine has been isolated from *Cabi paraensis*, an endemic malpighiaceous genus of the lower Amazon of Brazil. It has sundry uses in folk medicine, but it is apparently never employed as a hallucinogen.

Little indeed is known of the chemistry of additives of ayahuasca, caapi, and yajé. There is no question in the minds of field scientists, however, that many of these added ingredients greatly alter or heighten the narcotic effects of the drink. In the case of the *Datura* and the *Brunfelsia*, the addition to the β-carboline harmala alkaloids of tropane alkaloids—themselves highly hallucinogenic—is assumed.

One of the most significant recent advances in this field has been the discovery of alkaloids of the tryptamine type in several additive plants. In the westernmost Amazon—in Colombia and Ecuador—the admixture put into the drink basically prepared from the bark of *Banisteriopsis inebrians* commonly includes leaves of *B. Rusbyana*, known locally as *oco-yajé*. The bark of oco-yajé is apparently never employed—always the leaves. Recent studies have shown that the leaves and stem do not have the β-carboline alkaloids so characteristic of *B. Caapi* and *B. inebrians* but that they contain a very large amount of N, N-dimethyltryptamine. It is this alkaloid that increases the strength and duration of the visions. In addition, they contain as minor components N-methyltryptamine, 5-methoxy-N, N-dimethyltryptamine, 5-hydroxy-N, N-dimethyltryptamine, and Nβ-methyltetrahydro-β-carboline. The tryptamines are ineffective in the human body unless they are taken with some monoamine oxidase inhibitor. The β-carbolines act as this inhibitor, allowing the tryptamine to have its hallucinogenic effect in man. One wonders how peoples in primitive societies, with no knowledge of chemistry or physiology, ever hit upon a solution to the activation of an alkaloid by a monoamine oxidase inhibitor. Pure experimentation? Perhaps not. The examples are too numerous and may become even more numerous with future research.

Another additive utilized in several widely separated localities of the Amazon are leaves of *Psychotria viridis.* This species has been shown to contain N, N-dimethyltryptamine.

An interesting report of yajé intoxication by a botanical collector in the Colombian Putumayo stated that, after preparing the concentrated drink by long boiling of stems or bark of *Banisteriopsis inebrians,*

> . . . they add to the yagé the leaves and the young shoots of the branches of the *oco-yagé* or *chagro panga.* . . . The addition of this plant . . . produces the "bluish aureole" of their visions. These are cinematographic views, and occur after about half a liter of the drink has been consumed in portions an eighth of a liter each at intervals of half an hour. Thereafter, the Indian falls into a profound sleep, during which he is in a state of complete insensibility and anaesthesia. During this period, the subconscious activity acquires enormous intensity. The dreams follow each other with extraordinary precision and clearness, giving to the intoxicated person . . . the power of double vision and of seeing things at a distance, like certain mediums in their trances. Upon awakening, he retains clearly the hallucinations and fantastic visions which he experienced in unknown regions. . . .

The foregoing report described the effects of a preparation containing presumably harmine, or harmine and harmaline, fortified with N, N-dimethyltryptamine. The effects of the drug without the admixture of tryptamine, though different, are startlingly narcotic. In addition to the mode of preparing the drug, these effects depend in large measure on the social and physical environment in which the drug is taken, as well as upon the age, health, and mental state of the partaker. Commonly reported aspects of harmine intoxication in sophisticated subjects of Western cultures are nausea and vomiting, brachycardia, hypotension, tremor of the extremities and body vibrations, noises such as humming and buzzing, waviness of the environment, numbness, a feeling of sinking together with the sensation of flight, mental confusion, drowsiness, some amnesia, euphoria, and visual hallucinations, often of frightening objects such as jaguars, birds, and reptiles.

Ceremonial use of ayahuasca, caapi, and yajé differs greatly from tribe to tribe, but one early account will suffice as a general illustration. The discoverer of *Banisteriopsis Caapi,* the explorer Spruce, wrote in 1852 that the Tukanoan peoples of the Vaupés of northwestern Brazil prepared their caapi by beating part of the lower portion of the stem in a mortar with water, sometimes adding the slender roots of a vine called *caapi-pinima,* the identification of which still remains problematical.

When sufficiently triturated, it is passed through a sieve, which separates the woody fibre, and to the residue enough water is added to render it drinkable. Thus prepared, its color is brownish green and its taste bitter and disagreeable. . . . In the course of the night, the young men partook of caapi five or six times, in the intervals between the dances. . . . The cup-bearer—who must be a man, for no woman can touch or taste caapi—starts at a short run from the opposite end of the house, with a small calabash containing about a teacupful of caapi in each hand, muttering "Mo-mo-mo-mo-mo" as he runs, and gradually sinking down until at last his chin nearly touches his knees, when he reaches out one of his cups to the man who stands ready to receive it. . . . In two minutes or less after drinking it, its effects begin to be apparent. The Indian turns deadly pale, trembles in every limb, and horror is in his aspect. Suddenly contrary symptoms succeed: he bursts into a perspiration, and seems possessed with reckless fury, seizes whatever arms are at hand, his murucu bow and arrows or cutlass, and rushes to the doorway, where he inflicts violent blows on the ground or the doorposts, calling out all the while, "Thus would I do to mine enemy . . . were this he!" In about ten minutes, the excitement has passed off, and the Indian grows calm but appears exhausted. Were he at home in his hut, he would sleep off the remaining fumes, but now he must shake off his drowsiness by renewing the dance.

Spruce, Koch-Grünberg, and others have written about "other kinds" of caapi. Spruce, for example, mentioned *caapi-pinima* or "painted caapi" and suggested that it might be an apocynaceous plant that had reddish veins and blotches in the green leaves—the reason for its name. This apocynaceous plant, identified with reservations by Spruce as *Haemadictyon amazonicum* (now *Prestonia amazonica*), was thought to have been an additive with the *Banisteriopsis*.

In 1948, a hundred years after Spruce's sojourn in the same area, I discovered that the Makú Indians of the Rio Tikié, a Brazilian affluent of the Amazon, prepared an intoxicating drink from the malpighiaceous genus *Tetrapteris*: from a species called *T. methystica*. It is an extensive forest liana, the bark of which is utilized, with no admixtures, to make a bitter drink. The drink was yellowish, not brown, the usual color of caapi. I learned by experiment that it had strong hallucinogenic properties, very similar to those of *Banisteriopsis Caapi* itself. One wonders whether or not the "painted caapi" reported by Spruce could have referred to the kind of caapi that makes this unusual yellowish drink. More field work must be done before we understand the full significance of this "other kind" of caapi—*Tetrapteris methystica*. No chemical analysis has as yet been possible, but the chances are good that the hallucinogenic principles are the same as or similar to those in *Banisteriopsis Caapi*.

MYRISTICACEAE

One of the most fascinating hallucinogens—and one of the most recently discovered—is a snuff prepared in the northwest Amazon from the bark-resin of several species of *Virola*.

What appears to be the earliest report of this narcotic is by Koch-Grünberg (1909), who stated that the Yecuana Indians of the headwaters of the Orinoco had a very toxic snuff:

> Of an especial magical importance are cures during which the medicine man inhales *hak-ú-dufha*. This is a magical snuff used exclusively by medicine men and prepared from the bark of a certain tree which, pounded up, is boiled in a small earthenware pot, until all the water has evaporated and a sediment remains at the bottom of the pot. This sediment is toasted in the pot over a slight fire and is then finely powdered with the blade of a knife. Then the medicine man blows a little of the powder through a reed . . . into the air. Next, he snuffs, whilst, with the same reed, he absorbs the powder into each nostril successively. The *hak-ú-dufha* obviously has a strongly stimulating effect, for immediately the medicine man begins singing and yelling wildly, all the while pitching the upper part of his body backwards and forwards.

In 1938, the botanist Adolpho Ducke associated an intoxicating snuff with the leaves of *Virola theidora* and *V. cuspidata*. The snuff was called *paricá* in the Rio Negro basin. In 1939 he reiterated that, according to information he received "from natives in two localities in the upper Rio Negro, the paricá powder comes from the leaves of certain species of *Virola*. . . ." We now know that leaves are probably not employed to prepare the snuff, but this report represents the earliest association of a narcotic snuff with *Virola*.

In 1954, I reported the preparation and utilization of a snuff made from *Virola calophylla* and *V. calophylloidea* among sundry tribes of the Vaupés area of Colombia. In this westernmost region of its use, the snuff is taken only by medicine men or shamans, never generally and hedonistically by the male population as a whole, as in the case of *Anadenanthera* snuff among certain Orinoco groups today. This snuff—called *yákee* by the Puinave, *yató* by the Kuripako—is employed by at least a half dozen tribes in the Colombian Amazon.

It gradually became evident from sparse and scattered reports that *Virola*-snuff might be much more widely used in the Orinoco headwaters in Venezuela and on the northern tributaries of the Rio Negro of Brazil. This suspicion has now been fully substantiated through the collection of voucher specimens from numerous far-separated localities and tribes, but the complete picture of the utilization of this in-

Fig. 11.

teresting myristicaceous resin across the vast area of its use will require
many more years of careful field studies.

In 1967, Holmstedt and I were able to study the manufacture and
employment of *Virola*-snuff among several groups of Wãiká Indians
north of the Rio Negro in Brazil. The species used is *Virola theidora,*

although reports—apparently without voucher specimens—indicate that several other species may also be employed.

There are a number of methods of preparing the snuff, which is called *epená* or *nyakwana* by the many "tribes" which I include under the generic term *Waiká*. Some scrape the soft inner layer of the bark of the tree, dry the shavings by gentle roasting over a fire, and store them until they are needed for making the snuff. They are then crushed and pulverized, triturated and sifted. The resultant powder is fine, homogeneous, chocolate-brown, and highly pungent. Then, when the Indians desire it (but not always), a dust of the powdered dry leaves of the aromatic acanthaceous weed *Justicia pectoralis* var. *stenophylla* is added in equal amounts. The third, and invariable, ingredient is the ash of the bark of a rare leguminous tree, *Elizabetha princeps*. This tree is known as *amá* or *amasita* by the Waiká. These ashes are mixed in approximately equal amounts with the resin, or resin and *Justicia* powder, to give a brownish-gray snuff.

Other Waikás follow a different procedure, at least when they are preparing the snuff for ceremonial purposes. The bark is stripped from the *Virola* tree, the strips laid over a gentle fire in the forest, and the copious blood-red resin is scraped into an earthenware pot. It is boiled down and allowed to sun-dry. Then, alone or mixed with the powdered *Justicia* leaves, it is sifted and is ready for use.

The surprisingly high content of tryptamines in the resin of *Virola theidora* is responsible for the excessively rapid and strong intoxication of epená snuff. The Waikás snuff prepared from the resin alone, with no admixtures, possesses high concentrations of 5-methoxy N, N-dimethyltryptamine in addition to small amounts of other related tryptamines.

There are suspicions, still unconfirmed, that *Justicia pectoralis* var. *stenophylla*, often an admixture of *Virola*-snuff, may itself contain tryptamines and, consequently, be active. Tribes of the upper Orinoco basin may possibly use this weedy plant alone in preparing a hallucinogenic snuff.

Epená or nyakwana snuff is employed occasionally in what appears to be a nonritualistic or purely recreational context. Many tribal groups, however, utilize it only in ceremony. Often the shamans take it to induce a trance in connection with the diagnosis or treatment of disease. The ritual commemoration of death or, in some tribes, the annual endocannibalistic memorial of the dead of the preceding year, always requires considerable snuffing of epená. Dancing, chest-beating, and occasional fighting are characteristic before the onset of a long period of stupor during which, with visual and auditory hallucinations, the Indians commune with the spirit world, the *hekula*.

Intoxication by *Virola*-snuff sets in with extreme rapidity—within minutes after a large dose of the powder is blown into the nostrils through the bamboo or bird-bone tubes or is self-administered. Numbness and tingling of the limbs, twitching of the facial muscles, inability to coordinate muscular activity, nausea, visual hallucinations, and a deep stupor are characteristic. Macroscopia is frequent, entering into Waiká belief about the spirits that dwell within the plant. Levitation, or a sensation of floating in air or flying, is often reported.

My own experiences with snuff prepared from *Virola calophylla* may illustrate several points of interest:

The dose was snuffed at five o'clock. Within fifteen minutes a drawing sensation was felt over the eyes, followed very shortly by a strong tingling in fingers and toes. The drawing sensation in the forehead gave way to a strong and constant headache. Within a half hour, the feet and hands were numb and sensitivity of the fingertips had disappeared; walking was possible with difficulty, as with beri-beri. I felt nauseated until eight o'clock and experienced lassitude and uneasiness. Shortly after eight, I lay down in my hammock, overcome with drowsiness, which, however, seemed to be accompanied by a muscular excitation except in the hands and feet. At about nine-thirty, I fell into a fitful sleep which continued, with frequent awakenings, until morning. The strong headache lasted until noon. A profuse sweating and what was probably a slight fever persisted throughout the night. The pupils were strongly dilated during the first few hours of the intoxication. No visual hallucinations nor color sensations were experienced.

Among the Witotos, Boras, and other tribes of the Putumayo drainage areas of Colombia, the resin of *Virola theidora* is ingested in the form of small pellets when shamans desire to "talk with the little people" and to work charms against malevolent magic from distant medicine men. The soft inner bark is gently scraped and kneaded in cool water to remove the brownish "resin." The water is then set to a slow boil until only a thick syrup remains. This syrup is then formed into small pill-shaped portions which are coated with an alkaline powder prepared by boiling down water that has been allowed to leach through the ashes of any of several plants, commonly the bark of a species of *Gustavia*. The resin thus prepared is active because of the presence of β-carboline alkaloids (in addition to the tryptamines) which act as monoamine oxidase inhibitors.

Certain nomadic Makús on the Rio Pira-Paraná in the Colombian Vaupés prepare a snuff from the resin of *Virola elongata*. These very primitive Indians are said sometimes to take the crude resin orally when time is short for its proper preparation.

There are indirect indications that Venezuelan Indians may smoke the bark of *Virola sebifera* as an intoxicant.

RUBIACEAE

Psychotria

No rubiaceous plant is known to be employed alone as a narcotic in the New World. *Psychotria viridis* plays an important role, however, as an additive to the hallucinogenic drink prepared from *Banisteriopsis*

Fig. 12.

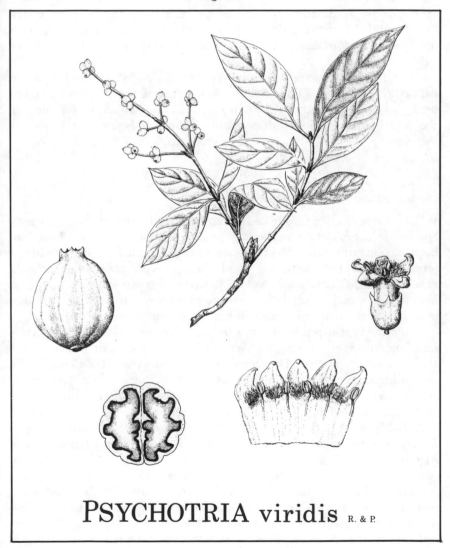

PSYCHOTRIA viridis R. & P.

Caapi. Its utilization as an admixture has been reported from widely separated localities in the Amazon of Ecuador and adjacent Colombia, in Peru and in Brazil. This wide range indicates that its use is a long-established culture trait.

The report that *Psychotria psychotriaefolia* was similarly used was based on a misidentification of botanical material, but the possibility does exist that other species of *Psychotria*—or even closely related rubiaceous genera—may also be so employed.

Recent chemical research has discovered the presence in *Psychotria viridis* of N, N-dimethyltryptamine—the first time this compound has been found in the family. It is curious that the same tryptamine has been found in another additive to the ayahuasca-caapi-yajé drink —the leaves of *Banisteriopsis Rusbyana.*

Psychotria viridis apparently is not employed alone to prepare a hallucinogenic drink. The tryptamine would not be active when taken orally without a monoamine oxidase inhibitor, which is supplied in the β-carboline alkaloids that occur in *Banisteriopsis Caapi* and *B. inebrians.*

SOLANACEAE

Datura, Latua, Methysticodendron

Datura has long been one of the most widely employed hallucinogens. Species have been used in both hemispheres, but the New World can boast the greater number of species valued for their psychotomimetic properties and for the intensity of their role in aboriginal societies. For in North, Central, and South America, this well-known genus has long played a major role in divination, prophecy, sorcery, diagnosis, and curing, as well as in adolescent initiation rituals.

The New World representatives of this genus are classified botanically into four subgenera or sections: Section I, *Stramonium,* in which *Datura stramonium* is placed; II, *Dutra,* with *D. inoxia;* III, *Ceratocaulis,* containing one species, *D. ceratocaulis;* and IV, *Brugmansia,* comprising all of the South American tree species. Species in all four sections have been utilized for their narcotic properties.

Probably most tribes in North America north of Mexico esteemed *Datura* for its strong psychotropic and narcotic characteristics. The Algonkian Indians of eastern North America administered *wysoccan,* an intoxicating medicine containing Jimson weed, or *Datura stramonium,* to youths about to undergo initiation into manhood. The boys experienced a kind of violent madness for twenty days, lost all memory, unliving their former lives and starting adulthood by forgetting that they had ever been children. California and Southwestern tribes similarly employed *Datura inoxia (D. meteloides)* or *toloache* in initiation rites. The Yumas took this drug to gain occult powers during these rituals, and the Yokuts valued it in a spring ceremony to ensure future good health and long life to adolescent initiates. The Luiseño gave it to youths who danced, screaming wildly "like animals," and finally fell into a stupor to find their adult life.

The Zuñis call *Datura inoxia a-neg-la-kya* and utilize it extensively as a medicine, narcotic, anaesthetic, and, in the form of a poultice, for treating wounds and bruises. The rain priests, who are the only ones permitted to collect the plant, put the powdered root into their eyes to see at night, to commune with the feathered kingdom, and to commune with the spirits of the dead to intercede for rain. The Zuñis ascribe a divine origin to the plant.

Several species of *Datura,* especially *D. inoxia,* played and still play very important magic roles in the life of many Mexican Indians. Its utilization goes far back into pre-Conquest history, when it was valued as both a medicine and a narcotic. Hernández reported that *toloatzin* was a major native medicine among the Aztecs, employed as an anodyne. He warned that excessive use could drive the patient to madness and "various and vain imaginations." The plant is still highly esteemed in Mexico. The modern Tarahumara, for example, add *Datura inoxia* or *tikuwari* to *tesgüino* (a fermented drink prepared from sprouted maize) to strengthen its effects, and the roots, leaves, and seeds of this species are the basis of a beverage employed ceremonially to induce visual hallucinations, which the medicine man values in diagnosing disease.

One of the most interesting Mexican species is *Datura ceratocaula,* a fleshy plant, with thick, forking stems that grows in shallow waters or swamps. Ancient Mexican Indians invoked the spirits of this plant in treating certain diseases.

All the native South American *Daturas* are arborescent and belong to the subgenus *Brugmansia,* sometimes treated as a distinct genus. They are all native to the Andean highlands—*D. arborea, D. aurea, D. candida, D. dolichocarpa, D. sanguinea, D. vulcanicola*—or to the warmer low-lands—*D. suaveolens.* They are handsome trees, well known in horti-culture, but they appear to be chromosomally aberrant cultigens un-known as wild plants. Their classification has long been and still remains uncertain: usually considered to represent six or seven species, the tree *Daturas* have recently been thought to comprise three or four species and a number of cultivars.

In South America, the preparation and use of *Datura* differ widely. It is most frequently taken in the form of pulverized seeds, sometimes dropped into beverages. The intoxication, fraught with grave dangers because of the extreme toxicity of the alkaloids, is marked by an initial

Fig. 13.   Flowers of *Datura suaveolens*. Mocoa, Colombia.

state of violence so furious that the partaker must be restrained until a deep, disturbed sleep overtakes him. The visual hallucinations are interpreted as spirit visitations.

Among the Ecuadorian Jívaro, for example, *Datura* is employed to correct refractory children in the belief that ancestral spirits carry out the admonishing. The ancient Chibcha of Colombia gave women and slaves potions of *D. aurea* to induce stupor prior to being buried alive with their deceased husbands or masters. The Inca are also known to have valued *Datura* as an intoxicant. It is still important in many areas from Colombia to Chile, along the Pacific coast of northern South America, and in certain parts of the Amazon.

There is a report that *curanderos* of the Ecuadorian highlands were recently taking lessons from Jívaro medicine men to reintroduce the use of *Datura* into the populous and now civilized Andean tribes.

The Kamsá and Ingano tribes of Sibundoy in the southern Colombia highlands use *Datura* extensively. They employ *Datura candida, D. dolichocarpa,* and *D. sanguinea* and even preserve for use and propagate vegetatively several highly atrophied named clones of *D. candida.* These clones are propagated merely by planting a piece of stem of the parent plant in wet soil. Some of these clones or "races" —representing possibly incipient "varieties" as the result of mutations— are such monstrosities that their parent species has, until recently, not been known. The natives have names for them and employ them for different purposes, since they apparently vary in chemical composition and produce slightly different effects one from another.

Identification of the species used by the tribes for special purposes leaves much to be desired in the way of accuracy, but since most species are known to contain similar tropane alkaloids—hyoscyamine, nor-hyoscyamine, and scopolamine, usually varying only in relative concentrations—this problem is not so serious as in the case of certain other narcotics.

Latua

Latua pubiflora is a spiny shrub or small tree found only in the coastal mountains of central Chile. A very strict endemic, known locally as *latué* or *árbol de los brujos* ("sorcerers' tree"), it was employed formerly by sorcerers in the Province of Valdivia for nefarious purposes. It is a virulent poison capable of producing a state of delirium and visual hallucinations, leading often to permanent insanity. Whether or not any cult or ritual surrounded its use is not known, but it was widely recognized and feared by the native population. A madness of any duration might be induced at the will of the practitioner, and dosages were a closely guarded secret. Many accidental poisonings were reported, partly because the shrub resembled closely a shrub known as *tayu (Flotowia diacanthoides)* which was a commonly employed medicinal plant of the region.

Known also, and probably more widely, under the synonym *Latua venenosa,* it is apparently nowhere abundant. Chemical studies of *Latua pubiflora* have reported alkaloids, presumably of the tropane series, but analyses with modern techniques, which are now underway with carefully vouchered collections, may provide a better understanding of the composition of this highly toxic hallucinogen.

Methysticodendron

Closely related to the genus *Datura*—and possibly an extraordinarily atrophied clone of a *Datura* instead of a distinct genus—*Methysticoden-*

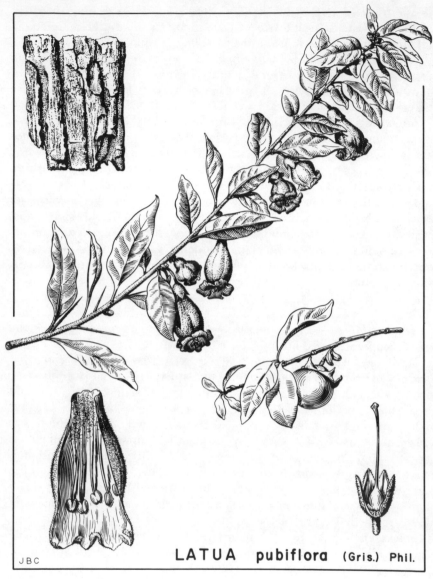

LATUA pubiflora (Gris.) Phil.

JBC

Fig. 14.

dron Amesianum represents a cultigen known only from the high Andean valley of Sibundoy in southern Colombia.

The Indians of the valley—Kamsá- and Ingano-speaking tribes—assert that this plant, known as *culebra borrachera*, is more potently hallucinogenic than *Datura* and more dangerous to use. It is taken in infusion by medicine men for divination, prophecy, and the practice of sorcery, and plays a role in native medicine as well.

The chemical constitution of *Methysticodendron Amesianum* supports the Indians' contention of the potency of the drug: it contains 1-scopolamine and hyoscyamine with minor amounts of other bases, but up to 80 per cent of the total alkaloid content is scopolamine.

SOME REMAINING PROBLEMS

Finally, there are a number of little-known psychotomimetics the chemistry and cultural uses of which urgently require further study before the societies that employ them disappear forever—and with them, much useful knowledge. Space does not permit more than brief mention of some of these:

Canada. Certain Indians chew the root of sweet calomel, *Acorus Calamus*, for its medicinal and stimulant effects. In large doses, this root can induce strong visual hallucinations.

Mexico. Yaqui medicine men in Sonora smoke the blossoms of *Genista canariensis*, a post-Conquest import from the Canary Islands. Its effects indicate possible borderline hallucinogenic characteristics. The plant is rich in cytisine, a toxic alkaloid also found in the hallucinogenic *Sophora secundiflora* of the Red Bean Cult. In southern Mexico the Mixtecs of Oaxaca employ two puffballs, *Lycoperdon mixtecorum* (*gi-i-wa* = "fungus of the first quality"), and *Lycoperdon marginatum* (*gi-i-sa-wa* = "fungus of the second quality") as hallucinatory divinatory agents. What makes these two gastromycetes unusual is the fact that they seem to produce auditory rather than visual hallucinations. As Furst (1970) has noted, a potentially very fruitful subject for ethnohistorical, ethnobotanical, and ethnographic study is *Erythrina*, the reddish seeds of which, known as *colorines*, are often sold in Mexican herb markets together with the red beans of the hallucinogenic *Sophora secundiflora*. The *Erythrina* is the legendary divinatory *tsité* tree of the *Popol Vuh*; its beans were also employed in the ritual *patolli* game of central Mexico. Some species of *Erythrina* contain indole or isoquinoline derivatives, but their possible use as a narcotic is not well known. The ancient Mexicans may also have valued two species of *Rhynchosia* —*R. pyramidalis* and *R. longeracemosa*—as narcotics. Oaxacan Indians today sometimes refer to *Rhynchosia* seeds as *piule*, a term they also occasionally apply to the seeds of the hallucinogenic morning-glories.

A recently discovered Mexican hallucinogen is the composite *Calea Zacatechichi*, widely used in folk medicine. The Chontal of Oaxaca take it to "clarify the senses."

Along with the curious hallucinogenic mint *Salvia divinorum,* which was evidently used also in prehispanic times, the Mazatec of Oaxaca are said to value two species of *Coleus* for their psychotomimetic properties. The Indians recognize all these mints as members of the same "family." *El macho* ("the male") is *Coleus pumilus. El nene* ("the child") and *el ahijado* ("the godson") are two forms of *Coleus Blumei.* Both are actually imports from the Old World and so could not have been used before the Conquest.

South America. In Ecuador, the fruits of the well-known toxic *Coriaria thymifolia,* called *shanshi,* were recently reported to have hallucinogenic effects. They are eaten to induce inebriation, with the sensation of flight. Also in the north, the solanaceous *Iochroma umbratica,* known in southern Colombia as *borrachero,* is said to be employed as a hallucinogenic narcotic by the Indians of Sibundoy. Farther south, *keule* or *hualhual (Gomortega Keule)* was formerly utilized as a narcotic by the Mapuche of Chile. Several species of the genus *Pernettya* have toxic fruits which induce hallucinations and other psychic and motor alterations—some, indeed, are said to cause permanent insanity. The best-known are *Pernettya furiens,* the *hierba loca* ("crazy herb") of Chile, and *P. parvifolia* of Ecuador. The leaves of a very restricted Chilean endemic, *Desfontainia spinosa* var. *Hookeri,* are also employed narcotically. *Brunsfelsia,* a solanaceous genus with many uses in folk medicine and apparently containing tropane alkaloids, has been employed as a narcotic in Amazonian Ecuador and Bolivia, either to strengthen the effects of ayahuasca or as the principal basis of a hallucinogenic drink. An interesting problem is the highly aromatic *Justicia pectoralis* var. *sphenophylla,* the dried and pulverized leaves of which are occasionally added to the snuff prepared from resin of the *Virola* tree. They may be employed alone as the source of a hallucinogenic snuff. There are suspicions, still unconfirmed, that *Justicia* possesses tryptamines. The Mapuche Indians of Chile reputedly smoke the leaves of *Lobelia Tupa,* known locally as *tupa* or *tabaco del diablo,* for their narcotic effects. This species has numerous uses in folk medicine—Chilean peasants, for example, use the juice of the leaves to relieve toothache—but whether the narcotic effects are truly hallucinogenic is still not certain.

In addition to these plants, the botanical identity of which is known, there are still a number of New World hallucinogens for which we have only Indian names. What, for example, was the source of the Mexican hallucinogen mentioned by several chroniclers as *popomatli* or *poyomate?* What is the *guayusa* taken by Jívaro to have "small dreams" in connection with hunting or warfare? Might this be the caffeine-containing *Ilex Guayusa,* taken alone, or in combination with other plants?

Another enigma is the narcotic known among the Arawakan Mojo Indians of Bolivia as *mariri*, taken by shamans to communicate with the spirits. Metraux reported that it looked like "our verbena" *(Verbena officinalis?)*. The Tanimuka Indians of Amazonian Colombia employ an as-yet unidentified liana to brew a hallucinogenic drink for boys in an adolescent initiation ritual. The effects are said to be similar to yajé, but the liana is not the well-known *Banisteriopsis Caapi*. Clearly, much more field work is required to solve these problems of botanical identification and chemistry.

Fig. 15. An early European view of tobacco smoking and fire making among the Tupinamba, on the east coast of Brazil. From a woodcut by A. Thevet, *Les Singularités de la France Antarctique, autrement nommée Amerique*, Paris, 1558.

TOBACCO AS A PSYCHOTOMIMETIC

All discussion of tobacco (*Nicotiana* spp.) has been purposely omitted from this overview of New World hallucinogens. There are some forty-five extratropical species indigenous to North and South America. While there are hundreds of references to the use of tobacco by American Indians in religious, magic, curing, and intoxicating practices, writers of the past have hardly begun to explore the real role and significance of the tobaccos in belief and ritual. Nevertheless, the literature from 1492 to the present leaves no doubt about the supreme ritualistic and mythological status accorded to these plants by the indigenous peoples of nearly all parts of the New World. There is also ample evidence that in many areas tobacco has been employed to trigger ecstatic states very similar, perhaps even identical, to those induced by the "true hallucinogens."

Whether or not some species of *Nicotiana* have chemical constituents with real hallucinogenic activity remains to be seen. The possibility exists, of course, that the solanaceous *Nicotiana,* belonging to a family rich in hallucinogenic principles, may, when fully investigated, yield interesting phytochemical data, supporting the ethnobotanical literature that ascribes "hallucinogenic" effects to certain tobacco preparations. In any event, the genus *Nicotiana* must be counted among the most important native psychotropic plants of the Western Hemisphere. At the present time, however, I prefer to leave it to qualified ethnographic investigators to assess its significance in the intellectual cultures of the New World.* On the basis of such comprehensive studies, it will be easier and more meaningful to evaluate and direct research in the botanical and chemical fields.

* See the following chapter, by Johannes Wilbert.

2

JOHANNES WILBERT

Tobacco and Shamanistic Ecstasy Among the Warao Indians of Venezuela *

Tobacco (*Nicotiana* spp.) is not generally considered to be a hallucinogen. Yet, like the sacred mushrooms, peyote, morning-glories, *Datura*, ayahuasca, the psychotomimetic snuffs, and a whole series of other New World hallucinogens, tobacco has long been known to play a central role in North and South American shamanism, both in the achievement of shamanistic trance states and in purification and supernatural curing. Even if it is not one of the "true" hallucinogens from the botanist's or pharmacologist's point of view, tobacco is often conceptually and functionally indistinguishable from them.

We know that Indians from Canada to Patagonia esteemed tobacco as one of their most important medicinal and magical plants and that some employed it as a vehicle of ecstasy. We also know that everywhere and almost always in prehistoric and more recent historic times its use was strictly ritualistic. Its increasing secularization among Indians is

* The author expresses his appreciation to several colleagues, including Peter T. Furst, Michael D. Coe, and Floyd G. Lounsbury, for discussions which helped clarify some of the theoretical implications of this paper; to Karin Simoneau for her efficient research assistance; and to Franklin L. Murphy, Jr., for his assistance in the field. Field research on which this paper is based was funded through the Venezuelan Indian Project of the University of California at Los Angeles and cosponsored by the Centro Latinoamericano de Venezuela (CLAVE). Financial assistance rendered by the Creole Foundation of Caracas has greatly aided the research work. I also gratefully acknowledge the logistic assistance of the Capuchin Mission, Guayo, Orinoco Delta. But most of all I am indebted to the shamans of the Winikina-Warao, who gave me their trust and friendship.

a modern development, adopted from Europeans (to whom tobacco was of course unknown prior to the first voyage of Columbus).* Nevertheless, ancient ritual meanings associated with native tobacco persist: in many tribes the tobacco they themselves cultivate or collect in the wild state is reserved for ritual and ceremonial use, whereas the white man's tobacco, or "Virginia tobacco," a hybrid domesticate of *Nicotiana tabacum,* is freely smoked.

Tobacco was and continues to be used in many ways, of which smoking (in cigarettes, cigars, or pipes) is the most common. This is related to the many esoteric meanings of tobacco smoke in shamanistic ritual, especially curing ceremonies. Zerries (1969:314) points out: "The power of the shaman is often linked with his breath or tobacco smoke, both of which possess cleansing and reinvigorating properties which play an important part in healing and in other magic practices."

Of the techniques other than smoking, the best-known are snuffing, drinking, chewing, eating, sucking, and licking. Even smoking is performed in different ways and with different meanings. Smoke may be blown (in supernatural curing or in feeding the supernaturals with tobacco smoke) or swallowed ("eaten") in enormous quantities to induce trance states. For example, in his curing ritual, the shaman of the Tenetehara Indians of Brazil will dance, chant, and shake his rattle, stopping

> . . . from time to time to take deep drags on a long cigar made of native tobacco rolled in *tawarí* bark. He soon becomes intoxicated from the smoke combined with the rhythm of the song and the dance. This process is known as "calling" the spirit. The spirit responds only to its distinctive songs and he himself is only prepared to receive the spirit after gulping large quantities of tobacco smoke. . . . During this time the "spirit is strong" and he falls unconscious (Wagley and Galvão, 1949:111).

Like smoke, snuff may be inhaled for its psychoactive effect or blown out, depending on the supernatural need. Tacana shamans in lowland Bolivia, for example, blow tobacco powder into the air to repel malevolent supernatural beings threatening a patient or the community.

Sometimes tobacco is used in combination or association with true vegetal hallucinogens, such as *Datura, Banisteriopsis Caapi,* or psycho-

---

* In view of the many parallels between Siberian and American Indian shamanism, the following remarks by Wasson (1968:332) on tobacco are of interest: "Among Europeans and their descendants elsewhere it became a habit and an addiction but played no role in religion. But after tobacco reached Siberia, probably also in the latter part of the sixteenth century or at the latest in the seventeenth century, it is astonishing how quickly the tribesmen adapted it to shamanism, thus recapturing for it the religious meaning that it has always had for the American Indians."—Ed.

tropic cacti. Often it serves its primary sacred function as the super-natural purifying, mortifying, and reinvigorating agent during the long and arduous initiatory training of novice shamans. This is true especially among Carib and other indigenous language groups in lowland northern South America. We have graphic firsthand accounts of these initiatory ordeals by such eminent ethnographers as Theodor Koch-Grünberg (1917–28). The young Indian shamans are deprived of normal food for long periods, during which they become emaciated almost to the point of skeletonization (ritual death and skeletonization are important aspects of shamanic initiation in many parts of Asia and America). Instead of food they are repeatedly fed large quantities of liquefied tobacco, through both nose and mouth, to induce narcotic trances. In this state the novice makes his first celestial ascent to meet face to face with the spirits inhabiting the Otherworld. Later he begins to use other psychotropic plants as well, especially *Banisteriopsis Caapi,* in which, one shaman told Koch-Grünberg, "resides the shaman, the jaguar." This refers to the common conceptual identification of shamans with jaguars in much of Middle and South America, an identification often realized through the use of hallucinogens or psychotomimetic substances.

Tobacco may be one of several vehicles for ecstasy; it may be taken in combination with other plants, as we have seen, to induce narcotic trance states; or it may represent the sole psychoactive agent employed by shamans to transport themselves into the realm of the supernatural, as is the case among the Warao of the Orinoco Delta in Venezuela. That Warao shamans smoke enormous "cigars" as much as 50 to 75 centimeters long has been known since early contact times, but the meaning of tobacco in Warao intellectual culture has often gone un-noticed. This is not surprising; few outsiders can expect to penetrate a culture meaningfully in the limited amount of time usually available for field work. My own experience is instructive. In 1954, after an initial period of field work, I dimly perceived the religious complexity of the Warao culture with its three types of shamans and a temple-priest-idol cult (Wilbert, 1957). Since then I have worked for more than fifteen years with the Warao shaman to whom I owe much of what follows in these pages. At first we communicated through an interpreter, later in Spanish, and more recently in his own language. Only in 1969, however, did he finally consent to lead me step by step beyond the outer fringes of Warao religion into that complex supernatural world that opens up for the shaman through the act of intensive smoking.

THE WARAO *

The majority of Warao, a typically riverine fishing people, inhabit the labyrinthine swamps and waterways of the Orinoco Delta in eastern Venezuela. Smaller groups live to the west of the Delta, in the neighboring states of Sucre and Monagas, and still others are found southeast of the main distribution area, along the swampy coastal belt of Guyana and Surinam. The Warao have lived in this region of some 17,000 square kilometers since prehistoric times, protected by their difficult environment from Afro-Europeans and other Indian tribes, neither of whom succeeded in conquering their stronghold. For this reason the Warao are among the few South American Indian peoples still surviving as a numerically substantial and culturally thriving tribal society, relatively free of genetic and cultural admixture. Counting the estimated 500 or so Warao living in Guyana and Surinam, the total population should now stand around 14,000 or even 15,000.

The Warao believe they inhabit a saucer-shaped earth surrounded by a belt of water. The "stepped" celestial vault covers both earth and ocean and rests on a series of mountains situated at the cardinal and intercardinal points. Much of a Warao Indian's life is spent in propitiating a number of Supreme Spirits *(Kanobos)* who inhabit these mountains at the ends of the world and who require nourishment in the form of tobacco smoke from the people.

The priest-shaman *(wishiratu)* visits these spirits in his dreams or in a tobacco-induced trance and, on returning from such a visit, transmits the message of the Supreme Spirits to the community. One of the four major spirits is usually present among the people in the form of a sacred stone. The annual *moriche* festival, called *nahanamu,* over which the priest-shaman presides, is celebrated in propitiation of the Supreme Spirits who request that the ceremony be held and who will protect the community if their command is heeded. Sickness is believed to be caused by one or another of the deified *Kanobos,* who thereby expresses his dissatisfaction with man and sends his *hebu* (spirit) to do harm or even kill. Children especially are subject to such attacks. The priest-shaman is the only one who can intervene as curer because only he can relate directly to the Supreme *Kanobos.*

In addition to the priest-shaman there are two other important religious practitioners among the Warao. The "light" shaman is known as *bahanarotu.* He presides over an ancient cult of fertility called *habisanuka.* As we shall see later, the *bahanarotu* travels in his dream or tobacco-induced trance state to an eastern part of the cosmic vault.

* For a more detailed description of Warao culture, see Wilbert, 1972.

Fig. 16.   A Warao *wishiratu* shaman communicates with the supernatural after
smoking his cigar during a curing ritual. (Photo by Peter T. Furst.)

The celestial bridge of tobacco smoke which he frequents and maintains between his community and the eastern Supreme *Bahana* (spirit)
guarantees abundance of life on earth. In their aggressive shamanic
role, *bahanarotus* spread sickness and death among their enemies by

hurling magic arrows at them. Only a friendly *bahanarotu* can assuage such misfortune, through the use of tobacco and the widespread traditional shamanic technique of sucking out the illness-causing foreign bodies magically introduced by the malevolent sorcerer.

The "dark" shaman, known as *hoarotu,* maintains the connection between the Warao in the center of the universe and the powers of the West. This connection became severed in ancient times and can be re-established only by the *hoarotu.* The spirit beings in the West subsist through their medium, the dark shaman, on the blood and flesh of man. To procure this human food for his masters, the *hoarotu* kills his victims by means of magic projectiles, again through the medium of tobacco smoke.

Thus there exist among the Warao three religious practitioners who derive their shamanic power from three different cosmic sources. All three are ambivalent and can adopt either a benevolent or a malevolent role: the *wishiratu* can cause and cure *hebu* sickness; the *bahanarotu hatabu* sickness; and the *hoarotu hoa* sickness. Further, all three kinds of shaman use tobacco smoke as their principal ecstatic and therapeutic vehicle. In spite of existing regionalism with regard to underlying concepts, it is generally true that shamanic initiation, ecstasy, and curing are unthinkable among the Warao without the aid of tobacco.

The overwhelming magical importance of tobacco is all the more remarkable in view of the fact that tobacco was originally absent from the Orinoco Delta. Even today it is not generally cultivated and must be acquired through barter or purchase. Until very recently, smoking was the sole prerogative of the religious and magical practitioners, who obtained their supply from Creole settlers of the western Delta and from the island of Trinidad. *Wishiratus* and *bahanarotus* require considerable quantities of tobacco to feed the *Kanobo* and *Bahana* spirits through the smoking of their extraordinary cigars. Considering that propitiation of these spirits by means of tobacco smoke is an absolute *sine qua non* of Warao intellectual culture, and that shamans must use tobacco to achieve the required trance state for travel to the Otherworld, one may imagine that procuring the sacred plant provided the principal impetus for Warao excursions into the hazardous frontier regions and the open ocean.

In the old days, ordinary mortals hesitated to smoke for fear of precipitating an undesirable encounter with tobacco-craving spirits. Nowadays cigarettes and tobacco in every form are smoked freely by most Warao; even the women indulge more or less freely as evening falls. But the long indigenous "cigars" are exclusively shamanic. (Strictly speaking, the Warao "cigar" is really a long tubular wrapping made of the stipule of a *manaca* palm, called *wina moru* in Warao, into which plugs of tobacco are inserted and which is consumed along with the tobacco, rather than a true cigar whose wrappings as well as contents consist of tobacco.) Warao shamans must never attempt to feed the Supreme Spirits with "Virginia blends," because the foreign "perfumed" aroma is offensive to the spirits. (Unaware of this prohibition, on one ceremonial occasion I deposited a Camel cigarette as an offering in the sanctuary of the *Kanobo* spirits. The officiating priest-shaman immediately asked me to replace it with a piece of "black" tobacco. Not only would it be more suitable for the *Kanobos,* its smell would also be free of the offensive odor of the burning cigarette paper.)

The Shamanistic World of Light and Darkness

The Wishiratu

At the ends of the universe *(aitona)* there live four supreme spirits, three male and one female, called *Kanobos,* "Our Grandfathers." The *Kanobo* Supreme, named *Karoshimo,* inhabits the world mountain of the south, *Kanobo Ariawara* lives on the world mountain of the east, and *Kanobo Warowaro* on the mountain of the north. The female *Kanobo* is called *Daunarani,* the Mother of the Forest; her serpent body lives in the southwest and her spirit in the southeast.

Generally speaking, all four *Kanobos* are benignly inclined toward mankind, so long as men propitiate them with tobacco, *moriche* flour, fish or crabs, and incense. The *Kanobos* accept these offerings gratefully before returning everything except the tobacco to be ritually consumed by the people. The tobacco the spirits keep for themselves, for tobacco smoke is their proper nourishment. They appreciate it especially when it has been perfumed with incense. If neglected for a long period of time by the priest-shaman, the *Kanobos* may become vindictive and send *wishi*-pains and death down to earth. Pains are invisible and yet materially conceived agents of the *Kanobos,* who endow the priest-shaman with the power to control them—hence his name, *wishiratu,* literally "Master of Pains." This control over pains represents the actual power base of the *wishiratu* as shaman.

The Warao recognize lower- and higher-ranking *wishiratus.* The most prestigious *wishiratu* of any Warao community is always the keeper of the sacred stone image. This stone, said to measure no more than thirty centimeters in length and ten in width, with an irregular surface, is variously called "Image of *Kanobo,*" "Grandfather," and "Son of *Kanobo.*" Though wholly unworked, it is conceptualized by the Indians as a head, with a recognizable face. On the lower back of the head is said to be an open sore, constantly oozing blood. The Indians are convinced that if any ordinary person, whether a member of the tribe or an outsider, were to lay eyes on the sacred stone, he would instantly be struck blind. The mythic origin of the image goes back to a primordial "first time," when an ancestral shaman, anguished by death and pain in his community, undertook an arduous pilgrimage to one of the sacred mountains at the end of the cosmos to ask the *Kanobo* for an end to the dying. He begged him to come and live in the midst of his people rather than far away on the mountain. The *Kanobo* agreed to do so—in the form of the sacred stone image. He also promised to advise the shaman in the future and to refrain from sending his pains if an initial sacrifice of ten men was made and the people agreed to continue to make offerings of tobacco smoke. By the act of residing in the cult house or temple of the community in the form of the image, the *Kanobo* effected the actual transfer of control over pain to the first shaman and, by extension, to all future *wishiratus*. The ten men selected for the primordial sacrifice were laid side by side and killed by the *Kanobo's* jumping over them.

Ever since this first contract between the ancestral *wishiratu* and the *Kanobo,* Warao communities have identified themselves as "People of *Kanobo Karoshimo*," "People of *Kanobo Ariawara*," or "People of *Kanobo Warowaro*," respectively, depending on which of the three male *Kanobos* was visited on the primordial pilgrimage in the tradition of the local group. The temple of the *Kanobo* image is a small hut set apart from the dwellings and screened on all sides with palm fronds or walls of folded *temiche* leaves.

To fulfill the primordial promise of abundant sacrificial tobacco smoke, *wishiratus* smoke incessantly. Their "cigars," as we have noted, are between 50 and 75 centimeters long and contain several tightly rolled leaves of black tobacco sprinkled with the fragrant resin of the *Curucay* or *Tacamahaco* (*Protium heptaphyllum* [Aubl.]), called *shi-buru* tree by the Warao. Incense is offered either in special incense burners or together with tobacco smoke. Small granules are wrapped into the cigar with the tobacco or else a ball of the incense is held to the burning tip in the course of smoking.

The *wishiratu* is not only obliged to "feed" the *Kanobo* whose rock spirit is housed in the village temple; he must also offer tobacco and incense to the other *Kanobos* living at the ends of the world. The *wishiratu* carries out the "feeding" of these spirits by holding the long cigar vertically and pointing it in the direction of the supreme *Kanobos,* all the while inhaling with hyperventilation or swallowing the smoke.

The *Kanobos* travel over well-conceived roads: from the dancing platform in the middle of the village they ascend to the zenith. Here lives a lesser *Kanobo* by the name of *Yaukware,* who supplies them with fresh tobacco. From the zenith the roads lead along the curvature of the firmament to the cardinal and intercardinal points of the *aitona* —the end of the Warao universe. The roads of the major *Kanobos* all end on top of sacred mountains which look like giant tree trunks and which support the cosmic vault—reminiscent of the well-known Mesoamerican concept of world trees supporting the sky. *Kanobos* also travel along the *aitona* circle along the end of the world to visit one another.

A *wishiratu* frequents the same celestial roads but mostly visits the mountain inhabited by the patron *Kanobo* of his community. Here the shaman has his own little house. If he wishes to confer with his *Kanobo*, the *wishiratu* travels in the smoke of his cigar to the zenith. There, after more intensive smoking, he mounts a flying horse (*behoroida*, literally big dog) which takes him to the *aitona*. It is understood that only well-prepared and established *wishiratus* are able to do this—that is, those who carry three pairs of pains (*wishis*) in their breasts and who have successfully completed their initiatory trance journey to their *Kanobo*.

Yaukware, the *Kanobo* of lesser rank who lives at the zenith, was once also a *wishiratu*, the first shaman ever to make the celestial ascent (Wilbert, 1970:184–85). This *wishiratu* lived peacefully on earth with his mother, brother, wife, and son, until one day he came upon his wife and brother committing adultery. Deeply grieved, the *wishiratu* took his shaman's rattle, called his son, and sat with him on his shaman's box. He lit a long shamanic cigar, and, ignoring the pleading of his mother, slowly ascended with his son to the zenith within the smoke of the shaman's cigar. From the zenith *Yaukware* sent pains to kill the adulterers and to make other Warao ill.

Nowadays novice *wishiratus* have to be taught how to ascend to *Yaukware*'s house in the zenith by means of smoking tobacco. After undergoing instruction in the special knowledge of *wishiratus,* the novice chants and fasts for several days. Then the master *wishiratu* hands him a long cigar charged with *wishi* spirits. These are to become the young *wishiratu*'s spiritual *Kanobos* and special familiars. The candidate falls into a deep trance sleep and in this state finds himself embarking on his initiatory journey across the "Road of the *Wishiratus*" to the end of the world.

This maiden voyage into the Otherworld is the most crucial ecstatic flight the *wishiratu* will ever undertake. Not only must he overcome many obstacles, his very life is threatened by the ever-present possibility that his dream will be interrupted so suddenly that his roaming soul will not have time to return to his body. A novice suffering this fate will never get to practice and will soon die.

Once the *wishiratu* in his ecstatic tobacco trance has left *Kanobo* *Yaukware's* house in the zenith he sets out on one of the roads that lead to a *Kanobo* at the end of the world. It is a difficult journey and he would surely fail were it not for an invisible psychopomp, or soul guide, who leads the way and advises the young traveler. The first station he reaches is a *manaca* palm. As mentioned, it is from the epidermis of the *manaca* leaf stalk that the Warao make the *wina,* or tube, for their cigars. This palm is the shamanic tree of all *wishiratus,* who come here to carve their mark into its bark. The novice is advised to follow the example of his predecessors and told that his mark will remain fresh as long as he lives.

Next he and his soul guide come to a place of many water holes, where each living *wishiratu* finds his own reservoir of water for drinking and purification. Only upon his death will his water hole dry up forever. Further along the road, the novice shaman encounters another *manaca* palm, and here he rolls his first shamanic cigar (the initial one having been presented to him by his *wishiratu*-teacher).

Then the young *wishiratu* has to clear an abyss filled with hungry jaguars, snapping alligators, and frenzied sharks all eager to devour him. A vine hangs down over the abyss and, grasping it firmly, the novice swings himself across. But this is still not the end of his ordeal. Soon he reaches another obstacle. The path becomes extremely slippery, so that he can hardly keep his balance. To make matters worse, on every side are threatening demons armed with spears, waiting to kill any novice who falls.

Next there are four stations where the novice is tested by groups of people barbecuing the meat of boar, deer, tapir, and alligator, respectively. He is offered the meat of all, but no matter how hungry he is and how strong the temptation, he must reject all of the proffered meat except the venison. Greatly tempting also are the women he meets next; he sees them making bark cloth for pubic covers but must not linger with them, much less have sexual intercourse.

Escaping the powerful lure of these women, the novice reaches the terrifying place where, stretched out on its back before him, he encounters the giant hawk, devourer of young *wishiratus.* Its beak snaps, its claws grasp, and its wings flap open and shut. Without betraying fear, the novice must step over the rapacious bird and pass by a great pile of bleached bones—the sad remains of his less fortunate predecessors.

Finally the candidate shaman has to pass through a hole in an enormous tree trunk with rapidly opening and closing doors. He hears the voice of his guide and companion from the other side of the trunk, for this spirit has already cleared the dangerous passage and now encourages the fearful novice to follow his example. The candidate jumps through the clashing doors and looks around inside the hollow tree.

There he beholds a huge serpent with four colorful horns and a fiery-red luminous ball on the tip of her protruding tongue.* This serpent has a servant with reptilian body and human head whom the candidate sees carrying away the bones of novices who failed to clear the clashing gateway of the tree.

The novice hurries outside and finds himself at the end of the cosmos. His patron *Kanobo*'s mountain rises before him. Here he will be given a small house of his own, where he may sojourn in his future tobacco trances to consult with the *Kanobo* and where eventually he will come to live forever upon successful completion of his shaman's life on earth.

After this initiatory encounter with his patron *Kanobo* at the end of the world, the young *wishiratu* awakens from his tobacco trance as a new man. He carries with him six *wishi* spirits to assist him in curing men who suffer from spirit sickness. This sickness is caused by a hostile *wishiratu* who blows a "pain" into a victim. In his shaman's rattle, the *wishiratu* carries additional spirit helpers in the form of quartz crystals. These too assist him in curing by extracting sickness-causing *wishi* pains. As time goes by, the young *wishiratu* will become more and more familiar with the complex world of *Kanobos* and learn how to be wise in maintaining a contractual partnership between them and his people. This is a monumental spiritual obligation, weighing heavily on him, and involving a never-ending cycle of ritual observances and tobacco-induced ecstatic journeys to the ends of the cosmos.

The Bahanarotu

The "history of consciousness" of the Warao as a people has its origin in the "House of Tobacco Smoke," created *ex nihilo* by the Creator Bird of the Dawn. The House of Smoke is the birthplace of "light" shamanism, called *bahana*. Its materialization by means of solidified tobacco smoke took place through the conscious act of a bird spirit, who at the beginning of time arose as a young man in the East. The radiant body of this youth, his weapons, and his shamanic rattle were all made of tobacco smoke.

The following is a condensation of some twenty hours of conversation on the origin of the *bahanarotu* shaman, in March and July, 1970, with a Winikina-Warao shaman. It is not to be taken as verbatim translation, but I have endeavored to preserve as much as possible the original form and spirit of this remarkable tradition as I perceived it.

---

* Reminiscent of the well-known and very ancient Chinese and Indian motif of the sky dragon with the wish-fulfilling pearl.

The House of Tobacco Smoke

One day the youth who had arisen in the East spread out his arms and proclaimed his name: *Domu Hokonamana Ariawara,* "Creator Bird of the Dawn." With his left wing he held a bow and two quivering arrows, and his right wing shook a rattle. The plumes of his body chanted incessantly the new song that was heard in the East.

The thoughts of the Bird of the Dawn fell now on a house—and immediately it appeared: a round, white house made of tobacco smoke. It looked like a cloud. The singing Bird walked inside whirling his rattle.

Next he wanted to have four companions; four men and their wives. Rooms were already provided for each couple along the eastern wall of the House of Smoke.

"You, Black Bee," said the Bird of the Dawn. "Come share my solitude." And the Black Bee arrived with his wife. They transformed into tobacco smoke and chanted the song of the Bird of the Dawn.

"Wasp is next," called the Bird. The red Wasp arrived with his wife, transformed into smoke, and joined in the singing.

"Termite, now you," said the Bird of the Dawn. Termite's body and that of his wife were yellow. They took the room adjacent to Wasp, transformed into smoke, and learned the new song.

"Honey Bee, you are the last to be called." The Bees' bodies were blue. They occupied the room next to Termite. Like the others they transformed into tobacco smoke and joined in the chanting.

"I am the Master of this House of Smoke," exclaimed the Creator-Bird. "You are my companions. Black Bee is your chief, Wasp the constable, Termite and Honey Bee are workmen." Consenting to this, each companion approached the Master and stroked his head, shoulders, and arms so as to know him well. They chanted and smoked cigars. Thus they became the *bahanarao,* those who blow smoke.

The thoughts of the Bird of the Dawn fell now on a table draped in white and set with four dishes in a row—and there they stood in the middle of the house, all made of smoke. The Bird laid his weapons on it and said: "Now let us finish the Game of *Bahana.*"

On Black Bee's dish there appeared a sparkling rock crystal. On Wasp's dish there was a ball of white hair. On Termite's plate white rocks appeared, and on Honey Bee's there gathered smoke of tobacco—the fourfold set of the Game of *Bahana.**

Such is the House of Smoke of the Creator Bird of the Dawn. This is how it became the birthplace of *bahana,* the shamanistic practice of blowing

---

* Crystal, hair ball, rocks, and tobacco smoke, each identified with a specific insect and color, are the principal agents of the shaman's power. Like arrows and other objects, they can be dispatched through the air as magical carriers of sickness. For the techniques used by shamans to accomplish this supernatural feat and a description of the "Game of *Bahana,*" which is played in a kind of "tobacco seánce," see below.

smoke and sucking out sickness. The House of Smoke is situated to the East, halfway between the junction of earth and sky and the zenith of the cosmic vault. It came about long before there lived any Warao.

Then one day there appeared in the center of the earth a man and a woman. They were good people but their minds were unformed. However, they had a four-year-old* son who was very intelligent. He put his thoughts on many things. This way he came to think about the *Hoebo* place in the West with its stench of human cadavers, its blood, and its darkness. "There must be something in the East as well," reasoned the boy, "something light and colorful." He decided to go and explore the universe.

Now, although the young boy's body was relatively light, it was far too heavy for flight. The boy thought much about this until one day he asked his father to pile up firewood under his hammock. For four days he abstained from food and drink. In the evening of the fifth day he lit the wood with virgin fire and went to sleep. Then with the surging heat and smoke of the new fire the boy's spirit ascended to the zenith. Someone spoke to him, saying, "Follow me. I will show you the bridge to the House of Smoke in the East."

Soon the boy found himself on a bridge made of thick white ropes of tobacco smoke. He followed the invisible spirit guide until, a short distance from the center of the celestial dome, he reached a point where marvelous flowers began meandering alongside the bridge in a rainbow of brilliant colors —a row of red and a row of yellow flowers on the left, and lines of blue and green flowers on the right. A gentle breeze wafted them back and forth. Like the bridge they adorned, the flowers were made of solidified tobacco smoke. Everything was bright and tranquil. The invisible guide ushered the boy toward the House of Smoke. From a distance he already perceived the chanting of the *bahanarao*.

The bridge led right to the door of the House of Smoke in the East. The boy arrived there, listened to the beautiful music, and became so elated that he desired nothing more than to enter at once.

"Tell me who you are," demanded a voice from inside.

"It is I. The son of Warao."

"How old are you?"

"Four."

"You may enter," consented the Creator-Bird. It was he, the Supreme *Bahana,* who had questioned the boy. "You are pure and free of women," he said.

The boy set foot into the House of Smoke. He saluted the Creator-Bird of the Dawn and his four companions who came out of their quarters. The boy stood in front of the table with its four-part Game of *Bahana* and the weapons on top. He wanted to learn all about them.

"Which one would you rather possess?" the Supreme *Bahana* wanted to know.

* Four is the sacred number of the Warao, a concept they share with numerous North and South American Indian tribes.

"I take them all: the crystal, the white hair, the rocks, the smoke, and the bow and arrows as well." The boy was very wise.

"You shall have them."

"Now teach me your beautiful song."

And emerging from below the floor of the House of Smoke the boy beheld the head of a serpent with four colored plumes: white, yellow, blue, and green. They chimed a musical note like a bell. Projecting its forked tongue, the plumed serpent produced a glowing white ball of tobacco smoke.

"I know *bahana!*" exclaimed the youth.

"Now you possess it," said the *Bahana*. "You *are* a *bahana-rotu.*"

The serpent retreated. The insect-companions returned to their chambers and the boy awakened from his ecstatic trance. He rejected his mother's food for four days and more.

"You will die," she warned.

But he only appeared dead. He no longer desired *moriche* flour, fish, and water. He longed for the food of *bahana:* tobacco smoke.

On the fifth day the young *bahanarotu* experienced a strange transformation. His hands, his feet, his head began to glow. His arms and legs and finally his entire body turned brilliantly white. Then people appeared around his house: ten couples of Black Bee people, ten couples of Wasp people, ten couples of Termite people, and ten couples of Honey Bee people. And there were also many beautiful children among them.

"He is alive," they said.

"My name is *bahanarotu,*" said the youth. This was the first time the name "*bahana*" was uttered on earth. The *bahanarotu* built a small house, put his four-part Game of *Bahana* into a basket, and placed next to it his bow and arrows. The smoke of his cigars formed a path from the center of the earth to the zenith, where the bridge commences that leads to the House of Smoke in the East.

The *bahanarotu* kept his body light by eating very little. Tobacco smoke remained his principal food. His parents died, and, with no fellow Warao on earth, he married a beautiful Bee girl, a child like himself. They lived together but did not sleep together.

The young *bahanarotu* observed in the palms of his hands four dark spots right below each of his fingers. From there, through the arches of his arms, led paths of smoke into his breast to his four sons, the insect-companions, who were gradually taking form. Elder Brother Black Bee above Younger Brother Wasp was living on the strong right side of his chest. Elder Brother Termite above Younger Brother Honey Bee on the left. They were growing firmer while the *bahanarotu* kept feeding them smoke. In the tube of his cigar he rolled four portions of tobacco, one for each of his sons. Had he slept with his wife while the sons were still feeble, the spirit children would have died, and *bahana* would have vanished from this earth.

Instead the young couple abstained for four times four years, until the *bahana* sons had grown strong from the rich tobacco food. Then the time had come for the *bahanarotu* to talk to them.

"My sons," he said, "I will give you a mother. Do not be alarmed. Tonight I will show you your mother."

When the *bahanarotu* slept for the first time with his Bee wife he was very gentle. Only the head of his penis entered her vagina. The four spirit sons saw their mother and liked her. Also the mother beheld her white-smoke sons in a dream and found them pleasing and handsome. During each of the succeeding nights the *bahanarotu* penetrated further and deeper. Thus the first *bahana* family was established.

The insect-people who had been living about the *bahanarotu's* home returned now to the House of Smoke.

"We should go there too," said the *bahanarotu* to his wife. "It is lonely here."

They began to fast so as to lighten their bodies. They smoked and smoked and after eight days the *bahanarotu* ascended. His wife followed shortly, but when she entered the House of Smoke, the Supreme *Bahana* suffered a seizure.

"I know how to help him," said the woman. Walking up to the Supreme *Bahana* she transformed herself into a beautiful black sea bird.* She spread out her wings, shook them like rattles, and, while blowing tobacco smoke on the epileptic body of her patient, soothed him gently with her plumes. The Supreme *Bahana* recovered.

"You are a *bahanarotu* indeed," said he. "Remain here, *Sinaka Aidamo*, spirit of seizures."

So there they are, the *bahanarotu* and his wife, smoking, rattling, and chanting in unison with the *bahanarao*.

Much time elapsed, and when many people appeared in the center of the earth, they knew nothing about *bahana* and the bridge that reached from their village to the House of Tobacco Smoke. For this reason the *bahanarotu* rolled a cigar with two *bahana* inside and aimed it at a young man whom he had chosen to receive them. He sent Smoke for the right side of the youth's chest and Rocks for his left side. Smoke became the Elder Brother, Rocks the Younger. When they struck the youth he fell over as if dead. The *bahana* spirits entered his body and became his helpers. But when he woke up displaying his weapons and rattle of tobacco smoke, the people vanished from sight. They were transformed into River Crab people and became the Masters of Earth.

Finally many Warao appeared in the center of the earth. Again the young *bahanarotu*, who was himself a Warao, shot the same pair of *bahana* spirits down to earth from the House of Smoke. The young man who received them survived and learned how to travel the bridge of tobacco smoke in the sky. Here he received much advice on how to preserve his *Bahana* spirits and how to use them.

That is why *bahana* continued on earth to the present day. It is not so perfect or so powerful as it was long ago, when the first *bahanarotu* re-

---

* Probably the Magnificent Frigate Bird, *Fregata magnificens*, also known as the Man-of-War Bird, with a wingspread of seven or eight feet.

ceived four spirit helpers. Nevertheless, *bahana* prevails. And it is still very strong among the Warao.

This, in brief, is the origin tradition of the *bahanarotu* shaman. It is the charter by which he orders his conscious existence and evidently also his supernatural experience. It is taught to him by his master in long and arduous initiatory training, and so firmly does it become fixed in his psyche that, when he is considered ready for his initiatory tobacco ecstasy, the novice shaman himself relives the primordial shamanic experience. In other words, he becomes culturally conditioned for a specific ecstatic experience under tobacco narcosis.

A young man who has decided to embark on the road of the *bahanarotu* takes a gift to the house of an older and respected *bahanarotu* whom he has chosen to be his teacher. If the gift is accepted, the master prepares a cigar charged with four wads of black leaf tobacco.

"Smoke this," he says. "It contains four *bahanas* who come to open your chest."

These four *bahanas* are Black Bee, Wasp, Termite, and Honey Bee. Black Bee hits hard when the smoker inhales the first charge of tobacco. Then Wasp, Termite, and Honey Bee tear painfully into his body. It is said that the smoke does not reach the stomach. *Bahana* spirits reside around the heart. They cleanse the novice from polluted foods.

"Smoke it slowly, very slowly," advises the master *bahanarotu*. "You had better be cleansed thoroughly."

The smoking of this first cigar introduces four days of fasting. After successfully completing this period of purification, the novice *bahanarotu* undergoes four additional days of abstinence, during which he incessantly smokes cigars lit from a virgin fire (i.e., a fire on which no cooking has been done).

The novice falls into a trance; the Indians say, "He dies." And in this state, "All of a sudden it happens." The unconscious apprentice perceives the sonorous vibrations of the four *bahana* insect spirits. Louder and louder they grow, until the trees of the forest are transformed into gigantic rattles, swinging and swaying and emitting sounds that are most agreeable to his ears. He feels exalted and, euphoric with the marvelous sound, embarks on his initiatory journey across the celestial bridge and its rainbow of colors. Buoyant as a puff of cotton, he is wafted by the breeze toward his encounter with the *Bahana* Supreme in the House of Tobacco Smoke.

Awakening at last from his ecstasy, the new *bahanarotu* clutches his chest which encloses the gift of *bahana*: White Smoke and White Rocks. Still small and feeble, the spirits require much care. The young *bahanarotu* eats little but smokes a great deal. For more than a month he observes celibacy and avoids the touch of blood and odors like those of roasting fish, onions, lemons, and rancid oil. In the palms of his hands small brown spots appear which grow proportionately to the growing *bahanas* in his body. Nowadays, unlike the first *bahanarotu, bahanarotus* have only one *bahana* exit in each of their hands, through which their spirit sons leave them to assist during trances or curing sessions.*

"Now swallow this small stick," orders the master. "Let your *bahanas* transform it."

The stick travels past the spirit in the chest and through the arm of the new *bahanarotu* and is "born" white through the mystical hole in the palm of the hand. A second stick is swallowed which exits as a white stick through the other hand.

"Now swallow the white sticks," orders the master.

This act produces the final proof of a successful initiation. Now the white sticks travel past the *bahanas* in the chest and through the arms, this time to be born as white crystal beads.

"The *bahana* spirits are beginning to play," observes the teacher. He is satisfied. He blows tobacco smoke over the arms of his young colleague and bids him go, with this warning: "Should you take a bath now, you would drown. Should you cohabit with your wife now, you would die. Your spirit sons would return to me, whence they came. Do not send your arrows to cause evil."

But of course many *bahanarotus* do emit magic arrows to kill or cause illness; all *bahanarotus* have this capacity. *Bahanarotus* can see these projectiles fly through the night like fireballs. They know that somewhere a malevolent *bahanarotu* has swallowed a piece of glass, a twig, a human hair, a rock, or some other object and sent it on its way to enter the body of a victim and make him sick. This is done in the following way: the *bahanarotu* ingests the chosen object and lets it pass by his *bahanas* in his chest and through his arms to the wrist. Here it waits, moving slowly toward the exit hole in the hand. Now the *bahanarotu* takes a deep pull at his cigar, lifts the hand with the magic arrow to his mouth, belches out a ball of smoke and sends the projectile on its way. A *bahanarotu* shooting magic arrows of sickness in this fashion is known as a *hatabu-arotu*, "master of the arrow." He

---

* All this, of course, is how it appears to the Indians, who see the shamanic phenomena through the eyes of faith and apprehend them as religious reality. I am reminded of the time when I was told by Sanema Indians in Venezuela that their shamans fly, or at least walk a foot or so off the ground. When I objected that I could see shamans walking just like ordinary people, I was told, "That is because you do not understand" (Wilbert, 1963:222). P. Martin Dobrizhoffer, who worked among the Abipon in Paraguay in the mid-1700's, had much the same experience when he tried in vain to convince the Indians that there was no such thing as shamans transforming themselves into jaguars. "You fathers do not understand these matters," was the Indians' answer (Dobrizhoffer, 1822:78).

works his malevolent magic during the night, when he can follow with his eyes the glowing puff of tobacco smoke in which the arrow travels. The impact of a *bahana* arrow is painful. It may hit any part of the body and only a benevolent *bahanarotu* knows how to extract it.*

If summoned to treat a patient, a *bahanarotu* waits until evening, when the heat of the day has cooled off. He places his hand on the affected part of the body and his *bahana* spirit helpers diagnose the nature of the arrow of sickness. The healer then sucks it out, inhales great quantities of tobacco smoke, and lets the magic arrow travel through his arm and through the exit hole into his hand, where it is "born" for the patient and his relatives to see.

During the night the malevolent *bahanarotu* appears to the curer in his dream. He tells him what it was that provoked him to send an arrow of sickness and warns the victim not to offend him again. The following morning the message is conveyed to the convalescent.

Since *bahanarotus* can see *bahanas* in the dark, they sometimes get together for a tobacco seánce to play the supernatural Game of *Bahana,* before the eyes of the awestruck villagers. Exhaling puffs of smoke, they send the four pieces of their *Bahana* Game one after the other to travel like luminous bodies through the dark house. The quartet of *bahana* spirits delight in this game. Generally they are said to be the aforementioned "power objects"—rock crystals, hair, rocks, and puffs of tobacco smoke—but a bullet, a piece of glass, or a button will also serve as a magic projectile. They drift through the air, seeking out one or the other of the spectators, but since this is only a game, they do not enter his body. The people in the room are fearful of this supernatural demonstration of shamanic power. But the "fathers" of the roving *bahanas* always call their "sons" back if the game threatens to get out of hand. They blow tobacco smoke to intercept the flight of the spirits and put them back in their baskets.

Bahanarotus travel frequently to the House of Smoke in the East, and when they die they go to live there forever.

* Warao beliefs concerning the ability of shamans to shoot sickness projectiles through a tube in the arm from an exit hole in the hand with the help of tobacco smoke are closely paralleled among the Barama River Caribs of Guyana (formerly British Guiana). According to Gillin (1936:173), these techniques are taught to the neophyte shaman by his teacher, who "places a spirit stone in the novice's mouth and draws it from the mouth through the shoulder and through the arm three times, in order to make the tube in the arm through which the shooting is done." Elsewhere (p. 140) he writes: "It is believed that a tube somewhat like the barrel of a gun extends from the piaiyen's [shaman's] neck to the elbow joint, and from the latter point to a small opening between the bases of the first and second fingers. . . . With the "shots" held above the elbow joint, the piaiyen, when ready for action, takes a long inhalation of tobacco smoke and extends the right forearm in the intended direction. The force of the smoke is believed to be the physical agency necessary for the ejection of the shot."

The Hoarotu

The Scarlet Macaw (*Ara chloroptera*) is the Supreme *Hoa* spirit who rules over the Abode of Darkness, called *Hoebo*. This place is situated at the end of the world to the West. Here live all the souls of deceased "dark" shamans, the *hoarotus,* as beings half human and half animal. The stench of human cadavers and clotted blood saturates the air, and the stream of *hoarotu* shamans who come from all parts of Warao-land with cadavers hanging head down from their shoulders is endless. It has to be endless if the Supreme *Hoa* and spirit companions, called *hoarao,* are to continue living: the former by eating human hearts and livers, the latter by devouring the bodies. All *hoarao* in the *Hoebo* drink human blood from a gigantic canoe made of human bone.

The Abode of Darkness has existed since the beginning of time. Originally the Supreme *Hoa* and his companions sustained themselves with human blood supplied through a long umbilicus-like artery reaching from the end of the world in the West across the water to the Warao village on earth. The artery was connected in the *Hoebo* to a gigantic structure of rock (or iron), where it was illuminated by one yellow and one white light. From there it followed the curvature of the celestial vault to the zenith and dangled down from the heavens over the dancing platform of the Warao village. The end of this duct was provided with a brilliant ball of light which at night sought out the heads of sleeping Warao in order to penetrate through the skull down to their hearts and drain their blood. The blood flowed through the umbilicus to the *Hoebo,* to nourish its spirits. No one could see this cosmic artery, nor did the Warao die after being thus drained—they felt weak but recovered.

One day this arrangement was changed through a violent act of jealousy. The bridge of blood in the sky disappeared and *hoarotus* became the sole providers of the spirits in the western world of darkness. This came about as follows:

There was an old man by the name of Miana (Without Sight). As his name implies, he had no eyes. He lived alone in the zenith and begot a son whose name, like that of the Abode of Darkness, was Hoebo. Hoebo had learned to sing like his father, in order to activate the search for blood by the celestial umbilicus. One day Hoebo wanted to visit the Supreme *Hoa*. Father and son set out on their journey. They heard the humming chant of the Spirits of the West when they had gone only half way. They also beheld the bright lights of white and yellow penetrating the darkness of the *Hoebo.*

"See the *hoa ahutu* artery," said Miana to his son. "Listen to its humming."

The youth became very anxious to reach the Supreme *Hoa*. Then his eyes fell on a beautiful girl below him in the Warao village. He decided to marry her. But when he lowered himself head first from the *hoa ahutu* umbilicus to the dancing platform in the center of the village, a jealous rival for the girl cut off Hoebo's head. The sphere at the end of the blood duct fell to the ground and disappeared. All the people present suddenly felt sick with a sharp pain in their stomachs. The elastic blood duct snapped back to the West.*

Thus was severed forever the connection between the Warao on earth and the *Hoebo* at the end of the world in the West. Hoebo's soul still remains above the village, a short distance in a westerly direction from the zenith. But the umbilicus has gone, and from the zenith to the *Hoebo* there now leads only a black road. This is the path taken by the *hoarotus*, who have to carry their human victims along it to the West in order to feed the hearts and livers to the *Hoa* Supreme and the bodies to the *hoarao* who inhabit the *Hoebo*. The victim is always carried head down, dangling at the *hoarotu's* back from his knees; this is to express extreme mockery and ridicule for the victim.

Hoarotus dislike having to kill their fellow men with magic arrows. But what would become of mankind if they stopped providing human blood and flesh for the *Hoa* Supreme and the *hoarao* in the western world of darkness? All would come to an end. So there must be *hoarotus* who provide this service.

The Hoa *Snare of Tobacco Smoke*

To become a *hoarotu* shaman, a young man has to submit to severe initiatory ordeals. He feels bitterness within himself for a long time

* Cf. Wilbert, 1969: 56–60. A remarkable parallel to this concept has been recorded by Tozzer (1907:153) among the Maya of Southern Mexico:

> According to the information obtained from the Mayas in the vicinity of Valladolid, this world is now in the fourth period of its existence. In the first epoch there lived the Saiyamwinkoob, the Adjustors. These composed the primitive race of Yucatan. They were dwarfs and were the ones who built the ruins. This work was all done in darkness before there was any sun. As soon as the sun appeared, these people turned to stone. . . . It was at this period that there was a road suspended in the sky, stretching from Tuloom and Coba to Chichen Itza and Uxmal. This pathway was called *kusansum* or *sabke* (white road). It was in the nature of a large rope (*sum*) supposed to be living (*kusan*) and in the middle flowed blood. It was by this rope that the food was sent to the ancient rulers who lived in the structures now in ruins. For some reason this rope was cut, the blood flowed out, and the rope vanished forever.

It may also be noted that in the Maya area and elsewhere in ancient Mexico the Scarlet Macaw is the Sun Bird, a concept that seems to survive in attenuated form in sacred mushroom rituals of Oaxaca, for which the Scarlet Macaw feathers are considered indispensable. Both the *wishiratu*-temple-idol complex and the *hoa* complex of the Warao are in fact strongly reminiscent of Mesoamerican religion and ritual. In the context of the present paper it is impossible to include an analytical discussion of these interesting and, from an ethnographic point of view, puzzling parallels. They are presented here for the first time only as they relate to the use of tobacco.

before he finally decides to ask an accomplished *hoarotu* to teach him to make and cure malevolent *hoa* magic. If accepted, the novice is taken by the master to a small hut in the forest, where the two men will remain secluded for five days. Smoking incessantly, the candidate waits to be taken to the zenith to visit the *Hoebo*. But first he must learn the many *hoa* songs—one kind to cause sickness, another to cure it. Finally the master lights a long cigar, turns it around with the fire in his mouth, and blows into it. Now the cigar contains two *hoa* spirits ready to enter the body of the apprentice and become his "sons." The master hands the *hoa* cigar to the apprentice, and one after the other the two *hoas* tear violently into his body. The pain is excruciating. Now comes the first test: do the *hoas* want to accept him as their father? Has he kept his body strong? Will he be a good provider?

If he proves acceptable to them, the two *hoa* sons remain in the young man's breast. While he continues to sing the *hoa* songs, he experiences increasing pressure at the base of the sternum, where his *Kaidoko*, the *hoarotu*'s snare of tobacco smoke, begins to grow. From now on, the *Kaidoko* tendrils will snake from the corners of his mouth each time he begins to chant or speak ritually with a loud voice.

To increase the effective length of his *Kaidoko*, the *hoarotu* novice has to fast and smoke incessantly for approximately one month. During this period he is repeatedly asked by his teacher, "Did anything happen to you last night?"

Finally one night something does happen. In his ecstatic dream state induced by tobacco, the novice meets a spirit who beats him across the neck with a heavy club.

"I was like dead," reports the novice. "But I did not die." His teacher is very pleased with this dream.

A second dream follows. This time the murderous spirit kills the novice and places him in a hollowed-out tree.*

"But I was not really dead," explains the novice. "I was lying there in my coffin when I discovered a small hole in the palm-leaf wrapping. Through this I escaped."

Then the novice *hoarotu* has a third dream. This time the demon leads him to a human cadaver.

"Eat this," he commands.

But the novice finds it repulsive and impossible to swallow the piece of human flesh he takes to his lips. The demon proffers a cup of human blood but the novice is revolted by it also. He lifts the blood to his lips but cannot bring himself to drink it.

The master *hoarotu* is pleased also with this dream.

---

* Warao traditionally bury their dead in dugout canoes or hollowed-out tree trunks.

"You will never die," he tells the agitated novice. "You will live forever."

Finally there comes a fourth dream. Sometimes weeks pass before the novice embarks on it. His body is so emaciated that he can hardly move or perform the most essential functions. He is truly near death. In his trance state the demonic spirit appears once more to lead him to his grave. This time it is made of stone slabs. Inside it is very cold and pitch black. The foul stench of decay and putrefaction is nearly unbearable. He feels like fainting and is terrified that he might wake up —because if that happened he really would die and remain in his grave. Day breaks and with the rising sun he discovers a crack between the stone slabs that cage him. Again he makes his escape.

The master *hoarotu* is pleased. He calls for his wife, who feeds the novice slowly and patiently to bring him back to life. The community has a new *hoarotu*, who will handle the *hoarao* of the West with great prudence, propitiate them, and provide them with sacrifices only when absolutely necessary.

The *Kaidoko* snare of a powerful *hoarotu* is infinite. The two front ends emerge slowly from the corners of his mouth. First they appear like short white tendrils, but they continue to grow and to travel toward their victim.* Invisibly they wind themselves around his neck and begin to weaken him through strangulation. The Indian falls ill. When he has become sufficiently debilitated, the *hoarotu* prepares to kill him, so that his organs and his body may be fed to the spirits of the West.

"*Mianaa warao akwamo saba,*" he sings. "Without looking it is going for a Warao's head!"

He smokes six long cigars while singing, and with the final word of his chant he puffs out a cloud of smoke and pulls the snare shut. It

---

* *Kaidoko*-like tendrils occur also in the ceremonial art of the Maya, where they are identified as characteristics of the Sun God, and in Veracruz. Earlier still they appear on certain Olmec face masks, such as one, believed to date to a Late Olmec period, in the Peabody Museum at Harvard. Here the tendrils in the corners of the mouth are associated with a triangular toothlike projection in the center of the upper jaw. This same association is found on certain tall cylinders depicting the Sun God of the Night from the Classic Maya site of Palenque, Chiapas. Michael D. Coe, in a letter, points out that one of the Maya names for the Sun deity is *Kinich Kakmoo*, literally "Sun-eyed Fire" (i.e., Scarlet Macaw). Is the triangular projection perhaps a stylized frontal view of the macaw's beak? If so, this would strengthen the correspondence between Warao and Maya. Long ribbon-like tendrils are also associated with the Maya bat. Barthel (1966) discusses the composite Maya glyph "*Schleifen-Fledermaus*" (ribbon or tendril bat) in connection with an anthropomorphic bat demon depicted in a Chama-style Classic Maya cylinder vase. Long tendrils emerge from his mouth. Barthel suggests that glyphs associated with this supernatural being may signify drilling or boring into, or sucking from the head—reminiscent of the function of the *Kaidoko* in Warao shamanism. The Maya associated the bat with the East (the rising Sun) and death, and Barthel suggests that it may have been conceptually linked by them with the Scarlet Macaw, the Sun Bird of the West.—ED.

takes the entire next day for the *Kaidoko* to contract and completely return to the breast of the *hoarotu*. Then, during the night, the sorcerer smokes again and throws the (living) soul of the victim over his shoulder to carry it to the zenith and from there to the *Hoebo* in the West. Here the soul is clubbed to death, bled, and dismembered.

It is impossible for a *hoarotu* not to kill. For example, when the two *hoa* "sons" who live in his breast approach him in his dream and beg for food, he can delay and propitiate them at least four times with to-bacco smoke and *yuruma* (*moriche* palm starch). But when they come a fifth time and demand their proper food—human blood—he can no longer turn them away unsatisfied.

The following day he goes alone into the forest. In complete solitude he sits down on a log and lights a cigar. The cigar contains his *hoa* sons. While smoking, he chants his *Miana* song, and with this the ends of his *Kaidoko* snare of tobacco smoke slowly begin to emerge from the corners of his mouth. The *Kaidoko* travels toward its victim, be he near or far, and when it arrives at its destination, the *hoarotu* pulls heavily at his cigar, turns it around, and, holding the fire in his closed mouth, blows into it. Out come ribbons of smoke, and these now transport the *hoa* arrow over the tree tops to the intended sacrifice. The magic arrow enters below the rib cage and searches for the heart.* And the instant that the *Kaidoko* snare of smoke closes, the *hoa* enters the heart to kill.

It is excruciatingly painful when the *hoa* enters the chest of the victim. And people are well aware of what is going on. They have observed the *hoarotu* depart alone for the forest. So, when someone in the village or in a nearby community starts complaining of a sharp pain in his breast and falls ill, he and everyone else know why.

Only a friendly *hoarotu* can prevent death when a person has been struck by *hoa*. His *hoa* sons know all their fellow *hoas*. He begins to smoke and sing the curing chants, and as soon as he divines the nature of the illness-causing *hoa* (e.g., the *hoa* of a particular species of tree, an animal, or the like), his own *Kaidoko* snare of tobacco smoke pries it loose from the victim. The intrusive sickness-causing object jumps into the massaging hand of the curer who blows it into the forest in a puff of tobacco smoke. This effects the cure.

Some *hoarotus* "kill" a person each time their *hoa* "sons" come and ask for flesh and blood. This kind of *hoarotu* kills more people than he cures. However, since other *hoarotus* are almost constantly occupied with curing victims of *hoa* magic, a kind of equilibrium between neg-

---

* Reminiscent of the flint knife with which Aztec priests opened the breast of the sacrificial victim in order to tear out his heart, which, like the blood, organs, and bodies of *hoa* victims, was fed to the gods to give them strength.

ative and positive forces is established. In some communities there is nearly perpetual competition between *hoarotus* that kill and others that cure—lucky the village that can rely on a powerful *hoarotu* who knows how to keep the Scarlet Macaw and his spirits of the West appeased with a minimum of sacrifices, while maintaining the strength of his own group by saving his fellows from the *hoa* snare of malevolent *hoarotus*.

Throughout their lifetime *hoarotus* travel often to the *Hoebo* in the West, always using tobacco as their means of ecstasy. They too have a house in the Otherworld in which they will dwell forever after death. But while the house of the *bahanarotu* is in the East, the land of light, that of the *hoarotu* is in the West, the realm of darkness.

CONCLUSION

So far as I have been able to determine, tobacco is the only psychotropic substance available to the three kinds of Warao shamans. The *Curucay* resin employed by the *wishiratu,* and to some extent also the *bahanarotu,* appears to lack any hallucinogenic properties. All three supernatural practitioners—*wishiratu, bahanarotu,* and *hoarotu*—employ tobacco extensively to put themselves in ecstatic trances. They achieve this trance state exclusively by smoking, rather than through infusions of liquid tobacco, as do novice shamans of some other Indian groups.

At the same time, as in many aboriginal societies in North and South America, tobacco smoke figures prominently in sorcery and, conversely, in curing: tobacco smoke is clearly as essential to the healing process among the Warao as it is elsewhere in Indian America—even where some other true hallucinogen is central to belief and ritual. Among California Indians we find tobacco side by side with *Datura*. In lowland South America novice shamans undergo their initiatory training with powerful infusions of liquid tobacco before they are introduced to *Banisteriopsis Caapi*. In eastern Bolivia shamans of the Tacana employ ayahuasca (*B. Caapi*) to place themselves in trances but also utilize tobacco as a magical deterrent against malevolent spirits. In northern Peru liquefied tobacco constitutes an essential ingredient in contemporary folk healing with the hallucinogenic *San Pedro* cactus.[*] Even in a society so totally committed to a single psychotropic plant as are the Huichol to peyote, we find tobacco playing a crucial role, not only in shamanic curing but in the peyote rituals themselves.[†] Indeed, just as the tobacco gourd is an identifying characteristic of Aztec priests in the codices, so it is the insignia *par excellence* of the Huichol

---

[*] See D. Sharon, below.
[†] See P. Furst, below.

Fig. 17. A *wishiratu* shaman "feeding" the *kanobo* spirits by directing his
burning cigar to the zenith and the world directions (except the west).

peyote seeker to this day and, as Lumholtz noted more than seventy years ago, is treated with great reverence throughout the pilgrimage.

Tobacco belongs to Our Grandfather, the Fire Shaman, who led the first peyote hunt of the supernaturals and cured them of their ailments with its help. Preuss (1908:377) describes an important ritual, performed by the Huichol shaman at intervals of about ten years, which re-enacts the curing with tobacco smoke of the whole group of leading supernaturals. The ritual takes place in early summer at the beginning of, or shortly before, the rainy season. The illness of the gods consists of the fact that they are not giving sufficient rain, and the long nocturnal song cycle recited by the *mara'akáme*, the shaman-priest, describes the healing process. This is not very different from ordinary shamanic curing among the Huichol—or, for that matter, the Warao and other groups. *Tatewari*, the Fire Shaman and principal supernatural, lets the smoke from his tobacco pipe flow over each ailing god in turn, while his spirit helper, the Sacred Deer *Kauyumarie*, sucks out the intrusive disease object, or "arrow of sickness." In the same way shaman and tutelary deer spirit cooperate in the curing of human patients.

While tobacco thus shares curative powers with the hallucinogenic peyote among the Huichols, there is nothing in Warao tradition to indicate that any other psychoactive plants were ever used in the past, either before or since the advent of tobacco. Naturally such negative evidence cannot be taken as definitive. In any event, the ritual use of tobacco itself is of respectable antiquity in the Americas as a whole: in Mexico, for example, the earliest clay tobacco pipes date to Olmec times, *ca.* 1200–900 B.C.,* and it is probably safe to assume that consumption of tobacco without the aid of imperishable instruments goes back a good deal further.

Whether or not one accepts tobacco as one of the ritual hallucinogens —and thus far neither botanists nor pharmacologists would classify it as such—it is clear that the role of tobacco as a vehicle of the vision quest in Warao shamanism does not differ qualitatively from the role which the various psychotomimetics of plant origin play in other Indian societies. Also, as with other psychotropic preparations used ritually, cultural traditions clearly influence the kinds of vision experienced by the shaman in the Warao tobacco trance. It would be too much to speak of "programming," but there is obviously cultural conditioning toward specific ecstatic experiences that have nothing to do with the chemical action of the tobacco plant itself. Through long instruction by his master, and as a child of his culture, the novice learns the precise nature of a Warao's "non-ordinary reality." Indeed, if the

---

* Peter T. Furst, personal communication.

promised cosmic landscape failed to appear for him in his trance state, the failure would be his, and he might well die. Thus there exist powerful cultural stimuli which interact with the chemistry of the tobacco plant to produce the kinds of vision required for the shaman's vital role in his society.

This brings me to another important point, namely, the nature of the initiatory ordeals of the novice Warao shaman, and the nature of Warao shamanism as such. It will have been immediately apparent to anyone familiar with the literature on shamanism that the Warao experience contains much that is near-universal, or at the very least circum-Pacific. Fasting, purification, skeletonization, symbolic death and resurrection after a trance, dismemberment, gashing, shamanic trees, celestial ascent by rainbows etc., replacement of internal organs and introduction of magical power into the shaman's body in the form of pebbles, rock crystals, and so forth, killing of the neophyte by initiatory demons, travel on flying animals, sexual abstinence, magical arrows of sickness, sucking, blowing, tutelary spirits, cannibalistic tests, animated "pains" as sources of power and causes of illness, almost all can be found in shamanistic initiation and the quest for shamanic power in a wide variety of native societies, from Australian aborigines through Indonesia, Japan, China, Siberia, across to the American Arctic, and southward through North America and Mexico into South America (Eliade, 1964).

I would like to single out the initiatory celestial quest for shamanic power of Warao neophyte shamans as a case in point. That it should closely resemble the quests of other tribes in South America and even North America is perhaps not so surprising as is its remarkable correspondence to the neophyte's quest for supernatural power among Australian aborigines—not only in general content but specific detail:

Among the Wiradjuri the initiatory master introduces rock crystals into the apprentice's body and makes him drink water in which such crystals have been placed; after this the apprentice succeeds in seeing the spirits. The master then leads him to a grave, and the dead in turn give him magical stones. The candidate also encounters a snake, which becomes his totem and guides him into the bowels of the earth, where there are many other snakes; they infuse magical powers into him by rubbing themselves against him. After this symbolic descent to the underworld the master prepares to lead him to the camp of Baiame, the Supreme Being. To reach it, they climb a cord until they meet Wombu, Baiame's bird. "We went through the clouds," an apprentice related, "and on the other side was the sky. We went through the place where the Doctors go through, and it kept opening and shutting very quickly." Anyone whom the doors touched lost his magical power and was certain to die as soon as he had returned to earth (Eliade, 1964:135–36).

Compare this Australian account with the initiatory journey of the
Warao *wishiratu;* the candidate, we recall, has to pass through a hole
in a tree with rapidly opening and closing doors. Inside is a great
serpent with colored horns and a fiery-red luminous ball on the tip of
her tongue; her servant is another snake whose task it is to clear away
the bones of neophyte shamans who failed to clear the clashing doors.*

As Eliade (1964) demonstrates in his classic work on shamanism, the
motif of the rapidly opening and closing passage (e.g., floating islands,
cliffs, icebergs, mountains, knives, snapping jaws, spears, razor-edged
dancing reeds, grinding millstones, etc.) is one of the characteristic
themes in shamanism, found in many parts of the world in both funerary and initiatory mythologies. Along with its associated motif of the
narrow and perilous bridge connecting this world to the celestial regions
or the underworld, it survives well beyond the limits of the shamanistic
ideology in which it had its remote origin, but most characteristically
in contemporary indigenous societies which retain strong vestiges of
an ancient shamanism. In a recent study of Huichol conceptions of the
soul, for example, Furst (1967) identified the motif of the dangerous
passage in no less than four different forms (clashing rocks, stone trap,
snapping jaws, and fiery solar curtain) along the path of the soul and
its shamanic guardian from this to the Otherworld. The gateway of
clashing clouds that bars the entrance to the sacred peyote country is
yet another version of the same theme. This multiplicity of what
Eliade has aptly called the "paradoxical passage" is characteristic also
of the Warao account of the neophyte *wishiratu*'s ecstatic initiatory
journey: the snapping jaws of jaguars, alligators, and sharks in the
abyss across which he swings himself on a celestial vine; the slippery
path lined on both sides with demons who jab their spears at him;
the snapping beak, grasping claws, and flapping wings of the giant

---

* An account by the Hungarian ethnologist Vilmos Diószegi (1968:66) of a Siberian
shaman's journey to the chief shaman in the Otherworld also contains remarkably
close parallels to the initiatory trance journey of the Warao *wishiratu*. The Siberian
shaman reaches the supreme spirit shaman by passing through a series of trials
culminating in a clashing gateway in which the inept are crushed. Also, like the
Venezuelan Indian, he comes first upon a special shamanic tree—in this case a pine—
into whose bark he and other shamans carve their symbols. "Whoever places his
marking, his *tamga,* upon it," Diószegi quotes his informant, "then becomes a real
shaman. It happens sometimes that a certain tamga 'falls down,' it disappears from
the tree. Then its owner dies." This is exactly the case with the *wishiratu*: his mark
on the tree and the shaman live a parallel existence. One cannot help but wonder
whether such common experiences by shamans in widely separated regions of the
circum-Pacific area are to be explained in terms of real historical relationships, survivals perhaps of some ancient shamanic substratum predating the settling of the
Americas from Asia, or in terms of the unconscious and the language of symbols by
which it communicates (e.g., Jung's "archetypes"). Perhaps there is something of both
here; in any event, the correspondences between Asian and American shamanism
are far too close and too numerous to be explained away as mere coincidence.—Ed.

hawk; and, finally, the opening and closing doorway to the giant tree trunk. Universally, the promised land lies beyond the dangerous passage, and its attainment requires that the traveler be "light" and that he have transcended the human condition—i.e., become shaman or spirit.

It will have become apparent that the various forms of shamanism practiced today by the Warao with the aid of tobacco occupy a central position in tribal culture. They seem to me to constitute true survivals of a more ancient shamanistic stratum with roots in Mesolithic and even Paleolithic Asia, introduced into the Americas 15,000 to 20,000 or even more years ago. Although attenuated and certainly overlaid with more recent features, including some characteristic of more advanced social systems in Mesoamerica and western South America, they seem to belong to what some anthropologists, including La Barre, Furst, M. D. Coe, and myself, have come to see as an archaic shamanistic substratum underlying and to some extent uniting all or most aboriginal American Indian cultures.

I am convinced that a true Warao community cannot exist without this very powerful shamanistic ideology. Its loss, I feel, would seriously disturb the social and psychic equilibrium of the local community, and eventually that of the entire indigenous society. Rooted in an ancient Paleo-Indian past, and beyond that in the total human experience, with its focus on tobacco as the vehicle of ecstasy, it represents a very special elaboration of Warao culture. Its undermining through Creole and Mission contact would probably dislocate this *axis mundi* of the Warao seriously enough to put an end to one of the earliest and most successful aboriginal social and cultural systems in South America.

3

GERARDO REICHEL-DOLMATOFF

The Cultural Context of an Aboriginal Hallucinogen: *Banisteriopsis Caapi* * †

The geographic distribution of the hallucinogens prepared from *Banisteriopsis* in various parts of South America has recently been traced by Friedberg (1965). In Colombia, these hallucinogens are used by virtually all tribes of the Amazon basin and the Orinoco Plains (Uscátegui, 1959). The custom can also be observed among the Noanamá and Emberá Indians of the Chocó, a rain-forest region on the Colombian Pacific coast, whence it has spread as far as Panama (Reichel-Dolmatoff, 1960:130–32). Here we shall describe its use by the Tukano Indians of the Territory of Vaupés, in the northwest Amazon region of Colombia, with the object of placing this custom in its cultural context and linking it to other activities and expressions characteristic of this aboriginal population. The data presented are based for the most part on my own research among the Tukano.

As Schultes has pointed out, the vernacular terminology for *Banisteriopsis* and the drink prepared from it varies considerably. *Yajé*, or *yagé*, is commonly used in the northwest Amazon region, but the plant is also known by many other names, depending on the local Indian language. For example, in the dialects of the Tukanoan linguistic

* Translated from the Spanish by Michael B. Sullivan.

† I owe my gratitude to the University of the Andes, Bogotá, Colombia, which in 1967 and 1968 sponsored research on which this paper is based in part. My sincere thanks go to Dr. Roberto Galán Ponce of the Department of Biology of that institution for having read and commented on the original manuscript in the Spanish language. Needless to say, the responsibility for the data and ideas expressed herein is exclusively my own. An earlier Spanish version of this paper appeared in the *Revista de la Academia Colombiana de Ciencias Exactas, Fisicas y Naturales*, Vol. XIII, No. 51 (Bogotá, Colombia: 1969).

family (the Eastern Tukano of the Vaupés), it is called *caapi*, or more correctly, *gahpi* or *kahpi;* among the Cubeo, *mihi;* the Guahibo of the eastern llanos, *kápi;* the Noanamá of the Chocó, *dápa;* and the Embera, *pildé.* In the *montaña* regions of Peru and Ecuador the plant is widely known by the Quechua term *ayahuasca.* These differing names, sometimes synonymous but often simply generic terms which the Indians give to any hallucinogenic plant, have wrought such confusion in the literature that it is often difficult to know exactly what botanical species is being talked about.* For the sake of brevity, I will call this widespread hallucinogenic plant simply by its common northwest Amazonian name, *yajé.*

The phytochemical and pharmacological study of the psychotropic substances derived from the Colombian Malpighiaceae began over a half-century ago and continues to attract diverse investigators. Fischer (1923) appears to have been the first to isolate a crystalline alkaloid from yajé, which he called *telepatina,* but he did not undertake a rigorous botanical identification of the species he used; nor did his contemporaries Barriga Villalba (1925), Albarracín (1925), or Perrot and Hamet (1927a, 1927b) do so. Barriga and Albarracín called the alkaloids they isolated *yajeina* and *yajeinina.* This imprecision of botanical determinations in the laboratory analysis of materials became a serious obstacle to the identification of chemical components, especially since there was the unresolved problem of just what the Indians used in making their hallucinogenic drinks, a process that sometimes included mixing in certain plants that had not yet been clearly identified.

There was also the problem of the numerous ways in which the drink could be prepared, a detail about which the available data were not always complete. According to the existing literature, Indians in certain regions (Putumayo, Caquetá) would prepare a boiled infusion several hours before taking the drug; others (in the Vaupés, for example) would mash it in cold water. In some instances, leaves and other parts of different plants were added, depending on the tribe and the desired results. These other plants were occasionally added to reinforce the hallucinogenic effect of the basic potion. The use of these additives continues to be of great importance to current studies, since the results of laboratory analysis depend, of course, on their precise identification.†

---

* The botanical and ethnobotanical characteristics of the various kinds of Colombian *Banisteriopsis* have been studied in detail by Schultes, whose research in this field is fundamental (Schultes, 1957; 1960; 1963a; 1963b; 1967b; 1969). Other authors who should be mentioned in this connection include Bristol (1966b), Cuatrecasas (1958), García Barriga (1958), Pérez Arbeláez (1956), and Uscátegui (1969).

† Some observations on this aspect of research can be found in Schultes (1957, 1970) and in his essay in this book, above.

In 1928, Elger (*q.v.*) showed conclusively that the alkaloid described by Fischer (1923) was identical to the harmine isolated years earlier from a shrub found in the Near East, *Peganum Harmala*, the hallucinogenic properties of which had been known since antiquity (Gunn, 1937). The terms *telepatina, yajeina,* and *banisterina* that had been employed by researchers in the past turned out to be mere synonyms for harmine. Later on, as botanical identification became more precise, it was possible to detect the presence of harmine in *B. Caapi* (Chen and Chen, 1939) and in *B. inebrians* (O'Connell and Lynn, 1953). Furthermore, Hochstein and Paradies (1957) found other derivatives of the beta-carbolines in stems of *B. Caapi*—for example, harmaline and d-tetrahydroharmine (Bristol, 1966:115–16; Naranjo, 1967:394; Schultes, 1969: 250). *B. Rusbyana* was found to contain appreciable quantities of N, N-dimethyltriptamine (Agurell, Holmstedt, and Lindgren, 1968).

The psychotropic effects of these components of *B. Caapi* and other species of Malpighiacea have been described by several authors, who refer in their studies to schizophrenics, to normal individuals, to observations made among indigenous peoples, and even to personal experiences (see, among others, Harner, 1968; Naranjo, 1965, 1967; Pennes and Hoch, 1957; Turner, 1963). Generally, the ingestion of an infusion or maceration of *Banisteriopsis* is said to cause vertigo, nausea, and vomiting, followed by more or less clearly defined states of euphoria or even aggressive excitation. Suddenly, brilliantly colored visual hallucinations appear, which may be of sublime beauty but which may also involve anxiety or even stark terror. Animals sometimes appear in these visions—usually felines or reptiles. Sometimes the individual finds himself flying on the winds, visiting far-off places, or communicating with divinities, demons, or tribal ancestors.

The circumstances under which the hallucinogenic beverage is taken vary considerably among the Indians of the northwest Amazon. Some take it in conjunction with collective ceremonies of a magico-religious nature, such as initiation rites for youths, funeral ceremonies, or the rite of *yurupari* (described below). In other contexts it is taken only by a shaman or curer, for the purpose of diagnosing an illness or divining its cure or to establish the identity of a presumed enemy. Neither women nor prepubescent youths are allowed to take the drink, but both may be present while it is ingested by the men.

According to Rocha (1905), who did not take yajé himself but instead reported information provided by the Indians and Mestizos of the Mocoa region, the hallucinations of the first thirty to forty-five minutes are extremely pleasurable; the individual perceives beautiful landscapes, delectable fruits, and lascivious dances performed by half-nude women, all accompanied by music. Some men believe themselves to be powerful chieftains or have visions of angels and celestial virgins; others fancy themselves consuming food and drink, after which they turn into jaguars and chase after the tapir and deer that roam the forest. Following this there is a short period of somnolence, and immediately thereafter terrifying visions appear: serpents and demonic beings attack the individual and abuse and humiliate him.

In 1852, Spruce attended a yajé ceremony of the Tukano of Urubú-Coará near Ipanoré on the Vaupés River. His description of the effect on those who drank the potion is quoted by Schultes (pp. 39–40).

Spruce drank a small amount himself, but only succeeded in making himself sick. He reports:

> White men who have partaken of *caapi* in the proper way concur in the account of their sensations under its influence. They feel alternations of cold and heat, fear and boldness. The sight is disturbed, and visions pass rapidly before the eyes, wherein everything gorgeous and magnificent they have ever heard or read of seems combined; and presently the scene changes to things uncouth and horrible. These are the general symptoms, and intelligent traders on the Upper Rio Negro, Vaupés, and Orinoco have all told me the same tale, merely with slight personal variations (Spruce, 1908, II:419–21).

Koch-Grünberg, who a half century later attended several ceremonies of the Tukano of the Tiquié River, reports the following:

> According to what the Indians tell me, everything appears to be larger and more beautiful than it is in reality. The house appears immense and splendrous. A host of people is seen, especially women. The erotic appears to play a major role in this intoxication. Huge multicolored snakes wind themselves around the house posts. All colors are very brilliant (Koch-Grünberg, 409, I, 299).

On one occasion Koch-Grünberg drank two small cups of the drink. He describes his reaction in these words (p. 318): ". . . after a while, and especially when I went out of the house into the darkness, there appeared before my eyes a strange flickering and intense light, and when I attempted to write, something like red flashes passed rapidly across the page." Although this author provides excellent descriptions of the ceremonial gatherings, he does not go into detail regarding the hallucinations or, more important, their function. He notes that yajé is taken on the occasion of reunions between two phratries* and during initiation rituals, and he considers that the use of the hallucinogen may also be related to a warrior ritual, when it is ingested so that men might become brave under its effect.

Goldman (1963) described the use of yajé by the Cubeo Indians of

* Local tribal subgroups based on consanguineal kinship. Such phratries are exogamous.

the Cuduyarí River, where the plant is called *mihí*. Of its effects he says:

> This sequence of *mihí* transports a man from vague and mild visions of white-ness to intense hallucinatory experiences, bursts of violence, and finally loss of consciousness. . . . At the beginning, the Indians say, the vision becomes blurred, things begin to look white, and one begins to lose the faculty of speech. The white vision turns to red. One Indian described it as a room spinning with red feathers. This passes and one begins to see people in the bright coloring of the jaguar. When the final strong forms of *mihí* are taken the hallucinations begin to assume a disturbing and fearful form. One be-comes aware of violent people milling about, shouting, weeping, threatening to kill. One is seized with fear that he no longer has a home. The houseposts and trees come alive and take the form of people. There is a strong sensation that an animal is biting one's buttocks, a feeling of the feet being tied. The earth spins and the ground rises to the head. There are moments of euphoria as well, when one hears music, the sound of people singing, and the sound of flowing water. The Cubeo do not take *mihí* for the pleasure of its hallu-cinations but for the intensity of the total experience, for the wide range of sensation. I spoke to no one who pretended to enjoy it (Goldman, 1963:210–11).

Father Brüzzi participated in two yajé ceremonies of the Tukano of the Carurú-Cachoeira, where he drank a small amount but did not have hallucinations. However, some of the participating Indians af-firmed having seen "luminous flames or globes." His negative experience made Brüzzi think that "the effects of the drug on the Indians can be readily explained by the easy excitability of their imagination" (1962: 230–32).

Schultes, who took yajé on several occasions, says (1960:70): "The narcosis . . . is pleasant, characterized . . . by colored visual hallucina-tions. In excessive doses, it is said to bring on frighteningly night-marish visions and a feeling of extreme reckless abandon, but con-sciousness is not lost nor is use of the limbs unduly affected." Later on (pp. 175–76), referring to the concoction of *B. inebrians* taken in the Upper Caquetá and Putumayo regions, he says:

> . . . the drink had a very strong psychotropic effect. Its intoxication had an initial stage of giddiness and nervousness, followed by profuse sweating and nausea. Then began a period of lassitude, during which the play of colors, at first mainly a hazy blue, increased in intensity. This eventually gave way to a deep sleep, interrupted by dreams and accompanied by feverishness. No uncomfortable after-effects save a severe diarrhea were felt the next day.

Referring to the cold maceration generally prepared only from *B. Caapi*, as used in the Vaupés, he writes (pp. 176–77):

As far as I was able to judge from six or seven experiences with *caapi,* the effects differ little from those of the boiled concoction used in the Putumayo. The intoxication is longer in setting in, and much more of the drink must be taken, but the symptoms of the intoxication and their intensity seem to be very similar.

Of particular interest is the work of Mallol de Recasens (1963), who was able to obtain from a Siona Indian several colored drawings representing his hallucinations under the influence of yajé, together with the informant's personal commentary and interpretations provided by the shaman to whom the informant had communicated the content of his visions. In her analysis of the drawings, Mallol de Recasens observes that the yajé plant occupies a central position and symbolizes a concept of female fecundity. Other symbolic features are given a sexual interpretation as well, but some are seen as expressions of profound conflicts, involving maternal images, the authority of the shaman, and the influence of the Catholic missions. Although the author considers her work a mere methodological contribution, it is in fact a most important attempt to place the hallucinatory experience in a wider cultural context.

The social and physical environments in which the Indians of the Vaupés take yajé, as described by the above authors, are generally as follows: Several pieces of the fresh *Banisteriopsis* vine, about the thickness of a finger, are mashed in a wooden trough, with cold water added later. The liquid is passed through a sieve to remove fibrous material and small pieces of bark and is then collected in a decorated ceramic vessel made especially for this purpose. When night falls, the men, adorned with feathers, their bodies painted, gather in the communal house (*maloca*) where, seated on small stools, they recite myths, converse, and sing. Sometimes groups of them rise and dance to the sound of Panpipes, rattles, and the beat of large wooden tubes pounded on the floor. One or two men distribute the drink, offering it in small calabashes to those present, who swallow it with expressions of disgust. The men who portion out the drink approach the others with ritualized gestures, sometimes jumping as they walk, and exclaiming rapidly, "*ma-ma-ma-ma-ma-ma*" (take-take-take-take-take-take). The dancing and singing continue, and in the intervals more doses are administered, sometimes up to six or seven.

Following is an account of my own experiences, recorded on tape after I had taken six doses of yajé on the Pira-Paraná:

The drink was consumed on the occasion of the celebration of an alliance between two exogamous phratries. The vines were cut between

3 and 4 P.M. in a nearby section of jungle. According to the Indians, three classes of yajé were represented: "yajé of *guamo*" (stems of a light hazel color, with somewhat fluted surfaces, collected about three meters from the ground); "mammalia yajé" (hazel-colored stems with light spots and a smooth surface, taken from a height of about two meters); and "head yajé," (dark hazel-colored stems with nodes and protuberances, picked close to the ground). These three groups of stems were obtained from three different plants, growing within twenty meters of one another. So far as I could make out, all belonged to the same botanical species. Some twenty-five pieces, each about sixty centimeters long and approximately one centimeter in diameter, were then macerated for over an hour. Finally eight liters of water were added. The liquid was passed through a sieve and kept in a painted ceremonial vessel.

The event lasted from 6. P.M. until 6 A.M. Twenty men and twelve women took part in the ceremony. The men were painted and adorned with large feather crowns, wore rattles, and carried painted staffs and stomping tubes. The entire ceremony unfolded in an atmosphere of intense solemnity. It began with a recital of the Creation Myth, followed by dances accompanied by chants in which reference was made to the fertility of the animals and the women. The first drink was distributed at 8:15 P.M., when the participants were already perspiring profusely. The second drink was administered at 9 P.M., the third at 9:30 P.M., the fourth at 10:15 P.M., the fifth at 11:05 P.M., and the sixth and last at midnight. In the intervals the men danced and sang, sometimes at an accelerated pace, sometimes more slowly. The precision of the steps of the dancers and the beat of the music became more perfect as more yajé was consumed, and at no time was there any dissonance or false step. No food was taken, except that after every drink of yajé a portion of slightly fermented maize beer was administered. The music, as much vocal as instrumental, did not let up for a moment, varying in intensity but maintaining a hypnotic rhythm. The whole event took place in the semidarkness of a large *maloca* (communal house) and in the light of but a single torch.

After the second drink, some men began to vomit and shortly thereafter claimed to have visions which they proceeded to describe in low voices and with much gesticulating. My own experience: first drink, pulse 100, light euphoria followed by transitory sleepiness; second drink, pulse 84; fourth drink, pulse 82, strong vomiting; sixth drink, pulse 82, strong diarrhea. Almost immediately when I closed my eyes I had visions of a multitude of intricate motifs of marked bilateral symmetry in spectacular colors passing slowly in oblique bands across my field of vision. The visions continued, modifying themselves, for more than twenty minutes, disappearing only briefly on two occasions. There were no acoustic phenomena or figurative images. The dances and songs continued until daybreak, without producing any disagreeable aftereffects in myself or in any of the other participants. The text of the tape follows, with the activities of others indicated by parentheses:

(Music from Panpipes which comes and goes with the coming and going of the dancers.) I'm seeing something . . . well, like . . . it's dark, but I see something like the tail of a peacock . . . but at the same time it's like . . . everything in movement . . . like fireworks, no? Much like a . . . the background of, let's say . . . of certain Persian miniatures. There's something Oriental about all this. Oh, tapestries, Tibetan tapestries. . . . Sometimes it makes me think of . . . that decorative Arabic script, some *sura* of the Koran. Rather in dark colors; sometimes it appears white, but more often than not it is a dark red. It passes . . . it is gone from . . . it is oblique in my field of vision. It goes from top left to bottom right. There is a very gentle flow. Now it is changing . . . all the colors of the spectrum, as . . . yes, undulating . . . but in some way the arches of each undulation separate and form different motifs. At the bottom it is yellow; it changes continually and then passes through all the colors of the spectrum. Rather they are motifs like . . . yes, everything is curvilinear: semicircles, shapes like hearts that are intertwined and then become flowers; suddenly, shapes like a Medusa. Sometimes there are . . . yes . . . again these effects of fireworks. But when . . . no, it isn't three-dimensional . . . it's flat and fairly dark. Now it's gone. *(Some sounds of the flutes; the dancers rest now.)* Something comes from above, from the right: they are . . . it is like water from a fountain, but the light passes through the jets of water, like a rainbow. These lines cross, but they aren't lines, in fact they are interrupted by intervals. Points, with a . . . dark center, the exterior yellow . . . then, like a flower, like ostrich feathers, curled. And again, feathers like a peacock's. Sometimes like moss; like these mosses. Now very much like fungi, like those fungi in the lens of a camera; iridescent. A flower, but with three petals . . . three . . . yes *(The vision disappears for two minutes; the dancing starts over again.)* I am very much awake again. When I open my eyes wide open, I see the *maloca,* the darkness, the people; but this way, when I half-close them, I again see these motifs. Sometimes they are like microphotographs of butterfly wings, or of marine corals. Sometimes the colors aren't . . . aren't pleasant. Now there are more definite motifs: arabesques, horizontal bands. Yes, just about everything comes in parallel bands, each a different color. Yet always in motion. Often in these bands there appears a kind of net, a mesh. Centers form themselves. *(The music becomes more intense.)* This mesh is relatively static, only the centers are in motion, they spin and change colors. Again . . . now this whole scheme tilts, and moves about . . . almost 45 degrees . . . but, now almost vertical. *(Strong rattling.)* Now the pattern is becoming more horizontal. The bottom is almost black. Sometimes there are concentric waves that move, like very black waters in which a stone has fallen. Yes, yes, but all very symmetrical. Hardly ever is there a motif which is not symmetrical. Sometimes, like . . . ancient locks, these ancient ornate plates on the lock

of a door. It is all so baroque! *(Dance with much percussion.)* A number of semicircles, like trees of some sort, dark against a lighter, almost bluish background. But it changed already! Like . . . like microphotographs of plants; like those microscopic stained sections; sometimes like from a pathology textbook. *(Some people are vomiting. All are saying that they are having hallucinations; they claim that they see the whole interior of the* maloca *painted in colors. But they go on dancing.)* Now there is a change on the right side . . . now . . . there is a Tibetan quality, blue Buddhas, and around them a yellow-red-blue halo or flames that end in little dots. *(The dancers rest; there is talking.)* It's like that sometimes. It isn't pleasant. Yes, it is spectacular as a color! And always this increase and decrease of shapes, of lights. They duplicate themselves . . . a circle appears, it doubles, it triples, it multiplies itself. Yes, they spin . . . everything moving very quickly. Like . . . like . . . that's it, like bubbles, transparent bubbles, those soap bubbles. And now darkness. No, I see no more. But I am feeling well. It's almost one o'clock. I have taken six cups of yajé: pulse 84, a light headache. After the fourth cup, I vomited violently, and after the fifth I started to get diarrhea. But otherwise I'm all right. A bitter taste in my mouth, nothing more. *(About two minutes go by.)* I continue to see things. Hexagons, all like a ceiling full of hexagons, some tilted 35 degrees, and at the center of every four of them, a blue dot. It's changed, now they are small stars . . . how many there are! They come and go, come and go; that is, they approach and recede, approach and recede. . . . Now they have almost disappeared. *(Monotonous ritual conversation beside me; virtually no music.)* Hmmm . . . like a basketry design. Ah yes, yes . . . Rouault's paintings, like stained-glass windows . . . colors . . . blots, surrounded by a thick black line. *(High-pitched sounds of flutes.)* Yes . . . or large, different-colored eyes. That symmetry doesn't exist any more! These things drawing near are like bodies . . . now they are like large caterpillars, with a lot of quills and fur . . . with a little ball at the end of each hair. But again . . . like a microphotograph. It has changed now . . . like little red hairs, is it not? But now it's changing; those little bubbles are lengthening, and now they are gone. Again . . . well, it's so difficult! Now there appears a dark red color, crossed by a series of yellow rays; the center is to the right, but I can't see it. These rays fall as if on a forest of little red hairs. Everything is tilted . . . again, above to the left and below to the right. It has now changed, now . . . they are like thousands and thousands of stylized palms in perspective. They are like tapestries, aren't they? They change, they change, like stylized little trees. Yes, all of that is, for the most part, like certain ties in bad taste. Yes, now it is all disappearing. I see no more.

Up to this point we have merely summarized the observations of various authors, myself included, but now we must ask, what is the significance of this custom? What is the meaning of the hallucinatory experience to the Indian? What role does it play in social organization? How does it relate to his mythic traditions, his religion, his symbolism, to all his mental and psychological processes? In short, what is the cultural dimension of the use of this hallucinogen? In the following pages I will try to provide at least partial answers to some of these questions.

THE MYTHOLOGICAL CONTEXT

In the course of my research among the Tukano I collected a series of myths in which there are numerous references to yajé. According to the Tukano of the Vaupés, the yajé plant was created in the mythical period at the beginning of the world and constitutes one of the most important elements of their culture. The following is an abstract of the Tukano Creation Myth:

The solar deity is a fertilizing male principle, phallic in nature. This phallus, symbolized by the Sun's rays and the shaman's ceremonial staff, at a certain moment in time placed itself vertically upon a fixed topographic point at the equator. On the day of the vernal solstice, at midday, the vertical rays of the Sun cast no shade whatever on the upright faces of certain rocks that lay on the banks of the rivers. This portentous sign marked forever the central and sacred places where the Sun had fertilized the earth. Among these sacred places are the rocks of the rapids of Ipanoré (lower Vaupés) and the rock of Nyí, near the rapids of Meyú (lower Pira-Paraná). The ancient petroglyphs found on these rocks commemorate the primordial event. From this phallic staff (the Sun's ray) drops of semen fell to earth and became man.

The first men took to the rivers, floating inside an enormous anaconda which served them as canoe (a mythic element that embodies as much uterine as phallic symbolism).* The long voyage of the anaconda-canoe represents the dispersal of humanity which took place along the course of the rivers wherever there were major rapids. For the rapids themselves possessed the uterine quality of gestation and spewed forth successive social groups as the canoe stopped at them. In the course of this long voyage, the mythical divine hero who steered the canoe likewise created a series of cultural institutions and principles and established their social and moral code as he traveled along.

According to a myth of the Desana, one of the Tukano phratries, at one of these way stations, called *dia vii* (House of the Waters), located below Ipanoré, there appeared a woman named *gahpí-mahsó*, Yajé Woman. While the men were gathered inside the house, drinking *chicha* (maize beer), she gave birth to a child in front of the house. The infant turned out to be the yajé plant. The woman brought the child into the house, which caused great consternation among the men. It had a human shape, but, according to the myth, "the child had the form of

* For a detailed explanation of the interpretation see Reichel-Dolmatoff, 1968, 1971.

light, it was human but it was light, it was yajé." When they saw the child the men stood as if intoxicated, because

> . . . the woman suffocated them with visions. "Who is the father of this child?" she demanded. One man sitting in a corner with saliva trickling from his mouth tore off the child's right arm and shouted, "I am!" The others followed suit; they grabbed the child and tore him limb from limb, scattering his parts. They seized the umbilical cord and . . . our ancestors obtained yajé.*

The symbolism underlying this mythic tale is very complex. The key concept here is expressed in the term "suffocated," and to clarify it I would like to refer to another mythic cycle, specifically that which is related to the *yuruparí* ritual. *Yuruparí,* a word stemming from the *lengua geral* of Brazil, in most of the Amazon Basin refers to a rite in which several short trumpets of bark play a central role. These trumpets have a sacred character and must be neither seen nor heard by the women, the rite being conducted solely by a group of initiated men.†

To the Tukano of the Vaupés, the *yuruparí* rite represents the commemoration of an act of incest which the Sun Father committed with his own daughter in the time of Creation, and the principal motivation behind the ceremony in which these trumpets are played is the promulgation of the strict exogamous laws that are characteristic of the Tukano. In most of the Tukano dialects, *yuruparí* is called *miriá-porá,* from *miríri* (to suffocate or drown oneself or to submerge oneself), and *porá* (children, descendants). According to my Indian informants, the term alludes to procreation or coitus, an act which the Tukano often compare to a state of drowning, drunkenness, or hallucination. During the sexual act a man "drowns" or "sees visions." Thus, if a person dreams he is drowning, this signifies a forthcoming inebriation. The term *miríri* also embodies the feeling of saturating oneself, confusing oneself with something, gratifying or losing oneself. The term *miriá-porá* therefore alludes to the sexual act, particularly in the incestuous sense in which it appears

---

* The myth of the origins of yajé exemplifies a cycle of widely distributed myths that deal with a bloody sacrifice in which a group of men participates and from which subsequently there emerges something of benefit to mankind. For an Old World example, see the myth of Dionysius. The first peyote of Huichol mythology is similarly dismembered (see P. Furst, below), as was the Pygmy who became the first hallucinogenic *eboka* plant of the Fang of Gabon (see J. Fernandez, below).—ED.

† A strikingly familiar motif of sacred trumpets which women must neither see nor hear is found among Australian aborigines, Pygmies of the Ituri Forest in the Congo, and several other South American Indian populations. In all these widely separated regions and cultural contexts the trumpets have their origin in the mythical first times and in all of them the penalties for women who violate the taboo are very severe, for the survival of the social order and man's balanced relationship to the supernatural are at stake.—ED.

in the myth describing the transgression of the solar divinity. When Yajé Woman "drowns" or "suffocates" the men, the text actually reads, *"gahpí noméri miria-vaya,"* "yajé images she drowned them with." The word *noméri* means figures or images, and one of the informants, who had been in a Catholic mission, used the term to describe the brilliant reflection of fireworks in a nocturnal sky. On the other hand, the word *noméri* also describes the actions of a woman who paints her face ceremonially with small red dots. One informant says, "When one takes yajé, one sees red things that jump and move about. Yajé is feminine and produces images." We are now in a better position to interpret the meaning of the yajé origin myth: intoxication under this hallucinogen is compared in the first place to a sexual act which, in the second place, has the connotation of being incestuous.

According to another version of the Creation Myth, the origin of yajé took place near the rapids of Mihí. It was there that Yajé Woman conceived her child, having previously been fertilized through an eye. In the symbolism of the Tukano, eye and vagina are frequently equivalent, and in this case the act of fertilization is designated by the word *inyásaase,* from *inyase,* to see, and *saase,* to deposit, in the sense of impregnating. When the labor pains began, all the men became "giddy" (*vihsipeo*), a word which also means to become lost or go astray, and which is used for a psychic state in which an individual's behavior becomes overtly self-contradictory. This term is employed to describe an aberrant mode of behavior, one that would violate religious norms, and it is in this sense that the men were disoriented. The condition of the men worsened as the Yajé Child was born and increased even more as he and his mother came in through the door. From there she moved toward the center of the house, where there was a hearth and where had been placed a box made from plaited leaves, containing the dance ornaments which the Creator had given to the men. It was a moment of anguish, of great agitation. Here the myth reads, *"beetëonyati paro* (Oh, it was unsufferable!)."

We must now interrupt this Tukano narrative to refer to some symbolic aspects of the scene. In the first place, to the Tukano the large communal houses have a uterine symbolism and are in fact overtly referred to as "uterus of the sib." The door of the house symbolizes the vagina, and the center, the most sacred area, is the location where on certain occasions ceremonial objects are placed. Secondly, the hearth itself is another uterine symbol, since it is a place where transformation occurs, where one of the most important components of life is produced— namely, food. The box containing the ornaments likewise symbolizes a female element, since it holds inside itself the "ornaments"—to be interpreted in seminal or fertilizing terms—of the men. The scene in which Yajé Woman comes through the door and penetrates into the house, much to the agitation of the men, is therefore equivalent to a sexual act.

However, one of the men present did not lose his mind, and as the others fell upon the Yajé Child to tear him to pieces, it was he who "took hold of the first sprig of yajé." Then one after the other the rest of the men, each according to his social rank, took possession of "his yajé."

There is now a change of scene in the myth. Along with the men there were also many animals in the house, and some of them, especially the tapir and some monkeys, had become profoundly affected by the intoxication of the yajé—that is to say, by the sexual act. In a tumultuous scene and amid the laughter and exclamations of the men, these animals began to devour their own tails. Now, an animal's tail, and monkeys as a whole, symbolize among the Tukano the penis and masculine sexuality, incestuous and untamed. One frequently hears in the obscene language of Tukano men expressions alluding to this symbolism. According to our informants, "to eat one's tail" has the meaning of coitus, and they also report that the animals who were eating their tails were cohabiting with one another under the influence of yajé. At the same time the men armed themselves with a ceremonial staff, the same phallic staff whereby humanity had descended to earth, and with it they drove the influence of yajé from the house. One of the commentaries says, "With this staff they repelled it. Yajé was supposed to bring only pleasant sensations, but in some it produced just the opposite, and for this they drove it away. They drove it away with a penis."

The myth continues: "The visions came to an end. They had found their potion. All the people thus acquired their traditions, their rituals, and their songs." The narrator explains that the Tukano phratry took the second sprig of yajé and that "*too mihsi këhëa vaaro mëha*" (from there the line continued), indicating that the line of descent was to be compared with a long vine.

In another myth, again narrated by the Tukano, the Yajé Child survived bodily and lived to be an old man who jealously guarded his secret of hallucinogenic power. The myth says, "From that old man they formed semen, since he was the Owner of Yajé. The desire to have this penis led to the creation of semen. The old man was Owner of Yajé, that is to say, of the sexual act. They are the children and he is the father."

Therefore, in the context of Tukano mythology, yajé has a marked sexual character. Hallucination and coitus are equivalent, not in the sense of procreation or gratification but rather as an experience full of anxiety, because of its relationship to the problem of incest.

THE RITUAL CONTEXT

We have observed that in these myths the yajé vine is identified with a human being and during the dismemberment of the Yajé Child each man availed himself of a certain portion of its body. This identification is important to the Tukano, since it is the basis of the criteria by which certain parts of the vine are selected over others in the preparation of the drink. In this manner each phratry (Tukano, Desana, Pira-Tapuya, Uanano, Barasana, etc.) has its specific yajé, as chosen by its ancestor during the sacrifice of the child. Today, each exogamous Tukano phratry consumes its own kind of yajé, a determination based on the external appearance of the vine and its particular hallucinogenic effect. The Desana, for example, mention at least four classes of yajé that are traditionally "theirs," to wit, "knotty yajé" (*korepida*), "yajé of *guamo*" (*merepida*), "yajé of *tooka,*" and "yajé of *duhtú-puu-sereda.*" * The Pira-Tapuya (Fish People), another Tukano phratry, are said to use a kind called *gahpí-da-vaí,* yajé-branch-fish. The Barasana of the Pira-Paraná are said to use at least three types: "yajé of the red jaguar," used to familiarize themselves with the general effects of the hallucinogen and to have visions in yellow colors, which relate to tobacco and coca; "yajé of *guamo,*" taken to have hallucinations referring to the ceremonial songs; and "yajé of blood," to have visions in red. In addition, they mention a "yajé of the jungle animals," which produces predominantly red and blue visions, and a "snake yajé," which apparently is no longer found in the area. Another variety, called "fish yajé," is said to be reserved exclusively for shamans of the Tukano phratry, who take it to establish contact with the Master, or Owner, of the Animals. This hallucinogen is also said to produce visions that refer to the fertilizing power of the solar rays and male dominance over women. The Karapana phratry have their own particular variety, called "flesh yajé." In this manner each Tukano phratry sees its "own" hallucinations. This does not mean, however, that they are completely exclusive, for a member of one phratry may see in his hallucinations visions that "belong" to another phratry. They are partial visions that enter into a total perspective and are immediately distinguished as "foreign" or "alien."

From each yajé plant the Indians choose branches or pieces of different colors, for example, green, red, or white. These colors do not refer solely to the external appearance of the vine but above all to the predominant color of the hallucinations experienced through its use. A yajé taken by

---

* *Tooka* or *too* is a small plant, as yet botanically unidentified, which plays an important role in the seminal symbolism of the Tukano. *Duhtú* is a kind of *Xanthosoma;* the term derives from *puu* (leaf), the suffix *da* expressing the idea of a string, thread, or vine.

the Desana produces visions of "jumping feather crowns," or snakes shaped like necklaces that coil themselves around the houseposts. Another kind of yajé is said to produce hallucinations of "snakes that jump." It goes without saying that what we are concerned with here are not different botanical species but a magico-religious classification established by the Indians. However, it is possible that at the base of this classificatory system there lies traditional knowledge that certain parts of the vine—roots, portions of the lower trunk, or young sprigs—contain different concentrations of the hallucinogenic component and therefore cause different visions. As a matter of fact, one of the chief concerns in the preparation of the drink is precisely the knowledge of how to combine portions of different vines. The combination is causally related to the desired effect, and this also depends upon the occasion when the drink is taken. Each ceremony and, more important, each dance requires a specific preparation. It is therefore a question of controlling the intensity and quality of the hallucinations.

We know that the effects of yajé can be pleasant or disagreeable, and that they cause states of euphoria or terror. It is possible that these two opposite effects follow one another as chronological stages in the course of the same intoxication. But it is also a fact that some people undergo more agreeable experiences than others. The ideal, according to the Indians, is to have only pleasurable and beautiful visions which the individual can enjoy passively, in a state of relaxation. On the other hand, a nauseating experience, or one that results in uncontrollable behavior or terrifying visions, is considered dangerous. Some persons are said to become aggressive and start haranguing their fellows; others tear off their ornaments and even their loincloths; they urinate and defecate in public and in general behave "like animals."

Obviously, the effect depends on a number of factors that are difficult to control, such as the properties of the plant, means of preparation, social and psychological atmosphere of the gathering, and personality of the drug taker. The effect is therefore highly unpredictable, and the consumer of yajé runs the risk of having some extremely unsettling experiences. This fact worries the Indians, who, apart from the combination of components used, attempt to influence the effects magically to eliminate the more unpleasant aspects. To this end there is a long series of spells and songs to be recited while the drink is being prepared. When a spell is put on stems of yajé, a formula for exorcism of certain diseases is employed, summarized in the exclamation: *"ahkipo suu tooka aí tuun-yeanugukama,"* meaning that the noxious component should "become anointed with milk, anointed with *tooka,* and driven away." Informants agreed that milk (whether mother's milk or the whitish sap of certain plants), as well as *tooka,* a small as yet unidentified plant that contains a white sap, possess a marked seminal character. We are dealing therefore with a symbolic sexual act, an insemination of a curative nature that neutralizes the danger (Reichel-Dolmatoff, 1968:133–42). When this formula is pronounced over the stalks of yajé, the *dehkó-bogá,* "force of the liquid," in this case the noxious component, is eliminated and cast away to "the mouths of the rivers."

In theory, the preparation of yajé is a highly formalized and complex process with a series of requisites and restrictions. The stalks should be cut by the men in a certain part of the jungle at a specified time of day, in accordance with their position on the vine. Immediately following this, the stalks should be mashed up in a wooden trough, using a heavy club or masher that strikes them with a determined rhythm and intensity of sound. We should add at this point that there is a definite possibility that the Tukano increase the potency of the hallucinogen by the addition of other ingredients. In a description of the ritual obtained from the Desana, we find that members of this phratry as well as the Pira-Tapuya sometimes add a plant called *bayapia,* which "makes us nauseous" *(irá ya bayapia arika iritá soyaró ahpaka).* Unfortunately we lack further details on this interesting practice. The maceration of the stalks is always conducted outside the house, and it is there that the cold water is added and the liquid filtered into a special container.

This ceramic vessel, about 25 centimeters in height, globular in shape, with two small handles on the edge of the lip and a high cylindrical support, is an important ceremonial object. The handles are perforated, so that when a string is passed through them the vessel can be carried or hung up. The yajé pot *(gahpí soró)* should be made by an old woman who smooths and polishes the inner and outer surfaces with a hard, smooth yellow stone. The Tukano view this stone as "a phallus which shapes" the vessel, which in turn is considered to be a uterine receptacle. As a matter of fact, the yajé pot represents the uterus, the maternal womb, and hence is a cosmic model of transformation and gestation. On the outside the vessel is decorated with a series of polychrome designs in white, yellow, and red. The first two colors represent the principle of fertilization, while the third symbolizes fecundity. On the cylindrical base there is sometimes a painted vagina and clitoris, symbolizing the "door." When the yajé vessel is not in use it is suspended from a rafter outside the house, under the overhanging roof; when yajé is prepared it is cleaned of dust and, if necessary, the paint is touched up. Before use, the pot is purified with tobacco smoke, as is the stick with which the drink is stirred shortly before consumption. When the pot has been filled with the liquid it is brought inside the house and placed in a dark corner.

Of course all this corresponds to ideal behavior, as promulgated in the myths and narratives which explain ritual norms. In practice, however, the preparation of yajé is often conducted with minimal observance of ritual.

Turning now to the collective consumption of the hallucinogenic drink, what follows is the procedure, in brief, as we ourselves observed it:

The men, adorned and painted, seat themselves on their stools, their backs turned to the entrance. When night falls, they light a large torch of pitch, located approximately in the center of the room. This torch gives off an intense red light. Now there begins a long ceremonial dialogue between the representatives of the household and those of the exogamous phratry invited to the event. The Creation Myth and the genealogies of the phratries are recited. The origins of humanity are commemorated with the phallic staff, which, equipped with a small sound chamber, serves as a rattle. Shortly thereafter, various musical instruments are played, such as flutes and whistles. The dances that follow are performed to the accompaniment of songs and the beating of large wooden tubes whose lower sections the men pound against the floor. In addition, the men wear seed rattles on their ankles and elbows. One musical instrument consists of a turtle shell with a piece of wax attached; the shell is held under the left arm while the wax is rubbed rapidly by the right hand, producing a sound like the croaking of a frog.

Each distribution of yajé is introduced by the blowing of a trumpet made of clay and decorated with polychrome paintings. The yajé vessel is placed before the headman of the house, who stirs the liquid with a small stick, producing as he stirs a clattering noise like that of a wooden rattle. He then fills two small gourd vessels (*gahpí-koá*) with the drink and these he offers to the men, chanting rapidly, *"ma-ma-ma-ma-ma-ma"* (take!). Walking in front of the row of seated men, he gives each a cup and then returns to his place to refill the cups. According to ritual, the distributor of the drink should approach from "beneath" (the back end of the house) and "ascend" toward those attending the ceremony with rapid steps. He should suddenly crouch and tread heavily on one foot, a ritual posture called *gubúro moári,* "to make feet." On other occasions, when crouching in this manner one foot is raised, a posture called *yuri meneri.* Other ritualized gestures include the following: the man drinking the liquid assumes expressions of displeasure, purses his lips, and spits in an exaggerated manner, indicating that he has to force himself to get the drink down. Sometimes the distributor of the drink forcefully beats his chest, producing a soft thud which is accompanied by the exclamation *"tsavé!"* to show happiness and gaiety.

Generally six or eight small cups of the drink are passed out, at approximately hourly intervals. In between these dosages there is singing, dancing, and conversation. It should be pointed out that in these dances of the men there are no pelvic or any other movements suggestive of the sexual act. As the effects of the yajé increase, so does the precision of the dancers' movements. The general rhythm and individual movements of the dancers become ever more coordinated until, at a certain point, the entire group appears to become one body, moving in a highly controlled and precise rhythm. Frequently a man will seize a staff or war club and, assuming a posture of ritualized defiance, exclaim, "This is how I would split my enemy's head!" Sometimes this theme is elaborated upon, and the others rise and gesticulate violently. Another ritualized activity consists of heaping abuse on the yajé vessel. The men shout, "I'm going to drink your contents, but then I'm going to kick you around! When you are empty I'm going to urinate on you! I'm going to fill you with excrement!" The men address themselves to the vessel as they would to a female being who had defied them, presenting a danger they are ready to confront.

The hallucinations are referred to by the generic term *gahpí-gohóri,* yajé images.* According to our informants, the word *gohóri* derives from *gohsisé,* reflection, aureole. *Gohóri* is "something which is seen," but they add that it is neither tangible nor imaginary—it is a projection. The Indians say that the order of the hallucinations is fixed and that certain images are seen only after the third cup, others after the fourth, and so on. They also emphasize that to have hallucinations that are bright and pleasant, it is essential that one abstain from sexual intercourse and eat only a light diet on the days immediately preceding the ceremony, and that one must participate actively in the dances and be covered with sweat during the ritual drinking.

There is a rhythmic and cyclical quality to the entire ceremony, a concept of "rounds" or encounters. The trumpet is blown, the drink ingested, and dancing follows. Then there is a brief rest until the hallucinations appear. This goes on until the trumpet is again sounded and the whole process is repeated. In each of these "rounds" the individual does not know ahead of time what will happen to him. Some see colors and jumbled forms, some experience an entire mythological scenario, others vomit and see nothing at all. There is a sense of chance, an intense expectation that hangs over the men.

On some occasions an old man or anyone who lays claim to esoteric knowledge explains his hallucination as though all were seeing the same thing. He says, for example, "This trembling which is felt are the winds of the Milky Way," or "That red color is the Master of the Animals."

The women are seated in the gloom of the other end of the house. Their function is to keep up the men's spirits by laughing shrilly every

---

* The symmetric motifs of the initial stage of the hallucinations are sometimes called *too-puri,* from *too* (plant), *puu* (leaf), *ri* (clusters, plural *ri*). The expression *toondári* (cluster) is also used.

now and then or by shouting words of contempt or defiance at the "cowards" who continue to vomit or who refuse the drink.* Frequently the men reply by shouting, *"nuri mahsá"* (people of cohabitation) or *"koré-mahsá"* (vagina people), but these exclamations are not directed at individual women or at anyone present in the *maloca*—rather, they are aimed in an impersonal way at the feminine element of the phratries with which there exists an exogamous relationship.

The strict ritualization described above is not, of course, adhered to on every occasion. Sometimes it is simply a group of men who get together to take yajé and hum and chat in a corner. Even on important occasions many of the traditional gestures and ritual words are held in abeyance.

THE SYMBOLIC CONTEXT

The objective reason for which an individual or a group habitually takes a hallucinogen is naturally of great interest to anthropologists. Does it consist of an escape from reality? a religious rite? a philosophical experience whereby one attempts to attain a state of sublimation, of equilibrium, of integration? Or is it a quest for a new life-dimension, another "reality," or simply a search for a Dionysian orgiastic experience? In our case the answer to the question will lead to the profound and complex dimensions of the psycho-cultural mechanisms of the group concerned and will uncover intimate and hidden motivations that manifest themselves only rarely in other aspects of social behavior.

According to our informants of the Vaupés, the purpose of taking yajé is to return to the uterus, to the *fons et origo* of all things, where the individual "sees" the tribal divinities, the creation of the universe and humanity, the first human couple, the creation of the animals, and the establishment of the social order, with particular reference to the laws of exogamy. During the ritual the individual enters through the "door" of the vagina painted on the base of the vessel. Once inside the receptacle he becomes one with the mythic world of the Creation. In evidence of this, the drawing on the vessel is called *gorosíri*, place of origin, uterus, and, what is particularly significant, place of return, place of death. This return to the uterus also constitutes an acceleration of time and corresponds to death. According to the Indians, the individual "dies" but is later reborn in a state of wisdom, because on waking from the yajé trance he is convinced of the truth of his religious system, since he has seen with his own eyes the personifications of the supernaturals and the mythic scenes.

* Some informants reported that on rare occasions an old woman can also take yajé, but we were unable to confirm this as fact.

On the other hand, a return to the womb is considered an incestuous act, since the person becomes identified with a phallus which enters into the maternal cavity, where he now passes through an embryonic stage to a state of rebirth. The transformation occurring during these hallucinations is considered to be an extremely dangerous process, for not all know that to comprehend it as a purification the individual must completely surrender that which is corporeal and earthly. Some continue to keep ties with the profane world, and when they enter into the sacred one, they suffer the terrifying consequences of an unnatural act.

According to the Tukano, after a stage of undefined luminosity of moving forms and colors, the vision begins to clear up and significant details present themselves. The Milky Way appears and the distant fertilizing reflection of the Sun. The first woman surges forth from the waters of the river, and the first pair of ancestors is formed. The supernatural Master of the Animals of the jungle and waters is perceived, as are the gigantic prototypes of the game animals, the origins of plants—indeed, the origins of life itself. The origins of Evil also manifest themselves, jaguars and serpents, the representatives of illness, and the spirits of the jungle that lie in ambush for the solitary hunter. At the same time their voices are heard, the music of the mythic epoch is perceived, and the ancestors are seen, dancing at the dawn of Creation. The origin of the ornaments used in dances, the feather crowns, necklaces, armlets, and musical instruments, all are seen. The division into phratries is witnessed, and the *yurupari* flutes promulgate the laws of exogamy. Beyond these visions new "doors" are opening, and through their apertures glimmer yet other dimensions, which are even more profound. One crosses over cosmic levels, perceiving more and more strongly each time the fertilizing energy of the Sun, in an atmosphere of yellow light.* It is also true that, while male personification and the animals of the jungle are clearly distinguishable, female personifications and fish appear only in symbolic form.

However, not everything is seen in one hallucination, nor, for that matter, at all times.

On some occasions the individual awakens from his trance in a state of great calm and profound satisfaction; on others he is nearly overcome by the nightmare of the jaguar's jaws or the menace of snakes that draw near while he, paralyzed with fright, feels their cold bodies winding themselves around his extremities.

For the Indian the hallucinatory experience is essentially a sexual one. To make it sublime, to pass from the erotic, the sensual, to a mystical union with the mythic era, the intra-uterine stage, is the ultimate goal,

---

* One informant said, "Man needed supernatural communication and for that reason searched for yajé (*igú duharagu irikoa amari arimi gahpi koapure*)."

attained by a mere handful, but coveted by all. We find the most cogent expression of this objective in the words of an Indian educated by missionaries, who said, "To take yajé is a spiritual coitus; it is the spiritual communion which the priests speak of."

THE HALLUCINATORY EXPERIENCE AND THE ORIGINS OF ART

The interpretation of these ideas belongs in the realm of psychology and psychiatry. For the anthropologist, it is most intriguing that the Indians maintain that everything we would designate as *art* is inspired and based upon the hallucinatory experience. This idea is of course of paramount importance and presents us with a surprising problem.

The Tukano, at least those groups that still live in relative isolation, sometimes cover the fronts of their houses with large geometric or representational paintings executed with mineral pigments on the walls of bark. When asked about the significance of these paintings they answered simply, "These are the things we see when we take yajé; they are the *gahpi gohóri*—the yajé images." This was the same answer we were given when we asked about other artistic expressions, such as the ornaments used to decorate various utensils. These decorated objects are mainly pottery, bark cloths, benches, calabashes, rattles, trumpets, and the sounding tubes used in dances.

When these objects are examined closely, one finds that certain decorative motifs are consistently repeated. We find, for example, the same motif painted on the wall of a house, carved on a rattle, and adorning a loincloth made of bark cloth. They are decorative elements that coincide with one another, form series, and later combine with other designs, thus forming the style of art characteristic of the Tukano. When they noticed our interest in these decorative motifs, the Indians explained in the most natural way that these were simply designs they had observed in their hallucinations, while under the influence of yajé.*

But we obtained results even more surprising than this. It is practically routine for an ethnologist to give drawing materials to members of the group he is studying and invite them to draw whatever comes to their mind. In this manner drawings can be obtained that usually show elements of the social or natural environment—e.g., a house, a tortoise, a fish. Many such examples of "primitive art" have been published. But these cannot be considered representative of a personal creative artistic expression, for they are little more than replicas of a real model, manufactured in accordance with the manual abilities of the painter. In the

---

* The Indians contend that they do not simply witness visual hallucinations but also hear music and see dances. They say that both their present-day dances and their music are based on hallucinations.

Fig. 18.   Painted *maloca* (communal house) of the Tukano of the Pira-Paraná,
         Colombia.

course of our research on yajé, we asked the Indians to depict their
hallucinations and soon obtained a long series of drawings.

We offered the men a choice of twelve colored pencils and some sheets
of white paper 28 by 22 centimeters, mounted on a wooden tablet. They
were all adult males who frequently took yajé; further, all were non-
acculturated Indians who did not live in contact with civilization and
none of whom spoke Spanish. The men showed great interest in and
concentration on this task and spent from one to two hours finishing
each drawing. Some immediately made their own drawing utensils, using
canes and fine fiber cords—to wit, a long ruler, a shorter one, a ruler

with an undulating edge, a semi-circle, and a circle. The models for these implements were the much larger ones they used to paint the walls of the communal houses. For our drawings, they first traced a rectangular frame and then divided the space into convenient sectors. Many times, before drawing the motif on the paper they first traced it in the dust on the ground and then copied this model onto the page. The colors they selected spontaneously were exclusively red, yellow, and blue, on very few occasions adding a shade of hazel brown. There were comments that there was not a good choice of the various tones of the basic colors, since the Tukano discriminate carefully between a number of shades of the same pigment, such as clear yellow, orange yellow, reddish yellow, etc., and evidently would have preferred to execute the drawings in a wider range than allowed by each of the basic colors. When each drawing was completed, we recorded on tape the explanation the artist gave for his work. Some comments were extremely concise; others were long and detailed explanations.

Once we had obtained a short series of drawings, we observed that they consistently repeated certain design elements. We therefore prepared a series of numbered cards. On each we painted a motif, selected and copied from the large drawings. We then showed these cards to a large number of men who had not done drawings for us and asked for their interpretation of each. We found that in the majority of cases their interpretations coincided. We could therefore conclude that these motifs were codified, each having the fixed value of an ideographic sign. At the same time we observed that the interpretation of these signs often made reference to aspects of sexual physiology and, in direct relation to this, to the laws of exogamy.

Taken one by one, the motifs appear as follows:

1. Male organ	11. Exogamy
2. Female organ	12. Box of ornaments
3. Fertilized uterus	13. Milky Way
4. Uterus as passage	14. Rainbow
5. Drops of semen	15. Sun
6. Anaconda-canoe	16. Vegetal growth
7. Phratry	17. Thought
8. Group of phratries	18. Stool
9. Line of descent	19. Rattles
10. Incest	20. Cigar holder

Before entering into a discussion of the individual motifs, we must say a few words about the color symbolism of the Tukano. The colors yellow and off-white symbolize a seminal concept and are always associated with the idea of male or solar fertilization. The various tones represent differing grades of intensity of this fertilizing energy, with orange-yellow the highest grade. Yellow and off-white are also the colors of natural materials which have a markedly seminal character for the Tukano and which symbolically are the equivalents of *semen virile:* saliva, dew, the juice of certain plants, the gelatinous component of certain fruits, the starch from *yuca* (manioc), cotton, bees' honey, the rays of the Sun, and other phenomena. The color red, on the other hand, signifies the opposing complementary principle, since it symbolizes female fecundity. It is the color of the uterus, of fire, of heat. These two colors, one "cold," the other "hot," one male, the other female, are essentially beneficent. The third fundamental color is blue. Blue is considered sexually neutral and morally ambiguous. Above all, it symbolizes a principle of communication, which is expressed by thought, by the smoke of tobacco that is smoked ritually, and by songs and spells. Since communication can have motivations or results as much beneficent as injurious, the color blue can be good or evil, its character depending to a large extent on its significative combination with other colors. For example, if one finds the colors yellow and red together, then one is dealing with a beneficent principle, a relationship that is both complementary and reciprocal. However, when red appears with the color blue, there appears a component of opposition which, although it can be institutionalized (as in the case of two exogamous phratries), can also symbolize a principle of conflict, in which the "evil" attempts to impose itself on the "good."

Let us now turn to the list of codified motifs given above. We have presented these motifs in highly schematic form, each the bare outline of the motif which the Indian later completed in detail. For example, the main lines of the motif can be doubled or tripled; they can branch into smaller lines and be traced in different colors. Similarly, size can vary widely. Naturally, these elaborations depend on the individual artist; what we list here is merely the basic outline. Nonetheless, the patterns are unmistakable in each motif.

1. The male organ is indicated by a triangle accompanied on each side by a vertical line ending in a spiral. This sign is called *vahsú,* a name given to the fruit of the rubber tree (*Hevea pauciflora* var. *coriacea*). This fruit is edible and represents, during the rainy season, a favored if not always available food. To it is attributed a marked seminal character, as much for its latex, a milky-colored liquid, as for the gelatinous mass that covers the fruit. Both are associated with semen.

2. The female organ (*koré*) is represented by a diamond. A small circle added to its center indicates fertilization.

Fig. 19. Codified motifs of the Tukano.

3. An ellipse or oval containing several circles or semi-circles represents a fertilized uterus.

4. A U-shaped element represents the entrance to the uterus and in a figurative sense a "door" or the "heavens." It symbolizes the break from one cosmic level and the transportation to another dimension of perception. The motif should be viewed as a casing for a cavity with a small vertical body in the center representing the clitoris.

5. Rows of circles or round dots symbolize *semen virile* and in a figurative sense a line of descent, or life itself.

6. Several undulating and parallel lines, painted horizontally and in different colors, represent the anaconda-canoe in which humanity arrived.

7. A diamond with a solid dot in the center represents a phratry. According to the color of the dot, "our people," or "other people" are indicated.

8. A cluster of diamonds, in red or blue and with central dots of the opposite color, represents the opposition of a group of exogamous phratries.

9. A vertical row of diamonds, sometimes simplified in the form of a zigzag line, represents a line of descent, a concept of fecundity and of social continuity.

10. A spiral symbolizes incest and represents women who are forbidden. It is the *yuruparí* sign. It is said that this motif is derived from the imprint of a *yuruparí* flute when it is placed mouth down on the ground. These flutes consist of a tube of bark rolled into a spiral. Because of the similarity of forms, it is associated with the snail.

11. A motif resembling a *fleur de lis* symbolizes exogamy and women who are potential marriage partners. It is said to have derived from the look of two fish traps placed back to back. These traps, which are woven from thin canes, have a sexual character and are compared to a vagina into which the fishes, here considered phallic symbols, swim.

12. Two or more concentric rectangles symbolize the box containing dancing ornaments and have a uterine association.

13. Vertical rows of small dots represent the Milky Way.

14. Parallel semicircles represent the rainbow, which in turn symbolizes a vagina.

15. The sun motif represents the fertility principle. Several concentric circles may also symbolize a vagina.

16. This stylized design symbolizes vegetal growth in general.

17. Undulating vertical lines symbolize creative thought and, on some occasions, the energy of the solar creator himself.

18. Small rectangles containing short parallel lines symbolize the men's wooden stools, which they adorn in this manner. Sometimes these benches have a ritual character.

19. This motif represents the gourd rattles and by extension the songs and spells that accompany these instruments.

20. A bifurcated motif symbolizes the wooden fork in which the ritual cigar is placed. It also has a marked sexual character.

This series of twenty symbols could be expanded upon, since there are other motifs that appear to have ideographic meaning, but this sample will suffice to present the problem. Naturally, in addition to these motifs, there are other more or less stylized drawings of men and animals, flowers and fruit. All the drawings contain lines, blots, or splotches of colors and ill-defined motifs that do not appear to have a precise significance. These are simply considered as "things which are seen."

How should one attempt to explain the Indians' contention that during the hallucinations all participants, or at least most of them, perceive the · same basic motifs? Could it be that a certain component of the hallucinogen results in visions of the same kind, a constellation of the same shapes and colors, which are apprehended in the same way by different individuals? Our informants report that the motifs described above appear mainly in an initial stage of the hallucination, and that in later stages they see mythic scenes and the shapes of men and animals, less stylized and well-defined than the visions of the first stage.

In the first place, it is evident that when the Indian interprets his visions, certain projective and feedback processes are at work, as well as earlier cultural experiences; he is therefore influenced by his visual and circumstantial memory. Since infancy, the individual has been aware of two types of models: those offered by nature, and those represented by human artifacts. The models that appear in the physical environment are the vegetation of the Amazonian rain forest, rivers, sandy beaches, clouds, flowers, fruits, butterflies, birds, and so on. In the interpretation of the hallucinations, flowers and fruits appear frequently, as do petals, vines, branches, reeds, and other vegetal forms. Several kinds of birds are referred to, as well as such phenomena as the stars, rainbow, Milky Way, and so forth. We must bear in mind that in the semi-darkness of the forest, the bright colors of the jaguar are extremely striking, and many snakes also possess vivid coloring. On the other hand, we have the manufactured objects of material culture. Again, since infancy the individual has seen the design motifs painted on pottery and pieces of bark cloth and the large paintings that adorn the walls of the houses, and their meaning has been explained to him. Even the adolescents who have not yet taken yajé already have a vague idea of the more common signs: male, female, incest, exogamy.

It would seem, therefore, that in a state of hallucination the individual projects his cultural memory on the wavering screen of colors and shapes and thus "sees" certain motifs and personages. There is nothing secret or intimate about the hallucinations the individual Tukano experiences. On the contrary, these are discussed openly, and, what is more striking, one individual will describe his visions to another even while he is undergoing the hallucinatory experience and will ask for an explanation of its significance! This open communication of experiences could lead to a consensus, to a fixation of certain images; in this manner, no matter what the vision, its interpretation could be adapted to a cultural pattern.

In the second place, it could also be that certain motifs or images are produced more or less consistently by the biochemical effects of the hallucinogen. Motifs such as rainbows, stars, circles or bright dots, undulating multicolored lines, all figure in a wide range of hallucinations, related to the taking of other drugs as well as *B. Caapi,* thus constituting a common base for the hallucinatory experience. Paintings and drawings executed by individuals under the influence of LSD, mescaline, peyote, and other drugs, or attempting to fix the hallucinogenic visions after the primary effect has worn off, frequently have common characteristics. It would be difficult to attribute this commonality solely to the cultural experiences held in common by these artists. There exists an element of rhythm, of pulsation, that seems more likely to be organically based than determined *only* by a visual and culturally molded memory.

The problem becomes more complex if we consider it from the perspective of artistic inspiration. It is amazing to note how frequently the design motifs dealt with above appear in the petroglyphs and pictographs of the region and areas far beyond it (Reichel-Dolmatoff, 1967). It would not be difficult to find parallels to these motifs in other prehistoric artifacts, such as the decorations of ceramics or the rock carvings of ancient indigenous cultures. It could be argued that we are dealing with such elementary motifs that they could have evolved independently in any place and any era, for they are simply circles, diamonds, dots, and spirals, and nothing more. But are they really that elementary? It would be difficult to claim that the sign of the "door" or that for exogamy are basic forms. Instead, it might be possible to conceive of vast cultural zones wherein, since time immemorial, a certain hallucinogen had been consumed and where, based on its use, traditional interpretations had been formed that thus created a certain artistic style. Could archaeology lead us to a zoning of these symbolic systems? If we suppose that the use of hallucinogens by the American aborigines is a very ancient practice, and that in general it is related to the magico-religious sphere, we may also assume that ceremonial objects were manufactured and decorated by specialists, or at least by persons who were thoroughly immersed in the religious symbolism of their culture.

It is interesting also in this connection to bear in mind those subjective images that appear in our field of vision in darkness or half-light, independent of any external light source, and that, originating in the eyes or brain, constitute a perceptual phenomenon common to all human beings. These phosphenes can be produced spontaneously or by such stimuli as electric impulses or hallucinogenic drugs. It has been observed that, when they are produced by drugs, they frequently appear as abstract motifs. Recently Max Knoll, in a study performed on 1000 individuals, was able to establish a series of fifteen of these images which largely conform to the codified motifs of the Tukano.

But we must distinguish between form and meaning. Why are the

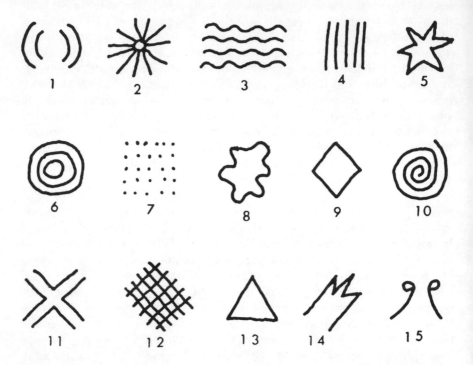

Fig. 20.   Motifs based on phosphenes. After Max Knoll.

motifs experienced by the Tukano in their hallucinations interpreted for the most part in terms of incest and exogamy? Certainly, the hallucination not only induces the projection of supposed or observed forms, but possibly also induces to a more intense degree the projection of latent psychological conflicts extant in the culture. The problem of incest preoccupies the Tukano greatly and, like many other societies, they have devised a considerable elaboration of rules which, of course, go far beyond the narrow biological meaning of the term. For the most part, their mythology and rituals revolve around these themes and conflicts, groping for a solution to the dilemma. The return to the uterus thus might be seen to constitute a means of alleviating the tension.

Before concluding we must make a brief observation on the frequency with which images of jaguars and snakes appear in the hallucinations. Both animals (or groups of animals, since we are dealing with felines and reptiles in general) appear not only in the most menacing forms but frequently as inoffensive and even beneficent to man. This ambivalence of their symbolic value makes their interpretation difficult, but it is important to note that to the Tukano and other Colombian tribes they sometimes represent principles of fertility and protection. In no way do they invariably appear as negative and dangerous forms. It is therefore interesting to record that felines and reptiles have always played a central role in the aboriginal religions of America, whether in the high civilizations of Mesoamerica and the Andes or among groups that had not evolved complex social orders. The symbolic importance of these animals can be traced back archaeologically at least to the second millennium B.C., and it continues into the present in the shamanistic religions of many indigenous groups. If the images of these animals were to be related to the nucleus of conflicts that refers to the theme of incest and exogamy, this would be a question to put to psychologists to consider.

One more point needs to be emphasized in relation to the cultural context in which the Tukano of Vaupés are seen to use *B. Caapi*. The inexorable processes of acculturation modify not only indigenous culture but also the natural environment. The Indians' age-old knowledge about the properties of many plants is of extraordinary potential value to us; yet it is being lost under the avalanche of accelerated acculturation. Here is an enormous field of research for anthropologists which must be investigated before it is too late. In the face of the current world-wide popularization of the use of hallucinogens, it is of the greatest importance to investigate, on an interdisciplinary basis and transculturally, not only the motivations but the psycho-biological effects of these substances. If this comparative material from primitive and fast-disappearing cultures is not obtained, humanity will have lost an important reference point on which to base informed opinion and decisions on the use of hallucinogens in advanced cultures.

4

DOUGLAS SHARON

The San Pedro Cactus in Peruvian Folk Healing *

Only recently have social scientists and other students of human behavior turned their attention in any depth to the widespread phenomenon of folk therapy with hallucinogens in northern Peru. Gillin (1945) was the first investigator to observe and record the role of the hallucinogenic cactus known as San Pedro (*Trichocereus pachanoi*), which contains mescaline as its active ingredient. His work was followed by that of Gutierrez-Noriega and Cruz Sanchez in the late 1940's, and a decade later by that of the French ethnobotanist Friedberg (1959, 1960, 1963), who traveled extensively through the north classifying plants and describing folk medicine. It was not until 1967, however, that scholars began to concentrate seriously on *curanderismo* (or folk healing) and its function in contemporary Peruvian society, especially among the urban and rural poor. In that year a team of investigators, including social psychiatrists and anthropologists, converged on the town of Salas, reputed to be the capital of north coastal healers, to study folk healing from a variety of points of view. As a result there is a growing body of literature † on a widespread system of therapy that represents a blend of prehispanic Indian, Western, Eastern, and idiosyncratic beliefs and techniques in which traditional hallucinogens, especially San Pedro,

* Field work on which this paper is based was made possible through a President's Fellowship from the University of California at Los Angeles. The author also expresses his appreciation to Christopher Donnan and William A. Lessa for their guidance and encouragement throughout the project, and to Clement W. Meighan for his support. Most of all, he owes a debt of gratitude to the curandero Gálvaez, who so generously shared his knowledge and wisdom, and to Gálvaez' family, whose hospitality was boundless.

† See, among others, Gutierrez-Noriega and Cruz Sanchez (1947), Cruz Sanchez (1948a, 1948b), Gutierrez-Noriega (1950), Friedberg (1959, 1963, 1964), Chiappe (1968), Dragunsky (1968). Dobkin (1968, 1969a, 1969b, 1969c, 1970), Schultes (1967), and Rodriguez Suy Suy (1970).

114

Fig. 21. A ceramic vessel of the Chavín culture (1200–600 B.C.) depicting a jaguar in close association with columnar cactus. This suggests that the hallucinogen *San Pedro* played an important ritual and magical role in northern Peru at least 3,000 years ago. Coll. Munson-Williams Proctor Institute, Utica, N.Y. (Photo by André Emmerich.)

play a catalytic role. Although they are extralegal, these hallucinogens clearly have a considerable following among the local population.

The ritual and symbolic importance in northern Peru of the hallucinogenic San Pedro (or a columnar cactus closely related to it) has recently been demonstrated to date back at least three thousand years, on the basis of its association with jaguars and spirit beings on ceremonial pottery and painted textiles of the Chavín horizon (Furst, 1971b). As Furst has noted, the identification of *Trichocereus pachanoi* or a related species on ritual burial ceramics and weavings of the Chavín period makes this the second hallucinogen for which we have very ancient evidence, the first being snuff. For the latter, there is even earlier archaeological proof in the form of snuffing paraphernalia almost four thousand years old, from the site of Huaca Prieta on the Peruvian coast.

My own interest in folk healing with hallucinogens came about through exposure to these practices during archaeological exploration work conducted in Peru from 1961 to 1966. It was discovered that, for trips considered hazardous, the only way to secure the services of guides and porters was to hire a *curandero,* or folk healer,* to accompany the expedition. In 1965, while cooperating with a Peruvian archaeological restoration committee working on the ruins of Chan Chan, near Trujillo, I made the acquaintance of a local curandero who was the artist in charge of adobe frieze reconstruction. He extended several invitations to participate in his curing sessions, but a busy work schedule and frequent absences from Trujillo for archaeological reconnaissance in the Andes prevented me from accepting his offer before leaving Peru in 1967. It was not until the summer of 1970 that a grant from UCLA made it possible for me to return to Peru and study the practices of this curandero in some depth. This paper is the result of an exploratory study undertaken to familiarize myself with the curandero's application of his art and to "gain membership" to the curandero community by following the approach of Slotkin (1955–56) and Castaneda (1969).†

As will soon be apparent, contemporary folk-healing practices in northern Peru are syncretic in nature, combining many Christian elements with older beliefs surviving from pre-European times. In this respect they strongly resemble the sacred mushroom cult as it is practiced today in Oaxaca, Mexico (see Wasson, pp. 185–200, below). Nevertheless,

---

* The English term hardly begins to convey the pervasive role that these modern shamans play in their communities as spiritual mentors and guardians of traditional lore—functions that include, but are not restricted to, medical therapy.

† Slotkin, who studied the peyote cult as practiced within the Native American (Indian) Church as an anthropologist, eventually became a full-fledged member of that Church. Castaneda apprenticed himself to a "man of knowledge" (Castaneda calls him a sorcerer) of Yaqui Indian origin while doing field work for his doctoral degree in anthropology. His apprenticeship continued for several years and included the use of various hallucinogenic plants employed by his teacher, don Juan.

it is correct to say that the core of the folk-healing system in Peru (as in Mexico) is shamanistic, and that the curandero himself is more of a shaman, in the traditional meaning of that term, than anything else —the various modern or folk-Catholic elements of contemporary curanderismo notwithstanding. The shamanistic component is especially apparent in the attitude toward, and use of, the hallucinogenic cactus. San Pedro is the catalyst that activates all the complex forces at work in a folk-healing session, especially the visionary and divinatory powers of the curandero himself. What the curer has to say about this phenomenon and his relationship to San Pedro and other magical plants is reminiscent of what one reads about shamans and peyote, mushrooms, yajé, and other psychotomimetics.* On the other hand, the contrast between my experiences with San Pedro and those of the indigenous curandero should demonstrate that much more than the psychotropic cactus itself is at work in "learning to see," which is the goal of every folk healer. To "see," to attain vision beyond what we would call the "real" world, requires hard work, lengthy training, and, most important, a very special kind of psychological predisposition combined with cultural "conditioning."

The Curer Gálvaez

My mentor-to-be, whom I shall call Gálvaez,† was born forty-one years ago in Trujillo, where his parents had settled after migrating to the coast from the Andean highlands. Much of his life history is unique, and yet in many ways he is typical of north Peruvian folk healers, for they are all extraordinary individuals. His father was a skilled artisan, adept in many trades, especially shoemaking. Gálvaez worked from an early age to help support the family; at sixteen he enrolled in religious studies in the hope of becoming a priest, but he soon became disillusioned. For a time he intended to study medicine; but this proved unfeasible. Nevertheless, some of what he learned in those early years stayed with him for the rest of his life and entered into his later practice of curanderismo. He was gifted in the fine arts, especially sculpture and ceramics, and for a year studied at the School of Fine Arts in Lima, using money he had earned as a bricklayer to support himself in the

---

* It is interesting to note that the curandero with whom I worked is himself well aware of the antiquity of the San Pedro cactus in Peruvian ritual. He knew, for example, that the hallucinogenic cactus is depicted on burial ceramics of the Mochica culture, dating back some 1500 years and more, an identification also made by Friedberg (1963).

† Since this was written, I returned to Peru (in the summer of 1971) for another season's research with the same curandero. By then his confidence in me had progressed to the point of permitting me to use his real name, Eduardo Calderón Palomino, in my published reports. He also agreed to accept me as full-fledged assistant in his curing rituals.

capital. He was married for the first time at age twenty, but the marriage soon dissolved, and his wife kept their infant daughter. Gálvaez then turned to fishing as a livelihood. At twenty-three he met his present companion, the daughter of a fisherman, herself a skilled potter. As of August, 1970, they had nine children—four girls and five boys.

At the time of his second marriage, the Peruvian fishing industry was just beginning to expand, and Gálvaez and his wife began to move to Chimbote, south of Trujillo, each fishing season. Soon he was foreman of a tuna clipper crew. In the off-season he returned to Trujillo, where he worked as a stevedore and earned extra money by making wood-carvings and ceramics on the side. In 1962 a hospital ship put into port for a year, and Gálvaez worked almost full time copying pre-Columbian ceramics for the vessel's crew and staff. Eventually he bought his own small fishing boat and began fishing near Trujillo, where he had first learned his trade. Here he became an innovator, introducing modern fishing methods for the first time to the local fishermen. Then, at age thirty-five, fortune turned against him, and he lost everything. However, not long after he was appointed artist in charge of restoring the famous adobe friezes at Chan Chan, political and economic center of the pre-Inca kingdom of Chimor. He held this job until 1969, when restoration work was terminated, and during this period he also produced some 2000 ceramic copies of ancient pottery vessels for sale to tourists. Apart from this close association with the remote Indian past and the Indian origins of his parents in the Peruvian highlands, there was obviously nothing very Indian about Gálvaez' lifeway—on the contrary, he was a typical Mestizo, Spanish-speaking, literate, Catholic in religion, apparently with only the most tenuous ties to native Indian culture.

However, throughout his long career in a variety of jobs, Gálvaez the artist and family man was also evolving as Gálvaez the curandero. His early interest in the priesthood had been an attempt to realize what he regarded as a "calling to serve humanity." He experienced dreams urging him to prepare himself and felt a deep and idealistic yearning to help alleviate human suffering. His attempt toward the priesthood was a disappointment, and medicine was out of reach. Then, aged only twenty-two, he suddenly fell ill with a mysterious ail-ment that failed to yield to modern medical treatment. Both of his grand-fathers had been curanderos in the highlands, and so he decided to see if a folk healer might help where the doctors had failed. He underwent treatment and was cured. He did not understand what had happened but felt an urge to learn.*

---

* Gálvaez' experience is obviously akin to "sickness vocation," a common phe-nomenon in shamanism, in which the future shaman feels himself "called" through a

His second wife had an uncle who was noted as a curandero working with hallucinogens and a *mesa* (literally table, a kind of altar containing numerous standardized and idiosyncratic "power objects"). At twenty-four Gálvaez began his apprenticeship under this relative. Fishing in Chimbote kept him from entering as deeply into his vocation as he wished, but between voyages he gained sufficient experience to serve as *rastreador* (literally "tracker," one who helps the curandero "see" during the curing session). In Chimbote he was also exposed to curanderos who specialized in "raising" the luck of fishing crews.

When he remained in Trujillo he had enough time to develop his powers to the point where, during one momentous session, he suddenly felt that the "Christ of the mesa" had chosen him to effect a part of the curing ritual. After that session Gálvaez decided that he had outgrown his teacher. But he did not yet feel ready to establish his own mesa. Instead he went north to work with famous curanderos in Chiclayo, Motupe, and Ferreñafe. When he returned, at age twenty-eight, he was still hesitant to practice on his own, although he had had four years of training. Then a cousin of his fell seriously ill. The girl's father, Gálvaez' uncle, was in financial difficulties and could not afford doctor bills. He suspected that his daughter was suffering from *daño*, witchcraft, and implored Gálvaez to take her case. Despite his doubts, Gálvaez decided to try. In two sessions he uncovered the cause and effected a cure using the hallucinogenic San Pedro cactus. Thus his career as a curandero working with his own mesa was launched. In gratitude to God, Gálvaez made a vow never to abuse his powers and to work only for good in the service of humanity. This, then, was the man who had agreed to become my teacher.

SAN PEDRO

San Pedro, a smooth, relatively thin, often spineless, columnar cactus of the *Cereus* family, was first described and classified as *Trichocereus pachanoi* by Britton and Rose (1920), who gave the area of its distribution as Andean Ecuador, where it is also called *agua-colla*, *giganton*, and *San Pedrillo*. How and why it came to be called "Saint Peter" was not stated. Backeberg (1959) agreed with the Britton and Rose classification but expanded the distribution area to include northern Peru and Bolivia. Friedberg (1959) submitted a voucher specimen to Poisson (1960), of the Faculty of Pharmacy at Paris, and Poisson identified mescaline (1.2 grams per kilo of fresh material) as the active alkaloid in *T. pachanoi*. The presence of mescaline was verified by

serious illness that fails to respond to normal treatment and requires supernatural intervention.—ED.

Gonzalez Huerta (1960) and also by Turner and Heyman (1961), although there was some confusion of the relevant species in the latter report. There may be alkaloids other than mescaline in San Pedro, but this will have to be determined by future pharmacological studies.

Britton and Rose reported San Pedro growing at altitudes ranging from 2000 to 3000 meters above sea level. However, I found San Pedro growing at an altitude only 24 meters above sea level in a suburb of Trujillo. The presence of San Pedro in other areas near the city was also confirmed to me by Michael Mosely of Harvard University's Moche–Chan Chan Project. (It should be noted that no voucher specimens were collected and that the identification of the cactus was not made by trained botanists.)

According to Gálvaez there are several types of San Pedro, distinguished by the number of longitudinal ribs. The kind most often used by curanderos has seven ribs. Four-ribbed cacti are very rare and are considered to have special curative properties. The varieties found in the Andean highlands are said to be the most potent, whatever the number of ribs, because of the higher mineral content of the soil.

The preparation of San Pedro for use in the folk-healing session is a very simple process. At noon on the day of the session, four short cacti (the thinnest cacti are believed to make the best brew) are sliced like loaves of bread, placed in a five-gallon can of water, and boiled for seven hours. For most cases brought to the folk healer, nothing is added to the boiled San Pedro infusion. However, in cases of illness caused by a sorcerer's magic concoction, such as powdered bones, cemetery dust, or dust from archaeological ruins, certain botanically unidentified plants, known as *hornamo blanco, hornamo amarillo, hornamo morado, hornamo cuti, hornamo caballo,* and *condor purga,* are boiled separately for addition to the portions of San Pedro served to the patient. Also, a separate purgative brew made from another unidentified plant *(condorillo* or *yerba de la justicia* or *mejorana)* is prepared to be taken after San Pedro and the *hornamos* to induce vomiting. Finally, a portion of the San Pedro infusion is set aside to be added to the ingredients mixed to produce *tabaco,* a liquid prepared from tobacco and other ingredients and imbibed via the nostrils during the curing ceremony.

Many curanderos in the Chiclayo area add *Floripondio* or *Floripondium (Datura arborea)*—one of the numerous *mishas,* or *Daturas*— to San Pedro, but Gálvaez does not. He was initiated by healers who used these potent plants and is aware of their toxic properties and adverse effects on many patients. He does not feel that such drastic shock therapy is necessary to alleviate the ailments of those seeking his services.

Gálvaez described San Pedro as follows:

Fig. 22.   Sections of *San Pedro* ready for cutting and boiling in the preparation
of the hallucinogenic potion used in curing.

San Pedro, Huando Hermoso, Cardo, Huachuma [are] various names
applied to this cactus. . . . It is medicinal. It is applied, for example, to
cutaneous infections. It is diuretic.* It is utilized in general for cases of
healing and witchcraft. . . . It is used . . . for both [types of] magic—white
and black. . . . It is always recommended that after taking San Pedro one
must follow a diet: not eat any food that contains hot peppers, salt, animal
fat or grease, or anything that "entangles," for example, foods that grow on
climbing vines, such as beans, peas, lentils, etc. . . . It has been represented
in archaeological ceramics, possibly to represent its power, its application,
its use. . . . San Pedro has a special symbolism in curanderismo, for a reason:
San Pedro is always in tune with ("accounted" with) the saints, with the
powers of animals, of strong personages or beings, of serious beings, of beings
that have supernatural power. . . . The symbolism of San Pedro is to locate
in all the regions of the territory the elemental thought and potentiality of
man.

Another interesting power claimed for San Pedro is the protection
of houses:

* The terminology used here is the result of his assimilation of modern medical
knowledge through correspondence courses and reading.

It cares for the house . . . as if it were a dog. It is accounted for [in the curanderismo traditions], it is in tune [with the curandero's own powers and with his other magical artifacts and herbs], and it is raised* with *tabaco* in the proper manner. Then it cares for the house. It serves as guardian. In the night it appears to strangers who want to enter as a man in white, wearing a hat. Or else it whistles. It whistles with a peculiar sound so that anyone who enters who is not of the household . . . comes out at top speed, like a bullet.

San Pedro is only one—thought to be the principal one—of a great number of "magic" plants. These plants—some of which are medicinal as well as magical—are carefully distinguished from the overwhelming number of purely medicinal plants known to the curandero. The great majority of magical plants are herbs collected on the hillsides of sacred lagoons in the Andes at altitudes of 12,000 to 13,000 feet above sea level. There are several areas in the northern highlands where such lagoons are found, but the most important, called collectively Las Huaringas, are found above the town of Huancabamba near the border between Peru and Ecuador. Many curanderos make periodic pilgrimages to Huancabamba to collect these herbs or have friends who do this for them. The herbs are then placed in the curandero's *seguro,* a special glass jar, where they are kept in a state of preservation by several perfumes accompanying them. The seguro is one of the focal points of the curandero's attention during the curing division of a session. According to Gálvaez, these plants, once activated by the ceremonial part of a session and by the drinking of San Pedro, "talk" to him when he is concentrating on the seguro. Some merely indicate representative symbols of the curing art and the causes of a patient's ailment during diagnosis, while others, which have both symbolic and medicinal value, indicate what herb or herbs should be used in the cure during treatment. Most of these plants can be purchased at the herb stands in the markets of the coastal towns and cities of Peru.

This is how Gálvaez explains the action of the magic plants and their relation to San Pedro and to himself:

According to my evaluation as a curandero, the herbs have their spirits, because they speak [and] direct the activities in the realm of curanderismo during the nocturnal session. . . . Their spirits are susceptible to the curandero who manipulates them. They can advise or warn him. . . . They indicate to him how the cure is to be effected by means of the San Pedro infusion, which is the principal base of curanderismo. They enumerate the dangers to watch

---

* "Raising," in the idiom of curanderismo, has both descriptive and symbolic meanings. In the curing ceremony San Pedro, *tabaco,* and other potions are in fact raised high before they are taken orally or through the nose. However, the context in which Gálvaez used the term here suggests he was not referring solely to the physical act of lifting. See below.

out for, and what is to be done about the sickness. If one does not drink San Pedro, there is nothing. . . . The herbs . . . have power to manifest themselves. It seems that possibly they have a spirit that is matched with the power of San Pedro and the intellectual power of the curandero. . . .

When asked about the force of the magic plants, he explained:

The curandero or *brujo* [sorcerer], upon invoking the power of the plants within his curative power, also influences them. He imposes his personal spiritual force over the plants . . . giving them that magic power which becomes, let us say, the power that plants contain as a result of having been rooted in the earth and partaken of its magnetic force. And, since man is an element of the earth, with the power of his intelligence . . . he emits this potentiality over the plants. The plants receive this influence and return it toward man, toward the individual in the moment when he invokes. In other words, all of the spirit of the plants is . . . fortified by the influences—intellectual, spiritual, and human—of man. He is the one who forms the magic potentiality of the plants. Because of the fact that they are in an isolated place, a place untouched by strange hands, by foreign elements, the plants together with water produce the magic power by virtue of their duality.

It would seem, then, that once the inner power of the curandero is activated by the hallucinogenic San Pedro cactus, the magic plants provide a medium by which his contact with the earth is renewed in a reciprocal flow of energy.

THE SYMBOLISM AND POWER OF THE MESA

Every curandero has his mesa, which, as mentioned, is a collection of numerous power objects laid out on the ground in altar-like fashion for the curing sessions. These objects are of either a positive or a negative nature. The mesa symbolizes the duality of the world of man and nature and of the spiritual realm, as manifested in the struggle between good and evil. The opposites among the power objects are complementary rather than irreconcilable, rather like two sides of a coin.

To the curandero, the existence of opposite forces does not mean splitting the world in two (the "sacred" and "profane") or establishing a rigid dichotomy between "this" world of matter and the "other" world of spirit. On the contrary, the curandero seeks to perceive unity in the dynamic interaction between the forces of good and evil through the attainment of "vision." Such a view of the world is very flexible and adaptable; it leaves room for the acceptance of new symbols and ideas and allows competing elements to enter into one's structuring of reality and the behavior determined by such structuring.

This manner of perceiving reality probably explains Gálvaez's ability to resolve apparent contradictions in his daily life (e.g., sensitive artist —rugged fisherman and stevedore, etc.). He clearly has developed a

Fig. 23. *Mesa* of a *curandero,* with staffs and other "power objects" used in divination and curing with *San Pedro.*

capacity to inhabit, with apparent ease, two religious worlds at once, one traditional, the other Roman Catholic; his faith in the power of the "ancients" and the hallucinogenic San Pedro cactus is as absolute as his belief in Christ, the Virgin, and the saints. Witness the following statement:

> I salute the ancients, the powerful ones, men who have lived in antiquity . . . for their intellectual force, their power, their magnificence, and the saints for . . . their intellect, their personality . . . their great power as philosophers, writers, poets . . . [so] that they will help me intellectually in search of these inconveniences [i.e., the causes of the patient's problems] in order to discover a solution. I always invoke the ancients, brujos, curanderos who have died [and] who are alive, calling their spirits, their personalities. They attend and deliver ideas that can bring one out of trance, out of the wrong path that he may be following. Therefore I [also] call on St. Augustine, Moses, Solomon, St. Cyprian, St. Paul, for advice, for help in moments of doubt.

Similarly, Gálvaez sees no contradiction between modern medicine and traditional curing and, depending on the situation and his diagnosis, readily employs pharmaceutical products in his work. Nor does he see modern medicine as a threat to his vocation; on the contrary, he is seeking to assimilate scientific knowledge and techniques into his practice by taking correspondence courses and reading medical literature. Also, for advanced organic or chronic disorders, he recommends immediate medical and hospital treatment to augment his own.

To return to the mesa: in accordance with the concept of complementary opposites, the mesa is divided into two major (though unequal) zones, called *campos* (fields) or *bancos* (benches), which are kept apart by a "neutral" area. The left and smaller side of the oblong mesa is called the *Campo Ganadero* (Field of the Sly Dealer, Satan). It contains artifacts associated with the forces of evil, the underworld, and negative magic, mainly fragments of ancient ceramics and stones from archaeological ruins, along with cane alcohol, a deer foot, and a triton shell. This zone is governed by Satan, whose negative powers are concentrated in three staffs—called Satan's Bayonet, Owl Staff, and the Staff of the Single Woman—placed upright in the ground behind the artifacts of the *Campo Ganadero*. A witch or sorcerer would use this negative zone for sorcery or curing for lucrative gain; a benevolent curer like Gálvaez needs it for consultation in cases of witchcraft, adverse love magic, or bad luck, since this is the realm responsible for such evils and consequently capable of revealing their sources.

The right and larger side of the mesa, called the *Campo Justiciero* (Field of the Divine Judge or Divine Justice), contains artifacts related to the forces of good or positive magic—including images of saints, positive power objects such as stones, shells, bowls, a glass, a dagger, and a rattle, and certain substances, including three perfumes, holy water, tobacco, sugar, lime, and a five-gallon can of San Pedro infusion. This zone is governed by Christ, whose positive powers are focused in eight staffs—called, respectively, Swordfish Beak Staff, Eagle Staff, Greyhound Staff, Hummingbird Staff, Staff of the Virgin of Mercy, Sword of St. Paul, Sabre of St. Michael the Archangel, and Sword of St. James the Elder—positioned behind the artifacts. The neutral field (*Campo Medio*) contains artifacts of a neutral nature, in which the forces of good and evil are evenly balanced. This zone is governed by St. Cyprian (a powerful magician who was converted to Christianity), whose neutral powers are focused in a Serpent Staff. The "neutral" or "balanced" objects are a bronze sunburst, a stone symbolizing the sea and the winds, a glass jar containing magic herbs, a statue of St. Cyprian, a "fortune stone," and a crystal "mirror." These are symbolic of forces in nature and the world of man that can be used for good or for evil, depending on the intention of the individual. This part of the mesa is the focal point of the curandero's "vision." Because of its neutral quality, it is considered capable of reflecting the case under consideration without distortion, usually in the glass jar of magic herbs or in the crystal mirror.

The artifacts of the mesa are not just a random collection of standard objects. Rather, they are gradually accumulated over the years of a curandero's practice. Gálvaez started his practice with the bare essentials —utensils and a few key artifacts for each of the three campos. As his skills improved he enlarged the collection and replaced objects with others considered to have more power. Each was carefully selected and acquired under special circumstances, and each has unique personal significance to the curandero, along with its own *cuenta,* or "account," which is activated by the catalyst San Pedro. Many artifacts were made by Gálvaez from carefully selected materials of special significance to him as an artist and fisherman. Obviously, within the standard symbolic framework passed on from curandero to initiate, there is room for personal elaboration, once mastery has been gained over the curing art. The same is true of the curandero's *tarjos,* or chants. He learns the traditional rhythms and song cycles but, as with the various power objects, he elaborates on the basic complex with his own particular talents and according to the inspiration he receives from a variety of extrapersonal and supernatural sources.

One of Gálvaez's most important power objects, activated by the hallucinogenic San Pedro and utilized in certain especially virulent cases of witchcraft or sorcery, is "the cat." His account of how he obtained it and how it is used is of particular interest, not only because of the role of cats in European witchcraft lore but also because of the intimate relationship of felines to traditional South American shamanism and the considerable feline symbolism to be found in the ancient ritual art of Peru:

In my case I have some talismans that I prepared by means of my own ideas and illuminations that I have had in my dreams. The cat plays a principal role in witchcraft and its glance has great power. When a cat dies . . . the eyes remain open. Then there is reflected all concerning the tragedy that has happened in the hour of its death. And it carries in its pupils the moment of [its] abduction toward the tomb. . . . Therefore, I purposely prepared this talisman. I grabbed a cat and killed it and drank the blood three times. I sucked the blood from the neck of the animal three times and then I took out the eyes. After I took out the eyes I cut off its right paw, the right claw. And this I gathered together and placed in a receptacle with *agua cananga* (dark perfume) during one complete cycle of the moon. . . . After that I added *agua florida* (scented water, another perfume). And after the *agua florida* I added cane alcohol at the end in order to give this feline bravery and power to intoxicate with his glance. Those eyes I sewed together with green and red silk thread and tied them to a flint arrow-head that I found in an ancient archaeological tomb. This talisman I carry with me and I use it at night when I want to countercheck the power of a cat, of a feline, of some exterior spirit attack of a sorcerer who wants to attack or perturb me. All I do is launch my savage cat by means of a few sparks made with the flint arrowhead. And it has its power. The cat goes out to the hills screaming and screeching. . . . I use it on a block of crystal. This block of crystal is like a mirror, and the cat sees what moves in this mirror. For whatever [disturbance] it is there, looking. The eyes light up as if they were light bulbs. This is one of the talismans purposely prepared by us in accordance with the idea that one has, or the inspiration of a dream, or the intuition of each one.

The whole concept of the mesa with its numerous power objects typifies the fusion of European-Christian and traditional Indian symbolism in contemporary curanderismo. All shamans have power objects, and many of those owned by Gálvaez are characteristic of shamans in many cultures, as is the manner in which they are obtained. Saints, Christ, Satan, the Virgin, etc., of course are Christian, but their functions are very similar to those of negative and positive forces in aboriginal shamanism; duality, or the complementary nature of opposites, likewise is characteristic of many indigenous symbolic systems.

To understand how the artifacts function it is important to remember that to the curandero they are not lifeless objects. Each is a focal point of a particular force. Collectively, they are a projection of his own inner spiritual power, which becomes activated whenever the mesa is manipulated in conjunction with the drinking of the hallucinogenic San Pedro infusion. This is clearly demonstrated in Gálvaez's account of what happened when he found an ancient sorcerer's kit in an archaeological site and took it home in the hope of "dominating its accounts" for use in his own work:

I took it in order "to track" (*rastrear*), to see what type it was. As a result these artifacts rebelled. Rare animals and monstrous beasts issued forth with hunger and desire to seize people. Then, when I placed the kit on my mesa, everything was distorted and turned black. The artifacts began bleeding. Several personages with huge fangs gushing blood came forth and demanded my wife and children. Then I tried to throw them out. I purified the kit with holy water and burned it because the day that I brought it home there had also begun a noise on my roof like the galloping of wild beasts. And they didn't leave me alone until I made cabalistic thrusts with my swords to countercheck these influences. . . . For me [the kit] was of no use. It was a black artifact, an artifact of witchcraft. That is, this was used in witchcraft . . . in remote ancestral times by the Mochica or Chimú peoples . . . to destroy farms, crops, [human] organs, etc. [*Question:* And this evil power remains preserved there for centuries, right?]. . . . Yes, all the evil has been preserved for centuries for one reason, which is that this [the kit] is designed or "accounted" (*contado*) under the influence of a person of this character. . . . When accounted, the object absorbs the potentiality, let us say, the intellectual potentiality of the man who manipulates it and remains impregnated forever.

Once the curandero has set up his mesa he is ready to begin the curing session. There are two parts to this: (1) ceremonial acts, and (2) curing acts. The ceremonial part lasts generally from about 10 P.M. until midnight; diagnosis and/or treatment lasts from midnight until about 4 A.M. The entire session takes place in the open, usually in an area enclosed by a wall or fence, and can be performed any night of the week except Monday, the "day of the spirits," when dead souls from purgatory are supposed to be roaming about.

The ceremonial part consists of prayers, invocations, and chants (accompanied by the rhythmic beat of the traditional shamanic rattle) addressed to all the supernaturals of the aboriginal and Roman Catholic faiths. The three perfumes mentioned earlier are used to "purify" the mesa and the San Pedro infusion. At specified intervals everyone present must imbibe a mixture called *tabaco* (see below for ingredients) through the nostrils. This process is known as "raising," most likely because the receptacle containing the fluid is lifted high and poured into the nostrils. However, as we have noted, the term may also have symbolic significance. Finally, at midnight, when the ceremonial acts have been completed, all present must drink one cup of the hallucinogenic cactus brew, after which they are ceremonially "cleansed" by the curandero. The ritual drinking of San Pedro is initiated by the curandero, who takes the first cupful, and concluded by his two assistants, who are the last to drink.

The curing part, which follows, consists of a standard series of therapeutic acts that must be performed by the curandero for all participants. Each takes a turn in front of the mesa. The curandero chants a tarjo in his name, whereupon everyone concentrates on the vertical staffs at the head of the mesa. One of these staffs, the focal point of the patient's ailment (or of the life history of a healthy visitor who has accompanied a sick one to lend moral support), is supposed to vibrate. When consensus has been reached as to which staff moved it is handed to the patient to hold in his left hand. The curandero chants the tarjo of the staff, which focuses his "vision" and activates the power of the staff and associated artifacts on the mesa. This is followed by a lengthy divinatory discourse by the curandero, relating events and describing people from the patient's life. Others present may share some of the curandero's visions. During this phase the curandero "sees" the cause of *daño* (witchcraft), *enredo* (love magic), or *suerte* (fate or bad luck), depending on which of these is bothering the patient. Once the evil has been exorcised, the curandero's two assistants "raise" the patient (i.e., stand behind and in front of him or her and imbibe through the nostrils one or all of the ingredients of the tabaco mixture, as specified by the curandero). Then the patient raises the staff to the level of his face and at the same time pours the substance selected by the curandero into his nostrils. After this one of the assistants "cleanses" the patient by rubbing the staff all over his body. Next the assistant slices the air with the staff, takes a liquid indicated by the curandero (lime juice, perfume, San Pedro, etc.), into his mouth and sprays it on the staff, after which he returns it to its place at the head of the mesa. Once everyone has taken a turn at the head of the mesa, the curandero ends the session and all depart after a final purification ceremony.*

Thus, through elaborate ceremony, music, perfumes, brews, and symbolic contact, the curing session stimulates the five senses of the patient in a familiar cultural environment. In addition, during his turn before the mesa, everyone present gives attention to the patient and his problem in a supportive fashion. All this, added to the hallucinogenic nature of the San Pedro infusion, is intended to render the patient susceptible to therapy.

The liquid *tabaco* which is imbibed through the nostrils by all present during the ceremonial acts and prior to the drinking of the pure hallucinogenic San Pedro infusion, is individually prepared for each participant by mixing the following ingredients in a bivalve shell: dried leaves of a wild, unprocessed tobacco plant (the principal ingredient from which the mixture gets its name); the hallucinogenic San Pedro, for its catalytic action; sugar candy and lime juice, symbolizing sweetness, intended to render the patient's spirit susceptible to therapy; two perfumes, one to reinforce the action of the sugar and lime, and the other, of a dark color, symbolizing fire or the purifying agent against evil; scented water, symbolic of magic plants which it helps to preserve; and *aguardiente,* cane alcohol, symbolic of the intoxicating force of the powers of evil (which must be invoked to get at the causes of disharmony). The purpose of the tobacco in the mixture was given by Gálvaez as follows:

> Pure tobacco (*sayri* or *huaman tabaco*—the famous falcon, as the ancients called it) gives power to "visualize" . . . and very rapid sight, mind, and imagination. It is for this reason that in ancient times they used *rapé* made from ground tobacco to "clear" the mind. It is in exactly the same fashion that we . . . the curanderos . . . utilize tobacco: to "clear" our minds and speed

* The fact that other observations of the San Pedro curing ritual conform in their major features to those reported by Sharon suggests a shared tradition, though with some idiosyncratic variations or innovations. Another anthropologist, Scott Robinson (personal communication), for example, had much the same experience with another San Pedro practitioner as did Sharon with Gálvaez. In Robinson's case the curandero preferred an entirely open space among the dunes, without walls or fences; also, lime juice was not administered in a mixture with tobacco juice but given separately afterwards, and the patient's body was cleansed or purified with a "doll" or figurine rather than with the staff. Otherwise the ritual proceeded along much the same lines and with similar paraphernalia as that conducted by Gálvaez.—Ed.

our thoughts toward the ends that we seek. (*Question:* Why do you take it through the nostrils?) Because it is near certain motor nerves that transmit it to the brain. There it touches these olfactory papillae that go directly to the brain. Then its power is more rapid.

THE SAN PEDRO EXPERIENCE: CURANDERO AND PATIENT

What emerges from many hours of taped conversation with Gálvaez and participation in his curing sessions is that the hallucinogenic San Pedro cactus is experienced as the catalyst that enables the curandero to transcend the limitations placed on ordinary mortals: to activate all his senses; project his spirit or soul; ascend and descend into the supernatural realms; identify and do battle with the sources of illness, witchcraft, and misfortune; confront and vanquish ferocious animals and demons of disease and sorcerers who direct them; "jump over" barriers of time, space, and matter; divine the past, present, and future —in short, to attain vision, "to see." And "seeing," in the sense in which this word is used by the curandero, is very different from "looking at." The effects of San Pedro, according to Gálvaez:

. . . are first a slight dizziness that one hardly notices. And then a great vision, a clearing of all the faculties of the individual. It produces a light numbness in the body and afterward a tranquility. And then comes a detachment, a type of visual force in the individual inclusive of all the senses: seeing, hearing, smelling, touching, etc.—all the senses, including the sixth sense, the telepathic sense of transmitting oneself across time and matter. . . . It develops the power of perception . . . in the sense that when one wants to see something far away . . . he can distinguish powers or problems or disturbances at a great distance, so as to deal with them. . . . It [also] produces . . . a general cleansing, which includes the kidneys, the liver . . . the stomach, and the blood.

When asked how San Pedro helps him vis-à-vis the patient, and the effects it has on the latter, Gálvaez replied:

San Pedro has great power . . . as it is "accounted" with the saints . . . with all the hills, ancient shrines, lakes, streams, and powers . . . that one must "account" with the saints. That San Pedro I "raise" intellectually, with my mind, with my five senses, in all the radius around us, according to the way my focus of action, that is, my power, irradiates [it]. Then San Pedro tends to manifest itself [in the patient] in the form of vomiting, perspiration . . . sometimes in dancing. At times during diagnosis a patient automatically starts to dance alone, or to throw himself writhing on the ground. And there unfolds the power (i.e., the ailment, or evil power) placed into the person. It seems that . . . not all of us are resistant. Some are very susceptible, very unstable, and San Pedro tends to reach the subconscious . . . and the conscious, in such cases. It penetrates the blood . . . rises to, let us say, the intellectual nervous system. Then it "visualizes" and opens up a sixth sense.

. . . Then the individual, sometimes by himself, can visualize his past or . . . the present, or an immediate future.

What did the concept of the "subconscious" mean to him? Here is his answer:

> The subconscious is a superior part (of man) . . . a kind of bag where the individual has stored all his memories, all his valuations. . . . One must try . . . to make the individual "jump out" of his conscious mind. That is the principal task of curanderismo. By means of the magical plants and the chants and the search for the roots of the problem, the subconscious of the individual is opened like a flower, and it releases these blockages. All by itself it tells things. A very practical manner . . . which was known to the ancients [of Peru].

It might be noted that Gálvaez distinguishes between "psychological sickness" and "sickness very different from that"—i.e., sickness caused by witchcraft.*

Again and again Gálvaez returned to the curandero's attainment of "vision" as the major focus of the curing session. "Vision" not only involves seeing problems "at a great distance" but also refers to his experiences on ecstatic journeys, in trances induced by San Pedro:

> I called certain saints, hills, ancient shrines; and I disappeared. There was an unfolding of my personality. . . . I was no longer at the mesa. . . . That is to say, my personality had departed to other places. . . . The human mind has great power, a supernatural power. And one must exercise it, of course, in order to conduct a session. . . . During my sessions at times I have been looking for a certain force, for example, an ancient shrine or a hill, and suddenly [while] I was whistling and singing, the "account" was activated, and I felt myself enter the hill which opened all its passages, all its labyrinths. And suddenly I returned again. I had "seen" and I had "visualized" with my spirit.

He also told me that the curanderos of northern Peru had their own sacred lagoons, called Las Huaringas, where one traveled to bathe and to learn about all the magical plants that grow there—"those for good and those for evil." I asked him if he had ever personally visited these sacred lagoons. Physically, no, he said, but supernaturally, yes, through the agency of his jar of magical herbs.

When an illness has been produced by the concoction of a sorcerer, the spirit of that concoction

* That this cultural syndrome is recognized as a separate and legitimate category which is shared with the patient and not simply as another psychological ailment, as it is often characterized by Western psychology, may give curanderismo great therapeutic value and may explain its persistence. Our knowledge of the extent to which culture influences psychological disturbances is weak, to say the least. Can we deny witchcraft the status of a separate, legitimate category in contemporary Latin American culture when great numbers of people accept it as such and act accordingly?

. . . comes to look for what it is lacking. A light in the form of a fire-fly blinks on and off and comes looking for its "bone," which the sorcerer has introduced into the patient's stomach, killing him, consuming him. And until the patient throws up that element, the firefly is there, circling.

In certain serious cases, the illness-causing forces are believed to be powerful enough to attack the patient during the actual curing session, in an effort to thwart the curandero's therapeutic measures. This is extremely critical and requires vigorous emergency action. The curandero seizes one of the swords of his mesa and charges into the open, beyond the mesa and the patients. Here he conducts a ferocious battle with the attacking forces (which only he can see in his San Pedro trance vision), violently thrusting and slicing the air with his blade. Then he performs seven somersaults in the form of a cross, while grasping the sword in both hands with the sharp edge held forward. This is intended to drive off the attacking spirits and shock the sorcerer who is directing them.*

If sufficiently strong, these hostile forces may even attack the curandero himself. In that case he must rely on the aid and protection of higher beings:

> In certain trances, on paths closed to most men, rare beasts have confronted me with harmful intentions. And the presence of the Lord and His power-ful light have helped me out of these places unharmed. And I always get out unharmed because there are beings in the other "mansion" [realm] such as great curanderos. . . . [By] calling these spirits via the prayers that I know, they come and assist in any trance.

To summarize, within the indigenous framework the hallucinogenic San Pedro infusion is the magical substance that activates the curer's inner powers, as well as those inherent in the objects of his mesa. For the patient it opens his subconscious "like a flower" and renders the forces that made him sick visible and susceptible to the curer's thera-peutic powers. By means of San Pedro the curer awakens all of his senses, including a vital sixth sense, and by their interaction attains "vision"--the true focus of the curing session and the supreme achieve-

---

* Here the pre-European shamanistic tradition is again obvious. Such trance experi-ences as visits to sacred lakes or water holes which belong exclusively to the super-natural practitioners (see, for example, Wilbert's account of the supernatural initiatory journey of the shaman of the Venezuelan Warao), entering the earth or hills, spirit projection, physical combat against disease demons and ferocious animals doing the bidding of sorcerers, foreign objects magically introduced into the body to cause illness, assistance from dead shamans and benevolent supernaturals, etc., all are typically shamanistic. Somersaulting also is a not uncommon shamanistic phenomenon, utilized especially for purposes of transformation. In neighboring Bolivia, for example, shamans of the Tacana perform somersaults in one direction to turn themselves into jaguars (their alter egos) and in the opposite direction to reassume human form (cf. Hissink-Hahn, 1961).—Ed.

ment of the curandero. For aid, guidance, and protection during these arduous and dangerous sessions, the curandero places his faith in higher spiritual beings, including those of the Christian faith as well as the aboriginal Indian pantheon.

THE SAN PEDRO EXPERIENCE: THE APPRENTICE

During my field work in 1970, I was able to participate in only three curing sessions as more than an observer. Thus there was insufficient time for me to develop even the beginning of "vision," as understood by Gálvaez, or to make an adequate analysis of the process. The problem was aggravated by the trappings of my anthropological subculture: tape recorder, notebook, and a felt need to collect ethnographic data on a phenomenon about which little had been written by trained observers. As a result, my first subjective experiences leave much to be desired in terms of content. However, this very paucity may prove useful, in that it illustrates the role of cultural factors in the "psychedelic" experience. It is with these limitations in mind that the following should be evaluated.

In the first session, the San Pedro infusion produced no observable effect whatever. I taped the ceremonial phase of the session until midnight. After drinking the infusion and taping the tarjo addressed to the first patient, I put the tape recorder away and began to participate in the curing phase. I did not notice any effects on myself, nor did I "see" any of the dogs, rats, or stars that the curandero and others present seemed to be perceiving together. After the session concluded, at about 5 A.M., I retired and slept soundly until noon. Throughout the afternoon, after rising, I experienced a very slight headache in the region of the frontal lobes, which passed by evening.

During the second session, fourteen days later, San Pedro did take effect, despite the fact that I was busy taping the entire session. The morning after the session, as soon as I awoke I jotted down the following notes:

> Finally had some results with San Pedro. Felt warm and relaxed. At 3 A.M. began to see what Gálvaez calls a *remolino*, a whirlpool of red and yellow light spinning inward before my eyes and lightly printed on everything I looked at. Also noticed flashes of light out of the corners of my eyes when I moved my head suddenly. . . . Was fully conscious of my surroundings and felt no strange sensations or dizziness—just very relaxed. Still don't see what everyone else sees, but did notice patients under "attack," leaning crazily backwards as if pulled by some force. Noticed a white ghostlike outline around each patient as each took his turn before the mesa out in the darkness. Also the outline of one patient seemed to melt around the edges. Gálvaez said this patient was in a state of indecision!

Actually saw one of the twelve staffs "vibrate" while the others remained stationary, on two occasions. Both times these were the staffs given to the particular patient taking his turn before the mesa. . . .

When we returned home and I finally got to bed (5 A.M.), as I began to doze off all kinds of designs in every color imaginable unfolded before my eyes—whether open or closed (although the latter made vision easier). There was a whole kaleidoscope of patterns, shapes, and designs which appeared very faintly and softly before my eyes. I slept till 8 A.M. (three hours), after which I was up and about with no ill effects or unpleasantness (other than fatigue from lack of sleep).

When the *remolino* first appeared, I waited for a break in the sequence of curing acts to ask Gálvaez about this phenomenon. He was quite familiar with it and said it was common in the early stages of San Pedro usage. From this it would follow that the objective sensory impressions triggered by San Pedro might be fairly standard for all users no matter what their culture. Culture influences how these objective impressions are conceptualized or processed. For example, even though San Pedro was clearly taking effect during my second experiment and the patient seemed to lean "crazily backwards as if pulled by some force," I still did not "see what everyone else sees." Everyone else, it seemed, was seeing a monster of some sort pulling his hair and trying to abduct him. From the participants' comments during the session and their obvious state of panic, it appeared that all except myself were sharing this perception together and at the same moment.

Later I discovered that, as in my own case, this was only the second time these patients had used San Pedro. Yet they had experienced something *together* that had completely escaped me. Thus it cannot be that they were physiologically more susceptible than I to the effects of mescaline through longer use. Rather, it seems more likely that the degree of their susceptibility and their common vision were due to culture—that, unlike myself, they were culturally conditioned to certain experiential expectations under the influence of San Pedro, within the context of a curing session. It is likely also that these expectations are held in common in that sector of north Peruvian society which accepts curanderismo as a valid and effective system of therapy. These expectations, reinforced by the long history of curanderismo in the north and the traditional shamanistic beliefs and practices in which it is rooted, would tend to determine the way in which neutral sense impressions produced by the action of San Pedro are processed—i.e., perceived—by northern Peruvians. I, on the other hand, would perceive these "neutral" impressions according to my own cultural conditioning—i.e., as the sympathetic but "objective" observer.

The experiences of my third session, seven days later, were similar to those of the second—warmth, relaxed feeling, *remolino,* flashes of light, the white ghostlike outline around the patients, and colors after the session— except that the *remolino* occurred earlier, at 1 A.M. instead of 3 A.M. and there were no "attacks." However, my impressions were much less intense than during the previous session, despite the fact that Gálvaez gave me a double dose of tabaco and San Pedro and the fact that, in an effort to give myself over completely to the hallucinogen, I did no taping whatever. Instead I spent the entire evening "concentrating" as hard as I could on participation, since I had soon to return to the United States and this was to be my last session. Gálvaez—wise man!—said later that my second session had been more successful (in the sense that the effects of San Pedro had been stronger) because my conscious mind had been occupied with the mechanical processes of taping and so had been kept out of the way, allowing my subconscious to take over completely. In my first and third sessions, on the other hand, I was acting as I had been taught to act in a learning (or apprentice) situation—tense, alert, "concentrating" with my conscious mind. The Peruvian patients, by contrast, backed by their cultural heritage, had simply relaxed, allowing San Pedro and the curandero to take hold of them completely.

That Gálvaez himself is well aware of the role of culture in one's subjective experience with a hallucinogen such as San Pedro is evident in his reply when I asked why people from other cultures seem to have such difficulty seeing what his own people see:

> That perhaps is due to the geographic position or the cultural heritage of the *raza*. For example, the *raza* of Peru is rooted in the very origin of the universe, it is one with the universe and its beginnings. And all the characteristics of our ancestors—race, blood, religion, intellectuality, culture—these are to be taken into account in an *ambiente* such as curanderismo. Possibly in Europe also, in antiquity, there was this [art], but it is according to one's geographic position. I believe this because people who have come to experiment, such as various friends of mine and my *compadres,* among them two ex-Peace Corps volunteers, never have had immediate certainty in capturing these things, except by means of exercise. And I also claim that exercise is primal in these operations. The more one practices the more one enters into the power. That is to say that all exercise is equal to the gain, to the appreciation of the *ambiente* in which one wants to introduce himself, in which one desires to live.*

The life of Gálvaez is testimony to the fact that wisdom is the universal property of all men, whatever their "cultural conditioning" or "geographic position." The profound wisdom embodied in Gálvaez' art is a tribute to the human spirit.

---

* *Raza:* literally race, but here meaning a people sharing a common cultural and genetic heritage. *Ambiente* is difficult to render into English; it is used to refer to a socio-cultural environment or milieu. *Compadre,* a ritual kinship term, literally "co-father," defining a relationship usually established at the baptism of a child.—Ed.

5

PETER T. FURST

To Find Our Life: Peyote Among the Huichol Indians of Mexico *

> And they knew the qualities, the essence of herbs. The so-called peyote was their discovery. These, when they ate peyote, esteemed it above wine or mushrooms. They assembled together somewhere in the desert, they sang all night, all day. And on the morrow, once more they assembled together. They wept; they wept exceedingly. They said [thus] their eyes were washed; thus they cleaned their eyes.
> —SAHAGÚN, *History of the Things of New Spain*, Book 10.

> Life is a constant object of prayer with the Huichols; it is, in their conception, hanging somewhere above them, and must be reached out for.
> —CARL LUMHOLTZ, *Unknown Mexico*, 1902

PERSISTENCE AND CHANGE IN HUICHOL RELIGION AND RITUAL

Fr. Bernardino de Sahagún, the greatest of the early Spanish chroniclers and, as author of the monumental mid-sixteenth-century *History of the Things of New Spain (Florentine Codex)*, the first scholarly ethnographer of an American Indian civilization, credited the primitive

* Field research on which this paper is based was funded in part by Ford Foundation International and Comparative Studies grants awarded through the UCLA Latin American Center. The Cora-Huichol Coordinating Center of the *Instituto Nacional Indigenista* in Tepic, Nayarit, and the Center's former director, Prof. Salomon Nahmad Sittón; its medical officer, Dr. Enrique Campos Chavéz, and staff member Carlos Rodriguez assisted in diverse ways in the filming and recording of the 1968 peyote pilgrimage, as did my wife, Dee Furst, who contributed numerous insights to the present paper. The author also benefited greatly from discussions on shamanism and non-Western religions with Johannes Wilbert and especially from a critical reading of the manuscript by Barbara G. Myerhoff. Above all, our gratitude goes to the late Ramón Medina Silva, his wife, Guadalupe, and their fellow *hikuri* seekers, who allowed us to witness "what it is to be Huichol."

northern desert hunters he called "Teochichimeca" with the discovery of the hallucinogenic cactus known to the Aztecs as *peyotl,* to the Huichol as *híkuri,* and to botanists as *Lophophora Williamsii* (Lemaire) Coulter.* As he described the Teochichimeca peyote ritual Sahagún might have been speaking of the modern peyote hunt, for even today, small bands of Huichol each year still "assemble together somewhere in the desert" 300 miles northeast of their homeland in the Sierra Madre mountains of western Mexico, still "sing all night, all day," still "weep exceedingly," and still so esteem peyote above any other psychotropic plant that the sacred mushrooms, morning-glories, *Daturas,* and other indigenous hallucinogens of which they have knowledge are consigned to the realm of malevolent sorcerers. Only the powerful native tobacco, *Nicotiana rustica* (*ye* in Huichol, *macuche* in Mexican-Spanish), plays an honored, indeed indispensable, role.

La Barre (1970c:1201) has suggested that the contemporary Huichol peyote rituals are "probably the closest extant to the pre-Columbian Mexican rite," a judgment that my own studies confirm. Present-day Huichol peyote rituals and their underlying mythology—accepted as valid, with varying degrees of participation, by most of the 10,000 speakers of the Huichol language †—may well be virtually unchanged since Cortés. In any event, the symbolic religious complex that has the peyote quest as its sacred center appears to be the only survival on a major scale of relatively pure Indian religion and ceremonial, without substantial admixture of Catholic elements, in Mexico today.

A variety of factors contributed to the new religion's failure to take hold among the Huichol even after the nominal conquest in 1722—two centuries later than the conquest of Mexico as a whole—of the Cora-Huichol country in the Sierra Madre Occidental: the incredibly rugged terrain, with endless chains of mountains slashed by precipitous canyons and rivers that are impassable in the long rainy season; the almost total lack of communication except for precarious Indian trails; the absence of economic incentives for intensive colonization; the Indians' stubborn

---

* "*Lophophora* has a latitudinal distribution of about 1200 km. from latitude 20° 54′ to 29° 47′ north. It is found along the Rio Grande drainage basin and southward into the high central plateau of northern Mexico lying between the Sierra Madre Oriental and Sierra Madre Occidental. Generally, the elevation of the localities increases to the southward. Those along the Rio Grande near Reynosa, Tamaulipas, are less than 50 m., while localities in San Luis Potosí exceed 1800 m. in elevation. Ecologists describe this large desert area of Texas and northern Mexico as the Chihuahuan Desert" (Anderson, 1969: 301).

† The actual name of the people for themselves and their language is *Wixárika,* "Huichol" being a Spanish Colonial corruption of an Indian tribal name which has passed into general usage. Although many Huichol adults know Spanish, and some speak it well, they customarily converse among themselves only in Huichol, a tongue which, like that of the Hopi of Arizona, the sixteenth-century Aztecs, and many contemporary Indian groups, belongs to the Uto-Aztecan language family.

refusal to abandon their characteristic pattern of scattered, independent, extended-family farmsteads *(ranchos* or *rancherías)* in favor of larger settlements in which they might receive sustained instruction by the clergy; internal contradictions and dissension within the complex colonial structure; the small number and physical and social isolation of missions established in the Sierra after 1722, and their early abandonment *; language difficulties (unlike the early friars, later missionaries hardly ever bothered to learn the native tongue); the relative isolation of the Indians from the mainstream of national life; and, perhaps most significant, the fulfilling nature of their traditional world view.

Like so many American Indians, the Huichol understand the natural phenomena—including man—in terms of immanent and innate powers of creation through transformation. In such a view, all the different manifestations of the biosphere are capable of transformation or metamorphosis. Further, the various phenomena are held to be qualitatively equivalent and imbued with a life force—indeed, even supernatural power. This, of course, is the antithesis of the Judeo-Christian credo that all creatures and other phenomena were created by an omnipotent deity and that man is commissioned by God to assume mastery over —rather than be in and of—nature.

Whatever the reason, at the present time only a small number of Huichol can be regarded as more than nominal converts to Christianity, and of these many have adopted enough other traits of the surrounding majority culture to be classified as Mestizo more than Indian. Nor are there any nativistic Christo-pagan cults comparable to, say, the North American Indian peyote religion, which some scholars trace back to northern Mexico, perhaps even to the Huichol themselves. Not every Huichol has participated in a peyote hunt—some have not even tasted peyote—but so completely integrated is the sacred cactus into the native ideology and ritual that there has been no dilution of the traditional indigenous beliefs regarding peyote nor any tendency to substitute more readily available substances, despite the considerable distance that separates the Huichol homeland in the Sierra from *Wirikúta (Real de Catorce)*, the sacred peyote country in the north-central state of San Luis Potosí.† On the contrary, as will be seen, the very duration,

---

* The early missionaries among the Huichol were mainly Franciscans; those among the Cora, Jesuits. However, in 1767, only forty-five years after the conquest of the Sierra, the Jesuits were expelled from the Spanish colonies. Although their role as missionaries in the Sierra was taken over by the Franciscans, by 1789 only about a dozen friars in all Nayarit were engaged in missionary work.

† Lumholtz (1902) reported that the Tepecano sometimes substituted *Cannabis sativa* for peyote when the latter was difficult to obtain. More recently, Williams García (1963) also described the substitution of marihuana for peyote in the curing rituals of the Tepehua of Veracruz. See W. Emboden. below.

itinerary, privations, and other difficulties of the peyote pilgrimage are themselves an integral part of the peyote quest and its meaning in Huichol culture, somewhat comparable to the privations North American Plains Indians underwent in their vision quests.

This is not to say that European Christian ideology, national life, and material culture have left no imprint on Huichol life. The Huichol still use the traditional digging stick to cultivate their maize plots, but apart from the dog and the native stingless bee, domestic animals are of colonial origin, as are such ubiquitous elements of economic life as coffee, sugar, fruit trees, fiddles, metal tools, and money. On the ideological level, there is a degree of syncretism in part of the ceremonial cycle, resulting from the non-Indian religious rituals that have been added since 1722. For example, as elsewhere in rural Mexico, such Catholic observances as Good Friday and Christmas play an important role in the annual ceremonial round. What sets the Huichol apart from other Indians is that Christian, or Christo-pagan ("folk Catholic"), rituals and supernaturals have not superseded the pre-European ones even nominally, but rather have augmented an already rich native tradition without affecting it in any fundamental sense. Whereas the highland Maya, to cite only one example among many, learned early in the colonial period at least to adopt the names of Christian supernaturals for many of their ancient deities, or to ascribe to the former the attributes and functions of the latter, the old Huichol gods continue to form their own closed system, while the traditional rituals—especially those related to peyote and agricultural fertility—remain largely intact, without significant admixture or substitutions from missionary sources.

Old images of saints, introduced into the Sierra by the early clerics, are acknowledged and play a role in the Christo-pagan ceremonies. They may even be found among the paraphernalia of an otherwise purely traditional ritual. Likewise, many Huichol accept the Virgin of Guadalupe as a legitimate, though minor, deity, or else identify her with the celestial eagle mother *Tatéi Wérika 'Uimári* (Our Mother Young Eagle Girl). Nevertheless, Christian saints and Biblical events are not generally found in the context of aboriginal mythology, except where a traditional story and one introduced by missionaries happen to overlap.* While the traditional myth cycle has thus remained basically unaffected by Christian influences, there is a fascinating independent

---

* For example, the pre-European Huichol version of the widespread deluge myth might be embellished with elements taken from the Biblical flood account—e.g., adding certain familiar domesticated animals of European origin to the contents of the wooden box or dugout canoe that survived the drowning of the earth. The myth that underlies the peyote pilgrimage, however, contains no Christian elements whatever, nor do the traditional stories of the origin of people, animals, plants, fire, sun, moon, etc.

Christo-pagan cycle of tales of which portions are chanted by the shaman-singers on Good Friday and at other ceremonials of missionary origin. This cycle illustrates the degree to which traditions belonging to an alien cultural context tend to become transformed and distorted over time. For instance, according to one Huichol version (there are several) of the New Testament, *Jesucristo* was the offspring of the Virgin of Guadalupe and *Tayaupá*, the Sun Father, who took pity on Guadalupe when she was deserted by her husband, San José (Joseph), because she fell in with "a bunch of drunken Spaniards." *Jesucristo* subsequently rose to eminence by winning a violin-playing contest!

Such stories are not meant to be irreverent. The Huichol customarily parody the clergy in their native rituals (for example, during peyote ceremonies following the pilgrimage to *Wirikúta*) but generally are quite respectful of the religious beliefs and practices of others, asking only that others respect theirs in the same way. It is more a case of adapting to their own cultural experience something the missionaries did not permit them (especially the children enrolled in mission schools) to ignore, but which they could not, or would not, accept completely as presented.

Thus Good Friday is observed with great solemnity, but the total effect of these "Christian" celebrations is rather less Christian than a missionary might wish. Similarly, certain aspects of the ceremonies attending the periodic installation of local Huichol governors are more traditional Indian than Colonial Spanish (although the institution of government itself is, of course, of European origin). The Huichol lack the ladder system of rural Indian-Mestizo Mexico and Guatemala, in which the men of the community actively seek ceremonial offices *(cargos)* of successively higher prestige and correspondingly higher expense to the aspirant, who is expected to make gifts to church and community commensurate with his rise on the scale of public duty and private prestige.

Among the Huichol there is no campaigning for office. The names of the future *gobernador* (governor) and important officials are often "dreamed" by the ranking *mara'akáme* (the singing shaman of the *túki*, or community sanctuary) and approved in consensus by a council of elders. The expenses of the installation, involving much ritual drinking, are largely borne, not by the chosen individuals, as in the *cargo* system, but by the community. A poor man is often preferred as governor, since his poverty is taken as proof of his honesty.

In practice, despite the existence of civil government, few—if any— major decisions are arrived at without the decisive participation of the ranking *mara'akáme*. He consults the supernaturals, among them especially *Tatewarí* (literally Our Grandfather, the deified Fire, often referred to simply as *Mara'akáme,* in the sense of First Shaman), *Tayaupá* (Our Father, the Sun), and other leading potencies, and communicates their wishes to the civil authorities, who act accordingly. The authority of some of these shamans is unmistakable. I have even heard Indians refer to Nicolás, the prestigious and wise old ranking *mara'-akáme* of San Andrés Cohamiata, one of the truly great religious and intellectual personalities of the Sierra, as *Tatewarí*: "*Tatewarí* lives among us here, he lives in 'Colás," they say. "Our *mara'akáme* is *Tatewarí*."

Lumholtz (1902:151) confirms the status of the leading *mara'akáme*:

> [He] ranks higher than any other shaman, and his dignity is even greater than that of the guardian of Grandfather Fire. In fact, he is the spiritual head of the community, and sets the dates for all the feasts and observances in accordance with communications he is supposed to receive direct from the gods themselves. This singing shaman . . . is the actual chief and even superior to the tatowan, or gobernador.

This total identification of a ranking *mara'akáme* with *Tatewarí* is of course of a different order than the temporary apotheosis of the leader of a peyote hunt into *Tatewarí*. The chief of the peyoteros is often a full-fledged shaman, or at least a novice, who "becomes" *Tatewarí* and is so addressed for the duration of the journey, because it was *Tatewarí* who led the first peyote pilgrimage, of which each such journey is the ritual re-enactment. In the same way, the other participants assume the identities of the deified ancestors who followed *Tatewarí* to *Wirikúta* "to find their life."

Clearly, then, the Huichol are unique among contemporary Indians north of the tropical rain forests of South America in that not merely certain individuals or groups but, practically speaking, everyone is an active or a passive participant in a pre-European philosophical and ritual system. The primary focus of this system is the "peyote hunt." It is a "hunt" in the literal sense, because to the Huichol, peyote and deer are synonymous. The first of the sacred plants to be seen by the leader of the hunting party contains the essence of Elder Brother *Wawatsári,* "master" of the deer species, and manifests itself as deer, which in turn explains why it is first "shot" with bow and arrow before being dug from the ground and ritually divided among the participants in the hunt. At the same time Deer-Peyote embodies the equally sacred and life-giving Maize, so that deer, peyote, and maize together form a symbol complex. On the peyote pilgrimage, or "hunt," these three elements become fused, the mythic "first times" that existed before the separation of man, plants, animals, and "gods" are recreated, man reunites with his ancestors, and contradictions between what is and what is thought to be or desired, between life and death, and between the sexes are resolved, bringing about that state of unity and continuity between past and present, "between man, nature, society, and the supernatural," that epitomizes the Huichol view of "the good" (Myerhoff, 1968). This is what the Huichol mean when they say that on the peyote hunt "we go to find our life."

THE "DIABOLIC ROOT"

That the Indians of the Sierra Madre Occidental used peyote ritually in a variety of contexts became known not long after the arrival in western Mexico of the ruthless and avaricious Nuño de Guzmán—one of the most unpleasant characters in the drama of the Spanish Conquest—and the subsequent founding of the province of Nueva Galicia in the early sixteenth century. Although not native to the region, the use of peyote by West Mexican Indians was common enough to be mentioned repeatedly and denounced with righteous fervor by Jesuit and Franciscan clerics of the seventeenth and eighteenth centuries—i.e., considerably before the actual conquest of the Cora-Huichol country in the rugged Sierra.* The Spanish clergy saw the spineless little psychotropic cactus as a principal medium by which the natives of northwestern Mexico maintained communication with the "devil." One man's devil being another man's god, this assessment was wrong only in its resort to European demonology. Understandably, the good friars recognized peyote as a serious threat to effective Christian instruction and rigorously sought to destroy any vestiges of a peyote cult among Indians under their control—clearly without success.

The most widely quoted of these early denunciations of peyote is that of P. José Ortega, who coined the term "diabolic root" in his *Historia del Nayarit*, published in Spain in 1754. Ortega convinced himself that with the conquest of the Sierra, the Indians, though for two centuries valiant defenders of their lands and beliefs, had quickly embraced Christianity, becoming "as lambs" and resolutely turning their backs on their former heathen practices. A rather less sanguine assessment comes from an eighteenth-century Franciscan writer, P. José Arlegui, who had firsthand experience with the tenacity of native religion and ritual among the "lambs" of the Province of Zacatecas, which included part of the mountain tribes of the Sierra.† Arlegui (in Santoscoy, 1899)

* Santoscoy (1899) makes the interesting suggestion that *Sierra de Xicora,* a common seventeenth- and eighteenth-century Spanish name for the then as yet unconquered mountain regions of Nayarit, was actually a corruption of the Cora-Huichol term for peyote, *hikuri,* and that Sierra de Xicora was therefore nothing else than the Sierra del Peyote.

† For the persistence of the ritual use of peyote and other indigenous hallucinogens in central Mexico in the seventeenth century we have the testimony of Hernando Ruíz de Alarcón (1629) and Jacinto de la Serna (1656), among others.

writes that, of all the herbs used by the natives, peyote was the most venerated and that, ground and mixed with water, it was imbibed for all manner of infirmities and also to attain "fantastic imaginings" and knowledge of the future. He complained that this "infernal abuse" persisted not only among Indians out of the reach of the missionary fathers but even among Christianized natives of his province. These, he reports, were adept at procuring the "horrendous drink" and cleverly concealing it from the watchful eyes of the ministers, so that they might inebriate themselves with it to procure knowledge of future happenings. As an especially brazen example he cites the case of Indian elders (*"políticos"*) who, in place "of the four Gospels one gives to the children in Spain," concealed peyote in the bags carried by their sons, claiming "without embarrassment or fear" that peyote would make them wise, skillful matadors and agile tamers of horses.* Arlegui tells us that such abuses were severely punished.

Nearly a century earlier, the Jesuit writer Fr. Antonio Arias de Saavedra (in Santoscoy, 1899), in a lengthy *carta* to his superiors describing the conditions and customs of the unconquered "Gentile" Indians of the Sierra of Nayarit, reported that the Cora drank decoctions of peyote to seal their pacts with their spirits. The "creator of peyote" was said to be *Naycuric*, a principal spirit who resided in the earth and who had the form of a crayfish. Santoscoy quotes another report on the use of peyote in western Mexico, dated January 20, 1659, in which the *cura* of San Pedro Teocaltiche, P. Andrés Estrada Flores, complained that the inhabitants of the Caxcana region in northern Jalisco drank peyote ceremonially as well as medicinally, for "different indispositions and convulsions," and that when they intoxicated themselves with peyote for their ceremonies they saw "horrible visions." †

The early Jesuits who labored among the Indians on the rugged northwestern frontier in Sinaloa, north of the Cora territory, and among the so-called Laguna Indians of Coahuila, to the north of the

---

* It is interesting that the Indians chose to emphasize those qualities they thought might favorably impress the Spaniards. They have been doing it ever since. Klineberg (1934: 446–60), for example, reports that when he asked some Huichol what they saw in the peyote vision, the answer was, "the saints"! He was given—and seems to have naively accepted—the same explanation when he inquired about the purpose of the native "god houses."

† Teocaltiche is the site of an important burial ground dating to the second century A.D., where polychrome pottery figurines with curious mushroom-like capped "horns" on their heads have been found. Together with representations of what may be mushrooms and mushroom spirits among the burial ceramics of Nayarit and Colima, this has given rise to speculation that the ancient mushroom cult of southern Mexico and Guatemala may have extended into western Mexico. Interestingly enough, in the summer of 1970 I came across a Huichol tradition according to which hallucinogenic mushrooms were used "in ancient times" by non-Huichol Indians of western Mexico. Characteristically, the mushroom-users were referred to as "sorcerers."

sacred peyote country of the Huichol (and Cora) in San Luis Potosí, were also much perturbed by the continued ritual use of peyote by the native population. According to the accounts of the Jesuit fathers, particularly Andrés Pérez de Ribas (1645), peyote was generally consumed in liquid form. Pérez de Ribas, who went to Sinaloa in 1604 and remained for sixteen years, says that, although it had medicinal properties, peyote was forbidden and its use punished by the clergy because it was inextricably bound up with "heathen rituals and superstitions" and used to conjure up evil spirits and "diabolical fantasies."

The widespread use of peyote in colonial times by the native peoples of western Mexico, from Jalisco north to Sinaloa, left the impression that peyote must be indigenous to the area. Even today one reads occasionally that *Lophophora Williamsii* grows not only in north-central Mexico but also in the Sierra Madre Occidental. That it does not, and that at least the Huichol travel long distances to procure it ritually each year, became generally known with the publication by Lumholtz of his observations among the Huichol between 1895 and 1898 (Lumholtz, 1900, 1902).* His contribution is all the more outstanding when one considers the lack of scholarly precedent, the enormous gulf between his own European system of interpreting the world and that of the Indians, and the difficulties of travel, communication (both cross-cultural and physical), and sheer survival that he had to overcome during his travels in the Sierra.

Although Lumholtz did not himself participate in a peyote pilgrimage,† he did observe and report in detail certain ceremonies connected

* A Mexican, Rosandro Corona, official engineer of the State of Jalisco, preceded Lumholtz by several years in reporting that peyote, not being native to the Sierra, was procured by the Huichol on long ritual pilgrimages to San Luis Potosí. Corona visited the Huichol *gobernancia* of Santa Catarina in December, 1888, where he observed the welcoming ceremonies for a group of returning peyote pilgrims. His account was subsequently published by Santoscoy in 1899 in his collection of documents pertaining to the history of Nayarit. In the introduction Santoscoy wrote that "patriotic impulse" and the recent work in the Sierra of two foreign scholars, the Frenchman Leon Diguét and the Norwegian Carl Lumholtz, inspired him to rush his volume of historical materials into print. A year later the American Museum of Natural History published the first monograph by Lumholtz on Huichol symbolic art.

† No anthropologist observed an actual peyote hunt until December, 1966, when the author and Barbara G. Myerhoff, of the University of Southern California, accompanied Ramón Medina Silva, a traditional Huichol artist then aspiring to become a *mara'akáme* (shaman), on his fourth peyote trek, and 1968, when the author and his wife were allowed to participate in, and record on film and tape, Ramón's fifth peyote pilgrimage, on which he became a full-fledged *mara'akáme*. Another non-Huichol who witnessed a peyote hunt in the 1960's, and whose work deserves attention for its wealth of detail and literary quality, is the Mexican writer Fernando Benítez. Although not a trained ethnographer, Benítez is a sensitive observer of Mexican Indian culture. His numerous publications on Huichol and Cora shamanism and on the cultural meanings of peyote and other sacred hallucinogens in indigenous religion and ritual,

with it and was also given an excellent description of the trek itself by his informants. What Lumholtz said of the pilgrimages and its meaning in Huichol culture was confirmed not only by ourselves but also by Benítez (1968a, 1968b). Indeed, I doubt that any of us would have been able to absorb as much of the ritual as we did had we not had Lumholtz at hand. Not only is this a tribute to his powers of observation and his ability to inspire trust in his Indian friends; it also demonstrates how little change there has been in the ritual in nearly eighty years. This fact gains in significance when one considers that it is precisely this period that has seen the greatest impact of the outside world on Huichol life.

THE PRIMORDIAL PEYOTE QUEST

This comes to us from ancient, ancient times. The times of my great-great-grandfathers, those who were the fathers of my great-grandfather, fathers of my grandfather who was the *mara'akáme,** fathers of my father. This is a story from those very ancient times. . . .
Those ancient ones of whom I speak, they began to say to one another, "How will it turn out well, so that there will be unity of all, this unity we have?" And another said, "Ah, that is a beautiful thing, that which is our life. It is the *hikuri* [peyote]." And another said, "It is like a beautiful flower, as one says. It is like the Deer. It is our life. We must go so that it will enable us to see our life."

So begins an account by my long-time Huichol friend Ramón Medina Silva of the original journey to *Wirikúta*—the primordial quest of the gods that provides the mythological model for the Huichol peyote pilgrimage.

According to the myth, the ancient gods had come together in the first *túki*, the prototypical Huichol sanctuary constructed by *Tatewarí*, so that each might have his proper place. When they were met together they discovered that all were ill—one suffered a pain in his chest, another in his stomach, a third in his eyes, a fourth in his legs, and so forth. Those responsible for rain were giving no rain; those who were masters of animals were finding nothing to hunt. It was a time of general malaise in the Sierra, and none knew how to "find his life." Into this assembly of the ailing gods entered the *Mara'akáme*, *Tatewarí*, tutelary deity of Huichol shamans. It was *Tatewarí* who had

---

although intended as literary reportage rather than ethnography, show not only anthropological insight but a rare gift of rendering his observations into literature (Benítez, 1968a, 1968b, 1970).

* This refers to the narrator's grandfather, who was a prestigious *mara'akáme*, or shaman-priest and singer. Ramón's sister, Concha, is one of the few female shamans in the Huichol Sierra today.

called them together, as the singing shaman of the temple to this day calls the supernaturals together "to take their proper places." "What can be ailing us?" they asked, and each spoke of his infirmities. "How shall we be cured? How shall we find our life?"

Tatewarí told them that they were ill because they had not gone to *Wirikúta* (Real de Catorce), the sacred land of the peyote, the place to the east where the Sun was born. If they wished to regain their health, they must prepare themselves ritually and follow him in their proper order on the long and difficult journey to the peyote. They must fast and touch neither salt nor *chile*. No matter how hungry or thirsty they became, they must nibble only dried tortillas and assuage their thirst with but a drop or two of water.

And so he placed them in their proper order, one after the other. No females were present—they would join the men later, at the sacred lakes or water holes called *Tatéi Matiniéri* (Where Our Mother Dwells), which lie within sight of the sacred mountains of *Wirikúta*.

Not all the divine peyote seekers completed the primordial quest. Some, like Rabbit Person and Hummingbird Person, were forced by hunger, thirst, or sheer exhaustion to leave the ritual file. They remained behind in their animal form in places which became sanctified by their presence and which, like the other stopping places of the divine pilgrims, were forever after acknowledged with votive offerings and prayer by those who journey to the peyote. But the principal male gods and the female ones—the Rain Mothers and those of the Earth-Ready-for-Planting and of fertility and children—they followed *Tatewarí* to the sacred mountains at the end of the world—"to the fifth level"—where the Deer-Peyote revealed itself to them in the ceremonial hunt. In this way they "found their life" and by their example taught the Huichol how to attain theirs.

Peyote pilgrimages may take place at any time between the end of the rainy season, in October–November, and early spring. Our own two pilgrimages were held in December, but Ramón and other Huichols have gone as late as February and even March. In general, however, the sacred hunt follows a fall ceremony in which children, the shamanic drum, new maize, and especially the first ripened squash play the principal roles. Although it does not require the use of peyote, this ceremony, which Lumholtz called "First Fruits," is actually a vital component of the whole peyote complex, for it is the principal ritual through which the shaman inculcates the children of the extended family homestead (often his own) or several related *rancherías* with the sacred itinerary of the peyote quest.

The "ceremony of the drum and the squash" is one of the few occasions in the annual ceremonial cycle when the *mara'akáme* employs the

Fig. 24. Ramon Medina, who led the pilgrimage described in these pages, taps a bow string with an arrow. The music of the "bow drum" is intended to tell the supernaturals that the pilgrims are on their way, and to charm the Deer-Peyote.

upright drum (*tepu*), a hollowed-out log of oak standing on three crudely carved legs, open at the bottom and closed off at the top with a head of deerskin. Like many of the characteristic archaeological ceramic drum miniatures from western Mexico, the Huichol drum has a hole ("mouth") in front through which sacred smoke emerges when burning pitch pine brands are placed beneath the drum to tighten and tune the skin to the proper pitch. Since the body of the drum can be considered to be female and the pitch pine brands male, as is the fire, this act has symbolic connotations as well as a practical purpose. The soot that builds up on the inside of the drum is considered to be therapeutic. The drum itself has great power and possesses a personality. To play it is the sole prerogative of the shaman and his assistants. As elsewhere in the indigenous cultural context, it is exclusively a ritual instrument, never used simply for dancing or other entertainment.* The deerskin head is beaten by the shaman with the palms of both hands, two rapid beats of the left complementing a single, stronger beat with the right. The children shake gourd rattles to accompany the drum.

Incessantly pounding the *tepu* and chanting all the while, the shaman proceeds to "transform" the participating children into hummingbirds and to lead them in magical flight from the Sierra to the country of the peyote:

> Look, you hummingbirds [he begins],
> Surely we are going where the peyoteros have gone,
> On their ancient pilgrimage of the peyote.
> Who knows if we are going to get there or not,
> Because this journey is very dangerous.
>
> One must fly high in order to pass over the wind,
> Light as air,
> We will make camp there,
> Under the highest trees.
>
> *Maxa Kwaxi* † gives them guidance,

* The widespread symbolic and ritual association of shamans and drums in indigenous culture leads me to interpret the well-known clay figurines of drummers from the tombs of western Mexico as representations of shamans intent on supernatural communication rather than as "musicians," as they are usually called in the literature on pre-Columbian art.

† According to Ramón, the "transformation" of the children into hummingbirds takes place by means of the *mara'akáme's* "secret"—i.e., his magical powers. The children "ascend" and fly eastward on the vibrations produced by the *mara'akáme's* rhythmic beating of the drum. Their flight in single file is symbolized by a string along which the children are arranged as puffs of cotton. One end is tied to the drum, the other to a thread cross or a pair of deer horns, representing the deer deity. The deerskin drumhead is symbolic of the deer deity Elder Brother *Maxa Kwaxí* (Deer Tail), who assists

He gives them the names of where they will fly,
So that they may enter there safely.

They rise, they rise,
Like a string of beads,
"How pretty is this pilgrimage,
How very pretty."
So says *Maxa Kwaxí.*

The chant consists of several hundred short verses, each repeated four times. Along the magical route the shaman points out the sacred landmarks: "Here the ancients made tortillas," "Here they rested," "Here Rabbit Person was left behind in the cactus thicket," "Here is the Place of Lost Water," "Here they ground their face paint,"* etc. Some of these are merely "overflown" or "circled," but at others the hummingbird-children alight, so that they may become familiar with the peculiarities of each of the sacred places, which presumably they will one day visit on an actual peyote quest.

Significantly, *Maxa Kwaxí,* speaking through the shaman, also warns the children of danger spots: "In this pueblo live bad Spaniards, avoid it." "Here they must not see you, they may try to capture you, do not light a fire" (literally, "do not light *Tatewarí*"). Or, conversely, "Here live people who are good and will help you." There may well be some historical basis for such statements, as there may be also for the story of the first peyote quest of deified ancestors under the leadership of a charismatic great shaman. References to "bad Spaniards who may capture you" could pertain to the colonial period, when peyote seekers from the Sierra must have made their way as much as possible in secret, perhaps traveling by night, ever fearful of discovery and capture, especially by slave raiders for the many Spanish silver mines of Zacatecas and San Luis Potosí. These mines took a fearful toll of Indians in the first two centuries after the Conquest. The peyote country itself must have been particularly perilous, since it is identical with the colonial silver-mining center of Real de Catorce. How many of those who set out for *Wirikúta* never returned?

---

the shaman as spirit helper on the bird-children's flight. Like Elder Brother *Káuyumarie,* he is conceived both in deer form and as a person wearing antlers; indeed, *Maxa Kwaxí* and *Káuyumarie* appear to be really two aspects of the same supernatural being. In the construction of the drum, the fitting of the deerskin (male) over the hollowed-out tree trunk (female) "completes" it—that is, makes it at once male and female. The symbolism of the hummingbird as the alter ego of Huichol children on the symbolic peyote quest is of interest in view of the frequent depiction of hummingbirds in pre-Columbian art and the role of the hummingbird in Aztec belief and ritual.

* *Uxa,* a yellow pigment obtained from a desert shrub, used to decorate the faces of peyoteros with the markings of the various supernaturals who participated in the mythological peyote quest. These markings serve the same purpose as the masks in the Indian Southwest.

The critical moment in the flight of the hummingbird-children is the dangerous passage through the "Gateway of Clouds," or "Where the Clouds Open and Close." In the actual peyote pilgrimage this mythological passage is located on a rise near the city of Zacatecas. The shaman invokes the aid of *Maxa Kwaxí,* and while the latter holds back the threatening clouds on either side with the points of his antlers, the bird-children fly quickly through the passage. The audience of children and their families may be held spellbound while the shaman, in his chant, relates how the clouds closed on the tail feathers of one little girl and how the shaman, "with his power," raised her from the ground and restored her ability to fly. Finally the children reach the sacred springs and places of fertility known as *Tateí Matiniéri,* "Where Our Mother Lives," the home of the Rain Mothers in the east. From here they set out on the final lap of their magical journey to *Wirikúta,* home of the peyote and the ancestral gods. Here the children are received by the Great Mother of Huichol children, *Niwetúka(me).** "Let us go where *Niwetúka(me)* is," the shaman sings. "Let us go, all of us, in order to know Our Mother. Let us go where the one who embraces us lives, the one who loves us much." The Mother Goddess greets them: "Now I am content, now I am happy. I will give them life. . . . Look, my children, I am the one who embraces you. I am the one who gives you your *küpúri* (life force, soul)."

Apart from its more subtle meanings and its obvious function of enculturation and education, the ceremony serves to imprint on the minds of Huichol youngsters a kind of subjective territorial map, on which all the sacred landmarks between the Sierra and the peyote country are indelibly engraved and by which they may one day orient themselves, geographically and culturally, on an actual pilgrimage. As Ramón put it, "In this way they begin to learn what it is to be Huichol."

METAMORPHOSIS AND SPIRIT POWER

Many Huichol pass their whole lives without ever going on a peyote pilgrimage: "one does or one does not go, as one wishes." Some participate in the rituals before and after the journey and take peyote at the various ceremonials but are not willing to submit themselves to the intense hardships and ritual abstentions from sex, salt, and normal nourishment required of the peyotero. Others have gone five, ten, even twenty times. Nicolás, the ranking *mara'akáme* of San Andrés, is said to have gone no less than thirty-two times.

---

* That the Huichol Mother goddess *Niwetúka(me)* is linguistically as well as functionally closely related to the Keresan Great Mother, *Iyetáku,* is only one of numerous cultural correspondences between the Huichol and Pueblo Indians.

Some go to *Wirikúta* in fulfillment of a vow, perhaps made in a moment of stress, or at the behest of a shaman when someone in the family fell ill. Ramón himself, and his wife Guadalupe, went on his sixth journey (and her third) because she was suffering from rheumatism and had made a promise to the supernaturals to make the difficult trek to obtain their aid for a cure. Although the pain in her legs was often so severe that she could barely stand up, in early 1970 she and Ramón walked the whole way to *Wirikúta*—over 300 miles!

Why do they go? "Patriotism," among many other reasons, says Lumholtz, by which he presumably means the same thing as Ramón's "being Huichol." "What does one go for?" asks Ramón. "One goes to have one's life." The pilgrimage helps one attain whatever one desires—health, children, rain, protection from lightning and sorcerers, or divine intervention against the ever-troublesome *vecinos* ("neighbors," Mestizos), who encroach illegally on the Huichol lands with their cattle and sometimes employ force to drive the Indians from their farms. Above all, one goes to attain visions of great beauty, to hear the voices of the spirits, the divine ancestors, and to receive their guidance.

In a sense, participation in a peyote journey makes of each man a kind of shaman or priest. For a long time following a pilgrimage its members acknowledge a ritual bond with one another. They recognize and greet each other in special ways. They have special names. They wear special insignia: the tobacco gourd of *Tatewari*, squirrel tails on the hats. The peyote journey also has the characteristics of initiation; one who has never gone is said to be "new," like a baby; he is a *matewáme* and must undergo special restrictions, because his tenderness makes him extraordinarily vulnerable to the malevolent magic of sorcerers.

But if all peyoteros have attributes of shamans (for one thing, because for the duration of the pilgrimage they can transform themselves, or are transformed, into spirit beings, a capability normally belonging only to true shamans), they are shamans on a very low level. Real and aspiring shamans feel that they are charged with a deeper purpose than ordinary pilgrims. Of course, they too have needs that they hope to have answered through the peyote pilgrimage—for health, children, calves, rain, maize. There are no full-time specialists, and shamans, like any other Huichol, must support themselves primarily through primitive *milpa* agriculture. But for them the peyote quest has deeper meanings.

A man who would assume the enormous burden, ritual and psychological, of a *mara'akáme*, who would make himself responsible for the welfare of his community, must first complete at least five peyote pilgrimages. But he must do this not as a follower, intent only on private thought and private vision. He must demonstrate on each such journey his capacity to be an effective soul guide, or "psychopomp," who escorts his spirit companions safely across the barriers of space and time, through the gateway of the clashing clouds, and to the sacred mountains at the end of the world in the east, where the ancestor spirits await them.

He must prove his capacity to endure not only lack of food and water but lack of sleep. Even at night, when his companions rest around the sacred fire, he must remain awake, alert, ever ready to defend their spiritual integrity against supernatural enemies. (Ramón, whom I have twice seen go without sleep for seven nights in a row in the course of the peyote pilgrimage, said a leader of peyoteros is "like one who is bent low under the heaviest carrying basket. Its ropes cut so deeply into his shoulders that they bleed.") They are all spirits, of course, for the duration of the journey. But he more than any other man must transcend the limitations of his bodily self and achieve that unique breakthrough that sets the shaman apart from ordinary men. If he lacks these qualities he will never "complete himself." It goes without saying that the leader must know the minutest mythological detail of the itinerary, as well as the correct sequence and proper manner in which each ritual is to be carried out at the sacred places along the way and, above all, in the peyote country itself. And he must "see" with an inner eye, for only he will recognize the tracks of the Deer-Peyote and see the brilliant rainbow-soul of Elder Brother *Wawatsári,* the Principal Deer, rise from the peyote plant as it is "slain" by his arrows.

I want to emphasize that this idea of completing a certain number of pilgrimages in order to become a shaman is not a matter of adding up so many miles, so many hardships, so many visions, to a required total—like collecting merit badges or battle stars. Rather, it is accumulation of spirit power, in geometric progression, through repeated and ever more intense metamorphosis. "Completing oneself" is really progressive minimization of matter and maximization of spirit to the point where temporary transformation makes the transition to spiritual exaltation and apotheosis.

It is my impression that this special condition of the shaman cannot be faked—that not only he himself but his companions really do know whether or not a man who lays claim to being a *mara'akáme* has what the Huichol call "balance"—that special, ineffable capacity to venture without fear onto the "narrow bridge" across the great chasm separating the ordinary world from the world beyond.

In the summer of 1966 Ramón gave us a memorable demonstration of the meaning of "balance." He took us to a spectacular waterfall, with a sheer drop of hundreds of feet to the valley below. This, he said, was "specially for shamans." While the other Huichol grouped themselves in a semicircle in a safe place some distance from the edge, Ramón removed his sandals and, after making a series of ritual gestures to the world directions, proceeded to leap—"fly" might be more appropriate—from one rock to another with arms stretched wide, often landing but a few inches from the slippery edge. Occasionally he would disappear behind a great boulder, only to emerge from an unexpected direction. Or he would stand motionless at the extreme limit of a massive rock, wheel about suddenly and make a great leap to the other side of the rushing water, never showing the slightest concern about the obvious danger that he might lose his balance and fall into space. We were frankly terrified, even annoyed, at such "foolhardiness," but neither his wife nor the other Huichol watching showed any real apprehension. The demonstration ended as abruptly as it had begun, without any explanation of Ramón's strange behavior.

The following day he asked if we thought he had been showing off. He said, "Perhaps you thought, 'Ah, Ramón is drunk with too much beer.' But no. I took you there to show what it means 'to have balance.' So you could see and understand. Because when one crosses over as a shaman one looks below, and then one perceives this great abyss filled with all those animals waiting to kill one. Those who do not have balance are afraid. They fall and are killed." In order to render intelligible something he feared our cultural experience might not have prepared us to understand, he had decided to give us a physical demonstration—a kind of literal translation—of a phenomenon basic to shamanism wherever it occurs.*

* In a lecture in the UCLA series on which this volume is based, Carlos Castaneda, author of *The Teachings of Don Juan,* told of a strikingly similar experience he had with a Mazatec shaman named don Genaro, the teacher of his own teacher don Juan. Although sixty-five years old, don Genaro took Castaneda, don Juan, and two assistants to a steep waterfall near Oaxaca, in southern Mexico, sat them down at the base, and started to make the perilous ascent to the top of the fall. On the way up he appeared repeatedly to be losing his footing and about to plunge to his death, but showed no concern whatever. Nor did don Juan. When he neared the summit, he "slipped" again and hung on only by his fingertips, looking down at Castaneda without any expression. Then he hoisted himself up, stood momentarily perched on top of the fall, almost at the edge. Holding on to a small rock with his feet, said Castaneda, don Genaro stood there, his body tensed, "like a feline about to leap." Then he literally flung himself through the air, landing on a little cone-shaped rock no more than six inches across, where he remained motionless for several minutes, after which he leaped without warning to the other side of the water, performed a sudden somersault to his left, and disappeared—all this within inches of the cliff face (see also Castaneda, 1971). As for Ramón's "great abyss" filled with dangerous animals, this is reminiscent of other shamanic initiatory experiences, including especially that described by J. Wilbert, above.

The Peyote Pilgrimage

So intense is the drama of the actual hunt for the Deer-Peyote in *Wirikúta* that certain prior events of crucial importance for the success of the quest tend to be overshadowed. The first of these is the ritual of confession and purification through which the participants are initiated into the sacred enterprise of the pilgrimage.

This is an extraordinary ceremony. Everyone—peyoteros as well as those who remain at home—is required to acknowledge publicly all his or her sexual adventures, from the beginning of adulthood to the present. Further, each sexual partner must be identified by name, regardless of the presence of spouses or lovers, although old people are allowed to telescope their love affairs and be less precise about names. No display of jealousy, hurt, resentment, or anger is permitted; more than that, no one is even allowed to entertain such feelings "in one's heart." Any show of hostility and any deliberate omission of sexual intimacy or a lover's name would jeopardize not only the offender but his companions and the entire sacred enterprise. The quest for life could prove fruitless. At the very least, even if the peyote country were reached, those who had failed to purge themselves or who carried "bad thoughts in their hearts" would probably fall victim to sorcerers, suffer terrible hallucinations, and perhaps even die. An extraordinary spectacle indeed—doubly so if one has been taught to regard jealousy and its expression as a "natural" human emotion, common to all people everywhere, rather than as an artifact of culture.

It may be that individual participants in the peyote rites do feel resentment, especially at an unexpected revelation of infidelity on the part of a spouse or lover. However, in neither of the two confession rituals I attended was there the slightest expression of hostility. On the contrary, there was an atmosphere of marked lightheartedness. Individual recitations of "transgressions" were frequently punctuated by laughter and ribald jokes, particulary when a wife found it necessary to jog her husband's memory by reminding him of an extramarital escapade he had overlooked.

On our 1968 pilgrimage the ceremony of confession was held late in the evening of the first day. The seventeen Indians—nine men, five women, and three children, the youngest only seven days old when we started on the trek—were seated or squatting in a circle around the ceremonial fire. As *mara'akáme,* Ramón was seated in his *'uwéni* (shamans' chair) on the west side, facing east across the sacred fire, flanked by his two principal assistants. Following incantations and the recitation of the story of the primordial gathering of the supernaturals for this same ceremony, Ramón gave the signal for the first of the participants to be brought before him. In his hands he held a sisal fiber string and his *muviéri*, or shaman's plumes. By his feet lay a pair of deer antlers, the likeness of *Káuyumarie*, the Deer spirit helper whose presence is indispensable for shamanizing; his *takwátsi*, an oblong basket in which ceremonial paraphernalia and power objects are stored; and a votive gourd bowl.

Serving as a kind of constable for this ritual and the remainder of the peyote pilgrimage was Crescenciano, who on this peregrination was the personator or likeness of Elder Brother *Párikuté*, patron of animals and hunting. Crescenciano-*Párikuté* led the peyote seekers in ceremonial circuits counterclockwise around the fire, ending in front of Ramón. Men came first, then women, and finally the oldest of Crescenciano's three children, a boy aged ten. Each gave a ritual recitation of past love affairs—except, of course, little Francisco, who shook his head, grinning from ear to ear, when Ramón addressed him and asked with perfect seriousness, "Well, little *matewáme* (novice), tell the *Mara'-akáme*, tell *Tatewarí*, how many women have you enjoyed in your life?" Everyone roared with laughter.

For each reported love affair Ramón made one knot in the cord. Those whose memory faltered were assisted by shouts of encouragement or a reminder of this or that extramarital escapade. As the personator of *Tayaupá*, the Sun, and oldest of the pilgrims, José was the first to come before Ramón; he named several women and then said, "I have led such a long life that my feet are already rotting in the earth; if I spoke here of all those whom I have enjoyed we would not leave here tomorrow or the day after tomorrow." This was hugely appreciated by all, and Ramón said, yes, for *Tayaupá** he would make only one knot, a very large one, or there would be no room left on the string for anyone else. Again, laughter. The entire ritual passed in this way, without tension of any kind.

Nevertheless, the lighthearted banter (which I understand is characteristic of every such ritual confession) should not be taken to mean that the ceremony is not in dead earnest—quite the contrary. Laughter, yes, cynicism, never; not the slightest hint at any time that all did not participate fully, "with their hearts," that they did not feel deeply the

---

* In accordance with the ritual reversal of terms and meanings which is also an integral part of the peyote pilgrimage, José, as the oldest, subsequently became known as *nunútsi* (baby), and was addressed as *Tayaupá* only on certain ceremonial occasions. Some reversals are institutionalized, such as nose for penis or sneezing for ejaculation, some are obvious (boy-girl, earth-sky, sand-water, night-day, hot-cold, etc.) and some are arbitrary, the important thing being only that opposites be employed as much as possible in conversation. The reason for this is not clear but one suspects that it serves to reinforce the general quality of metamorphosis in the peyote quest.

extreme seriousness of what they were doing, or that they did not
completely accept the potentially fatal consequences of any violation of
prescribed behavior. Rather, it seemed to me that the good-natured
badinage that accompanies the confessions serves primarily to reinforce
the ritual obligation to preserve good will toward each of the companions, no matter what.

In any event, if the potential sting of a confession is neutralized by
ritually required good humor, the manner in which the peyoteros are
"purged," as it were, of their sexual past leaves no doubt of the extreme
gravity of the occasion. As each peyotero completed the ritual recitation
and the last knot was tied for him or her, Ramón rose and brushed his
ceremonial arrow with its pendant hawk plumes (*muviéri*) over the
face, shoulders, arms, and chest, and down the thighs and knees to the
feet. He directed the pilgrim to face *Tatewarí*, the purifying fire, and
ask that he "burn away everything, everything, burn away all your
transgressions, burn it all away, so that nothing will remain, so that
you will be new. The *Mara'akáme* (*Tatewarí*) does and undoes (transforms)." Leaning into the flames, the peyoteros held first one hand and
then the other over the fire and followed the same procedure with
their feet. The women lifted their skirts so that the heat could travel
up their thighs. Some braver souls actually leaped over the flames, a
rite which they repeated several times on the trek and which seems to
suggest a former practice of ritual fire-walking.

When everyone—including Ramón himself—had completed his confessions and been purified, Ramón rolled the sisal fiber cord, now
crowded with knots, into a spiral and placed it on the fire. It flared
briefly and was soon turned to ashes. Ramón stirred these with the
brazilwood point of his ceremonial arrow and said, "Now you see that
you are new. Tatewarí has burned it all away. He has removed it all
from you. Now we can cross over there. The *Mara'akáme* does and
undoes."

How is one to understand this event? Lumholtz recognized its fundamental importance to the success of the peyote pilgrimage but interpreted it primarily in terms of sexual purity. The Huichol, he wrote
(1902:129–30), seek to achieve health, good fortune, indeed life itself,
by gathering peyote. For these goals to be attained, the participants
must purge themselves of all sin, i.e., their sexual experiences: ". . . inasmuch as the pure fire cannot benefit those who are impure, the men
and women must not only commit no transgression for the time being,
but must also purge themselves from any past sin." *

---

* Lumholtz refers to separate confessions by men and women, but no such separation
occurred in the two rituals we witnessed. Also, the confession was held on the
first night out, not the fourth, as Lumholtz reports. It may be that the sequence has

At first glance one might be tempted to explain the whole phenomenon in terms of Catholic influence. Why else would the Huichol, who sanction polygamy and who in any event are not noted for their sexual fidelity, equate sex with sin, or at least with transgression? Nevertheless, I see no reason to regard the Huichol rite as anything but purely aboriginal and pre-European. In the first place, confession was practiced in Mesoamerica long before the arrival of the Spaniards (an Aztec goddess to whom confessions were addressed was appropriately known as "The Eater of Filth").* Secondly, there are fundamental differences between the Catholic and Huichol rites that are obscured by the very term "confession." In Catholic practice the confessor admits to having sinned and, if the priest accepts his act of contrition and repentance as genuine, is absolved from the sins he has acknowledged. The Huichol does not repent but merely acknowledges a certain act as fact. In this sense "profession" might be more accurate than "confession," except that of course in the context of the peyote quest sexual intercourse per se is disapproved and hence a "transgression." But "transgression" of what and against whom?

I would suggest that the answer is to be found in the meaning of the peyote pilgrimage itself. Just as metamorphosis and return to origins are the *Leitmotif* and fertility the purpose of the peyote quest as a whole, so it seems to me to be metamorphosis, not absolution, that lies at the heart of the confession ceremony—metamorphosis from man to child, from ordinary mortal to spirit being. What is less obvious is the relationship this may bear to the concept of incest. Incest is a grave offense among the Huichol (incest and sexual intercourse with a "Spaniard" are the only offenses for which there is punishment after death), and incest on a symbolic level also enters into the quest for the peyote

---

never been rigidly structured, or else that it has changed somewhat due to the increasing use by the peyoteros of wheeled transportation for at least part of the itinerary. With respect to the latter, it is interesting that even when—as in our case—the peyoteros know full well that they will be traveling all the way by motor vehicle, they insist on behaving as though they were really on foot. In the primordial pilgrimage the gods "slapped down" their sandals in front of *Tatewari* and asked him to strengthen them for the long and difficult trek; our peyoteros did the same. Throughout the pilgrimage I heard references to our "walk" by car to *Wirikúta;* one peyote song I recorded on the first night in the peyote country had this refrain:

> The white machine, the white machine
> Which brought us here to *Wirikúta,*
> That white machine is so good for walking,
> So good for walking.

* As a matter of fact, the Huichol custom of making knots for each transgression and then burning the knotted cord is reminiscent of an Aztec confession ritual in which straws were drawn through the pierced tongue and then ritually burned in a sacred fire. "With this," reports the sixteenth-century chronicler Fr. Diego Durán (1971:247), "everyone felt he was cleansed and pardoned for his transgressions and sins, having the same faith that we hold for the Divine Sacrament of penance."

vision. It is in this direction that I suggest we must look for additional meaning in the confession ritual. (This dimension of the ceremony was not apparent to me in the first peyote pilgrimage and did not begin to take shape until some time after the second, when there had been an opportunity to stand back from the experience, compare observations, and analyze a good deal of visual data on film.)

Myerhoff (1968), who participated in the first pilgrimage in 1966, correctly recognized the journey to *Wirikúta* as a symbolic return to an original state. In order for ordinary mortals to undertake this sacred quest, she writes, "the pilgrims must be cleansed of all sexual experience, that is, they must return to the period of life when they were innocent, before they were mature, worldly adults." In that sense, she suggests (again correctly, I believe), the confession ritual is itself a journey to origins, as is the peyote pilgrimage as a whole. But why should shedding one's adulthood open the door to the sacred country? What, indeed, *is* the sacred country—that is, beyond the obvious answer that it is the place where the sacred cactus grows? Might the sacred country be a kind of "Great Mother"? If so, we would have at least one explanation for the emphasis on ridding oneself of all adult sexual experience before embarking on the journey, lest the whole enterprise come to naught or the offender go mad in *Wirikúta*. To "enter" the Mother as an experienced adult would be tantamount to incest, and incest is far and away the most unthinkable transgression in the social universe, an act that threatens not merely the transgressor but his whole group.* I want to emphasize that there is no overt equation of *Wirikúta* with a "Great Mother" in the Huichol peyote traditions. Nevertheless, it is implied: one need only recall the emphasis on the embrace of the hummingbird-children by the Mother Goddess *Niwetúka(me)* as they finally reach the sacred peyote country.

Many interpretations are possible, of course, within the over-all theme of the return to a mythical original state, the paradise for which all men yearn. Identification of the sacred country with a Great Mother almost certainly represents only one level in a very complex system built around the peyote quest, with others remaining to be probed (but not necessarily understood within the Western tradition). That this should be so is not surprising: there is really no such thing as a "primitive" people, and the Huichol, who may be characterized as a case of incomplete transition between a former life as food gatherers and hunters—with powerful vestiges remaining still of the world view typical of this type of culture—and their present existence as subsistence farmers in a rapidly changing world, are sufficiently complex ideologically for a lifetime of study.

* For comparable data, see G. Reichel-Dolmatoff, above.

I said earlier that metamorphosis is implicit in the confession ritual. The peyotero has been made over, "become new." He has shed one state of being, maturity, and assumed—or reassumed—another, that of childhood innocence. At the same time, transformation has occurred on another level, for the peyotero has "become" the likeness of one of the supernaturals of the original peyote quest. More than merely child, he has had to become spirit, for the gates to the Otherworld will open only for one who is spirit.

If the attainment of childhood innocence is the immediate purpose of confession and purification, just how far back into his own life is the peyotero supposed to be transported? The answer may lie, at least in part, in a second sacred cord into which the shaman "knots" the peyoteros as an integral part of the ritual preparations for the actual peyote hunt. From the manner in which these knots are tied (and eventually untied, following the return of the pilgrims from the peyote quest), it appears that the peyote seeker is really meant to be taken back to his very beginnings as a human being, or at least to the moment of birth. Indeed, as will be seen, for novices the reversal of their lives is complete in that they will soon find themselves in the total darkness of a simulated prenatal state.

Some time after the obliteration by fire of the sisal string with its accumulated sexual transgressions, Ramón took a second string, considerably longer than the first, from the gourd bowl by his seat. He uncoiled it, held one end to the back of his hunting bow, beat the bowstring several times with an arrow, and for some moments chanted quietly. Then he and José (*Tayaupá*), seated to his left, passed the cord twice around themselves, once in front and again in back. Ramón rose and walked with cord and *muviéri* (ceremonial arrow) to the far end of the circle of peyoteros. Moving from right to left, he stopped before each, touched him with the hawk feathers, and tied a knot. When the seventeen Indians, including the seven-day-old infant, had thus been knotted in by the *mara'akáme*, he made several additional knots for the observers, "so that we will all be of one heart."

Back in his chair, Ramón once more held the end (or beginning) of the cord to the back of his bow, beat the bowstring, and passed the cord to José-*Tayaupá*. While he continued to beat the bow in the manner of a drum, the knotted cord, stretched tight, traveled counterclockwise in back of the entire group and clockwise in front. When it was back in Ramón's hands, he coiled it in a spiral and tied it to the back of the bow.

The identity of this knotted cord and the string on which the hummingbird-children are symbolically arranged as puffs of cotton in the drum-and-squash ceremony is obvious. Also, there is no question that

for the Huichol, knots, knotting, and binding have much the same
magical significance as they have elsewhere: folk belief, customs, and
religion the world over "attribute to knots and bonds a function of
healing, a defence against demons, or of conservation of the magic and
vital forces" (Eliade, 1961:111).* However, in the context of the peyote
pilgrimage the knotted cord seems to have an additional dimension
which may even be its primary symbolic function: that of umbilicus.
This became apparent only after I had time to consider the implications
of a basic difference between the tying ceremony before the pilgrims set
out for the sacred country and an untying ceremony following their
return. In the first—at least as we observed it—it is the shaman who
ties the knot for each participant. In the second it is the pilgrim who
unties it. This seems to suggest the following: Just as the midwife ties
off the umbilical cord of the newborn infant, so the "new" peyotero
cannot tie the knot for himself but must have it done for him by the
mara'akáme, who in a very real sense acts as midwife for his passage
into the Otherworld, both at this point and later on in the journey.
But once the sacred goal has been attained and the pilgrims have returned from their quest for life, they regain their former status as
adults. This seems to be reinforced symbolically by the ritual untying
of the knots upon their return to western Mexico. In this ceremony,
the knotted string, which has been in the custody of the *mara'akáme*
throughout the pilgrimage, is passed twice around the circle of participants, once counterclockwise and once clockwise (to symbolize transformation, or, as the Huichol call it, "doing and undoing"). Then the
mara'akáme walks around the inside of the circle with the cord in his
hands, stopping before each pilgrim in turn to allow him or her to untie
his or her own knot, this time without the *mara'akáme*'s assistance.

It is this apparent identity of the knotted sisal fiber string with the
umbilical cord that explains why the *mara'akáme* ties the string with
the cotton puffs to his drum and why the end, or beginning, of the
knotted cord is held to the back of the bow before being passed around
the circle to be tied and, after the pilgrimage, untied. For drum and
bow are identical.† They are male-female, representing the maternal

* The literature on this subject is voluminous. A useful summary is Chapter III,
"The God who Binds and the Symbolism of Knots," in Mircea Eliade, *Images and
Symbols* (New York: Sheed and Ward, 1961).

† The bow serves as drum throughout the peyote pilgrimage. Its beat tells the supernaturals that the pilgrims are coming and guides them through the dangerous passage
of the Clashing Clouds. It is also played to "make Elder Brother happy" in the final
tracking and stalking of the Deer-Peyote in *Wirikúta*. According to tradition, "in
ancient times" the Huichol had no drum at all. Instead, the shaman used his bow as
drum, holding it with one foot, string-up, on an inverted gourd bowl and beating it
with two arrows. This "musical bow"—called "bow-drum"—is still used in the Huichol
territory today, although Lumholtz observed it only in the Cora region.

aspect, the Great Mother-Earth from whom her children receive nourishment through the umbilical cord and, at the same time, the male procreative principle.*

We can now shed some light on the previously suggested connection between incest and the confession and purification ceremony. We recall that before the peyote seekers enter the peyote country, they must visit *Tatei Matiniéri,* Where Our Mother Dwells, the desert water holes from which one catches one's first awesome glimpse of the sacred mountains of *Wirikúta.* It is here that one asks for rain and fertility. Here the *matewámete,* the novices, "emerge into the light" (quite literally, as we shall see). Here the peyoteros are ritually washed by the *mara'akáme,* as the midwife washes newborn infants. Here the containers are filled with the water that has the power of fertility. In the total context of the quest, the confession ritual, by canceling out adult sexuality (i.e., matter), facilitates metamorphosis to spirit. In relation to the specific confrontation, symbolic intercourse with the maternal, creative forces at the Place of Our Mother would be tantamount to incest were it not for the prior restoration of the "innocent" condition of childhood. At least that is one way of looking at it. The perilousness and ambiguity of the undertaking are underscored in the passage of the Place of the Clashing Clouds that threaten to crush those who would venture on the journey to the Otherworld.

The Dangerous Passage

That critical rites prior to and during the dangerous passage took place only a few yards from a heavily traveled highway seemed to matter not at all to the Huichol. As usual they acted as though the twentieth century had never happened—or, more accurately, as though the flow of time had been reversed. As a matter of fact, nothing we saw on the entire pilgrimage demonstrated more dramatically the time-out-of-life

*Dr. Enrique Campos Chávez, medical officer of the Cora-Huichol Center of the Instituto Nacional Indigenista (INI) in Tepic, Nayarit, who accompanied us on the 1968 pilgrimage, has recently made some important discoveries regarding the umbilical cord which shed new light on its importance in Huichol thought and ritual. According to Dr. Campos (personal communication) the umbilicus plays a vital role in Huichol conceptions of man's fate throughout his life. After parturition the umbilical cord is planted together with the seed of one or another fruit-bearing tree or large cactus, such as the *nopal.* The earth is "Our Mother the Earth Ready for Planting," who nourishes the seed and helps it germinate, as the Huichol mother nourished the unborn foetus through the umbilical cord. Seedling and child lead parallel lives and their fate is interdependent, similar to the relationship between "companion animal" and man in the Maya area. Should the young tree sicken or die, the child would suffer the same fate, and vice versa. Whereas the cord thus serves to link child and companion tree through the medium of the earth mother, the placenta is customarily placed by the mother or midwife into the high branches of a tree in a wrapping of grass (although some women nowadays bury it in or near the house).

quality of the whole enterprise than the sight of the *híkuri* seekers acting out their deepest beliefs on the very outskirts of the city of Zacatecas, within sight and sound of the rushing traffic, oblivious of the trucks and buses fighting the long grade.

There are two stages to the actual crossing of the critical threshold. The first is called Gateway, or Entrance, of Clouds; the second, Where the Clouds Open. They are only a few steps apart, but the emotional impact on the participants of passing from one to the other is enormous. From here one travels to the place called Vagina, and from there the trail leads through a series of named stations (the stopping places of the first peyote pilgrims) directly to *Tatéi Matiniéri,* Where Our Mother Dwells. However, one would search in vain on any map for places around this historic mining capital that bear such names, in Huichol or Spanish. For like other sacred loci on the peyote itinerary, these are landmarks only in the geography of the mind.

It was mid-morning of the fourth day out when we arrived at the outskirts of Zacatecas. The vehicles were parked and, assembling once more "in their proper order" (i.e., as decreed by *Tatewarí*), the pilgrims proceeded single file to some low-growing nopal cactus and thorn bushes a few hundred feet from the highway. Here they halted, and Ramón moved down the line, brushing each pilgrim with his *muviéri* and ritually pronouncing his or her new name as the likeness of one of the original *híkuri* seekers. They listened carefully as he related the relevant passages of the peyote traditions and invoked the protection of *Káuyumarie* and other supernaturals for the coming ordeal. At his direction, each then took one small green and red parrot feather from a bunch carried by a *matewáme,* or novice, and tied it to the spiny branches of a small bush. When the last feather had been fastened they filed by, muttered prayers, and returned to the vehicles. Instead of embarking, however, Ramón had the cars drive slowly ahead while the pilgrims followed on foot. This, he later explained, was so that *Káuyumarie,* whose likeness in the form of antlers and ceremonial arrows was mounted on the front of each vehicle, could act as guide and scout on this final approach to the Clashing Clouds (in a more traditional pilgrimage on foot the deer horns would be carried by the *mara'akáme*). Beyond their obvious symbolism of celestial flight, the feather offerings commemorate an event on the pilgrimage of the gods and serve as prayers for safe passage "to the other side." *

---

* We recall that on the mythical flight to *Wirikúta* in the drum-and-squash ceremony one of the bird-children lost tail feathers in the dangerous passage. Nonfatal injury, such as loss of feathers, a foot, or part of the stern of a vessel, is a common feature in many versions of this widespread motif of the dangerous passage, from the clashing rocks or Symplegades of ancient Greek tradition to funerary or shamanistic mythologies in Australia, Siberia, the Arctic, and the Americas. There are several versions of the

Some distance up the road the pilgrims were led to an open space that commanded a magnificent view of the valley from which we had just come. Here they formed a semicircle—men to Ramón's left, women and children to his right. Although everyone knew the peyote traditions by heart, all listened with rapt attention as he told them how the ancestors had "done this thing," and how with *Káuyumarie*'s assistance they would soon pass safely through the perilous Gateway of Clashing Clouds into the sacred country. But from now on, until they came to the Place of Our Mothers, those who had not yet traveled to the peyote would have to "walk" in darkness. For they were "new," he said, "new and very delicate," easily blinded by the glare emanating from the sacred country on the other side of the clouds and especially vulnerable to whirlwinds and other dangers which malevolent sorcerers cast in the way of *hikuri* seekers. Blindfolded they would be safe, but they would have to proceed with caution, holding on to the one in front and taking care not to stumble or fall. "It will be hard," he said, "very hard, this walk. It is a great penance, this journey to *Wirikúta,* and you will cry very much."

Starting with the women, Ramón proceeded to blindfold those who were "new and delicate." Even the three children had their eyes covered, although for the baby this act was only symbolic. He was very gentle with all of the pilgrims, in speech and touch, exhorting them, and especially the *matewámete,* to "be of one heart" and take good care as they walked, for soon they would come to the Gateway. It would be dangerous, but with his power (i.e., the power of *Tatewari*) and that of *Káuyumarie,* they would be "admitted" and pass safely "to the other side."

Although everyone took the blindfolding seriously (some actually cried), we were again impressed by the quick shifts between solemnity and humor. As Ramón came to those who, as veterans of previous journeys, did not require blindfolds, spirited and often very funny dialogues ensued. Was the companion well fed, had he quenched his thirst? Oh, yes, went the reply, the pilgrim's stomach was full to bursting with all manner of good things to eat and drink. And yes, he was happy to be "walking" such a long way in such ease and comfort. In truth none had had more than minimal nourishment for days. The reference to ease and comfort, by the way, had nothing to do with the fact that they were riding in a vehicle instead of walking. Several of the Indians even said that they much preferred walking, "because it is more beautiful." Rather, it was part of the aforementioned reversal of meanings, an integral part

---

motif of the dangerous passage (clashing rocks, stone traps, solar rays, snapping jaws, etc.) in Huichol mythology, in connection with the shamanic quest for supernatural power or the journey of the soul (and the shaman) to the Otherworld (Furst, 1967). Clashing rocks were also a feature of Aztec funerary belief, as they continue to be among Nahuatl-speaking Indians in Mexico to the present day.

Fig. 25. Peyote seekers line up by the side of the highway near the city of
Zacatecas for the blindfolding ceremony, which precedes the symbolic
passage through the incessantly opening and closing mythic "cloud
gates" and the entrance into sacred country.

of the peyote quest which intensifies as the pilgrimage progresses toward
its climax. Reversal was to become more common after we left the
paved highway ("oh, what a rocky path, so full of holes and stones!")
and entered upon desert or deeply rutted wagon trails ("ah, what a fine
highway, so well paved, so smooth!").

Following the blindfolding ceremony Ramón took the peyoteros some
hundreds of yards northeastward, to the fateful cosmic threshold which
only he, as shaman, perceived, but whose reality was evidently in no
wise doubted by the pilgrims. When he reached a certain point he
stopped abruptly, motioning to those behind him to do likewise.

Here, on a little rise of dusty adobe on the edge of Zacatecas, a place
entirely unremarkable to the untutored eye, was the mystical divide, the
Symplegades of the peyote quest. The pilgrims remained rooted where

they stood, intent upon Ramón's every move. Some lit candles. Lips moved in silent or barely audible supplication. Ramón bent down and laid his bow and arrows crosswise over his shaman's basket—bow and quiver pointing east in the direction of *Wirikúta*. He rose and conducted what appeared to be an urgent dialogue with unseen supernaturals, all the while gesturing with his *muviéri* in the directions of the world quarters and the sacred center.

Visually, the passage through the clashing cloud gates was undramatic. Ramón stepped forward, lifted the bow, and, placing one end against his mouth while rhythmically beating the string with an arrow, walked straight ahead, stopped once more, gestured (to *Káuyumarie,* we were told later, to thank him for holding back the cloud doors with his horns, at the place called "Where the Clouds Open"), and set out again at a more rapid pace, all the while beating his bow. The others followed close behind in their customary single file. Where the terrain was rough some of the blindfolded *matewámete* held on to those in front. Others

Fig. 26. Blindfolded *matewamete* (novice peyote seekers).

made it as best they could by themselves. Ramón's bow music sounded like a high-pitched drum beat, but with a recognizable tune.

Whatever the event might have lacked in visual drama for an uninitiated observer, there was no mistaking its impact on the participants. Their faces clearly reflected the emotional stress of this critical passage, their deep commitment to its truth, and their relief and pleasure that Ramón had proved to have the power to transport them safely through the clashing gates. At one point a battered and noisy dump truck crossed their line of march, drowning out the musical beat of Ramón's bow. To us, watching it roll over the sacred ground the Indians had just vacated, the symbolism was so stark, so explicit, as to be almost trite. Yet I doubt very much that the Huichol themselves even noticed its presence—or, if they did, that it disturbed them nearly so much as it did us.

Ramón himself showed the strain of all that had transpired here. He was solicitous of the blindfolded *matewámete*, assisting them in entering the cars and speaking soothingly to them, as one would to a frightened child. But he was also insistent that they hurry. For while all had gone well, one should not linger longer than necessary in such dangerous and sacred places.

The degree to which what we had just witnessed conforms to Eliade's analysis of the meaning of the Symplegades motif in shamanism and funerary and heroic mythologies is remarkable. According to Eliade (1964), the "paradoxical passage" opens only to those who are spirit—i.e., the dead or those who have become transformed. In Huichol mythology, the peyote pilgrimage seems to be the only occasion in which ordinary men, and not just shamans, souls, and supernaturals, can achieve the breakthrough from this world to the one beyond. They are able to do so because they are no longer "ordinary" but are transformed. Yet they are not allowed to forget that this condition is only temporary, even for the shaman—that they are men, not gods. Hence the required assistance of *Káuyumarie*. Hence also the lost feathers of the bird-child. It is after all only the dead and the supernaturals who are truly and permanently spirit.

The Springs of Our Mothers

We arrived at the sacred water holes the Huichol call *Tatéi Matiniéri*, in San Luis Potosí, in the late afternoon. Ramón would have preferred dawn, when the rising Sun Father is stronger and therefore a more effective protector than the setting Sun. A number of awesome things were to happen here, and the pilgrims were excited and tense with expectation. The physical setting was hardly inspiring: an impoverished Mestizo desert pueblo at the edge of a former lake, now dry; a few hundred yards beyond the last of its adobe huts, a cluster of water holes surrounded by marsh. On the peyote quest, however, it is not ordinary reality that matters, but the reality of the mind's eye. Accordingly, to the Huichol *Tatéi Matiniéri* is not a forlorn and probably polluted desert oasis. It is beautiful, they say, because Our Mothers live here, and because it is the wellspring of the water of life.

The pilgrims were conducted single file to the edge of the bog. They set down their bundles and the gourds, bottles, and flasks they had brought to be filled from the springs, and proceeded to pray with great fervor toward the east. The *matewámete* were again admonished to be very still. When Ramón motioned everyone to sit or squat he told the blindfolded novices to make themselves small and keep their heads down. Then things became very busy, with much going back and forth to the various water holes, each of which represented a different Mother and was known by her name. As one of his first acts Ramón inserted the wooden point of his *muviéri* into several of the cavities, stirred the cloudy liquid, and sprayed water in the world directions and on the pilgrims. (We had already observed something very similar at the confession-purification ceremony, when ceremonial and hunting arrows were used to spray water from bottle gourds on the women.) Meanwhile those who were not blindfolded unpacked offerings—ceremonial or votive arrows, thread crosses, animal crackers, yarn designs, candles, votive gourds, etc.—and laid them out carefully "for Our Mothers to see." Some were gifts or prayers to the Mothers themselves and would be left in their cavities; others were to be sacrificed by fire in *Wirikúta*. Whether intended as generalized offerings or more specifically as petitions for health, rain, fertility, luck in hunting, or whatever, such offerings gain greatly in effectiveness by being impregnated with the life-giving fluid of the springs.

For the blindfolded *matewámete,* the enforced period of sightlessness was about to come to an end, for much of what went on about them was designed to prepare the way for their "emergence" into the light. To a degree this was true also for the others, since everyone present, including Ramón, was to be ritually washed and internally purified with the water of Our Mothers. Only after this washing ceremony would they be capable of perceiving the sacred country all around them, and especially the mountains of the peyote country on the distant eastern horizon.

Although Ramón was obviously anxious to hurry the proceedings in order to finish before sundown, the preliminaries took a while. Some of what people did was then, and remains today, obscure; unfortunately, for much of what happens in these ritual situations there really is no clearer explanation than the stock answer, "That is the way one does this thing." Original meanings have been forgotten, or else the act requires no explanation because its meaning is known to everyone who belongs to the culture.

On the other hand, just as the blindfolding before the dangerous passage can be understood in terms of a return to the womb as well as metamorphosis (unborn children are spirits and become human only when they receive their essential life force through the fontanelle at the time of birth), so the manner in which the Mothers "receive" the pilgrims from the *mara'akáme* is seen to symbolize birth—or, better, rebirth. Consider the following:

Having dipped the *muviéri* into the cavity of one of the rain and fertility Mothers and ritually purified a gourd bowl, the *mara'akáme* requests that the pilgrims be brought before him one by one. The assistant selects one of the waiting companions and pulls him by the arm around the water hole and in front of the *mara'akáme*. The *mara'-akáme* asks whether the companion fed himself well on the journey and how much tequila and beer he consumed. Is his belly full? Is he happy? Is he warm and comfortable behind his blindfold "in the dark"? As before, the stereotyped reply is that yes, his belly is full and yes, he (or she) has drunk much and is snug and warm (in truth it is uncomfortably cold here at over 5000 feet in mid-December; at night the temperature often falls to the freezing point or below). This exchange brings on laughter and shouts of encouragement from everyone except the blindfolded *matewámete*, who remain very much subdued, kneeling or squatting motionlessly with their heads down and their shoulders hunched up. Then Ramón bends down, scoops up a gourdful of water, holds it behind his back, lifts the companion's hat or scarf, and, if he is a *matewáme*, removes the blindfold. With sweeping gestures he now points to the east, exclaiming, "There, companion, now you are able to see! Behold now the sacred places," or words to that effect, and suddenly pours the contents of the bowl over the latter's head. He instructs him to rub vigorously, working the sacred water into his hair, face, and eyes. Although the water is very cold and must come as a considerable shock, no one shows any indication of discomfort—quite the contrary. Ramón meanwhile takes up another gourdful from the water hole and holds it to the pilgrim's lips, telling him to drink it all down without leaving a single drop. Subsequently he is given his "first food," bits of tortilla and animal crackers which have been softened by soaking in sacred water. This is baby food, and its purpose is to reinforce the symbolic condition of "newness," i.e., of having just been born.

These rituals were repeated in more or less the same way for all, although more gently for the two youngest children. Then Ramón himself was ritually washed and "made to see" by one of the other men. It should be noted here that, with the exception of a required ritual bath and ritual washing of the hair at the beginning of the pilgrimage, this is the only occasion on which a *hikuri*-seeker is allowed to wash for the duration—even when the pilgrimage is on foot and takes up to forty-five days.*

Several things remained to be done before we could resume what the pilgrims insisted on calling our "walk." The naming of the baby, by now ten days old, had been put off because Ramón, who as *mara'akáme* was to do the naming, had agreed with the parents that it would be propitious for the child's health and proper growth if it were to be given its name in the presence of the Mothers. This was done by presenting it to the Mothers as well as to the Sun, the four quarters, and the sacred center and pronouncing the name, which had come to the *mara'akáme* in a dream.

Next the numerous containers had to be filled with the water of the Mothers. A small amount of this potent fluid was required for the rituals in the peyote country, but most was to be taken back to the Sierra for the rituals of agricultural fertility and other rites of the ceremonial cycle. *Tatéi Matiniéri* is not the only source of water to which magical potency is ascribed (indeed, in a sense all water and all bodies of water are sacred to the Huichol), but these desert springs on the way to the peyote country are believed to possess unique powers of fertility. It is no accident that one of the first acts of the returning pilgrims is to spray their wives with bouquets of flowers that have been dipped into gourds full of water from *Tatéi Matiniéri*—an act also performed in the peyote country itself by the *mara'akáme*. Water from the sacred maternal springs is utilized in numerous ways, all related to the concept of fertility and germination: it is drunk in small quantities at the rituals; added to *nawá*, the ceremonial maize beer, in the fermentation process; mixed with peyote infusions, and sprinkled or sprayed on fields, crops, animals, people, tools, hunting weapons, and the likenesses of supernaturals. It is also carried by shamans to the Pacific Ocean (Our Mother *Haramára*) for rituals designed to facilitate rain.

Characteristically, the manner of filling the gourds and other containers from the sacred springs is ritually prescribed. The way in which it is done can be interpreted as yet another symbolic act of sexual union and impregnation, with the ceremonial arrow serving as phallus and the empty container as uterus. Before the *hikuri* seeker can pour water into

---

* The traditional pilgrimage on foot was ritually fixed at twenty days in each direction. Although the Huichol do not have a formal ceremonial calendar or even the memory of one, it may be that the length of the pilgrimage was in some way related to the twenty-day "month" of the 260-day ceremonial calendar of prehispanic Mesoamerica. Such a calendar survives today in certain areas, especially the Maya region.

his bottle or fill it by submerging it in one of the water holes, the *mara'akáme* has to transfer a few drops from the cavity into the bottle with the long hardwood point of his ceremonial arrow. However, despite such readily apparent sexual symbolism, it would be simplistic in the extreme to reduce this particular ritual at *Tatéi Matiniéri* to the level of symbolic coitus alone. As already noted, the Huichol are by no means lacking in sensuality. Sex for its own sake is considered pleasurable. On the peyote pilgrimage, however, it is not sex that matters but fertility—the survival of the people and their natural and cultural environment. What the *mara'akáme* simulates with his ceremonial arrow, therefore, is not coitus but unity—the life-producing union of the male and female principles in all nature.

Not surprisingly, water from the sacred springs is considered to be a powerful agent against barrenness, and before the journey to *Wirikúta* was resumed, one of the pilgrims, a childless woman, asked Ramón to "cure" her so that she might conceive. The curing ceremony that followed differed little from traditional shamanic curing elsewhere in Indian America, with this exception: in addition to such familiar ritual acts as blowing tobacco smoke over her body, spitting, and sucking to remove the intrusive foreign agent believed to be making her ill (e.g., small stone, splinter, etc.), Ramón sprinkled water from one of the water holes on her bared stomach and spread it about with his fingers and the *muviéri*. Two days later, in the peyote country, he touched the region of her stomach with a peyote cactus and told her to do likewise. We also noted her special petition to the Deer-Peyote and the other supernaturals of *Wirikúta:* a small votive gourd decorated on the inside with the image of a child, in the form of a crude little stick figure of beeswax embellished with tiny colored beads and wool yarn.

The Hunt for Elder Brother

As has been said before, the peyote country is more or less identical with the Colonial Spanish mining district called Real de Catorce, in the high desert of northwestern San Luis Potosí. It is typical Chihuahuan-type desert country, 5000 feet or more in altitude, covered with creosote bush, mesquite, tar bush, agave, yucca, Euphorbia, and many kinds of cactus. The Huichol say "it is beautiful, very beautiful" here, and one has the feeling that they really mean it and are not just using ritual reversals. Presumably, when they say that the *Wirikúta* desert is covered with "flowers of brilliant colors" they are speaking of the peyote that grows here. In 1966 Ramón had taken us by the hand and pointed out everything that made survival and even a reasonably good life possible—edible leaves and seeds and roots, barrel cactus full of thirst-quenching liquid, herbs good for wounds and sickness of all kinds (peyote itself is considered the best medicine of all, effective not only against fatigue but infections and intestinal complaints), and the burrows and lairs of small animals. "One lives well here," he said, "if one has learned well and does not take more than one needs." That particular lesson in desert ecology came back to me later, when someone tried to convince me that the hallucinogenic properties of peyote "must" have been discovered accidentally, because "there is nothing to eat in the desert and the starving Indians were so desperate they tried everything and anything, even the bitter peyote." My own view, admittedly unprovable, is that the discovery of peyote, like many other sacred hallucinogens, was probably the consequence of a deliberate search for "mind-altering" substances by shamans engaged on the vision quest.

The sacred "Patio of the Grandfathers" is actually much more extensive than the area in which peyote is ritually collected. It lies between two mountain ranges about thirty miles apart. One is *Wirikúta* proper, and it is below its slopes that the Deer-Peyote is hunted. The other is called *Tsinuríta*. It is said that peyote also grows on the lower slopes of the latter, which the Huichol deluge myth identifies as one of the ends of the world and which is conceived as the mirror image of *Wirikúta*, the sacred mountains *par excellence*. The individual peaks of both ranges are said to be the abodes of the *Kakauyaríxi*, the generic name by which the Huichol address their supernaturals. No translation that makes sense in English is possible; the Huichol say it means "ancient, ancient ones," or ancestral gods. The most sacred of the *Wirikúta* peaks is *'Unáxu*, legendary birthplace of the Sun; its mirror image on the *Tsinuríta* range is the mountain of *Tatewarí*. *Tatewarí* also has his sacred mountain in Nayarit, close to the Pacific coast. The *Kakauyaríxi* do not always remain in their abodes but sometimes travel west, to the Huichol country and the Pacific coast. When they do so, they may assume the form of ducks —as do the supernaturals of the Pueblo Indians of the Southwest.* The analogy between *Wirikúta* and the sacred San Francisco Mountains of the Pueblos is striking, but it is only one of many traits that point to ancestral ties between the Cora-Huichol and the Pueblos of Arizona and New Mexico.

Between *Tatéi Matiniéri* and the peyote country proper there were to be two more camps. The second was only ten miles (in this rugged desert, two hours' driving time) from the area Ramón had selected in his mind for the hunt of Elder Brother *Wawatsári*. We broke camp before dawn, in bitter cold, waiting only for the first red glow in the

---

* One is tempted to relate these beliefs to the frequent naturalistic and abstract representations of ducks (but not geese) in the ancient art of Mexico—especially the tomb ceramics of western Mexico, which are rich in sculptures of ducks, in pairs, trios, and even quartets.

east so that the pilgrims might pay their proper respect to the rising Sun
Father and ask his protection. There was little conversation on this
final stretch. Everyone remained still, except for the times when the
vehicles had to be emptied of passengers to get past a particularly
difficult spot in the trail. Even then there were few unnecessary words.
Lupe and José lit candles the moment we started out and held them
the entire distance.

It was just past 7:00 A.M. when Ramón stopped the cars and told the
Indians to get out and assemble in single file by the side of the trail.
It was time to walk. For no matter how one had traveled thus far, one
must enter and leave the Patio of the Grandfathers exactly as had
Tatewarí and his ancient pilgrims—on foot, blowing a horn and beating
the hunting bow. In former times, and occasionally today, the horn was
a conch shell; José's was a goat horn, and one of the others used a
cow-horn trumpet.

As the *híkuri* seekers walked they picked up bits of dry wood and
branches of creosote. Little Francisco, who was carrying his two-year-old
brother, stopped to break off a green branch for himself and also stuck
a long dry stick in the little boy's hand. This was the food of *Tatewarí*.
It is another mark of the total unity of the *híkuritámete* that each
companion, down to the youngest, is expected to participate in the first
"feeding" of the ceremonial Fire when it is brought to life by the
mara'akáme.

This happened so quickly that we almost missed it. The line stopped,
Ramón squatted, and seconds later there was a wisp of blue smoke and
a tiny flame. *Tatewarí* had been "brought out" (fire is inherent in wood
and only needs "bringing out"). Now more than at any other time on
the pilgrimage, speed and skill in starting the fire are of the essence,
for one is in precarious balance in this sacred land and urgently requires
the manifestation of *Tatewarí* for protection. The fire is allowed to go
out only at the end, when sacred water is poured on the hot ashes, after
which the *mara'akáme* selects a coal, the *küpúri* (soul, life force) of
Tatewarí, and places it in the little ceremonial bag around his neck. Since
the ritual is repeated at each campsite there is an accumulation of
magic coals, which become part of the *mara'akáme*'s array of power
objects.

Chanting and praying, Ramón piled up bits of brush which quickly
caught fire. The others, meanwhile, arranged themselves in a circle with
their pieces of firewood and began to pray with great fervor and obvious
emotion. We saw tears course down Lupe's face, and there was much
sobbing also among the others. Such ritualized manifestations of joy
mixed with sorrow were to recur several times during our stay in
Wirikúta, especially at the successful conclusion of the "hunt," and

again when we were getting ready to take our final leave. After much praying, chanting, and gesturing with firewood in the sacred directions, and a counter-sunwise ceremonial circuit around the fire, the individual gifts of "food" were given to *Tatewarí,* and everyone went off to prepare for the crucial pursuit of the Deer-Peyote.

It was midmorning when Ramón signaled the beginning of the hunt. To my question how far we would have to walk to find peyote, he replied, "Far, very far. *Tamátsi Wawatsári,* the principal deer, waits for us up there, on the slopes of the mountain." I judged the distance to be about three miles.

Everyone gathered up his offerings and stuffed them in bags and baskets. Bowstrings were tested. Catarino Rios, the personator of *Tatutsí* (Great-grandfather), one of the principal supernaturals, stopped playing his bow to help his wife Veradera (Our Mother *Haramára,* the Pacific Ocean) cut a few loose strings from the little yarn painting she had made to give as a petition to the sacrificed Deer-Peyote. It depicted a calf. Catarino's bow music, we were told, was to make the deer happy before his impending death. Ramón conducted the pilgrims in another counterclockwise circuit around the fire, during which everyone laid more "food" on the flames and pleaded for protection. Ramón entreated *Tatewarí* not to go out and to greet them on their return. Then he led the companions away from camp toward the distant hills.

About 300 feet from camp we crossed a railroad track and beyond it a barbed-wire fence. The men had their bows and arrows ready. Everyone had shoulder bags and some had baskets as well, containing offerings. We had walked perhaps 500 feet when Ramón lifted his fingers to his lips in a warning of silence, placed an arrow on his bowstring, and motioned to the others to fan out quickly and quietly in a wide arc. I pointed to the distant rise—was that not where we would find the peyote? He shook his head and smiled. Of course, I had forgotten the reversals! When he had said, "far, very far," he really meant very close. Ramón now crept forward, crouching low, intently watching the ground. Catarino's bow, which he had sounded along the route "to please Elder Brother," fell silent. The women hung back. Ramón halted suddenly, pointed to the ground, and whispered urgently, "His tracks, his tracks!" I could see nothing. José-*Tayaupá* sneaked up close and nodded happy assent: "Yes, yes, *mara'akáme,* there amid the new maize, there are his tracks, there at the first level." (There are five conceptual levels; for a man to reach the fifth, as Ramón was to do here in *Wirikúta,* means he has "completed himself"—i.e., become shaman.) The "new maize" was a sad little stand of dried-up twigs. The hunters look for any growth that can be associated with stands of maize, for the deer is not only peyote but maize as well. Likewise, peyote is differentiated by "color," corresponding to the five sacred colors of maize—blue, red, yellow, white, and multicolored.

Ramón moved forward once more, José following close behind and to one side, his face lit up with the pleasure of discovery and anticipation. All at once Ramón stopped dead, motioning urgently to the others to come close. About 20 feet ahead stood a small shrub. He pointed: "There, there, the Deer!" Barely visible above ground under the bush were some flecks of dusty green—evidently a whole cluster of *Lophophora Williamsii.* Although I have seen peyote plants grow-

Fig. 27. A clump of *Lophophora Williamsii* in the San Luís Potosí desert. Characteristically the plants barely show above ground. These young peyotes, because they have five ribs, are considered especially precious by the Huichol, who regard five as the symbol of completion.

ing in full sunlight, more often it is found like this—in a thicket of mesquite or creosote, shaded by a yucca or Euphorbia (especially *Euphorbia anti-syphilitica*), or close to some well-armed *Opuntia* cactus, such as rabbit ear or cholla. Its broad, flat crown is usually almost level with the earth and so is easily missed by the inexperienced eye).

Ramón took aim, and the first of his arrows buried itself a fraction of an inch from the crown of the nearest *hikuri*. He let fly with a second, which hit slightly to one side. José ran forward and fired a third, almost straight down. Ramón completed the "kill" by sticking a ceremonial arrow with pendant hawk feathers into the ground on the far side, so that the sacred plant was now enclosed by arrows in each of the world quarters. The *mara'akáme* bent down to examine the peyote. "Look there," he said, "how sacred it is, how beautiful, the five-pointed deer!" Remarkably, every one of the peyotes in the cluster had the same number of ribs—five, the sacred number of completion! Later on, he was to string a whole series of "five-pointed" peyotes on a sisal fiber cord and drape it over the horns of *Káuyumarie* mounted on the vehicles.

The companions formed a circle around the place where Elder Brother lay "dying." Many sobbed. All prayed loudly. The one called *Tatutsí*, Great-grandfather, unwrapped Ramón's basket of power objects, the *takwátsi*, from the red kerchief in which it was kept and laid it open for Ramón's use in the complex and lengthy rituals of propitiation of the dead deer and division of its flesh among the communicants. Ramón explained how the *küpúri*, the life essence of the deer, which, as with humans, resides in the fontanelle, was "rising, rising, rising, like a brilliantly colored rainbow, seeking to escape to the top of the sacred mountains." Do not be angry, Elder Brother, Ramón implored, do not punish us for killing you, for you have not really died. You will rise again, Ramón was echoed by the pilgrims, we will feed you well, for we have brought you many offerings, we have brought you tobacco, we have brought you water from Our Mothers, we have brought you arrows, we have brought you votive gourds, we have brought you maize and your favorite grasses, we have brought you tamales, we have brought you our prayers. We honor you and we give you our devotion. Take them, Elder Brother, take them and give us our life. We offer our devotion to the *kakauyaríxi* who live here in *Wirikúta;* we have come to be received by them, for we know they await us. We have come from afar to greet you.

To push the rainbow-*küpúri*, which only he could see, back into the Deer, Ramón lifted his *muviéri*, first to the sky and the world directions, and then pressed it slowly downward, as though with great force, until the hawk feathers touched the crown of the sacred plant. In his chant he described how all around the dead deer peyotes were springing up, growing from his horns, his back, his tail, his shins, his hooves. *Tamátsi Wawatsári,* he said, is giving us our life. He took his knife from the basket and began to cut away the earth around the cactus. Then, instead of taking it out whole, he cut it off at the base, leaving a bit of the root in the ground. This is done so that "Elder Brother can grow again from his bones." * Ramón sliced off the tough bottom half of the cactus and peeled away the rough brown skin, carefully preserving the waste for ritual disposition later. Then he divided the cactus into five pieces by cutting along the natural ridges and placed these pieces in a votive gourd. The process was repeated by Ramón and Lupe with several additional plants, for there had to be enough to give each of the companions a part of "Elder Brother's flesh." Those who had made previous pilgrimages came first. One by one they squatted or knelt before Ramón, who removed a section of peyote from the gourd and, after touching it to the pilgrim's forehead (in lieu of the fontanelle hidden under the hat or scarf), eyes, voice box,† and heart, placed it into his or her mouth. The pilgrim was told to "chew it well, chew it well, for thus you will see your life." Then he summoned the non-Huichol observers and repeated the same ritual for them (as he had also included them in the knotting-in ceremony).

In the meantime Ramón had gathered up all the tobacco gourds *(yékwé,-te)* belonging to the pilgrims and placed them near the sacred cavities from which the peyote had been taken. As Lumholtz noted, these gourds are an indispensable part of the outfit of the *hikuri*-seeker, giving him, as it were, priestly status (the tobacco gourd was also a priestly insignia in Aztec times). I have heard it said that *yé,* tobacco, was once a hawk and the *kwé,* gourd, a snake. The tobacco is always the so-called wild species, *Nicotiana rustica*—the "tobacco of *Tatewari*"—which contains nicotine in far greater amounts than the domestic brands. Tobacco gourds are specially raised for the purpose. Those with numerous natural excrescences are highly valued, although smooth ones are

---

* Anderson (1969), who has been engaged in extensive field studies of *Lophophora* throughout its natural range from Texas to San Luis Potosí and Queretero since 1957, reports that "injury or harvesting by man induces the formation of many stems from a single rootstock. Single clones more than 1.5 m. across have been observed in San Luis Potosí, for example" (p. 302). The ritual practice of leaving part of the rootstock in the ground to induce new growth "from Elder Brother's bones" is common among Huichol peyote seekers. Clones growing from a single rootstock are considered especially sacred and powerful and are treated accordingly. Ramón, for example, would not allow anyone else to touch one such clone he had removed from the ground until it had been propitiated in the proper manner. Characteristically, he left part of the root where it grew.

† The voice box is obviously of great significance in a nonliterate culture, for, as Ramón said, "If one could not speak, how would his children know how to be Huichol?"

also employed, sometimes with a covering of skin from the scrotum of a deer. This, of course, makes them especially powerful.

All the *híkuri* that had "grown from the horns and body of Elder Brother" had been dug up and set on the ground. Bows and arrows were stacked against a nearby cactus. Votive offerings and prayers addressed to the Deer and the *kakauyaríxi* were placed in a pile in front of the holes where the peyote had been. The pilgrims were seated on the ground in a circle. Ramón touched the offerings with his *muviéri,* prayed, and set fire to one of the little wool yarn paintings he had made, depicting Elder Brother. As the wax melted, the flames licked at the ceremonial arrows, and soon the entire pile of offerings and the dry creosote bush itself were ablaze. Ramón muttered incantations and with his *muviéri* wafted some of the smoke toward the sacred mountains. Then he rose and with a gourd filled with peyote passed in a ceremonial circuit from right to left on the inside of the circle to give each his portion of "Elder Brother's flesh." Forehead, eyes, larynx, and heart were touched and the peyote placed into the mouth of each pilgrim in turn. The *matewámete* especially were exhorted over and over to "chew it well, brother [or sister], so that you will see your life, so that it will appear to you with clarity." When Ramón came to ten-year-old Francisco, all turned to watch. Peyote is not given in any quantity to young children, but after the age of three it can be a sign whether or not the child has the disposition to become a *mara'akáme.* If he or she likes the taste, which is exceedingly bitter and difficult to tolerate, it is taken as a positive omen. If it is rejected, it is a negative sign—though not necessarily definitive. Ramón touched Francisco on the head, eyes, throat, and heart and placed a small piece between his lips. "Chew, little brother," he admonished, "and we will see how you like it. Chew well, chew well, for it is sweet, it is delicious to the taste." There were smiles at this obvious reversal but no laughter—this was not a time for hilarity. After slight hesitation Francisco, who had not tasted peyote before, began to chew vigorously. He nodded—yes, he liked it. Later he participated with great enthusiasm in the search for peyote and that night ate a goodly amount himself, with no visible ill effect. He danced for hours, fell asleep smiling happily, and next morning was his old self. One *matewáme* who was obviously greatly moved by the whole experience was Veradera, a strikingly handsome girl apparently under twenty. Veradera ate more peyote than anyone with the exception of Ramón and Lupe, and later that night fell into a deep trance that lasted for many hours and caused everyone to regard her as specially sacred.

When every one of the companions had chewed a piece of the first sacrificial *híkuri,* Ramón took out his fiddle and one of the others a

Peter T. Furst

guitar (both homemade), and the veterans stood aside in a group to sing and dance the *matewámete* into a "receptive condition." In the meantime, another gourd had been filled with peyote cut into small pieces, and the initiates were not allowed to rise until they had emptied it. As the bowl was handed around, the others, led by Ramón, exhorted them over and over to "chew well, companion, chew well, for that is how you will see your life." Lupe then took a sizable whole plant, sliced off the bottom, lifted her long, magnificently embroidered skirt (like Ramón's clothes, it had been made specially for this journey), and rubbed the moist end of the cactus on her legs, especially on the numerous small scratches and cuts inflicted by spines and thorns during the trek through the desert. The others followed her example. Lupe explained that peyote not only discourages hunger and thirst and restores one's spirit but heals wounds and prevents infection.*

Hikuri-seekers know about a small cactus they call *tsuwíri*, which also grows in the north-central high desert and which they say is liable to manifest itself as true *híkuri* to those who have not properly purified themselves. Its effect, as described to me by Ramón, approximates the "bad trip." † Ramón having admonished the companions repeatedly to

---

* It might be argued (as has La Barre) that these medicinal qualities are ascribed to peyote by the Huichol, not on any real evidence, but on the basis of its inherent supernatural powers and its exalted place in Huichol belief and ritual. It is my impression, however, that Huichol shamans at least are accomplished herbalists, and that many of their medicinal plants really do possess at least some of the curative powers with which they are credited. That this applies also to peyote is supported by a recent scientific study. Researchers at the University of Arizona separated a water-soluble crystalline substance from an ethanol extract of *Lophophora Williamsii* which, they report, exhibited "antibiotic activity against a wide spectrum of bacteria and a species of the imperfect fungi. The name *peyocactin* has been given to the principal antimicrobial component contained in this partially purified substance. Of particular interest was its inhibitory action against eighteen strains of penicillin-resistant *Staphylococcus aureus*. Preliminary protection studies with mice suggest the *in vivo* effectiveness of peyocactin" (McLeary, Sypherd, and Walkington, 1960:247–49). As for the effectiveness of peyote against even the most extreme fatigue, we have, among others, the testimony of Lumholtz (1902:178–79). Totally exhausted after a long trek and unable to walk another step (to make matters worse he had just recovered from an attack of malaria), Lumholtz was given a single *híkuri* by his Indian friends: "The effect was almost instantaneous, and I ascended the hill quite easily, resting now and then to draw a full breath of air."

† Following our return to Tepic, Nayarit, one of the pilgrims gave me a specimen of the cactus the Huichol call *tsuwíri*, or "false peyote." It turned out to be *Ariocarpus retusus*, which does not actually resemble the true *híkuri, Lophophora Williamsii*, very closely but which is nevertheless called peyote in some parts of northern Mexico. Along with *Ariocarpus fissuratus*, which is said by the Tarahumara Indians of Chihuahua to be more powerful than *Lophophora Williamsii* and other members of this group, *A. retusus* does in fact belong to the same cactus subtribe (Cereeae) as *L. Williamsii* and like the latter has long been reputed to possess magical and medicinal properties. Two alkaloids also found in *L. Williamsii*, hordenine and N-methyltyramine, as well as some other alkaloids not previously detected, were recently isolated from tissues

Fig. 28. *Ariocarpus retusus*, called *tsuwíri*, or "false peyote," by the Huichol. Pilgrims who are not completely "pure," who have committed incest, or who have been insufficiently instructed by the shaman-leader of the pilgrimage may be misled into eating this cactus instead of peyote and suffer a "bad trip," madness, or even death unless they are cured in time by the shaman.

"be of a pure heart" and not be misled by *tsuwíri*, the actual *híkuri* harvest was ready to commence, and the pilgrims went off into the desert, alone or in pairs. *Híkuri* "hides itself well," and several of the companions had to walk a considerable distance before seeing their first peyote. Lupe, on the other hand, almost at once discovered a thicket of cactus and mesquite so rich in peyote that in a couple of hours she had filled her tall collecting basket. Occasionally she would stop to admire and speak quietly to an especially beautiful *híkuri* and to touch it to her forehead, face, throat, and heart before adding it to the others. We also saw people exchanging gifts of peyote. This seemed to us a very beautiful aspect of the pilgrimage. No ceremony in which peyote was eaten communally went by without this kind of ritual exchange, in which each participant is expected to share his

of *Ariocarpus retusus* (Braga and McLaughlin, 1969:87–94; Neal and McLaughlin, 1970:395–96). For a complete text of the *tsuwíri* tradition among the Huichol see Furst, 1971:182–87.

peyote with every companion. A man or a woman would carefully divide a peyote, rise, and walk from individual to individual, handing over a piece and receiving one in return. Sometimes an older participant would place his gift directly into the mouth of a younger one, urging him to "chew well, younger brother, chew well, so that you will see your life." But most often these ritual exchanges took place in silence.

No *híkuri* was ever dug carelessly or dropped casually on the ground or into a basket or bag. On the contrary, it was handled with tenderness and respect and addressed soothingly by the *híkuri*-seeker, who would thank it for allowing itself to be seen, call it by endearing names, and apologize for removing it from its home. As mentioned, small, tender, five-ribbed ("five-pointed") plants are considered especially desirable. Being young, they are also less disagreeable to the taste. Some plants were cleaned and popped directly into the mouth—after first being held to forehead, face, and heart. Lupe sometimes wept when she did this. She was also chewing incessantly, as was Ramón.

Toward four in the afternoon Ramón rose from where he had been digging peyotes and called out that it was time to return to camp. One of the *híkuri*-seekers had just spotted a sizable cluster and was reluctant to abandon so rich a find. Ramón admonished him: "Our game bags are full. One must not take more than one needs." If one did, if one did not leave gifts and propitiate the slain Deer-Peyote (just as one should propitiate the spirits of animals one hunts, the maize one harvests, and the trees one cuts), Elder Brother would be offended and would conceal the *híkuri* or withdraw them altogether, so that next time the seekers would walk away empty-handed. We would call this practice conservation; to the Huichol it is part of the principle of reciprocity by which he orders his social relationships and his relationship to the natural and supernatural environment. So the pilgrims gathered their gear and their bags and baskets, now heavy with peyote, and after a tearful farewell returned to camp as they had come, walking single file to the sound of the bow. On the way they stopped here and there to pick up "food" for *Tatewari*.

On arriving at camp they made the usual ceremonial circuit around the fire and offered thanks for its protection, without laying down their burdens. Again there was much weeping. Ramón's basket, held in one arm while he gestured in the sacred directions with the other, must have weighed a good thirty pounds. Though dormant, the ashes were still aglow, and new flames quickly licked through the growing pile of brush as each deposited some "food" for *Tatewari*. The green branches, wet with dew, sent thick clouds of white smoke billowing to the leaden sky. It was turning cold and damp.

The night was passed in singing and dancing around the ceremonial fire, chewing peyote in astounding quantities, and listening to the ancient stories. Considering the lack of food, the long days on the road, the bitterly cold nights with little sleep (by now, Ramón had not closed his eyes to sleep for six days and nights!), and above all the high emotional pitch of the sacred drama, with its succession of increasingly intense and exalted encounters, one might have expected them to feel some letdown now that they had successfully "hunted the deer" and to lapse into a dream state induced by the considerable quantities of *hikuri* they had already consumed. True, after their return from the hunt they were, for the most part, somewhat subdued and quiet. Some had actually entered trances. Veradera had been sitting motionless for hours, arms clasped around her knees, eyes closed. When night fell Lupe placed candles around her to protect her against attacks by sorcerers while her soul was traveling outside her body. But most of the others were wide awake, in varying states of exaltation, supremely happy and possessed of seemingly boundless energy. If the dancing and singing stopped it was only because Ramón laid down his fiddle to commune quietly with the ceremonial fire or to chant the stories of the first pilgrimage. Neither he nor Lupe was ever without a piece of peyote in the mouth. Yet they were never out of control—indeed, none of them was—and neither they nor any of the others, little Francisco included, showed the slightest adverse effect, then or later.

The singing, dancing, and speech-making, punctuated by laughter and trumpet-blowing, went on with few interruptions until well past midnight, when Ramón laid aside his fiddle and allowed the peyote to take hold of him completely, so that he might speak directly with *Tatewari* and the *kakauyaríxi* and listen to their counsel. It is in this dream state also that the *mara'akáme* obtains the new peyote names for the pilgrims (e.g., Offering of Blue Maize, Votive Gourd of the Sun, Arrows of *Tatewari,* etc.). These names are said to "emerge" from the center of the fire like brilliantly colored, luminous ribbons. They are conferred on the *hikuri*-seekers on the final day and preserved at least until the participants are formally released from their sacred bonds and restrictions by a ceremonial deer hunt some time after their return to the Sierra.

The Huichol regard their peyote experiences as private and do not, as a rule, discuss them with anyone, except in the most general terms ("there were many beautiful colors," "I saw maize in brilliant colors, much maize," or simply, "I saw my life"). Under certain conditions the *mara'akáme* might be called upon to assist in giving form and meaning to a vision, especially for a *matewáme,* or in a cure. This much is clear, however: beyond certain "universal" visual and auditory sensations, which may be laid to the chemistry of the plant and its effect on the

Fig. 29.   After midnight Ramón laid aside his fiddle and entered a trance state in which he listened to the voices of ("Grandfather") *Tatewari*, the old Fire Shaman, and the other supernaturals who reside in *Wirikuta*, the sacred land of the ancestors and the peyote.

central nervous system, there are powerful cultural factors at work that influence, if they do not actually determine, both content and interpretation of the drug experience. This is true not only between cultures but even within the same culture. Huichol are convinced that the *mara'akáme,* or one preparing himself to become a *mara'akáme,* and the ordinary person have different kinds of peyote experiences. Certainly a *mara'akáme* embarks on the pilgrimage and the drug experience itself with a somewhat different set of expectations than the ordinary Huichol. He seeks to experience a catharsis that allows him to enter upon a personal encounter with *Tatewari* and to travel to "the fifth level" to meet the supreme spirits at the ends of the world. And so he does. Ordinary Huichol also "experience" the supernaturals, but they do so essentially through the medium of their shaman. In any event, I have met no one who was not convinced of this essential difference or who laid claim to the same kinds of exalted and illuminating confrontations with the Otherworld as the *mara'akáme.* In an objective sense his visions might be similar, but subjectively they are differently perceived and interpreted.

The *hikuri*-seekers left as they had entered—on foot, single file, blowing their horns. Their once-white clothing was caked with the yellow earth of the desert, for during the night it had begun to drizzle—an astonishing event at the height of the dry season and an auspicious omen. Behind them a thin plume of blue smoke rose from the ceremonial fire. They had circled it as required. They had made their offerings of tobacco and bits of food and sacred water from the springs of Our Mothers. They had purified their sandals. They had wept bitter tears as they bade farewell to *Tatewari,* to Elder Brother, to the *kakauyaríxi.*

A few hundred yards down the trail they halted once more. Facing the mountains and the sun, they shouted their pleasure at having found their life and their pain at having to depart so soon. "Do not leave," they implored the supernaturals, "do not abandon your places, for we will come again another year." And they sang, song after song—their parting gift to the *kakauyaríxi:*

> What pretty hills, what pretty hills,
> So very green where we are.
> Now I don't even feel,
> Now I don't even feel,
> Now I don't even feel like going to my rancho.
> For there at my rancho it is so ugly,
> So terribly ugly there at my rancho,
> And here in *Wirikúta* so green, so green.
> And eating in comfort as one likes,

Amid the flowers, so pretty.
Nothing but flowers here,
Pretty flowers, with brilliant colors,
So pretty, so pretty.
And eating one's fill of everything,
Everyone so full here, so full with food.
The hills very pretty for walking,
For shouting and laughing,
So comfortable, as one desires,
And being together with all one's companions.
Do not weep, brothers, do not weep.
For we came to enjoy it,
We came on this trek,
To find our life.

For we are all,
We are all,
We are all the children of,
We are all the sons of,
A brilliantly colored flower,
A flaming flower.
And there is no one,
There is no one,
Who regrets what we are.

POSTSCRIPT

On June 23, 1971, Ramón Medina Silva died of wounds sustained
during a shooting incident at a fiesta held at his *rancho* in the Sierra
to celebrate the preparation of the soil for the planting of the new
maize crop. As is customary on such festive and sacred occasions, there
had been a good deal of ritual and recreational drinking. At the time
of his death at age forty-five, he had become widely recognized as
the leading Huichol artist, and as a *mara'akáme* of considerable and
very special gifts. His loss, to his people and to his friends, is in-
calculable.

6

R . G O R D O N   W A S S O N

The Divine Mushroom
of Immortality

I have often told the story of our visits to the remote mountains of southern Mexico in search of survivals of the cult of the sacred mushroom. Rather than repeat it here, I now prefer to give my readers this chapter of my life in perspective—that is, to say what I think the Mexican hallucinogenic mushrooms mean to us all, what bearing they may have on the origin of the religious idea among primitive peoples. I shall be writing retrospectively, after many years' absence from the Mazatec hills. I am told many things have changed there.

Let me start at the beginning. Those who do not know the story will be interested in learning how it came about that my late wife, a pediatrician, and I, a banker, took up the study of mushrooms. She was a Great Russian and, like all of her countrymen, learned at her mother's knee a solid body of empirical knowledge about the common species and a love for them that is astonishing to us Americans. Like us, the Russians are fond of nature—of the forests and birds and wild flowers. But their love for mushrooms is of a different order, a visceral urge, a passion that passeth understanding. The worthless kinds, the poisonous mushrooms—in a way, the Russians are fond even of them. They call these "worthless ones" *paganki,* the "little pagans," and my wife would make of them colorful centerpieces for the dining-room table, against a background of moss and stones and wood picked up in the forest. On the other hand, I, of Anglo-Saxon origin, had known nothing of mushrooms. By inheritance, I ignored them all; I rejected those repugnant fungal growths, manifestations of parasitism and decay. Before my marriage, I had not once fixed my gaze on a mushroom, not once looked at a mushroom with a discriminating eye. Indeed, each of us, she and I, regarded the other as abnormal, or rather subnormal, in our contrasting responses to mushrooms.

A little thing, some will say, this difference in emotional attitude toward wild mushrooms. Yet my wife and I did not think so, and we devoted a part of our leisure hours for more than thirty years to dissecting it, defining it, and tracing it to its origin. Such discoveries as we have made, including the rediscovery of the religious role of the hallucinogenic mushrooms of Mexico, can be laid to our preoccupation with that cultural rift between my wife and me, between our respective peoples, between the mycophilia and mycophobia (words we devised for the two attitudes) that divide the Indo-European peoples into two camps. If this hypothesis of ours be wrong, then it must have been a singular false hypothesis to have produced the results that it has. But I think it is not wrong. Thanks to the immense strides made in the study of the human psyche in this century, we are now all aware that deep-seated emotional attitudes acquired in early life are of profound importance. I suggest that when such traits betoken the attitudes of whole tribes or peoples, and when those traits have remained unaltered throughout recorded history, and especially when they differ from one people to another neighboring people, then you are face to face with a phenomenon of profound cultural importance, whose primal cause is to be discovered only in the wellsprings of cultural history.

Many have observed the difference in attitude toward mushrooms of the European peoples. Some mycologists in the English-speaking world have inveighed against this universal prejudice of our race, hoping thereby to weaken its grip. What a vain hope! One does not treat a constitutional disorder by applying a band-aid. We ourselves have had no desire to change the Anglo Saxon's attitude toward mushrooms. We view this anthropological quirk with amused detachment, confident that it will long remain unchanged, for future students to examine at their leisure.

Our method of approach was to look everywhere for references to mushrooms. We gathered the words for "mushroom" and the various species in every accessible language. We studied their etymologies. Sometimes we rejected the accepted derivations and worked out new ones, as in the case of "mushroom" itself and also of *chanterelle*.* We were quick to discern the metaphors in such words, metaphors that had lain dormant, in some cases for thousands of years. We searched for the meaning of these figures of speech. We sought for mushrooms in the proverbs of Europe, in myths and mythology, in legends and fairy tales, in epics and ballads, in historical episodes, in the obscene and scabrous

---

* A little yellow mushroom, in French also called *girolle*, in German *Pfifferling*.

vocabularies that usually escape the lexicographer, in the writings of poets and novelists. We were alert to the positive or negative value that the mushroom vocabularies carried, their mycophilic and mycophobic content. Mushrooms are widely linked with the fly, the toad, the cock, and the thunderbolt; and so we studied these to see what associations they conveyed to our remote forebears. Wherever we traveled we tried to enter into contact with untutored peasants and arrive at their knowledge of the fungi—the kinds of mushroom they distinguished, the names of the mushrooms, the uses to which they were put, and the peasants' emotional attitude toward them. We made trips to the Basque country, to Lapland, to Friesland, to Provence, to Japan. We scoured the galleries and museums of the world for mushrooms, and we pored over books on archaeology and anthropology.

I would not have my readers think that we ventured into all these learned paths without guidance. We drew heavily on our betters in the special fields we were exploring. When we were delving into questions of vocabulary, in working out an original etymology for a mushroomic word, we were always within reach of a philologist who had made of that tongue his province. And so in all branches of knowledge. Sometimes it seems to me that our entire work has been composed by others, that we served merely as *rapporteurs*. Since we began to publish, in 1955, people from all walks of life have come to us in increasing numbers to contribute information, and often the contributions of even the lowliest informants have been of the highest value, filling lacunae in our argument. We were amateurs, unencumbered by academic inhibitions, and therefore we felt free to range far and wide, disregarding the frontiers that ordinarily segregate the learned disciplines. What we produced was a pioneering work. We know, we have always known, better than the critics, the flaws in our work, but our main theme, which we adumbrated rather diffidently in *Mushrooms, Russia, and History* (1957), seems to have stood up under criticism. My recent volume on *Soma* (1968) is Ethno-mycological Studies No. 1. If I live and retain my vitality, you may see published over the coming years a series of volumes, and, at the end of the road, there may be a new edition of our original work, reshaped, simplified, with new evidence added and the argument strengthened.

I do not recall which of us, my wife or I, first dared to put into words, back in the '40's, the surmise that our own remote ancestors, perhaps 6000 years ago, worshiped a divine mushroom. It seemed to us that this might explain the phenomenon of mycophilia *vs.* mycophobia, for which we found an abundance of supporting evidence in philology and folklore. Nor am I sure whether our conjecture came before or after we had learned of the role of *Amanita muscaria* in the religion of several remote tribes of Siberia. Our bold surmise seems less bold now than it did then.

I remember distinctly how it came about that we embarked on our Middle American explorations. In the fall of 1952, we learned that the sixteenth-century writers describing the Indian cultures of Mexico had recorded that certain mushrooms played a divinatory role in the religion of the natives. Simultaneously we learned that certain pre-Columbian stone artifacts resembling mushrooms, most of them roughly a foot high, had been turning up, usually in the highlands of Guatemala, in increasing numbers. For want of a better name, the archaeologists called them "mushroom stones," but not one archaeologist had linked them with mushrooms or with the rites described by the sixteenth-century writers in neighboring Mexico. They were an enigma, and "mushroom stone" was merely a term of convenience. Some of these stone carvings carried an effigy on the stipe of a god or a human face or an animal, and all of these carvings were very like mushrooms. Just like the child in "The Emperor's New Clothes," we spoke up, declaring that the so-called mushroom stones really *did* represent mushrooms, and that they were the symbol of a religion, like the cross in the Christian religion, or the Star of Judea, or the crescent of the Moslems. If we are right—and accumulating evidence is strongly in our favor—then this Middle American cult of a divine mushroom, this cult of God's flesh, as the Nahua called it in pre-Hispanic times, can be traced back archaeologically at least to 500 B.C. and probably 1000 B.C. This places the ancestral mushroom cult in the culture of the highland Maya at a time when stone sculpture was making its first appearance in Middle America.*

Thus we find a mushroom cult in the center of one of the oldest civilizations in Middle America. These mushroom stones are stylistically among the finest we have. It is tempting to imagine generations of wooden effigies earlier still, mushroomic symbols of the cult that have long since turned to dust. Is not mycology, which someone has called the stepchild of the natural sciences, acquiring a wholly new and unexpected dimension? Religion has always been at the core of man's highest faculties and cultural achievements, and therefore I would suggest that we learn to contemplate the lowly mushroom in a new light: what patents of ancient lineage and nobility are coming its way!

It remained for us to find out what kinds of mushroom had been

---

* Some Middle American specialists may challenge my assumption of a connection between the "mushroom stones," which ceased to be made centuries before Columbus arrived on these shores, and today's surviving mushroom cult. For years I had only an assumption to go on, but now, thanks to discoveries made by the late Stephan F. Borhegyi and us, I think we can tie the two together in a way that will satisfy any doubter.

Fig. 30. A pre-Classic mushroom effigy stone from highland Guatemala, about 500 B.C. Many such stone carvings of mushrooms, dated between 1000 and 300 B.C., have been found in Guatemala, as well as in Tabasco and Veracruz in Mexico, with or without anthropomorphic and zoomorphic effigies at the base. The effigy here is a crouching jaguar with a human head, possibly signifying shamanic transformation under the influence of the hallucinogenic mushroom or depicting the guardian spirit of the sacred plant. Coll. Edwin Janss, Jr., Thousand Oaks, Calif. (Photo by Peter T. Furst.)

worshiped in Middle America, and why. Fortunately, we could build on the experience of a few predecessors in the field: Blas Pablo Reko, Robert J. Weitlaner, Jean Bassett Johnson, Richard Evans Schultes, and Eunice V. Pike. They all reported that the cult still existed in the Sierra Mazateca in Oaxaca. And so we went there, in 1953. So far as we know, we were the first outsiders to eat the mushrooms, the first to be invited to partake in the agapé of the sacred mushroom.* I propose now to give the distinctive traits of the Amerindian cult of a divine mushroom, which we have found a revelation, in the true meaning of that abused word, but which for the Indians is an everyday feature, albeit a Holy Mystery, of their lives.

Here let me say a word parenthetically about the nature of the psychic disturbance that the eating of the mushroom causes. This disturbance is wholly different from the effects of alcohol, as different as night from day. We are entering upon a discussion in which the vocabulary of the English language, of any European language, is seriously deficient. There are no apt words in it to characterize one's state when one is, shall we say, "bemushroomed." For hundreds, even thousands, of years, we have thought about these things in terms of alcohol, and we now have to break the bonds imposed on us by our alcoholic obsession. We are all, willy-nilly, confined within the prison walls of our everyday vocabulary. With skill in our choice of words, we may stretch accepted meanings to cover slightly new feelings and thoughts, but when a state of mind is utterly distinct, wholly novel, then all our old words fail. How do you tell a man who has been born blind what seeing is like? In the present case this is an especially apt analogy, because superficially the bemushroomed man shows a few of the objective symptoms of one who is intoxicated, drunk. Now virtually all the words describing the state of drunkenness, from "intoxicated" (which literally means "poisoned") through the scores of current vulgarisms, are contemptuous, belittling, pejorative. How curious it is that modern civilized man finds surcease from care in a drug for which he seems to have no respect! If we use by analogy the terms suitable for alcohol, we prejudice the mushroom, and since there are few among us who have been bemushroomed, there is danger that the experience will not be fairly judged. What we need is a vocabulary to describe all the modalities of a divine inebriant.

These difficulties in communicating have played their part in certain amusing situations. Two psychiatrists who had taken the mushroom

* This was on the night of June 29–30, 1955. In 1938 Jean Bassett Johnson had led a party to Huautla de Jiménez that attended a night-long mushroom ceremony, but they were not invited to partake of the divine mushrooms.

and known the experience in its full dimensions have been criticized in professional circles as being no longer "objective." Thus it comes about that we are all divided into two classes: those who have taken the mushroom and are disqualified by subjective experience, and those who have not taken the mushroom and are disqualified by total ignorance of the subject! As for me, a simple layman, I am profoundly grateful to my Indian friends for having initiated me into the tremendous Mystery of the mushroom. In describing what happens, I shall be using familiar phrases that may seem to give some idea of the bemushroomed state. Let me hasten to warn that I am painfully aware of the inadequacy of my words, any words, to conjure up for you an image of that state.

I shall take you now to the unilingual villages in the uplands of southern Mexico. Only a handful of the inhabitants have learned Spanish. The men are given to the abuse of alcohol, but in their minds the mushrooms are utterly different, not in degree, but in kind. Of alcohol they speak with the same jocular vulgarity that we do. But about mushrooms they prefer not to speak at all, at least when they are in company, and especially when strangers, white strangers, are present.* If you are wise, you will talk about something, anything, else. Then, when evening and darkness come and you are alone with a wise old man or woman whose confidence you have won, by the light of a candle held in the hand, and speaking in a whisper, you may bring up the subject. Now you will learn how the mushrooms are gathered, perhaps before sunrise, when the mountainside is caressed by the predawn breeze, at the time of the New Moon, in certain regions only by a *doncella,* an untouched maiden. The mushrooms are wrapped in a leaf, perhaps a banana leaf, sheltered thus from irreverent eyes, and in some villages they are taken first to the church, where they remain for some time on the altar, in a *jícara,* or gourd bowl. They are never exposed in the market place but pass from hand to hand by prearrangement. I could talk to you for a long time about the words used to designate these sacred mushrooms in the languages of the various peoples who know them. The Nahua before the Spaniards arrived called them God's flesh, *teonanacatl.* I need hardly draw attention to a disquieting parallel, the designation of the Elements in our Eucharist: "Take, eat, this is my Body . . ."; and, again, "Grant us therefore, gracious Lord, so to eat the flesh of thy dear son. . . ." But there is one difference. The orthodox Christian must accept on faith the miracle of the conversion of the bread into God's flesh: that is what is meant by the doctrine of transubstantiation. By contrast, the mushroom of the

---

* I am speaking of 1953–57. Conditions have changed in the past fifteen years.

Nahua carries its own conviction: every communicant will testify to
the miracle that he has experienced. In the language of the Mazatecs,
the sacred mushrooms are called *'nti¹ ši³ tho³*.* The first word, *'nti¹*, is a
particle expressing reverence and endearment. The second element means
"that which springs forth." Our muleteer in 1953 had traveled the mountain trails all his life and knew Spanish, although he could not read or
write, or even tell time by a clock's face. We asked him why the mushrooms were called "that which springs forth." His answer, breathtaking
in its sincerity and feeling, was filled with the poetry of religion, and I
quote it word for word as he gave it:

> *El honguillo viene por sí mismo, no se sabe de dónde, como el viento que
> viene sin saber de dónde ni porqué.*

The little mushroom comes of itself, no one knows whence, like the wind
that comes we know not whence nor why.

When we first went down to Mexico, my wife and I, we felt certain
that we were on the trail of an ancient and holy mystery, and we went
as pilgrims seeking the Grail. To this attitude of ours I attribute such
success as we have had. It has not been easy. For four and a half centuries
the rulers of Mexico, men of Spanish origin or at least of Spanish culture,
have never entered sympathetically into the ways of the Indians, and the
Church regarded the sacred mushroom as an idolatry. The Protestant
missionaries of today are naturally intent on teaching the gospel, not
on absorbing the religion of the Indians. Nor are most anthropologists
good at this sort of thing. For more than four centuries the Indians have
kept the divine mushroom close to their hearts, sheltered from desecra-
tion by white men, a precious secret. We know that today there are
many *curanderos* who carry on the cult, each according to his lights,
some of them consummate artists, performing the ancient liturgy in
remote huts before minuscule congregations. With the passing years
they will die off, and, as the country opens up, the cult is destined to
disappear. They are hard to reach, these *curanderos*. Almost invariably
they speak no Spanish. To them, performing before strangers seems a
profanation. They will refuse even to meet with you, much less discuss
the beliefs that go with the mushrooms and perform for you. Do not
think that it is a question of money: *No hicimos esto por dinero* (We
did not this for money), said Guadalupe, after we had spent the night
with her family and the *curandera* María Sabina. (For those who know
the Mazatecs this simple declaration will be all the more remarkable:
money is hard to come by in the Sierra Mazateca, and the Mazatecs are
notoriously avaricious.) Perhaps you will learn the names of a number

---

* The superscript digits indicate the pitch of the syllable, 1 being the highest of four.
The initial apostrophe indicates a glottal stop.

of renowned *curanderos,* and your emissaries will even promise to deliver them to you, but then you wait and wait and they never come. You will brush past them in the market place, and they will know you, but you will not know them. The judge in the town hall may be the very man you are seeking, and you may pass the time of day with him, yet never learn that he is your *curandero.*

After all, who would have it different? What priest of the Catholic Church will perform Mass to satisfy an unbeliever's curiosity? The *curandero* who today, for a big fee, will perform the mushroom rite for any stranger is a prostitute and a faker, and his insincere performance has the validity of a rite put on by an unfrocked priest. In the modern world religion is often an etiolated thing, a social activity with mild ethical rules. Religion in primitive society was an awesome reality, "terrible" in the original meaning of that abused word, pervading all life and culminating in ceremonies that were forbidden to the profane. This is what the mushroom ceremony was in the remote parts of Mexico.

We often think of the Mysteries of antiquity as manifestations of primitive religion. Let me now draw your attention to certain parallels between our Mexican rite and the Mystery performed at Eleusis in the first millennium B.C., and probably much earlier. The timing seems significant. In the Mazatec country, the preferred season for "consulting the mushroom" is during the rains, when the mushrooms grow, from June through August. The Eleusinian Mystery, a sacred rite of purification and initiation related to deities of the earth, was celebrated in September or early October, the season of the mushrooms in Europe. At the heart of the Mystery of Eleusis lay a secret. In the surviving texts there are numerous references to the secret, but in none is it revealed. Yet Mysteries such as the one at Eleusis played a major role in Greek civilization, and thousands knew the experience. From the writings of the Greeks, from a fresco in Pompeii, we know that the initiate drank a potion. Then, in the depths of the night, he beheld visions, and the next day he was still so awestruck that he felt he would never be the same man as before. What the initiate experienced was "new, astonishing, inaccessible to rational cognition."* One writer in the second century A.D., by name Aristides, pulled the curtain for an instant, with this fragmentary description of the Eleusinian Mystery:

> Eleusis is a shrine common to the whole earth, and of all the divine things that exist among men, it is both the most awesome and the most luminous. At what place in the world have more miraculous tidings been

* For this and the following quotation, see Walter F. Otto, "The Meaning of the Eleusinian Mysteries," in Joseph Campbell, ed., *The Mysteries,* Bollingen Series XXX, 2 (New York: Pantheon Books, 1955), pp. 20 *et seq.* Italics mine.

sung, where have the *dromena* called forth greater emotion, *where has there been greater rivalry between seeing and hearing?*

And he went on to speak of the "ineffable visions" that it had been the privilege of many generations of men and women to behold.

Just dwell for a moment on that description. How striking that the Mystery of antiquity and the mushroom rite in Mexico are accompanied in the two societies by veils of reticence that, so far as we can tell, match each other point for point! The ancient writers' words are as applicable to contemporary Mexico as to classic Greece. May it nót be significant that the Greeks were wont to refer to mushrooms as "the food of the gods," *brōma theon*, and that Porphyry is quoted as having called them "nurslings of the gods," *theotróphous?* * The Greeks of the classic period were mycophobes. Was this because their ancestors had felt that the whole fungal tribe was infected "by attraction" with the holiness of some mushrooms, and that they were not for mortal men to eat, at least not every day? Are we not dealing with what was in origin a religious taboo?

For me there is no doubt that the secret of Eleusis lies in the hallucinogens. I should like to think that the agent was a mushroom, and there are clues hinting that it was, but the plant world withholds from us in our modern times many mysteries that may have been known to the untutored herbalist of former times. The natural hallucinogens were the concern of the hierophants of Eleusis, and these exalted priests must have had several of them at their disposal to face any eventuality when the annual invitation went out far and wide. The cult never faltered for want of the miraculous potion.

All the utterances concerning Eleusis, such as the one from Aristides, quoted above, the awe and wonderment, the instinctive reticence, for me bespeak a hallucinogen. This reticence, observed to the end, deserves more attention than it has received. I believe that it was spontaneous, upwelling among the initiates before a great Mystery. It prevailed throughout the Greek world. Anyone could become an initiate on two conditions: that Greek was his tongue, and that he was not an unabsolved murderer. Even slaves could present themselves. Thus the reticence was not a self-imposed rule of an elite guarding a secret from the profane, as it was among the Aryans of India. Much has been made of the sanctions imposed by Athens for the slightest infraction of the secrecy. True, the law was severe. Many examples of its enforcement survive. Alkibiades, a rich, popular, handsome young Athenian belonging to the café society of his day, dared to impersonate the hierophant of Eleusis at a private party in his own home. By decree he suf-

---

* Giambattista della Porta, *Villa* (Frankfort: 1592), p. 764.

fered the loss of all his wealth.* But the Athenian rescript did not run throughout the Greek world, whereas the silence did, to the end of the age. I think the silence imposed itself, spontaneous and voluntary, precisely the same reticence that we found among the Mazatec Indians when we went there in 1953–55, precisely the same reticence that prevails in all circles when face to face with the deepest Mysteries of religion.

But how much could we have learned if the initiated of Eleusis had spoken? Perhaps only the details of their experience, whereas the secret of secrets, the identity of the hallucinogen, may well have been the arcanum of the hierophant and his next of kin. The Eleusinian cult, according to George Mylonas, flourished for about 2000 years without interruption.† The hallucinogens, whatever they were, seem never to have been wanting. The effects on the initiates were, as near as we can say, the same as follow the ingestion, in proper dosage, of peyote, of ololiuqui, of the hallucinogenic mushrooms of Mexico. Plants chemically allied to the Mexican hallucinogens may well flourish in the Aegean basin, their virtues still hidden from us. At present I am inclined to think that the potion of Eleusis did not contain the juice of the fly agaric of the forest belt of Eurasia, the Soma of the Aryans. The action of the fly agaric on the human organism is different: there is a period of abnormal somnolence, and then a phase in which the imbiber is stimulated to perform feats of physical endurance renowned both in Siberia and in the hymns of the Rig-Veda. We have no hint of these effects from the Eleusinian potion. The chemistry of the fly agaric is not the chemistry of the Mexican plants.

Now that we are struggling unsuccessfully to control drug addiction in our modern world, let us turn to our "primitive" kin to see how they handled the dangers inherent in all hallucinogens. Among the Aryans, only the Brahmans were privy to the secret of Soma; they alone knew how it was prepared and imbibed. Similarly, in the Valley of the Ob, in Siberia, the Vogul laid down a severe taboo on the ingestion of the fly agaric: only the shaman and his acolyte could consume the mushroom with impunity—all others would surely die. In Greece the initiates generally attended the celebration at Eleusis only once in their lives, a few being permitted to return for the second time the following year. In Mexico the shamans (*curanderos*) and their next of kin know which plants are hallucinogenic. In the Mazatec country the *curanderos* pre-

* See George E. Mylonas, *Eleusis and the Eleusinian Mysteries* (Princeton, N. J.: Princeton University Press, 1961), pp. 223 *et seq.*

† *Op. cit.,* p. 285; but see p. 257 for the one occasion when the celebration was called off.

scribe the dose that each will take. Throughout my sojourns in Mexico I was constantly being warned that the divine mushrooms were *muy delicados*, "very dangerous," and their consumption is hedged about with many taboos, differing from village to village, some of them inconvenient and arbitrary. As I said before, the Indians never abuse the plants, which they treat with respect, and I have known Indians, some of them alcoholics, who had taken the mushrooms only once in their lives. They spoke of the mushrooms with reverence but did not wish to repeat the experience. During an all-night session, the *curandero* (or *curandera*) watches solicitously over those who have taken the hallucinogen and is quick to act if there is sign of upset. The communicants are enjoined not to leave the house (a one-room hut) under any circumstances as long as the effect of the plant lasts. There is always one person, sometimes two, who do not share in the agapé and who stand guard against interruptions from without and any untoward happenings within. Afterwards, those who have participated whisper among themselves, exchanging confidences about the events of the night. All those who have shared in the communion feel close to one another, having passed together the unforgettable hours.

I would not be understood as contending that only the hallucinogens (wherever found in nature) bring about visions and ecstasy. Clearly, some poets and prophets and many mystics and ascetics (especially in India) seem to have enjoyed ecstatic visions that answer the requirements of the ancient Mysteries and that duplicate the mushroom agapé of Mexico. I do not suggest that St. John of Patmos ate mushrooms in order to write the Book of the Revelation. Yet the succession of images in his vision, so clearly seen and yet such a phantasmagoria, means for me that he was in the same state as one bemushroomed. Nor do I suggest for a moment that William Blake knew the mushroom when he wrote this telling account of the clarity of "vision":

> The Prophets describe what they saw in Vision as real and existing men, whom they saw with their imaginative and immortal organs; the Apostles the same; the clearer the organ the more distinct the object. A Spirit and a Vision are not, as the modern philosophy supposes, a cloudy vapor, or a nothing: they are organized and minutely articulated beyond all that the mortal and perishing nature can produce. *He who does not imagine in stronger and better lineaments, and in stronger and better light than his perishing eye can see, does not imagine at all.**

This must sound cryptic to one who does not share Blake's vision or who has not taken the mushroom. The advantage of the mushroom is that it puts many (if not all) within reach of this state without having

---

* *The Writings of William Blake*, Geoffrey Keynes, ed., vol. III, p. 108 (Italics mine).

to suffer the mortifications of Blake and St. John. It permits you to see, more clearly than our perishing mortal eye can see, vistas beyond the horizons of this life, to travel backward and forward in time, to enter other planes of existence, even (as the Indians say) to know God. It is hardly surprising that your emotions are profoundly affected, and you feel that an indissoluble bond unites you with the others who have shared in the sacred agapé. All that you see during this night has a pristine quality: the landscape, the edifices, the carvings, the animals— they look as though they had come straight from the Maker's workshop. This newness of everything—it is as though the world had just dawned —overwhelms you and melts you with its beauty. Not unnaturally, what is happening to you seems fraught with significance, beside which the humdrum events of every day are trivial. All these things you see with an immediacy of vision that leads you to say to yourself, "Now I am seeing for the first time, seeing direct, without the intervention of mortal eyes." (Plato tells us that beyond this ephemeral and imperfect existence here below is an ideal world of archetypes, where the original, the true, the beautiful pattern of things exists forevermore. Poets and philosophers for millennia have pondered and discussed his conception. It is clear to me where Plato found his ideas; it was clear to his con- temporaries too. Plato had drunk of the potion in the Temple of Eleusis and had spent the night seeing the great vision.)

And all the time that you are seeing these things, the priestess sings, not loudly, but with authority. The Indians are notoriously not given to displays of inner feelings—except on these occasions. One night my *curandera* devoted her attention to her seventeen-year-old son, who seemed to have been mentally retarded. She sang over him, and it was as though what she sang were a threnody of all the mothers of the world from the beginning of time, the Lament of the Grieving Mother, with- out artifice, without self-consciousness because a stranger was present, without reticence, her naked soul reaching out to the Divine Mother.

The singing is good, but under the influence of the mushroom you think it is infinitely tender and sweet. It is as though you were hearing it with your mind's ear, purged of all dross. You are lying on a *petate* or mat—perhaps, if you have been wise, on an air mattress and in a sleeping bag. It is dark, for all lights have been extinguished save a few embers among the stones on the floor and the incense in a shard. It is still, for the thatched hut is usually some distance away from the village. In the darkness and stillness, that voice hovers through the hut, coming now from beyond your feet, now at your very ear, now distant, now actually underneath you, with strange ventriloquistic effect. The mushrooms produce this illusion also. Everyone experiences it, just as do the tribesmen of Siberia who have eaten of *Amanita muscaria* and lie under the spell of their shamans, displaying as these do their astonishing dexterity with ventriloquistic drumbeats. Likewise, in Mexico, I have heard a shaman engage in a most complex percussive beat; with her hands she hit her chest, her thighs, her forehead, her arms, each giving a different resonance, keeping an intricate rhythm and modulating, even syncopating, the strokes. Your body lies in the darkness, heavy as lead, but your spirit seems to soar and leave the hut and with the speed of thought to travel where it listeth, in time and space, accompanied by the shaman's singing and by the ejaculations of her percussive chant. What you are seeing and what you are hearing appear as one: the music assumes harmonious shapes and colors, giving visual form to its harmonies, and what you are seeing takes on the modalities of music—the music of the spheres. "Where has there been greater rivalry between seeing and hearing?" How apposite to the Mexican experience was the ancient Greek's rhetorical question! All your senses are similarly affected: a whiff of the cigarette with which you occasionally break the tension of the night smells as no cigarette before had ever smelled; the glass of simple water is infinitely better than a *flûte* of champagne.

Elsewhere I once wrote that the bemushroomed person is poised in space, a disembodied eye, invisible, incorporeal, seeing but not seen. In truth, he is the five senses disembodied, all of them keyed to the height of sensitivity and awareness, all of them blending into one another most strangely, until, utterly passive, he becomes a pure receptor, infinitely delicate, of sensations. (You, being a stranger, are perforce only a receptor. But the Mazatec communicants are also participants with the *curandera* in an extempore religious colloquy. Her utterances elicit spontaneous responses from them, responses that maintain a perfect harmony with her and with each other, building up to a quiet, swaying, antiphonal chant. This is an essential element of a successful ceremony, and one cannot experience the full effect of the role of the mushroom in the Indian community unless one attends such a gathering, either alone or with one or two other strangers.) As your body lies there, your soul is free, with no sense of time, alert as never before, living an eternity in a night, seeing infinity in a grain of sand. What you have seen and heard is cut as with a burin in your memory, never to be effaced. At last you know what the ineffable is, and what ecstasy means.

Ecstasy! The mind harks back to the origin of that word. For the Greeks *ekstasis* meant the flight of the soul from the body. Can a better word than that be found to describe the bemushroomed state? In common parlance among the many who have not experienced it, ecstasy is fun, and I am frequently asked why I do not reach for mushrooms every

Fig. 31 A sixteenth-century drawing of the sacred mushroom of Mexico. The
bird-headed spirit atop the plants presumably symbolizes hallucinogenic vision. From the Florentine Codex, Book 11, by Fr. Bernadino
de Sahagun.

night. But ecstasy is not fun. In our everyday existence we divide experiences into good and bad, "fun" and pain. There is a third category,
ecstasy, that for most of us hovers off stage, a stranger we never meet.
The divine mushroom introduces ecstasy to us. Your very soul is seized
and shaken until it tingles, until you fear that you will never recover
your equilibrium. After all, who will choose to feel undiluted awe, or
to float through that door yonder into the Divine Presence? The un-
knowing vulgar abuse the word, and we must recapture its full and
portentous sense. A few hours later, the next morning, you are fit to
go to work. But how unimportant work seems to you by comparision
with the portentous happenings of that night! If you can, you prefer to
stay close to the house and compare notes, and utter ejaculations of
amazement with others who lived through that night.

As man emerged from his brutish past, millennia ago, there was a
stage in the evolution of his awareness when the discovery of a mushroom (or was it a higher plant?) with miraculous properties was a
revelation to him, a veritable detonator to his soul, arousing in him

sentiments of awe and reverence, gentleness and love, to the highest
pitch of which mankind is capable, all those sentiments and virtues that
man has ever since regarded as the highest attribute of his kind. It
made him see what this perishing mortal eye cannot see. How right
were the Greeks to hedge about this Mystery, this imbibing of the
potion, with secrecy and surveillance! What today is resolved into a
mere drug, a tryptamine or lysergic-acid derivative, was for them a pro-
digious miracle, inspiring in them poetry and philosophy and religion.
Perhaps, with all our modern knowledge, we do not need the divine
mushrooms any more. Or do we need them more than ever? Some are
shocked that the key even to religion might be reduced to a mere
drug.* On the other hand, the drug is as mysterious as it ever was:
"like the wind it cometh we know not whence, nor why." Out of a
mere drug comes the ineffable, comes ecstasy. This is not the only instance in the history of humankind where the lowly has given birth to
the divine. Altering a sacred text, we would say that this paradox is a
hard saying, yet one worthy of all men to be believed.

What would our classical scholars not give for an opportunity to
attend the rite at Eleusis, to talk with the priestess? They would approach the precincts, enter the hallowed chamber, with a reverence born
of the texts venerated by scholars for millennia. How propitious would
be their frame of mind if they were invited to partake of the potion!
Well, those rites take place now, accessible but unbeknown to classical
scholars, ignored by them, in scattered dwellings, humble, thatched,
without windows, far from the beaten track, high in the mountains of
Mexico, in the stillness of the night, broken only by the distant barking
of a dog, perhaps the braying of an ass. Or, since we are in the rainy
season, the Mystery may be accompanied by torrential rains and punctuated by terrifying thunderbolts. Then, indeed, as you lie there bemushroomed, seeing the music and listening to the visions, you know a
soul-shattering experience, recalling as you do the beliefs of some primitive peoples that mushrooms, the sacred mushrooms, are divinely en-
gendered by Jupiter Fulminator, the God of the Lightning Bolt, in the
Soft Mother Earth.

* The case made for the origins of Christianity in a mushroom cult in John Allegro's
recent book, *The Sacred Mushroom and the Cross* (1970) has not met with acceptance
among scholars, including some who are generally persuaded by Wasson's arguments
regarding the identification of Soma with the fly agaric and the role of hallucinogens
generally in the religious experience.—ED.

7

R. GORDON WASSON

What Was the Soma of the Aryans?

At the end of the last century, cultivated circles in the West were excited by the discovery and translation of a body of antique verse composed in a language related to ours and dating from the second millennium B.C. This was a collection of 1028 hymns, the Rig-Veda, which had been preserved by word of mouth among the Brahmans in India for thirty centuries and more. There was an agreed text, but the Vedic language presented thorny problems. A cluster of scholars of the highest eminence worked hard to arrive at the meaning of those lyrics, and a number of renderings in European languages made their appearance in the 1880's and 1890's. The hymns were an expression of the religion of the people who called themselves Aryans and who had invaded the northwest of India about 1600 B.C.

One of the divinities in this religion was Soma—the only plant known to have been deified in the history of human cultures. One hundred and twenty of the hymns were devoted entirely to extolling this plant and its properties (including the inebriating juice), not to speak of frequent adoring references to it in the other hymns. The role of Soma in the Rig-Veda pervades the entire collection of hymns. As the late Louis Renou said, the whole of the Rig-Veda is present in a nutshell in the themes centered on Soma.

Now, the strange thing is that in 1900 no one knew, no one has known until now, what plant Soma was. In India its identity had been forgotten millennia before the arrival of Westerners. In the West, which was learning of Soma for the first time, there were many guesses, but none of them carried conviction. By this time the botanical survey of India was well advanced, and among Indologists and botanists in India there was much puzzlement about the mysterious Soma. Perhaps the plant was extinct? Possibly it had never existed? But with the passage of time and no satisfying identification forthcoming, the enigma presented by Soma sank out of sight and nowadays has been almost forgotten except by Vedic scholars. Even they seem to be adjusting themselves to the absence of Soma, although this is a feat comparable to presenting the play of *Hamlet* with the Prince of Denmark absent. I now revive the question, proposing a botanical identification for Soma that is the subject of my recent book *Soma: Divine Mushroom of Immortality*. Soma, I suggest, was the mushroom known in the English-speaking world as the fly agaric, *Amanita muscaria*.

When I first approached the Rig-Veda in 1962 I was mystified not so much by the elusive Soma as by the inability of the learned fraternity to identify it. Given the free-wheeling nature of poets everywhere, always, who can suppose that scores of poets, for generations, probably centuries, composing their poems in different cultural centers, could devote themselves to extolling a plant and never use the descriptive terms that would make it identifiable for us? But let me remind you that we must read these hymns as poetry. Perhaps I was blessed by being unencumbered with problems of syntax, with ramifying questions of Indo-European philology, with the sweep of mythological concepts emanating from prehistoric times. However, I did possess some knowledge of the known plant hallucinogens of the world.

I will not tarry over the many suggestions that Soma was an alcoholic beverage, since they all do multiple violence to the text of the Rig-Veda and they merely reflect the obsession of the West with alcohol as *the* inebriant of this world. But I will point out that in the Rig-Veda there is no mention of the roots, the leaves, the blossoms, the seed, or the fruit of Soma. In fact, the Rig-Veda says* expressly that Soma was born without seed: the gods laid the Somic germ. The only plants that fill these requirements are mushrooms. The habitat of Soma is on the mountain heights. This means that the divine fungus grew in the Himalayas or the Hindu Kush or both, and not in the dry hot plains of the Indus valleys.

The fly agaric first appears as a fluffy ball the size of an egg wrapped in an envelope of white wool. As it grows and swells it bursts its woolly envelope, showing its dazzling red skin beneath. Fragments of the envelope remain on the cap, studding it with small white patches. In many, perhaps most, languages the "cap" of a mushroom is called the "head," and it is so called in Vedic, *mūrdhán* or *'síras*. The poets, with poetic license, also liken it to an "udder," *ūdhan*, which is "milked" of its holy ambrosia, called *pávamāna*. The full-grown fly agaric stands as

* IX, 83.3d.

a column, and the poets hyperbolically refer to it repeatedly as the "mainstay of the sky," the "pillar of the world." The stem, or stipe, is called the *am'sú*. In one place the poet actually says that Soma sloughs off its envelope, a figure of speech that a mycologist today might use in conversation. Its resplendent apparel is known as *nirnij*, the "vesture-of-grand-occasion." Vedic scholars, not aware that Soma was the stunning fly agaric, have always assumed that the *nirnij* was the milk with which the *pávamāna* was mingled after being pressed out of the "udder," and they were certainly right, but this does not prevent the *nirnij* from being also the dress of the mushroom. The two figures of speech support and strengthen each other, permitting the poets to revel in word-play. It is a question which meaning was the original one. The poet speaks of the dazzling red skin of the fly agaric as the hide of a bull, the red beast that the Vedic priests exalted above all others in nature, and he describes Soma's "dress" as of sheep—the woolly fragments that remain when the envelope bursts. Could more suitable metaphors be found? (The reader must bear in mind that the ball of the mushroom is fiery red speckled with white.)

Scholars have been puzzled by the five verses in which Soma is called the "single eye," *ékam áksi*. This metaphor now becomes clear: in its natural habitat the adored plant at one stage in its life cycle looks like a single eye, contemplating the world, taking it all in. The juice of Soma is pounded out, filtered through a woolen cloth, and then mixed with water, milk, honey, or barley water. But this filter, *pavítra*, is only one of three filters in the Rig-Veda. There is another transcendental filter of which the poets speak incessantly, the filter that permits the poet to say, "King, having the filter for chariot," and again, "With his 1000 knobs he conquers mighty renown." For the poet the divine juice comes down from heaven on the rays of the sun. Soma enters the plant while the rays remain caught on the skin. What a delicious figure of speech! What plant other than the fly agaric fits these poetic figures? Have not the Vedic poets exalted their adored Soma in terms that are unmistakable? The god is suitably enshrined in a plant radiantly beautiful, *hári*, resplendent. The steeds of the Sun-God are *hári* and so is Soma! By a miracle of nature the hallucinogen is clothed in vesture suitable to its high station.

Let me point out that these correspondences, shown strikingly in color photographs, recur without ceasing in the hymns; the poets play with them, ring all possible changes on them. I have yet to find a single verse in the Rig-Veda that is incompatible with my identification, and there are many verses whose figures of speech are in happy concordance with our regal plant. The poets repeatedly apply to Soma the word "navel," *nābhi*, and here we have analogies to this day in the fungal vocabularies of the vernaculars spoken from France and Russia through Turkey to Cambodia and Korea. The poet speaks of Soma as "dazzling by day, by night silvery white." Surely he is referring to the brilliant spectacle that the fly agaric presents in sunlight, and then to its aspect as the color fades out by night and only fragments of the silvery-white envelope remain visible in the light of the moon.

I now present converging evidence of startling character in support of my contention. I wish to emphasize that this evidence is not essential to my case, but, unless it is impugned, it alone is sufficient to prove that Soma was the fly agaric of Eurasian folklore and to suggest that the fly agaric may be the key to the religion prevailing throughout Eurasia in prehistoric times.

The fly agaric possesses a peculiar property, unique so far as we know in the whole plant world: it is an inebriant whose inebriating property passes quickly through to the urine. The tribesmen of the Chukotka and Kamchatka, in the far northeast of Siberia, used to drink the urine of those who had ingested the fly agaric, apparently by preference, I think because certain impurities are strained out as it passes through the human organism, the third of the Rig-Veda's three filters. Georg Steller* tells us that the urine so used transmits its potency to the urine of the second drinker, and to the third and fourth or even fifth "generation" of drinkers, when finally its virtue peters out.† Not all tribes have recourse to this practice: we have no evidence that the tribes who use the fly agaric in the valleys of the Ob and Yenisei do so. The sources are silent on this. The question may be asked how these northern tribesmen first discovered the potency residing in the urine of the fly agaric consumer. The answer may lie in the reindeer. The tribes live in intimacy with their great herds of reindeer, and these are addicted both to the fly agaric and to drinking urine, especially human urine. Fly-agaric inebriation is common among the animals, as every reindeer-handler knows.

When I read the Rig-Veda in translation I was naturally alert for evidences of urine drinking, and I think I have found them. The Rig-Veda is a collection of hymns written by poet-priests for priests to sing in the liturgy, and the priests were all, naturally, privy to the practices of their religion and to the singular attributes of Soma. We must expect

* See my *Soma: Divine Mushroom of Immortality*, Exhibit 5, pp. 239–40.

† Wasson's recent book *Soma: Divine Mushroom of Immortality* (1968) includes a complete anthology of the travelers, anthropologists, and linguists who have left accounts of the Siberian practice, some of whom describe in some detail the practice of urine-drinking in mushroom rituals. See especially the accounts of Georg Heinrich von Langsdorf (pp. 246–51), J. Enderli (pp. 261–64), and Waldemar Jochelson (pp. 365–72). —ED.

the allusions to be casual, incidental, not at all spelled out for us and the other excluded profane to grasp. They are in fact revealed in mythological contexts. In RV VIII 4.10 the poet addresses the god Indra:

> Like a stag, come here to drink!
> Drink Soma, as much as you like.
> Pissing it out day by day, O generous one,
> you have assumed your most mighty force.
> [Daniel H. H. Ingalls' rendering.]

When we drink tea or coffee or milk or beer, no one says that we later urinate tea or coffee or milk or beer. But *Indra pisses Soma*, just as the fly-agaric consumer in the Chukotka does. Whether the figure of a drinking stag in the verse we have quoted alludes to the confirmed addiction of deer to the fly agaric I hesitate to say. There is yet another verse (RV II 34.13) where deities in the shape of horses, known as the Rudras, seem to have pissed Soma. The tenor of these verses is clear: only with Soma is there Soma-urine. How did the priests learn this other than by drinking the Soma-impregnated beverage? In the Rig-Veda we find a number of allusions to the passing of Soma through the belly, the entrails, of Indra, some of these allusions expressing considerable anxiety. I say that these become meaningful if we understand that Soma is being passed through what the poets call the Third Filter, the human organism, into the urine, and that this act is attended by genuine dangers of misadventure. There is a verse, IX 74.4d, where the priests "with full bladders piss Soma quick with movement." Now this is a translation of Renou and also in essence of Geldner, both of them Vedic scholars of the highest eminence. They agree on the peculiar meaning of this verse. I believe other scholars dispute such a reading, but if Geldner and Renou are right, this verse alone is sufficient to clinch my case.

Although there are only two or three direct references to Soma-urine in the Rig-Veda, we find supporting evidence elsewhere, and this evidence comes just where we should find it in the circumstances, given the general acceptance in the priestly caste of all Soma's attributes and the sacred nature of the Mystery. Let me emphasize again that we must expect the references to occur casually, incidentally, like the accidental disclosure in a conversation of a secret known to all. According to a well-known Brāhmana story,* Indra drinks so much Soma that the sources say Indra exudes it from his ears *as well as pissing it*. In the

---

* *Taittirīva Samhitā* 2.3.2.5–6; *Satapatha Brāhmana* 5.5.4.8–9 and in most detail 12.7.1.1–9.

Avesta, Yasna 48.10, Zarathustra angrily excoriates those who use urine in the sacrifice: "When wilt thou do away with the urine of drunkenness with which the priests evilly delude the people?" The Parsis, descendants of the Zoroastrians, to this day consume urine in their religious devotions, although only in symbolic amounts and only bull's urine.* The Manichaeans, whose religion was an outgrowth of Zoroastrianism, exercised considerable influence in China for some centuries; from a late date in Fukien Province, two reports survive by a high civil servant to his superiors criticizing the religious activities of these Manichaean sectarians. In their devotions, he said, they consume too many *red mushrooms* and, moreover, were making use of urine, apparently human urine.† (Probably this civil servant had not himself attended the Manichaean rites and was reporting hearsay.) As a final citation, in the Mahabhārata we find a quaint apologue, interpolated late into the text, telling how a *mātanga* (the lowest of the low) invited the holy man Uttanka to drink his urine to quench his (Uttanka's) thirst and how Uttanka refused indignantly, only to learn later that the *mātanga* was Krishna in disguise, and that he had been offered—and had refused— Soma-urine! Uttanka thus lost forever the chance to join the immortals.‡

If my interpretation of the Rig-Veda in this crucial respect meets with resistance in the West, it has proved acceptable, even illuminating, in India in some quarters. An English woman writes me that she was in a circle of Indian ladies and one of them, a ranee, was dwelling on the infatuation of her husband, the rajah, for a certain *sadhu*, or holy man. Why, he even wished to drink the sadhu's urine, she said. The Indian ladies accepted this calmly, as though not surprised, and my correspondent therefore remained silent. Again, an Indian intellectual says that the present-day *sadhu* conveys his spiritual powers to his disciples in any one of four ways: (1) by a "laying on" of hands, precisely as in our church; (2) by having his disciples repeat incessantly for long periods a certain prayer or *mantra*; (3) by having him fix his gaze undeviatingly on the *sadhu's* countenance for long periods; and, finally, (4) by giving his favored disciples the privilege of drinking his urine. Do not these instances of contemporary urine-drinking come down from the time when urine was still impregnated with the essence of Soma?

Some skeptics are doubtless asking how it comes about that the iden-

---

* J. J. Modi: *The Religious Ceremonies and Customs of the Parsees* (Bombay: 1923; 2nd edition 1937). In 2nd ed., p. 93, and index entries under "gaomez," "nirang," and "nirangdin."

† *Un Traité manichéen Retrouvé en Chine,* traduit et annoté par Ed. Chavannes et P. Pelliot, Paris, 1912, pp. 292–340, especially pp. 302–05 and 310–14.

‡ A'svamedha Parvan, 14.54.12–35.

tity of Soma is being discovered only now, and by an outsider, one who knows no Vedic.

The Indo-Iranians coming down from the North exalted a plant in terms breath-taking for us. But for three millennia Soma, the exalted plant, has been absent. The Hindus strangely disclosed no curiosity about it; as for the West, our speculations in recent times have been only blind guesses, convincing no one, often not even those who propounded them. Of late I find more and more scholars receptive to the possibility that the Soma of the poets was for them little more than a mythological concept—that is to say, a non-plant. Nature abhors a vacuum, and in the absence of the genuine plant, our scholars, devising a myth to fill the vacuum in their own knowledge, seem ready to weave for the poets a myth that the poets never knew.

The trouble, I think, is clear and simple. The Vedists have allowed themselves to be miscast. When you seek the identity of a plant you go to a botanist, not to a Vedist. But then, why have the botanists not discovered it? A little reflection will give the answer.

Cultivated circles in the West were first alerted to the existence of the Rig-Veda in the second half of the last century. The Rig-Veda could be read only by the Vedists, a generation of scholars of the highest eminence tilling a field remote from the main thoroughfares of Western studies. The botanists had no access to the hymns, but, what was far worse, they thought they had. A number of translations tumbled from the presses, and botanists working in the Indian field read them. But the translations of the period—by Wilson and Cowell, Griffith, Langlois —were not intended for scholars or scientists. They were an effort to convey to cultivated circles the treasure house of early religious poetry that had just been uncovered in India, composed in a language related to our Western languages. The translators were not in the forefront of Vedists. Their translations sound like what refined ladies enjoyed reading in the Victorian age. They were "poetical" in the vein of the *Idylls of the King* but without Tennyson's powers of versification. They were flowery, rotund, some might say flatulent, giving a pseudo-sense to all passages that puzzled Vedists and that the translators had to guess at, and, moreover, bowdlerizing the text to caress the prudish Victorian ear. Small wonder that George Watt, the foremost botanist of the British *raj*, who knew no Sanskrit, much less Vedic, is quoted as saying, "the vague and poetical descriptions given of the Soma make any scientific identification impossible."*

And so the Vedists were left with the Soma problem. Unhappily they did not demur: they accepted the role of botanists, for which their

* Quoted from Max Müller, *Collected Works*, Vol. X (London: 1888), p. 223.

qualifications were not readily apparent. The world has ever since looked to them for an identification that they could not supply, could not be expected to supply. Speaking for the Vedists, Professor F. B. J. Kuiper of Leiden is a thousand times right in saying that "the complexities of the problem should not . . . be underestimated." He adds that the identification of Soma must take the seeker far beyond the confines of Indo-Iranian studies proper. This is where I have gone.

There was a further difficulty. British botanists in India performed a Herculean task in mapping the vegetation of that vast land in a long series of specialized monographs culminating in an admirable encyclopedic work, *Dictionary of the Economic Plants of India*, edited and partly written by George Watt. But they confined themselves to the phanerogams—the seed-bearing plants—and they neglected the fungal flora. No one suggested a mushroom for the role of Soma. This may seem strange, but the English people, mycophobes to the core, chose to ignore the fungal flora, the "toadstools," of India.

One more consideration: from a botanist's point of view the distinctive feature of Soma is that it belongs to the world that Louis Lewin, the pharmacologist, first called *Phantastica* more than forty years ago, that today is usually named the "plant hallucinogens," that the chemist and pharmacologist designate as the psychotropic or psychotomimetic plants. This restricts the area of inquiry. Specialized study of the natural hallucinogens is only a few decades old: before then there were only the old travel books and the field notes of anthropologists, difficult to come by and to collate.

Many have observed that discoveries in the realms of geographical or intellectual exploration arrive in a measured sequence, when the days are fulfilled that they should be made, and that only in recent years have we been able to approach the Soma problem with a hope of finding the answer. The fortunate person who makes the discovery is an accident of history, arriving as he does at precisely the right moment and happily possessed of the needed information derived from diverse disciplines hitherto not associated together. I am certainly one of the first persons with any botanical background to study the recent scholarly translation of the Rig-Veda concentrating on the Soma question. My late wife and I had been concerned with ethnomycological problems for decades. On the strength of the folklore of Europe and the etymologies of the fungal words in the languages of Europe, in the 1940's we had advanced to each other the daring idea that a mushroom had once figured in the religious life of our own remote ancestors. When we learned of the role played by the fly agaric in the shamanic rites of Siberian tribesmen, down to recent times, we were overjoyed, thinking that the Siberian usage in part vindicated our hunch. Little did we

Fig. 32.   "Pillar-of-the-World,"
"Mainstay-of-the-Sky."

imagine that we were on the road to a discovery of much larger scope.

In 1952 we were diverted to Mexico, where we later revealed to the world the part played by hallucinogenic mushrooms in the religious life of the Indians of southern Mexico. Thanks to the indispensable aid of Professor Roger Heim, then Director of the Muséum National d'Histoire Naturelle, upwards of a dozen hallucinogenic species received scientific identification for the first time. We took advantage of our Mexican explorations to extend our acquaintance to the phanerogamic hallucinogens.

Certain English scholars have lately dwelt with dramatic effect on the divorce that has taken place in our generation between the scientific and humane aspects of our culture. But for ethnobotanists (including ethnomycologists) these two aspects are still joined. As scientists, they know plants; as students of human cultures, they study the role plants play in man's daily life and in his spiritual perceptions. When I read the Rig-Veda as poetry, it was evident that the poets were deifying, in lyrical language of breath-taking poignancy, the hallucinogenic fly agaric of the Siberian taiga, *Amanita muscaria*, in prehistory the divine inebriant of all Eurasia.

What is this discovery that I think I have made? Have I done more than identify some plant or other that happened to be named in an ancient hymn? When the Vedic poet sang that most famous of all the verses of the Rig-Veda,

> We have drunk the Soma, we are become Immortals,
> We are arrived at the Light, we have found the Gods.
> What now can hostility do to us, what the malice of mortal,
>   O Immortal Soma!

he was giving utterance to the epitome of the whole collection. What are we to make of it?

The poet throughout the ages has pursued a serious calling intimately associated with prophecy. In this verse we feel the potent afflatus of Soma, the ecstasy inspired by the divine hallucinogen. The poet is certainly not performing an arid exercise in versification and music about a plant that he has never seen. Nor are we discussing merely an "invigorating" inebriant comparable to alcohol. We are dealing with the "enthusiasm" of the poet, in the original and now obsolete sense of that word, divine possession, poetic frenzy, supernatural inspiration. The engine behind the myth and ritual of the Rig-Veda is this "enthusiasm." If I am right, here is where we are arrived, this is the secret of our discovery. We have identified a plant understandably considered as miraculous by the people of long ago, and in so doing we have swung open the portals to ecstasy.

Daniel H. H. Ingalls, Wales Professor of Sanskrit at Harvard, has recently endorsed my identification of Soma,* and he added:

> The greatness of a discovery is in the further discoveries that it may render possible. To my mind the identification of the Soma with a hallucinogenic mushroom is more than the solution of an ancient puzzle. I can imagine numerous roads of inquiry on which, with this new knowledge in hand, one may set out.

I will venture now on one such "road of inquiry."

The fly-agaric complex of Siberia is of absorbing interest from many points of view. That the use of Soma, the inebriating mushroom, has survived there until recently, even if in a degenerate state and restricted

---

* Paper read at the annual meeting of the American Oriental Society in Baltimore, 15 April 1970.

to two shrinking areas, is a remarkable fact. In our own time the use of the fly agaric has been described in the Chukotka and also, far to the west, in the valleys of the Ob and the Yenisei. The words used for the fly agaric in the various tribes, the associated meanings of those words and their etymologies, the part played by reindeer in the urine-drinking of the natives, the personification of the fly agaric as little men, the petroglyphs dating from long ago—all these aspects of the fly agaric cult deserve attention. But I will pass over them to come to the point of my story.

Many students of the customs and folklore of the forest belt of Siberia have remarked on the reverence shown everywhere for the Siberian birch, a tree that is much taller and straighter than our birches. The birch is pre-eminently the tree of the shaman. He builds his tent around the bole of a birch, and in trance he climbs up the trunk to go on his travels to the land of departed spirits. The folklore of Siberia is saturated with the birch, even where the cult of the fly agaric has been given up. Why the birch? Every student of the Siberian forest peoples has asked this question, but no one seems to have found an answer.

For me the answer is clear. The birch is revered wherever it grows in Siberia because it is the preferred host to the fly agaric. This mushroom grows in mycorrhizal relationship with certain trees, and the tree that it prefers is the birch. It also grows at the foot of conifers, and I hold it to be no accident that the pine tree occupies a place second only to the birch as a cult focus for the forest tribesmen of Siberia. The relationship between birch and fly agaric has been known to mycologists only since 1885, but the natives of the Siberian forests have sensed it from time immemorial. If investigators have not discovered why the birch is a cult object, I think this is because they have not asked the right questions. The natives of the Chukotka and of the valleys of the Ob and Yenisei have not volunteered information that they regard as self-evident; in their world, any cretin would know why the birch is venerated. As for the mycologists, who certainly now know the birch–fly agaric relationship, they talk only to one another and *never* to anthropologists.

Uno Holmberg, in the *Mythology of all Races*, has summarized for us the folk beliefs that surround the birch. The spirit of the birch is a middle-aged woman who sometimes appears from the roots or trunk of the tree in response to the prayer of her devotee. She emerges to the waist, eyes grave, locks flowing, bosom bare, breasts swelling. She offers milk to the suppliant. He drinks, and his strength forthwith grows a hundredfold. The tale, repeated in myriad variations, clearly refers to the fly agaric, but none of Holmberg's sources has called this to his attention. What is the breast but the udder, *ūdhan*, of the Rig-Veda,

the swelling cap or *pileus* of the full-blown fly agaric? In another version
the tree yields "heavenly yellow liquor." What is this but the "tawny
yellow *pávamāna*" of the Rig-Veda? Repeatedly we hear of the Food
of Life, the Water of Life, the Lake of Milk that lies hidden, ready to
be tapped, near the roots of the Tree of Life. There where the Tree
grows is the Navel of the Earth, the Axis Mundi, the Cosmic Tree, the
Pillar of the World. What is this but the Mainstay-of-the-Sky that we
find in the Rig-Veda? The imagery is rich in synonyms and doublets.
The Pool of "heavenly yellow liquor" is often guarded by the chthonic
spirit, a Serpent, and surmounting the tree we hear of a spectacular
bird, capable of soaring to the heights, where the gods meet in con-
clave.

In brief, I submit that the legends of the Tree of Life and of the
Marvelous Herb had their genesis in the Forest Belt of Eurasia, the
tree being the towering Siberian birch, and the herb being the fly
agaric, Soma, the *pongo* of the Ugrian tribesmen. True, we are familiar
with this legend from the cuneiform inscriptions of Sumeria and the
countries lying to the west thereof. There the birch had become only a
memory, and it is an unanswerable question how much even their most
learned priests knew of the marvelous herb. But the legends were
powerful, speaking for the power of the original Soma, and they survive
in paintings, sculpture, and writings on clay. We must not forget that
the Sumerians, the shadowy Subarians, the Hittites, the Mitannians, and
yet others, known to us and unknown, had all hailed from the north,
and in their original homelands they or their neighbors knew the
marvelous herb by personal experience. They brought down with them
in their baggage all the tales about the herb and proceeded to write
them out in clay as soon as they had devised and mastered the art of
writing. It is a mistake to attribute the genesis of these ancient tales to
Mesopotamia and the Near East merely because these lands furnished
the clay on which they were first inscribed. Gilgamesh, our earliest epic
hero, dates from a recension written in the third millennium in Sumeria,
but he was already a legendary hero by that time. He went out to seek
the marvelous herb and found it in a watery place, only to have it
filched from him, as he slept, by the Serpent, its chthonic guardian,
more subtle than any beast of the field. The Semites at Mari and elsewhere lived in intimacy with the Sumerians and borrowed their stories,
as is well known, sometimes giving the stories a new twist. In *Genesis,*
is not the Serpent the self-same chthonic spirit that we know from
Siberia? The Tree of Life, is it not the legendary Birch Tree, and the
Forbidden Fruit of the Tree of Life, what else is it but the Soma, the
fly agaric, the *pongo* of the Ugrian tribesmen? The Indo-Iranians were
late-comers on the stage of history, but they brought down with them

the miraculous herb itself, and they bequeathed to us the strange, the breath-taking poems known as the Rig-Veda.

Hitherto the Soma-Haoma of the Indo-Iranians has been regarded as without parents or siblings. If my reconstruction of the legends holds good, the Soma of the Rig-Veda becomes incorporated into the religious history and prehistory of Eurasia, its parentage well established, its siblings numerous. Its role in human culture may go back far, to the time when our ancestors first lived with the birch and fly agaric, back perhaps through the Mesolithic and into the Paleolithic. We have here a web of interrelated beliefs that give to us a united field in a major area of primitive Eurasian religion.*

* And perhaps Amerindian religion as well. Much the same association of world (or shamanic) tree as symbolic *axis mundi,* with the pool of the water of life at its base, is found in the Americas, as is the chthonic guardian, the chimereal serpent. The prehistoric shaman's ascent of the sacred tree (and its functional counterpart in the great prehispanic religions, the ascent of the priest up the steep pyramidal stairway to the house of the god at the summit) still survives in some indigenous cultures of the New World. When applied to aboriginal beliefs and rituals in North and South America, Wasson's exploration into the origins and symbolic meanings of the tree of life support La Barre's recognition of powerful vestiges of the religions of Paleolithic and Mesolithic Asia in the religions of the American Indian. (See La Barre, below.)—ED.

8

WILLIAM A. EMBODEN, JR.

Ritual Use of *Cannabis Sativa* L.:
A Historical-Ethnographic Survey

Despite much writing to the contrary, there is but a single species of *Cannabis*—popularly called marihuana—and that is *Cannabis sativa* L., the cultivated hemp, so named by Linnaeus in 1753. Much of the confusion regarding the botanical identity of this historically and culturally fascinating plant stems from the botanical name changes it has undergone through time: to cite but a few examples, the pre-Linnaean botanists Bentham and Hooker treated *Cannabis* as a member of the nettle family, Urticaceae; later it was assigned to the mulberry family, Moraceae, and given its own tribe, Cannaboideae. More recently, anatomical and morphological studies assigned *Cannabis* to its own family, Cannabinaceae, within the order Urticales.

Although the common name "hemp" has come to be inextricably associated with this genus and species, there are actually more than twenty plant families that produce products known as hemp; the term can apply to any of a number of fibers of plant origin, so that *Cannabis* and hemp are not in fact synonymous.

There is only one species of *Cannabis,* but there is evidence to suggest that the plant has undergone natural selection and selection by man for perhaps 6000 years, and this fact, coupled with migration, has led to recognition of three varieties within the single species: *mexicana, americana (gigantea)*, and *indica*. The North American and Mexican varieties may achieve heights of up to twenty feet; the Indian variety (*indica*) is relatively small, but it produces a more potent resin and in greater abundance than the other varieties, which have developed in America since the introduction of *Cannabis* some time after the discovery and conquest of the New World.

Fig. 33.   A flowering plant of *Cannabis sativa.*

There is a certain degree of variation in the growth habits of *Cannabis;* most commonly it is found growing as an annual, which must be re-planted each year, but occasionally it assumes the habit of a perennial, developing in the process a heavy, woody stem. Sexes are usually found on separate plants (the dioecious condition), but occasionally a single plant is found to have both male and female parts, borne separately (the monoecious condition).* The leaves are digitate, with varying numbers of lobes and serrate margins.

All the plant parts bear trichomes, or hairs, of varying sorts. Some are simple and unbranched, others branched, and still others terminate in a gland which secretes resin. Another type of hair, called a scale, consists of a series of cells flattened in a plane parallel to the leaf surface; this type of trichome is also secretory. The frequency of capitate resin-producing glands supported by uniseriate or biseriate stalks is greatest on the female carpels. The frequency of glandular hairs is also greater on the female flowering parts than on the rest of the plant. The fruit coat covers the seed coat in such a manner as to conceal it and is densely

* Sex is determined by a $2n = 18 + xx$ or xy system, but variation in sex can be accounted for by heterozygous genes on x chromosomes and an occasional yy individual.

covered with glandular trichomes. Hairs with calcium carbonate deposits at the base are referred to as cystoliths. These are characteristic of *Cannabis* as well as of several genera in other families (cf. *Urtica*). The flowers of *Cannabis* are so minute on the female as to be quite inconspicuous, except as axillary clusters. On the male they are pendulous and conspicuous by reason of the yellow anthers, which produce pollen. After flowering (anthesis), the male plants die; however, the females persist until completion of fruiting.

The green pigment chlorophyll is essential to the growth of *Cannabis*. Therefore, we must regard as nonsense reports of seeds flushed into a sewer giving rise to plants that grew in darkness and were silver or white rather than green, and more potent than other plants. Accordingly, the oft-repeated tale of "Manhattan Silver" as an especially powerful variety of *Cannabis sativa* (Bloomquist, 1968) has no foundation in fact and is botanically unsound.

The herb that Linnaeus christened *Cannabis sativa* over two centuries ago originated somewhere in the desert region to the south and east of the Caspian Sea. As a cultivated plant it does not seem to be as old as some of the better-known Old-World food plants, but it certainly boasts respectable antiquity among cultigens. That it manifests itself today in a number of forms and that it has become adapted to a wide variety of climates and physical environments, ranging from the equator north to 60° latitude, is due largely or wholly to the intervention of man over a very long time: human exploitation of *Cannabis* is thought to reach back as far as 6000 years, with actual cultivation of *Cannabis* for a variety of purposes beginning only slightly more recently. If we are to believe Boyce (1900), a cloth made of the fibers of *Cannabis sativa* stem was found among 6000-year-old cultural remains in a cave in Europe. One may assume that the edible seeds of the plant were not ignored by the ancient cave dwellers. Of more exotic uses we cannot be certain. However, the earliest civilizations of Mesopotamia brewed intoxicating beer of barley more than 5000 years ago; is it too much to assume that even earlier cultures experienced euphoria, accidentally or deliberately, through inhalation of the resinous smoke of *Cannabis* while clothed in the coarse fibers of its stem?

THE CULTURAL USES OF *Cannabis*

China

It is quite certain that the ancient Chinese did not ignore the properties of this herb, for we have the pharmacopœia of the legendary Emperor Shen-Nung, allegedly compiled in 2737 B.C.* The ancient herbal recognizes both male and female plants, but there is a decided bias in favor of the female, or pistillate plant, evidently because it is the only sex that produces a significant amount of intoxicating resins. Shen-Nung, or "Divine Cultivator," is said to have founded Chinese medicine with the appearance of this herbal; during his experimentations with different plants he is said to have taken as many as twelve "poisons" a day. He must have tried exudate of *Cannabis* and given his approval, for he recommended it for "female weakness, gout, rheumatism, malaria, beriberi, constipation, and absent-mindedness."

By the fifteenth century B.C. the Chinese book known as the *Rh-Ya* was compiled, and in it there is mention of the herb *Ma*, the *Cannabis sativa* plant. Not only were the fibers and potent resins employed at this time, but the *Rh-Ya* describes the first ritualistic or shamanistic use of the plant.

The most detailed early account of the uses of *Cannabis sativa* in early China is to be found in the *Shu-King*, written in 500 B.C. (Bretschneider, 1870). When the plant grows under favorable conditions, the main stem becomes highly lignified, or woody. It was the practice of the early Chinese to carve this wood into the likeness of a serpent coiled around a rod (not unlike the caduceus or Staff of Aesculapius, which had its origin in the Greco-Roman world and is still with us as the traditional symbol of the physician). This image was used in curing rituals; a relative of the patient beat on the sickbed with the snake rod in order to dispel evil spirits.

Despite these descriptions, it is rather difficult to estimate the prestige of the plant in ancient China, for while we have early conservative warnings in which it is cursed as a "liberator of sin," we have equally ancient texts that call it the "giver of delights." In any event, its medical uses persisted in China for many centuries. In A.D. 220 the celebrated Chinese physician and surgeon Hua-T'o performed surgery using *Cannabis* resins mixed with wine, known as *Ma-Yo*, as an anesthetic, rather like the use of *Mandragora officinarium* roots and leaves mixed with *Atropa* leaves by the early Greeks. Both these preparations proved efficacious in relieving pain (*Cannabis* lulls the sensation of pain, while the mandrake and nightshade render the patient unconscious). Hua-T'o records testimonials by his patients praising their pain-free operations. Bloomquist (1968) states that the Chinese had no use for "technicolor

---

* Regarding the herbal of Shen-Nung, known as the *Pen Ts'ao Ching*, F. N. L. Poynter and H. L. Lei (1969) are of the opinion that it was really compiled in the late Han Dynasty, about the first century A.D. This is based on evidence that there was no written language in China in the third millennium B.C.

fantasies from hemp exudate"; I would suggest, rather, that the conservative element in China may have realized the potential threat to authority in a liberated younger generation given over to using the exudate of hemp, and for this reason inveighed against it. Conservative resistance was similarly manifested against the introduction of alcohol, tobacco, and even coffee.

Ancient Mediterranean

Nepenthe, that "potent destroyer of grief" of which the poet Homer wrote in the ninth century B.C. and which was first discussed in an Egyp-

Fig. 34.   The legendary Chinese Emperor Shen Nung, the "Divine Cultivator," who is credited with the introduction of agricultural implements and the discovery of the medicinal properties of plants in the third millennium B.C. His pharmacopoeia, which mentions both the male and female plants of *Cannabis sativa*, with their respective medical uses, is said to have been first compiled in 2737 B.C. Note the typically shamanic horns in the eighteenth-century French portrait, copied from an earlier Chinese painting.

tian papyrus dated *ca.* 1600 B.C., has been taken by some—most recently
Andrews and Vinkenoog (1969)—to refer to *Cannabis sativa.* I believe
this to· be in error. If we combine the testimony of Homer with that of
Diodorus Siculus, who wrote of the women of Thebes dispelling their
anxiety with nepenthe, we cannot escape the conclusion that the herb
or preparation in question was not *Cannabis* but the exudate of the
unripe capsules of the opium poppy, *Papaver somniferum,* or poppy milk
mixed with *Mandragora* (mandrake), *Hyosyamus* (henbane), *Atropa*
(deadly nightshade), and other herbs of similar soporific powers. Thus,
it was not *Cannabis* that Helen used to assuage her anguish but the milk
of the opium poppy. So popular was the latter that early Greek cameos
show the goddess of night, Nix, distributing poppy capsules; terra-cotta
figurines from Knossos with slit poppy capsules as coronas can also be
seen in museums. One city in early Greece was even known as Opion,
the City of the Opium Poppy.

Actually, the confusion should never have arisen in the first place. The
use of nepenthe and *Cannabis* was clearly differentiated. There is a
classic Greek term, *cannabeizein,* which means to smoke *Cannabis. Cannabeizein* frequently took the form of inhaling vapors from an incense
burner in which these resins were mixed with other resins, such as
myrrh, balsam, frankincense, and perfumes; this is the manner of the
shamanistic Ashera priestesses of the pre-Reformation temples in Jeru-
salem, who anointed their skins with the mixture, as well as burned it.
Cannabis is also the plant which Democritus (*ca.* 460 B.C.) knew as
potamaugis, and which he said was drunk with wine and myrrh to produce delirium and visionary states. Democritus observed the "immod-
erate laughter" that occurred erratically following a draught of this
decoction.* The first Greek botanist, Theophrastus (371–287 B.C.), wrote
of *Cannabis* under the name *dendromalache* and gave one of the first
accurate accounts of the plant.

Lucilius was the first Roman writer to give an account of *Cannabis,
ca.* 100 B.C. It was said to be so like hemp-agrimony in appearance that
some herbalists called it the cultivated hemp-agrimony.† There is no
doubt that the fiber obtained from the stem of *Cannabis* was prized over
that of *Agrimonium,* for the former was the cordage of most of the early
vessels; Hiero II, King of Syracuse, bought hemp fiber for the ropes of
his vessels in Gaul (France). So esteemed was the fiber that it figured

---

* Democritus himself was called by his compatriots "the laughing philosopher."

† Actually, the resemblance is superficial, in that both have palmate leaves with conspicuous serration along the margins. Both also produce a high-quality fiber from the
stem. However, hemp-agrimony (*Agrimonium cannabium*) belongs to the sunflower
family, Compositae, and no competent botanist could mistake the two plants. One is at
a loss to account for the choice of *Agrimonium* to adorn the cover of a book, by Andrews
and Vinkenoog (1969), which purports to be an authoritative history of *Cannabis.*

prominently in mythology: it was said to be the stuff that Penelope wove and tore apart to discourage her suitors during the absence of her husband, Ulysses, and the cord that Circe wove magically during the night. Could it also have been the mythical thread that *Atropos* measured out and severed in order to determine the life of a man? All these legends involve manufactured fiber as well as a mystical state of mind, and they are associated with cultures that were well aware of the plant, which embodied both economic and mystical properties.

Elaborating on the writings of the botanist Dioscorides, who preceded him by a century, the famous physician Galen (A.D. 130–200) spoke of *Cannabis* as a medicinal, but he also recorded a nonmedicinal, non-ritualistic use of *Cannabis* mixed with wine as a sweetmeat terminating heavy banquets. This confection promoted warmth and excited pleasure.

To ethnobotanists, one of the mysteries of the Ancient World is why the Egyptians should have preferred the cultivation of *Linum,* from which they obtained flax, or linen, to the cultivation of *Cannabis.* Certainly soil conditions and climate were favorable in the Nile Valley. Moreover, the fiber of *Cannabis* is in no way inferior to that of *Linum;* quite the contrary. Nevertheless, an analysis of the wrappings of numerous mummies has revealed that only flax fiber was used. Also, recent studies of embalming practices in ancient Egypt show that linseed oil, myrrh, balsam, and other oils and resins were used to coat the bodies, but not *Cannabis* resin. Both *Linum* and *Cannabis* provide an edible seed from which meal and oil can be obtained. Although both wine and beer were consumed in great quantities and also poured as libations to the gods, there is nowhere mention of hemp resins as part of such religious usage. Finally, it should be noted that no elements of any *Cannabis* cult are to be found in the Babylonian tablets relating the epic of Gilgamesh.

Arabia: Hasan and Scheherazade

Of the man from whom hashish got its name, al-Hasan ibn-al-Sabbah (A.D. 1124), only the sketchiest biographical data have survived.* He was probably a Persian by birth, some say from Tus. At an early age in the town of al-Rayy, he was tutored in the Batinite tradition. (The doctrine of *batin,* meaning inner, or esoteric, was founded in the ninth century A.D. by the Ismailites; its adherents believed the Koran should be interpreted allegorically and religious truth ascertained by the discovery of inner meaning, of which outer form was "but a veil intended to keep that truth from the eyes of the uninitiated.") A year and a half in

---

* For an authoritative analysis of Moslem sects, including that of al-Hasan, see Philip K. Hitti, *History of the Arabs* (London: Macmillan, 1968), from which some of the historical data in this section were drawn.

Egypt were sufficient to prepare him for his expected position as a missionary of the Fatimid caliphate, last of the medieval Moslem states, which had its center in Cairo. Back in his native land, it soon became obvious to those around al-Hasan that he was driven by strong personal ambition. He claimed to be a direct descendant of the Himyarite kings of South Arabia, and this assertion, together with his undoubted personal charisma, drew many young men to him. These dissenters from orthodox Moslem thought became known as hashishin, those of the "new word" (the full name of al-Hasan was Hashishin ibn-al Sabbah.) This term has become Anglicized as "Assassins."

In 1090 al-Hasan and his followers gained possession of the mountain fortress Alamut, situated in an extension of the Alburz mountain chain at 10,200 feet above sea level, near the towns of Baghdad and Basra. The name Alamut has been translated as "nest of the eagle," an apt description since it overlooked the shortest caravan route between the Caspian shore and the Persian highlands and thus gave al-Hasan and his men a most strategic position from which to launch surprise raids on those passing below.

The movement of the Assassins was essentially religiously motivated. Al-Hasan was not driven to assassinate those around him by bloodthirsty personal ambition, as has sometimes been claimed; rather, he and his followers felt that in order to promulgate their new religion, they first had to eliminate by whatever means necessary those who taught contradictory philosophies. As the sect developed, it drew away from the Ismailite tradition and became increasingly agnostic. The number of his followers grew to more than 12,000. All were part of a hierarchy, of which Hasan was "Grand Master," his closest companions "Grand Priors," those below them "Spreaders of the Faith," and those of the lowest order "Fiad'is," the executioners of all who were considered to be a threat to the faith. Alamut was maintained by the spoils derived from plundering the caravans from the East headed for Baghdad, and soon the fortress grew into elegant palaces, gardens, and pavilions of great wealth. Perhaps this was one of the attractions for the young men who joined the cult as "Fiad'is."

Marco Polo, who passed through the region in 1271, a half-century after al-Hasan's death, left this account of the "Grand Master's" court:

> He kept at his court a number of the youths of the country, from twelve to twenty years of age, such as had a taste for soldiering. . . . He would introduce them into his garden . . . having first made them drink a certain potion which cast them into a deep sleep. . . . When therefore they awoke and found themselves in a place so charming, they deemed it was Paradise . . . and the ladies and damsels dallied with them to their heart's

content. When the Old Man would have any prince slain, he would say to such a youth: "Go thou and slay So and So; and when thou returnest my Angels shall bear thee into Paradise."

There is no historical basis for the allegation that the slayers of al-Hasan did their work in states of malice or frenzy, intoxicated with hashish, or for the tales of depravity and debauchery at the court. These were promulgated by enemies of the Assassin cult and popularized by Marco Polo, among others. Most of the information we have about the Hashishin actually comes from the descendants of the Mongolian Hulagu, who in 1256 seized the fortress and palaces in Persia. At this time all the books and records of the cult were destroyed. In truth, the slaughter performed by the Assassins was less bloody and wanton than that which was then and later carried on in the name of another religious movement—Christianity. We do know that a member of the Assassins, Nizam-al-Mulk, was a founder of hospitals, observatories, and universities and was himself a statesman and scholar—hardly a picture that accords with the vicious character attributed to the sect and its adherents.

Attitudes of the time toward *Cannabis* are well reflected in that great favorite of Eastern and Western literary tradition, the Arabian epic *A Thousand and One Nights*. In a story told by Scheherazade on the 798th night, a Sultan in disguise has the misfortune of being deliberately urinated upon in the house of a *cadi*, or lowly magistrate, by another guest, a fisherman. The fisherman believed himself to be Sultan, for he had swallowed enough hashish "to destroy a hundred-year-old elephant." In the morning cadi and fisherman were called to the palace, where the Sultan revealed himself as the hapless guest of the night before. The cadi fell to his knees to beg for mercy, while the fisherman, to the Sultan's delight, replied, "What of it? You are in your palace this morning, we were in our palace last night." To the Sultan this truth was the "sweetest noise in all our kingdom," and he said to the fisherman, "We are both Sultans of this city." The implication, of course, is that the consumption of hashish was at least accepted, if not encouraged. This is supported also by the fact that at the beginning of the tale Scheherazade says, "Allah had willed that the cadi should also be given to the use of hashish." If hashish consumption had been beneath contempt, as al-Hasan's detractors claimed, tales of this period would hardly implicate Allah himself in the practice.

Asia Minor

The historically documented use of *Cannabis* in the funeral customs of the ancient Scythians, a nomadic people who ranged eastward as far as what is now central Siberia, appears to have originated with their defeat and brief domination by the Thracian Getae in the early sixth century B.C. The Getae were a well-organized society of horsemen and hunters, with a body of laws and a belief in the soul and a hereafter comparable to the Christian heaven or Germanic Valhalla. Their shamans, known as Kapnobatai, used hemp smoke to induce visions and oracular trances.

According to the German botanist Ludwig Wittmaack (1839–1929), we may assume from the discovery of *Cannabis* seed found in a Scythian funeral urn that the Scythians used hemp for nourishment and pleasure at least as early as the fifth century B.C. De Candolle (1869) goes so far as to suggest that the Scythians were disseminating *Cannabis* to other areas around 500 B.C. Non-Oriental Scythian shamanistic practices with *Cannabis* doubtless stemmed from the Getae. After anointing their heads, the mourners placed posts in the ground and wrapped them with cloth. They then rolled heated rocks from funeral fires and placed them in censers; it was on these rocks that the hemp was thrown, and the resulting vapors were inhaled. Herodotus, born in 484 B.C., tells that the Scythians howled with joy after such vapor baths, and that they danced and sang. An account by Aeschylus (525–456 B.C.) reports that the hemp was simply thrown on the fire and the smoke inhaled. Still another contemporary account tells of the smoldering herbs being covered with large skin blankets, which were periodically lifted so that all might inhale the accumulated vapors.

Herodotus makes no mention of shamanistic ritual in the ceremony, but he was given to such oversights. We can be reasonably certain that among the Scythians, as among other Turko-Tartar peoples, shamanic ecstasy played an important role in curing as well as funeral rites. It was one of the shaman's duties to act as psychopomp for the soul of the deceased, escorting it on its difficult journey to the netherworld. This the shaman was able to do by transporting himself into a state of mystical ecstasy, in which his soul left his body to serve as spiritual guide.* Then as now, psychotropic plant preparations played an important role. It is interesting that in a number of related Indo-European languages,

---

* The Soviet archaeologist S. I. Rudenko discovered additional archaeological evidence for the use of *Cannabis sativa* to induce trances in Scythian funeral rites during his excavations of the great burial mounds *(kurgans)* at Pazaryk, in the Altai, between 1947 and 1951. Rudenko found metal support rods and bronze censing vessels containing not only stones which had been heated to produce hemp-seed vapors but even the seeds themselves, some of them burnt. According to Rudenko, all these objects were used for purification ceremonies after the funeral, similar to those described by Herodotus in his report on the Scythians living on the shores of the Black Sea (Badasz, 1968: 65–66). The Swiss classical scholar K. Meuli (1935) suggests that the "howling" reported by Herodotus was nothing else but the characteristic shouting by shamans in their trances and that the entire purification rite must have been a form of shamanism, related to the shaman's role as psychopomp, the guide of the soul to the beyond. Interestingly enough, Meuli sees a relationship between the Scythian ecstatic vapor bath and the well-known curative vapor bath of Arctic peoples and American Indians.—ED.

bangha, the Iranian word for hemp, simultaneously refers to mushroom intoxication, hemp intoxication, and the hemp plant itself. Today in India, certain concoctions of *Cannabis* are known as *bhang,* and there are those who still insist that *bhang* is the Soma of the Vedic hymns, a contention with which R. Gordon Wasson especially has taken sharp issue.

Shamans or shaman-priests also used the ecstatic state for spiritual instruction. Zarathustra, the founder of Persian religious thought in the sixth century B.C., considered himself a shaman, or, as he himself termed it, a psychopomp. According to the Gathas, united in ecstasy with Zarathustra, the dead as well as the living disciples could commune between heaven and earth. Both melotherapy and versotherapy (music and chant) were necessary to the process, which had to occur in a *maga,* or enclosed space. This is curiously reminiscent of curing and divining rituals by shaman-like curers in Mexico and Peru, who intoxicate both themselves and their patients or supplicants with psychotropic plant decoctions in order to enter a mystical realm where causes and cures of illness or misfortune may be learned.

Sara Bentowa, of the Institute of Anthropological Sciences in Warsaw, has studied the original text of the Old Testament and its Aramaic translation, the Targum Onculos, and finds that the word for cane (*kane* or *kene*) appears both alone and linked to the adjective *bosm,* the Hebrew word for aromatic (in Aramaic *busma*) (Bentowa, 1936). According to the Polish scholar, both *kane bosm* of the Old Testament and the Aramaic *kene busma* refer to *Cannabis sativa.* In the Mishna, the collection of traditional Hebrew law, the *kanbos* bears an unmistakable affinity to the Assyro-Babylonian *kannab,* the Sanskrit *cana* and *sana,* and the Scythian *cannabis,* to mention but a few of the more than 100 synonyms compiled by Dr. Bentowa for this plant. She further traces the migration of the word with the migrations of the Semites through Asia Minor. A number of traditions developed around the hemp harvest that involved rituals based on intoxication from the volatile resins and oils. One such tradition was the offering of hemp seed as a sacrifice to one's ancestors. There seems to be an obvious link between such ritualistic gestures and the funeral ceremonies of the Scythians.

India

The most likely route of migration for *Cannabis* is from the tribes of Iran into India, where it did not grow indigenously. The contemplative nature of Hinduism had already led these people to the tranquilizing root of *Rauwolfia serpentina* and the sedative root of *Withania somnifera.* It may be that the prior acceptance of these plants facilitated the easy assimilation of *Cannabis* in India; in any event, it was soon inseparable from most of the religious philosophies. Consequently, the greatest vocabulary for *Cannabis* and its derivatives emerged from India. It became known as the "heavenly guide," and just as "Father Peyote" resides in the psychotropic cactus for some Indians of the southwestern United States, so a Guardian lived in the leaves of *Cannabis* for the early Indo-Iranians. Even a dream of the hemp plant was considered an omen of good fortune, and to long for it implied a future happiness. The resins had a pharmacological significance comparable to that outlined in the pharmacopœia of Shen-Nung. The Indian dispensaries claimed that it was efficacious in treating dysentery, sunstroke, phlegmatic tempers, indigestion, lack of appetite, lisping, and muddled intellect, among other disorders. It was believed that to experience *Cannabis* intoxication was to fix one's eyes on the Eternal. Hence, decoctions of *Cannabis* resin were used before reading holy writings or entering sacred places.

Andrews and Vinkenoog (1969) cite the hymns of the Rig-Veda in support of their contention that the sacred plant they celebrate (especially throughout the ninth book) as *soma* is *Cannabis*. However, although one of the earliest Sanskrit names for *Cannabis* is *sana,* meaning a hollow reed or cane, it cannot be equated with soma. Soma as a deity was the brother of Indra, and the Vedic hymns, which date prior to 1000 B.C., mention both Soma the god and soma as a plant. Although the two are inextricably intertwined and mention of the plant is made in at least three books of the Vedic hymns, none of the rather obscure descriptions fits *Cannabis*. R. Gordon Wasson, the undisputed authority on soma, has identified the sacred plant of the Rig-Vedas as the mushroom *Amanita muscaria*. Others have attempted to identify soma as *Sarcostemma acidum,* a leafless prostrate Asclepiad which is native to north India and Pakistan. Both *Amanita* and *Sarcostemma* have psychotropic properties, and either would be better suited to the descriptions of the Sanskrit soma than the distinctive leafy *Cannabis*.

It is true, however, that according to one tradition in India the resin of *Cannabis,* under the name *Vijaya,* was the favorite drink of the god Indra and that he gave it to the people so that they might attain elevated states of consciousness, delight in worldly joy, and freedom from fear. Hence it is customary for Hindus to throw idols into the river and rejoice with friends by embracing and drinking *bhang* * on the last day of the *Durga pooja*.

Africa

The route by which *Cannabis* entered Africa remains obscure, but presumably it came from India or Saudi Arabia. It seems to have been

---

* Bhang is a decoction of water, milk, *Cannabis* resin, cucumber and melon seeds, sugar, and black pepper.

in the Valley of the Zambezi in pre-Portuguese times—that is, before
A.D. 1500. None of the more elaborate techniques of using *Cannabis* in
the Mediterranean or the Near East accompanied the plant into Africa,
and practices in the central part of the continent in the thirteenth century were very simple. The confections which were known to Galen, such
as *Cannabis* wine, or the date, fig, raisin, nut, and *Cannabis* confection
of the North Africans, apparently had not reached central Africa at this
early date. The simple but efficacious practice of throwing hemp plants
on the burning coals of a fire and staging what might today be called a
"breathe-in" seems to have been popular initially. This was elaborated
into a ritual in which members of a given tribal unit would prostrate
themselves in a circle around the fire and each would extend a reed into
the fumes in order to capture the volatilized resins, without the accompanying irritation produced by standing over the vapors and inhaling.
At a later date the fire was elevated to an altar, where a man could sit
or stand while inhaling through a tube extending into the smoke.

The dervishes used *Cannabis* resins mixed with oils of seeds to produce
a "hypnotic" which, when drunk in that strength, induced a trancelike
sleep in which revelation was considered inevitable. In milder doses it
was used as a medicinal in cases of madness, hysteria, and convulsions
or spasms.

As the weed moved southward in Africa, the techniques of its consumption became more elaborated. The tribes of the Upper Zambezi
made a variety of pipes of gourds, bamboo stalks, and even coconut
bowls for smoking the resins and crude leaf material. It was the North
Africans who developed the water pipe, which cooled and to some
degree purified the smoke. Resins alone were used under the name *Kif*
in this apparatus.

When von Wissmann visited the Congo, in the late nineteenth century, he noted vestiges of *Cannabis* usage among the Balubas, a Bantu-
speaking tribe of the Belgian Congo. This was significant in that many
other tribes were subjugated by the Balubas, and their rituals were essentially the same. Hemp-smoking in this area seems to have originated in
1888, when Kalamba-Moukenge, then chief of the Balubas, ordered all
the ancient idols and fetishes of conquered territories to be publicly
burned. He realized that a multiplicity of tribal gods would hardly serve
as a unifying force, so he acted to strengthen his overlordship and bind
his subjects into one "nation" by replacing the old idols with a new and
more powerful one—*Cannabis!* On state and feast days, the Baluba
smoked hemp in gourd bowls one meter in circumference. In addition to
ritualistic use of *Cannabis,* men of the tribe frequently smoked hemp as
a pleasant evening pastime. Some subjects of Kalamba-Moukenge were

so impressed with the new *Cannabis* ritual that they united themselves under the name *bene-Riamba,* or sons of hemp.

The eminent composer and writer Paul Bowles, who has lived in North Africa for a number of years, identified more than twenty terms that apply to *Cannabis* or *kif* and its use in various guises among the North Africans (Bowles, 1962). So important is *Cannabis* in this area that, according to Bowles, the plant has been involved with some important areas of esthetics: "Music, literature and even certain aspects of architecture have evolved with *Cannabis*-directed appreciation in mind." Some homes actually have *kif* rooms, where family groups gather to sing, dance, and relate histories based on ancient cultural traditions.

North African men carry their *kif* in a *mottoni,* or pouch, of two to four compartments, each containing a different grade of *Cannabis.* Degrees of esteem or friendship are indicated by the quality of *kif* offered to another. Bowles points out that large numbers of Moslems have used *Cannabis* because alcohol is forbidden by Koranic law; any attempt to impose the Dionysian tradition upon these peoples, for whatever reasons, can lead only to a confusion of moral values. Although *kif* is outlawed in North Africa, the district of Ketama in the western Rif still produces crops of hemp on its steep hillsides and supplies most of Morocco. Lack of success in eradicating the habit is confirmed by recent visitors to the area, as well as by the trade in *chquofa,* clay pipes designed specifically for *kif* smoking.

Substitution of the physiologically addictive poison alcohol for the nonaddictive euphoriant *kif* seems to be inevitable in Africa. However, a new nationalistic trend, increasingly more apparent, may help to preserve the old traditions.

The Origin of a European Ritual

Although *Cannabis* must have been available in Western Europe since relatively early times, little interest was shown in the plant until *ca.* 1800, when Napoleon's battered army returned to France from the Egyptian campaign with hemp resins to sustain them. From Egypt itself the earliest records of hemp cultivation and the use of hemp resin date from the eighteenth century. The custom was not readily assimilated by the populace of cosmopolitan France, but in Paris a group of avant-garde writers and artists found considerable pleasure in this new euphoriant and founded a *Cannabis* ritual, well documented by Theophile Gautier, who wrote of the odd gathering in a *feuilleton* of *La Presse Medicale* (n.d.) and in the *Revue des Deux Mondes* of 1846. The ritual was certainly French in character, notwithstanding both Egyptian and Algerian antecedents.

A certain Dr. Jacques Joseph Moreau, of the Hôpital de Bicetre, was responsible for introducing the use of *Cannabis* resins in the hospital for the mentally ill. Dr. Moreau had investigated some of the potions used in the Middle Ages for treating mental illness and had used extractions of *Datura stramonium,* or Jimson weed, with some success in treating his patients. In 1841 Dr. Moreau substituted hashish for *Datura* and, after three years of experimentation, published his studies along with an appendix of observations by Gautier. Almost a decade before the association with Dr. Moreau, Gautier had attained his literary laurels with the perverse and brilliant *Mademoiselle de Maupin.* In the preface to this chronicle of a transvestite, Gautier proclaimed that abandonment to the senses was the will of God, an attitude that later became the manifesto of the decadents. It is not surprising that a man to whom the "superfluous" was the most essential element of life should found an organization devoted to the veneration of the senses in the form provided by *Cannabis.*

Le Club des Haschischins, formed in 1844, found a home in the elegant Hotel Pinodan on the fashionable Île St. Louis. Gautier's description of the hotel, built by Lauzun, suggests an atmosphere that was certainly conducive to hallucinations. Meetings were held monthly, as regularly as any religious service and with equal attention to the appointments to the ceremony—flickering lights, ceilings painted with mythological scenes, Venetian goblets, fine porcelain, velvet tapestries from Utrecht, and Egyptian chimeras, all provided elements of the phantasmagoria that was part and parcel of *Le Club.* Doctor Moreau would dispense the intoxicating resins from a crystal vase, pronouncing with each spoonful the sententious dictum, "This will be deducted from your share in paradise."

Each participant would down the green paste and then drink coffee in the Arab manner, without sugar and heavy on the grounds. A banquet followed the *Cannabis* hôrs d'oeuvres. It was not until the end of the feast that the members would begin to feel the intoxication that would culminate in hallucinations. The environment reinforced this vision state, and music was introduced for the further delectation of the guests. According to Baudelaire, the uninitiated were bound to be disappointed in their expectations of marvelous visionary experiences, for "man cannot escape the fatality of his physical and moral temperament. Hashish will be for a man's familiar thoughts and impressions a mirror that exaggerates, but always a mirror." However, it is difficult to assess the writings of Baudelaire on the effects of hashish, since he was so given to a mixture of opium and alcohol that the influence of the different drugs is likely to have been inseparable.

Perhaps the most interesting aspect of the European use of *Cannabis* is its ritualistic nature. Baudelaire had had access to *Cannabis* in his earlier travels in India, and Gautier had used this substance in his experiments with Dr. Moreau; however, they and the other members of *Le Club* preferred a group ceremony in which their visions might to some degree be shared with the other participants—shades of howling Scythians! *

A New World Ceremony in Mexico

Although *Cannabis* was unknown in the New World prior to the Conquest and most Indian groups continue to spurn it as alien to their indigenous culture, of late there have been reports of rituals in which marihuana has come to replace hard-to-get aboriginal hallucinogens. As early as 1902 the pioneer ethnographer Carl Lumholtz reported that "Tepecanos" (Tepehuano) in northwest Mexico sometimes substituted *Cannabis sativa,* which they called *rosa maria,* when peyote was not available from neighboring Huichol Indians.

A particularly interesting account of a Tepehua (no relation to "Tepecano") Indian ceremony with *Cannabis* was published in 1963 by the Mexican ethnologist Roberto Williams García of the University of Veracruz, Mexico.† The Tepehua, who live in scattered communities in the mountains of Veracruz, Hidalgo, and Puebla, belong linguistically and culturally to the Totonac of Veracruz, northernmost branch of the Maya language family, but their culture, especially the non-Christian elements in their religious beliefs and rituals, are very close also to those of Nahua and Otomí-speaking Indians of Veracruz and adjacent states in southeastern Mexico.

In his account of Tepehua religion and ritual, Williams García (1963: 215–21) describes in some detail a communal curing ceremony focused on a plant called *santa rosa,* "The Herb Which Makes One Speak," which he identified botanically as *Cannabis sativa:*

The ritual takes place in the community of San Pedro, under the direction of a diviner or shaman named Antonio. The reputation of the

---

* And, for that matter, of marihuana-using G.I.'s in Vietnam. CBS News in 1970 broadcast an extraordinary film of a marihuana "ritual" in which soldiers employed a shotgun—"anthropomorphized" as "Ralph"—to inhale large quantities of marihuana smoke. As depicted in the television news film, the combat unit's leader ejected the shells from his shotgun, inserted a lighted marihuana pipe in the breech and then blew the smoke through the barrel directly into the mouth of each of his men in turn! There are some interesting implications in such a use for a weapon of death, especially since bamboo was readily available to achieve the same effect (but without the same symbolism). The use of a gun here is reminiscent of the manner in which the Waika Indians of Venezuela blow charges of a powerful hallucinogenic snuff into one another's nostrils with a long tube. This tube, though shorter than the blowgun, is otherwise similar to this deadly hunting weapon. It is unlikely that the Army unit had access to this bit of anthropological information, so that their particular communal way of ingesting the euphoriant must be regarded as spontaneous ritualization.—ED.

† I am indebted to Peter T. Furst for this reference.

herb is great, for it is said to have the power to induce a fleeting "madness" which can be calmed only by the shaman. In the hut of Antonio there is an altar with candles, plates, crystals, and small archaeological clay heads used in divination. On an upper platform are images of saints, and especially of the Virgin, who is considered to be a companion of the divine Sun. Boxes beneath the altar contain cutout barkpaper spirit figures (*muñecas,* or dolls),* which are taken out for this ceremony of purification. Ashes, representing the extinction of life, and earth from the cemetery are symbolically placed on the altar to represent the sacred place where such a ceremony should properly be performed. They also have the effect of removing impure air and freeing the people of evil spirits.

Two female attendants wash the hands and feet of the diviner, and he in turn ritually washes ears of corn. He enters the room, distributes flowers, and squats to pray; upon rising he cleanses the participants with branches of lemon. *Costumbre* (native ritual) music is played by temple musicians while Antonio stands at the altar and arranges branches that have been purified by the smoke of a censer. The participants are invited to seat themselves, holding burning candles. Antonio prays, blows on a whistle, and rings a bell. He touches them on the shoulder with the purified branches, upon which they are required to spit.† One of the women does the same for Antonio. He then lights the altar candles and concludes the homage to the ancestors and the purification of the participants.

The group then moves to an adjacent hut which contains an altar bearing the Sacred Heart of Jesus and a plate, covered by a cloth, with the herb *santa rosa.* This is taken back to the temple and distributed ceremoniously to the participants, to be eaten by them. The female participants dance in a circle and speak in a high voice. The atmosphere is by no means solemn; rather, there is light conversation, occasionally interrupted by laughter. Leaving the temple the group moves to a cross in an adjoining patio, where they genuflect and prostrate themselves, after which they re-enter the temple. Speech now becomes oratory and the entire atmosphere changes to one of fervent music, song, declamations, ringing of bells, rhythmic movement, dancing, whistling, and prayer.

---

* These cutout spirit figures are characteristically Otomí, attesting to the strong influence Otomían culture has had on the Tepehua. Otomí shamans use them widely for curing and sorcery as well as in connection with fertility rituals for crops and fields, as do the shamans of the Tepehua. Although the art of bark-papermaking survives in several parts of Mexico, the real center of this ancient craft is the Otomí village of San Pablito, in the Sierra de Puebla, where bark paper is traded widely. The art of bark-papermaking is an old one; stone bark beaters have been found in archaeological contexts dating to 900 B.C.—ED.

† Spittle in general, but especially in a ritual context, is a symbol of transcendance.—ED.

One old man, who had been given a considerable quantity of *santa rosa* for assisting Antonio, is said to be speaking to the sanctified herb. Antonio prays and then dances with a handkerchief, an act signifying that children of the village who are sick with the grippe are now cured. Soon the music ceases and soft drinks are passed around. Day breaks, the intoxication is wearing off, and the ceremony is near an end. Only a few ritual ingredients remain to be used up by the participants before they return to their everyday pursuits.

According to Williams García, *santa rosa* is considered both herb and intercessor with the Virgin. It is worshiped as an earth deity and is thought to be alive and comparable to a piece of the heart of God. It is also dangerous: were it not for prayers and rituals, it could affect people adversely. It could assume the form of a man's shadow (soul) and make him sick, put him in a rage, or even lead to his death.

A recent personal communication from a North American ethnobotanist, David Wheeler, who has spent several years in the state of Oaxaca among several groups of Indians, provides interesting corroboration of Williams García's observations among the Tepehua. As is known, mushroom cults focused on several varieties of hallucinogenic fungi flourish in Oaxaca. Less well known is the fact that several other hallucinogenic plants, including *Heimia salicifolia, Calea zacatechichi, Genista canariensis, Salvia divinorum, Rivea corymbosa,* and *Ipomea violacea,* are also used in Oaxaca, either when mushrooms are unavailable or as the preferred mystical substance in curing and other rituals. *Genista canariensis,* as the name implies, is an introduction from the Canary Islands, and one of the mushrooms used ritually is also an importation from the Caribbean. In cultures so attuned to the use of psychotomimetics it is perhaps not surprising that yet another alien plant, *Cannabis sativa,* should have found ready acceptance, at least in one area of the highlands.

The advantages of growing *Cannabis* in the volcanic soils of the highlands are considerable. Of the nine-odd cannabinols found in *Cannabis sativa,* the delta-1 form is by far the most active. However, the amount of ultraviolet light striking these plants may convert relatively inactive isomers into potent forms. The agricultural traditions among the Indians here are very ancient; long experimentation has led to the production of a variety of excellent crops perfectly adapted to the varied climates and soil conditions of the mountains and valleys. It is hardly surprising that such experienced farmers should have discovered in short order that the finest *Cannabis* is derived from plants that do not flourish in the usual sense but have been "tortured" by an extreme environment and by unusual pruning practices.

According to Wheeler, when the plants are just beyond the cotyle-donary, or seedling, stage, they are pinched so as to remove the apical meristem which terminates the shoot tip. This part of the plant is responsible for the production of auxins, plant hormones, and the absence of this site of synthesis causes lateral meristems, or side shoots, to become active. Thus, instead of the usual tall cane, a small bush is produced. Once every week the plant is pinched in such a manner as to keep it within a few feet of the ground. The form it assumes in the course of such pruning is that of an urn. Shoots which would normally fill the interior are removed, so that as resins are formed they volatilize within the confines of the urnlike shrub. At maturity this strange crop resembles a topiary of sorts, the grotesque "urns" being so heavily coated with resins that the surface of the plant has a crystalline appearance. Pinching is so frequent as to interfere with the normal flowering of the females, and the auxin changes also lead to changes in pigmentation in some instances. Cyanins, which give a red appearance to plants, may accumulate, lending the plants an acharacteristic color as well as form. The leaf morphology is so changed that palmate leaves are no longer characteristic, being replaced by verticillate balls of entire leaves and abortive flowers. Indeed, the botanist would be hard pressed to identify the genus of these tortured plants.

That these practices figure in the syncretic Christo-pagan religious traditions of the local population is hardly surprising. The red color, the copious exudation of crystalline resin, akin in appearance both to sacred copal and to traditional shamanistic rock crystals, and the urn shape probably all contribute to ritualization of this psychotomimetic botanical import. Of great interest in this connection is the peculiar mode of harvesting *Cannabis*. As the bloodlike color begins to appear, the plants are "crucified" by inserting wooden splinters through the stem at right angles to one another just above the ground. The effects of this practice on the physiology of the plant are not known, but one might assume that this act of crucifixion has implications beyond the purely ritual, even if the Indians are concerned only with the latter. It is possible, for example, that wound hormones produced in response to the piercing with wooden splinters may enhance the quality of the resins even beyond what is accomplished by the pruning practices described above.

Be that as it may, the resultant material is especially effective, acting rather like hashish. However, it does *not* constitute the hashish of illegal drug traffic, since it is utilized exclusively in the area in which it grows and for ritual purposes akin to those involving the use of indigenous hallucinogens.

CHEMISTRY AND EFFECTS OF *Cannabis* RESINS

It is the resins of the *Cannabis* plant that are responsible for the euphoriating properties. In Nepal, one of the few areas of the world where marihuana use is now legal, the resins were once collected by having naked men run through the fields planted to marihuana and then scraping off the sticky substance that adhered to their skin; a more sanitary mode of harvesting was to have the men wear leather aprons which were scraped, eliminating body hair and perspiration that might impede marketability. At one time the resins were listed in the U.S. Pharmacopoeia as a tincture for treating fatigue, fits of coughing, rheumatism, asthma, delirium tremens, migraine headaches, and the cramps and depressions associated with menstruation. The Tax Act of 1937 imposed such rigid controls on the use of *Cannabis* that it was effectively eliminated from most drug dispensaries. Cannabinols, of which more than eighty have been isolated from *Cannabis sativa,* form the group to which the active principles belong. Although a number of these have been ascertained to be active euphoriants, the delta-1 form of tetrahydrocannabinol is believed to be of primary activity, and in laboratory synthesis the synthetic product obtained has most of the quality that occurs in resins.

The drug acts mostly on the central nervous system. In moderate doses the effects on laboratory animals and in man are the induction of euphoria, or a dreamy, nonaggressive, semisomnolent state. Unless one is working with synthetic THC (tetrahydrocannabinol), dosages are difficult to determine because of the qualitative differences in resins coming from different varieties of plants in nature.

Massive doses of the resins have been given to dogs without causing death, and there is no recorded fatality from overdosing with either the natural resins or THC in man, stories to the contrary notwithstanding. Fitzhugh Ludlow, who popularized *Cannabis* in alarmist language in a chronicle which appeared serially in *Harpers'* Magazine, owes much to his reading of De Quincey's *Diary of an English Opium Eater,* and one can hardly take his claims of "horrible addiction" seriously. The death of Baudelaire, attributed by some to hemp resins, may be more realistically laid to advanced tertiary syphilis, opiate addiction, and alcoholism.

Most *Cannabis* in the United States is smoked as a crude leaf material, known as marihuana. The "high" it produces lasts from two to four hours, whereas ingestion of the resins lasts twelve or more. The state produced has been described as having a duality in which the individual may be both high and objectively aware of his subjective state. Thus, it is possible for a person to be under the influence of marihuana and yet perform routine duties with considerably greater competence than an individual who is lightly intoxicated by alcohol. Surprisingly, this has been shown to apply even to driving an automobile, in tests conducted by the University of Oregon and the Oregon Department of Motor Vehicles with both alcohol and marihuana. (Needless to say, because of individual variability and other reasons, one would hardly advocate mixing marihuana smoking with driving.)

Perhaps the only noticeable effect of marihuana use is altered time and space perception, which also accounts for obviously altered speech pattern while under *Cannabis* influence. Weil and Zinberg (1969) have reported on interference with retrieval of information from immediate memory storage in the brain, but at this writing this is the only scientifically acceptable study that points to a "danger" from using moderate amounts of this material. We must await the findings of more scientific studies and long-term research to ascertain whether or not there might be other major health hazards associated with the use of these resins. Recently it has been pointed out that inexperienced individuals (the drug-naive group) show lessened motor coordination when under the influence of marihuana while experienced users may actually show improvement, as evidenced by standard performance tests (Weil, Zinberg, and Nelsen, 1968).* Other physiological changes, such as hunger, increased urination, etc., are curious but negligible effects.

SOME CONCLUSIONS

Available evidence to date suggests that *Cannabis* may have been used as a gathered, if not cultivated, plant as early as the Late Neolithic and that, with the exception of Egypt, it was one of the most prominent cultigens in Bronze and Iron Age civilizations. The Scythians may have

---

* Results of an interesting study on the disposition and metabolism of delta-9 tetrahydrocannabinol in man by four researchers of the National Institute of Mental Health were reported by Lemberger *et al.* in the journal *Science,* Vol. 170 (1970), pp. 1320–22. The researchers found that the major active component of marihuana, D-9-THC, administered intravenously to normal human volunteers persists in plasma for more than three days, that tetrahydrocannabinol is completely metabolized, and that the radioactive metabolites are excreted in urine and feces for more than eight days. The report suggests that THC, as a nonpolar compound, may accumulate in fat or other tissues, such as those of the lung, which have an affinity for drugs. "If, indeed, the D-9-THC is found in the lung, then in man this would be even more significant since inhalation is the usual route of administration," according to the researchers. THC accumulation in the tissues, they write, may explain in part the phenomenon of so-called "reverse tolerance" in chronic users of marihuana (who may need progressively smaller doses to achieve the desired euphoriant effect, in contrast to the need for ever-larger doses in addictive narcotics such as heroin); possibly, the report states, "a critical degree of tissue saturation must be attained before effective threshold levels of D-9-THC can be achieved." It may also explain in part why novice users of marihuana often report no effect whatever from their first experimentations with *Cannabis.*—ED.

cultivated the plant for some time before employing it ritually, for De Candolle in 1869 adduced evidence that they transported *Cannabis* from Central Asia and Russia during their westward migrations just before the Trojan War, or *ca.* 1200–1300 B.C. He mentioned that it might have been disseminated by earlier incursions of the "Aryans" into Thrace and Western Europe but was unable to produce evidence to support this.

Shamanistic traditions of great antiquity in Asia and the Near East had as one of their most important elements the attempt to find God without a vale of tears; that *Cannabis* played a role in this, at least in some areas, is borne out in the philology surrounding the ritualistic use of the plant. Whereas Western religious traditions generally stress sin, repentance, and mortification of the flesh, certain older non-Western religious cults seem to have employed *Cannabis* as a euphoriant, which allowed the participant a joyous path to the Ultimate; hence such appellations as "heavenly guide."

The North African tradition involving *Cannabis* is closely bound up with the Koranic injunction against alcohol. The cultural context of *Cannabis* use is the family tradition, in which the members gather in a special *Kif* chamber for the purpose of relating oral histories. Recent attempts to substitute alcohol for *Cannabis* amount to forced culture change, with potentially harmful effects on the traditional system.

The adoption of *Cannabis* by Mexican Indians into their syncretic traditional-Christian rituals and beliefs, especially in connection with curing, is particularly interesting since *Cannabis* is of Old World origin, introduced after the Conquest into a cultural area already strongly predisposed toward the use of mind-altering substances. It would be too much to say that *Cannabis* is replacing aboriginal sacred hallucinogens, such as morning-glories, peyote, or mushrooms. But it does appear to have taken root and even been sanctified in local areas, perhaps because more traditional psychotomimetics are difficult to obtain or, like *Datura,* are actually physiologically dangerous. Of some interest also is the spontaneous development of marihuana "rituals" in the United States, which is otherwise increasingly undergoing secularization. These rituals are in clear opposition to the cultural traditions of the larger society, which values aggressiveness and achievement as opposed to introspection and passivity.

Studies to date on *Cannabis* are inconclusive with respect to total physiological effects, especially on chronic users. Excessively large doses of hashish over a period of time may well have deleterious effects, but this would apply to a very small number of *Cannabis* users—a fraction, certainly, of the number of persons who habitually use alcohol to excess. Clearly much more research is needed, not only in Western societies, where *Cannabis* is rapidly becoming a "social drug," but historically in societies that have focused on *Cannabis* (and other psychotropic substances) in a ritual way. In the meantime, is it not obvious that the social costs of enforcing laws based essentially on the hysteria of the 1930's rather than on dispassionate scientific research are out of proportion to the actual or presumed harm done by this ancient euphoriant? Surely one of the most deleterious results of the law—modified recently, to be sure, but still punitive—is precisely a cause-and-effect relationship so often charged to *Cannabis:* that it leads to the use of other, more dangerous, and truly addictive drugs. The cause-and-effect relationship is not physiological, however, but social, because by having driven *Cannabis* underground the law forces young people into contact with criminal elements whose motivation is neither ritual nor altruistic but commercial.

There is an additional factor, which touches on the relationship of the dominant white society to its minorities. On a television program on drug abuse produced by KNXT, the CBS station in Los Angeles, in 1970, a young female participant from the Spanish-speaking community observed that marihuana had become so expensive that only affluent middle-class whites could afford it, while minority youth seeking momentary relief from unbearable pressures were forced by economics to resort to more readily available and cheaper amphetamines and other potentially far more harmful drugs.*

To an ethnobotanist concerned with the complex interrelationship, through time, between man and the plant kingdom, especially its numerous intoxicants and euphoriants, it is ironic that *Cannabis,* which only a few years ago was associated in the public mind exclusively with the poor black and brown minorities, should have joined the long list of social drugs of our drug-oriented, affluent, white middle-class society, while being priced out of reach of those on the bottom rung of the economic ladder. It is doubly ironic if we speculate that some of the remote Mediterranean, Near Eastern, and African ancestors of these minorities might have been among those who long ago used *Cannabis* as a divine plant and "guide to heaven."

---

* It may be recalled that it was the avowed intent of the U.S. Justice Department's "Operation Intercept" to drive the price of marihuana beyond the reach of young people by impeding its importation across the Mexican border. One could also attribute the widespread experimentation with potentially deadly, wild-growing plants for hallucinogenic purposes at least in part to the economics and legal dangers of the marihuana market. To cite only one example, a recent "underground" publication, *Herbal Highs,* by one "Maryjane Superweed," lists a number of deadly poisonous plants as psychedelics and encourages them as "legal highs." The popularity of this spurious guide is such that I was barely able to get the last copy in a Hollywood "head shop." Several of the listed plants are misidentified, as are some of the illustrations; on the whole these "alternatives" to marihuana are frightening. The author, whoever he or she may be, may be responsible for the death of or permanent injury to a number of misinformed youths.

9

JAMES W. FERNANDEZ

Tabernanthe Iboga: Narcotic Ecstasis and the Work of the Ancestors

Right at the start I am going to impose upon the reader a conceptual continuum and a confession. At least he is forewarned where certain habits of thought may reach. The continuum is the familiar one between instrumental behavior on the one hand and expressive behavior on the other. Instrumental behavior is behavior in which we seek to change things in the object world by manipulating them in some way, usually to the benefit of ourselves. Expressive behavior is behavior in which we seek to change things within ourselves by giving outward expression to inward states. In instrumental behavior we interiorize. We make as accurate a model as we can of the external world and, conforming our behavior to that model, we hope to influence the world. We have been more successful in this than Francis Bacon, the great interiorizer, could have ever hoped. In expressive behavior we exteriorize. We bring forth the lights and shadows of interior weather and let them play willy-nilly upon the object world, often to creative effect. The distinction we are making is sometimes made, as is appropriate in the age of polymers, between autoplastic and alloplastic action: that is, action that seeks to change the self, and action that seeks to change everything else. There are undoubtedly philosophic and behavioral difficulties with such a clean distinction. But we hope our discussion of an African narcotic will be of enough interest to carry us beyond the abuse of terms.

Now, here is the confession. When one chooses to become an anthropologist—as opposed to some other choice well within the mainstream of one's culture, such as businessman, lawyer, physician, or even theologian—one expects to have the experience of other cultural realities, other world views. One might say that the anthropological

career decision expresses, in most of those who make it, the conviction
that realities are not completely given but are always in important part
expressed and defined, and that men have available a multitude of
ways in which to define their situation. Most career decisions are quite
different in that they are instrumental. One asks: Given the realities
of the situation in which I find myself, what must I do to maximize
the values available to me and to others, and to minimize the afflictions
to which I and others are susceptible? Of course, anthropologists ask
such questions as these—the so-called minimax questions. But at the
very beginning, I think, the decided anthropologist, however otherwise
pragmatic, has questioned ontology itself. "Show me other realities: I
know how much the present one is consensual and not virtual!"

In any case, for me such a major premise has always been present
though inarticulated. And I have not been disillusioned. In fact I have
been privileged to have access to other realities, for which I am very
grateful. I would like to explore some of that experience in the present
paper. Given our over-all theme, I should perhaps state here and now
that this exploration has been for me almost entirely without benefit
of drugs. In fact, I have never had a complete drug experience. That
is not, as it turns out, my path to knowledge. The most that hallucinatory drugs produce in me is anxiety, nausea, some dissociation and
lightness of body. Perhaps that is because I hold too much to the
instrumental view that the sleep of reason produces monsters. Still, as I
have been saying, to a very important extent I am convinced that
"*la vida es sueño*." Hence, I am convinced we can learn important things
from the study of what we ordinarily regard as excessive psychological
states.

African Religious Movements

For the past decade I have been studying—interiorizing—religious
movements in various parts of sub-Saharan Africa: Gabon, South
Africa, Zambia, Dahomey, Togo, Ghana. These movements—often called
revitalization movements in the literature—are caught between the
lingering relevance of traditional religions and a certain authority which
they recognize in Christianity, compounded of some attractive aspects
of the Christian message, in particular the Old Testament (but not
excluding the moral vision of such New Testament messages as the
Sermon on the Mount), and the conviction and determination with
which missionaries undertook the evangelical enterprise.

We speak of these movements as revitalization movements for several
reasons. First, they attempt to create new wholes—new integrations of

dissonant experience—for the situation of culture contact is a situation of dispiriting disparities. Religious traditions with quite differing emphases on the nature of the supernatural, the shape of evil, and the importance of ritual face each other. There is even disagreement as to whether God is One or a Lineage of decreasingly powerful creators, and as to whether He is ever-present or a long-departed and now simply a philosophical first principle whose only purpose is to lay inquiry to rest. Secondly, these movements face the fact that the colonial situation imposes an inferiority and dependency which are devitalizing. These movements are in many respects self-isolating and seek a self-sufficiency that can arise only by dwelling in one's own universe rather than in a universe created and imposed by the Western civilization—a very instrumental one—of science and technology. For that is a civilization appropriated in virtually every particular by Western skills and know-how. Naturally, men are led to seek within themselves for other resources.

In response, then, to the confusions of culture contact and the affliction of implied incompetence, some Africans of talent and character have undertaken to celebrate their own world view by creating, in microcosm at least, their own religious world in which to dwell. Although these movements are pervasive throughout Africa and probably run into the many thousands—there are more than 1500 in South Africa alone—it is rare that more than a small minority of any population claims membership or actively participates. The figure would be not much more than 8 per cent of the population in any African state. These movements are of many varieties, ranging from those that, for all intents and purposes, are fully Christian to those that are very traditional-nativistic.

A convenient way to think about these movements is to type them on two continua: the one we have already defined, between instrumental and expressive behavior, and the other between a fully Christian symbolism and a traditional symbolism. These continua give us a biaxial coordinate system with four main types of movement: (1) *separatist movements* that have separated from missionary-founded churches for instrumental reasons—usually because they have objected to disparities in the distribution of power and resources between missionaries and African converts; (2) *messianic movements* that maintain a strong Christian orientation but are involved, not with manipulating the external world, but with giving vent to urgent internal feelings, often painful; (3) *reformative movements,* which are very much aware of their relation to the object world and eager to improve their position within it but have a commitment to traditional religious ways; and

(4) *nativist movements,* whose chief concern is to give expression to their commitment to traditional religious ways through traditional symbols.*

It would be even more convenient if we could say that those cults at the expressive end of the chart were those in which we find the use of psychoactive drugs, since such use would seem to imply a preoccupation with internal states—or at least lead to such a preoccupation—and with the exteriorizing of these internal states irrespective of the object world. But this cannot be said without qualification. First of all, drug use is not widespread in these movements in Africa. Although *Cannabis* in one form or another is used throughout Africa, and although there is, I believe, a tendency for expressive cults to employ marihuana, I have no evidence of a significant correlation unless we employ drug use as a defining characteristic of expressiveness, as I have not done. Cults that seem quite instrumental for most purposes use drugs. In fact, the cult we concentrate on here, *Bwiti,* has shown in many respects an instrumental object world orientation; I have typed it as reformative. But let us not belabor our own model. I intend it here as a convenience only. It would be useless to try to coerce all the data into its forms. The fact is that in Bwiti the use of the drug *Tabernanthe iboga (eboka)* seems to be quite practical and realistic as far as the members are concerned.

THE BWITI CULT OF GABON

I wish I could play the music of Bwiti to the reader as I did during the lecture on which this paper is based. That is the best way to convey a feeling for the expression in this cult, which is filled with music and dance—more than a dozen different dances and several hundred songs. The old saying well describes the attitude of the members of Bwiti: "He who knows the power of the dance dwells in God!" Well before the all-night ceremonies begin (after 8:00 P.M.), the insistent rhythms of the cult harp *(ngombi)* and the soft beat of the bamboo staves *(obaka)* build up in the membership an expectation and a spirit of engagement that are integral to successful cult performance. Men must be powerfully attracted to engage themselves in an all-night rite. And *eboka,* as we shall see, is a great aid to the success of their performance.

What seemed to me the most beautiful music is performed in the early morning hours, after the spirits of men and ancestors have mingled in the cult chapel and after the membership has achieved a state of what they call "one-heartedness"—*nlem mvore.* These concluding songs celebrate the state of grace or good luck *(okan)* which the membership

* A more extensive discussion of this classificatory scheme and particularly its dynamic qualities can be found in J. W. Fernandez, 1964, 1969.

has achieved and also bid farewell to the ancestors, departing again for the village of the dead. Dawn is faintly evident over the equatorial forest wall to the east. The first cock has crowed. All cult activities must be concluded before the sun rises, for Bwiti is a night cult, a cult of the female principle of the universe, Nyingwan Mebege, the Sister of God, who is the moon. There is deep satisfaction in the membership born of the fact that they have danced all night, achieved "one-heartedness," and can look forward to the fellowship of the communal meal, which comes immediately after the cultic activities. It is an afterglow brought to them by *eboka* as well, for the drug is not usually associated with undesirable aftereffects. The work of the ancestors *(eseñ bimvama)* has been satisfactorily completed.

There are actually two new cults among the Fang that use *eboka*: Bwiti and MBiri. Both have been adopted, at the time of World War I, by the southernmost subtribes of the Fang from more southern and western Equatorial people upon whom the Fang, a Bantu-speaking people, have intruded in their southward migration. (Southern Fang have always shown a greater diversity of cults and complexity of cult life than northern Fang, probably because of the frontier cultural influences to which they were constantly exposed.)

The Bwiti cult is a syncretism of influences from the Bwiti cult of the dead found among southern Gabonese cultures, particularly the Metsogo-Massango of the upper Ngounie, from the Bieri ancestral cult traditional to the Fang, and from Christian, primarily Catholic, evangelization. The cult has spread throughout Fang territory, although it is still much stronger in the south. It is polymorphous, and there are at least six branches of the cult. As is typical of Fang anarchic egalitarianism, cult organization beyond the village level is sporadic only. Local chapels of the same branch maintain contact, but usually on a casual basis. The cult and its branches have a number of purposes, but it seems to be devoted mainly to recreating through its microcosmogeny a satisfactory relationship with the dead who came to be ignored by virtue of evangelical pressures. The cult also seeks to offer its members the experience of a passage over to the afterlife *(si ayat)* and, hence, a coming to terms with death. There is heavy emphasis upon aesthetic form and the exact timing of ceremonial events in this cult, for it seeks to approximate heavenly activity.

MBiri is a curing cult which is very widespread and has even less organization than Bwiti. It is generally led by women, whereas Bwiti is led by men. It is an adaptation into Fang culture of the Ombwiri cults of the coastal peoples, in particular the MPongwe. The Ombwiri is a genie of water courses or the sea, associated with the search for fortune among the MPongwe, which afflicts men of ambition and instrumental

mentality particularly. The primary objective of MBiri among the Fang
is to assuage suffering brought about by intrusive spirits of one's own
lineage and the various ills associated with that intrusion. It seeks to
pacify these spirits by bringing their victim into direct communication
with them so that an accommodation might be obtained. A secondary
object of the cult is to obtain good fortune. A much higher regular
ingestion of *eboka* takes place in this cult. There is much less emphasis
upon logico-aesthetic integration and the work of the ancestors. For the
object of this cult is to make contact with the ancestors as directly as
possible and not to recreate the more perfect forms of the afterlife in
cult ritual.

The Narcotics Involved

There are four narcotics with hallucinogenic properties that are
in use among the Fang and that enter into cult rituals:*

Tabernanthe iboga—eboka
Alchornea floribunda—alan (pl. *malan*)
Elaeophorbia drupifera—ayañ beyem
Cannabis sativa—yama (beyama)

All these plants have had important ritual uses, but by far the most
important at the present time is *Tabernanthe iboga*.

Alan (malan). The root of this bush, ground up, powdered, and
dried, is consumed by those being initiated into the ancestral cult,
Bieri. The object is to "break open the head" *(akwia nlo)*. Consumed
in sufficient quantity, *alan* produces collapse and a vertiginous sense of
excursion interpreted as passing over to the land of the ancestors.
Initiates consume large quantities of this drug while sitting in the
village courtyard under the morning and midday sun. No doubt the
effect of the sun is also important in their vertigo. The pattern of
ingestion of this drug is followed in Bwiti. But the general opinion
in Fang Bwiti is that *malan* has less power than *eboka*. Cults in southern
Gabon which practice a version of Bwiti are known to mix *malan* with
eboka.

Ayañ beyem. *Elaeophorbia drupifera* has a number of uses in
equatorial pharmacopoeia. The latex, typical of the euphorbiae, is mixed
with oil to form eyedrops. It was employed in the ancestral cult among
the Fang when the ingestion of *malan* was slow in showing effect.
A parrot's red tail feather dipped in the mixture was brushed across
the eyeballs. The latex appears to affect the optical nerves, producing

---

* These four plants do not exhaust the list of Fang narcotics. Women, for example,
mix tobacco and ashes together into a ball *(adzugan)* which they hold in their cheek or
under their tongue. It is said to produce a state of pleasurable lassitude.

bizarre visual states and a generally dazed feeling. It is said that the latex was applied to the eyes of slaves and prisoners in the old days to baffle their sight, to daze them, and to make them quiescent.

Yama. Hemp, also called *nkot alok* (dry herb), is smoked in some branches of Bwiti after the ingestion of two or three teaspoons of *eboka*. The smoke is symbolic of the soul's leaving the body and wending its way to mix with the ancestors at the roof of the chapel. But in most branches *Cannabis* is rejected as a foreign plant, distracting the members' attention from ritual matters. In fact, hemp has long been smoked on the coast, and missionaries and administrators developed an antagonism to it very early in the colonial enterprise.* *Cannabis* tends to be more widely used in southern Gabon; there the plant pollen is eaten, which is more potent than smoking the leaves.

Eboka is the Fang name for *Tabernanthe*. The species name, as well as the Fang name, is taken from the Galwa-Mpongwe (Miene) term *iboga*. The bush, which is of several varieties, not always clearly distinguished botanically, is common to the equatorial underforest, but it is also grown in the open courtyards of Bwiti villages as a decorative bush. It produces yellowish or pinkish-white flowers and a small orange fruit whose sweetish pulp is edible, though not narcotic. The fruit is sometimes used in Bwiti as a medicine for barrenness in women.

The plant has long been known by Europeans. Edward Bowdich, in his "Sketch of Gabon and its Interior," mentions the *Eroga* under fetish plants as a "favorite but violent medicine," which he takes to be a charred fungus since he probably saw it in its powdered state (1819:445). French explorers knew the plant in mid-century, and Griffon du Bellay brought specimens back from Cap López (Lecomte, 1864). The plant was investigated intensively by the French after the turn of the century. Walker and Sillans give a bibliography of this work (1961:89–91). The Germans were interested in it in the 1880's, when references to it appear in the reports of district officers from Kamerun in *Mitteilungen aus den Deutschen Schutzgebieten* (in particular vol. I, 1888:49). In volume XI of this colonial journal (1898:29) the instrumental value of the root is recognized. It is pointed out that the plant has an "exciting effect on the nervous system so that its use is highly valued on long, tiring marches, on lengthy canoe voyages, and on difficult nightwatches." Old informants in northern Gabon, formerly German Kamerun, say that the use of *eboka* was permitted, if not encouraged, by the Germans in their work gangs and various colonial projects, such as the Douala-Yaounde railroad. This capacity of the

* Paul DuChaillu, the famous (and notorious) mid-nineteenth-century explorer of Gabon, mentions the eating of wild hemp (*liamba*) in the southern Ngounie in the early 1860's (1903:321).

Fig. 35. *Tabernanthe iboga*. The psychotropic *eboka* bush is cultivated in groves in and near the *Bwiti* villages. The roots, whose bark will be pulverized later, are dug up in the morning for the evening ceremonies.

plant to suppress fatigue has constituted one of its principal attractions to the Bwitist. He must dance all night and hence values the euphoric insomnia produced by the drug.

Myths of the Origin of Eboka

It is relevant when considering the known history of the drug to give the most central versions—there are several differing accounts—of the Bwiti myths of the coming of the drug. The importance of *eboka* in Bwiti is seen in the fact that the name is employed as a metonymic for the entire cult. In addition to *banzie* (angel), the term *ndzi eboka* (eater of *eboka*) is often used for a member of Bwiti. Eating *eboka* is synecdoche for the entire process of becoming a member of Bwiti. One speaks of the religion of *eboka (nyiba eboka)* and generally of *eboka* —meaning Bwiti—having done such and such for an individual.

The following origin myth of *eboka* is taken from the *Asumege Ening* (New Life) branch of Bwiti as given in two villages—Sougoudzap, District of Oyem, and Ayol, District of Mitzik, both in the northern Gabonese region of Woleu Ntem. All versions, whether of this branch or any other, consider *eboka* to be a gift from the Pygmies to the Fang and the other people of Equatorial Africa. Although the Fang themselves possess extensive knowledge of equatorial pharmacopoeia, they credit the Pygmies, who actually live within the forest without benefit of village clearings, with a greater knowledge than themselves. In the Fang legends of *Adzap Mboga,* the giant tree that blocked Fang migratory passage and that symbolizes the equatorial forest, it is the Pygmies who appear to save the Fang by instructing them on how to obtain passage and how to cope with the deep forest. The Fang must indeed have learned a great deal from the Pygmies.

Zame ye Mebege (the last of the creator gods) gave us *eboka*. He saw the misery in which blackman was living. He thought how to help him. One day he looked down and saw a blackman, the Pygmy Bitumu, high in an Atanga tree, gathering its fruit. He made him fall. He died and Zame brought his spirit to him. Zame cut off the little fingers and the little toes of the cadaver of the Pygmy and planted them in various parts of the forest. They grew into the *eboka* bush. Now the brothers of the Pygmy came to search for him but they could not find him. One day his wife, Akengue, went fishing deep in the forest. She found in a stream the bones of a man which she thought might have been her husband. She gathered them up and placed them on the bank for she intended to return them to the camp. But while she was fishing, a wildcat came along and gathered these bones so that when she returned up the bank they were gone!* In perplexity, she returned through the deep forest, losing her way. Suddenly across her path ran a porcupine pursued by a dog and then by a man.† Peering in the direction in which they disappeared she saw a cave, and there in the back was the pile of bones. As she entered the cave she suddenly heard a voice—as of the voice of her husband—asking who she was, where she came from, and whom she wished to speak with. The voice told her to look to the left at the mouth of the cave. There was the *eboka* plant. It told her to eat of its roots. It told

---

* The wildcat skin is important in initiation, for the *eboka* is eaten off it. The skin is symbolically important for its mottling—in leopard fashion—of red and white. These are basic colors in the cult.

† This revelatory configuration has celestial significance. Porcupine, dog, and hunter are the three stars in Orion's Belt in Fang astronomy. Tolo, Orion, and Lepus together is the most clearly marked constellation to the Fang—a constellation sometimes extended to boundaries of the stars Sirius, Aldebaran, Rigel, and Betelgeuse. Orion rises in October and is associated with the clear skies and the planting and growing of crops during the long, cold, rainy season (*sugu oyon*). It is a time when ancestral blessing is particularly important.

her to look to the right. There was the mushroom *duna*.* The voice told
her to eat of these two things. She ate and felt very tired. Now the voice told
her to look out of the cave. Suddenly the fly that flies into men's eyes,
Olarazen † flew into her eye and brought tears so that she could not see.
Then she was told to turn around in the cave. The bones were gone and in
their place stood her husband and other dead relatives. They talked to her
and gave her a name, *Disoumba,* ‡ and told her that she had found the
plant that would enable men to see the dead. This was the first baptism
into Bwiti and that was how men got the power to know the dead and have
their council.

Several elements in this myth deserve additional commentary. First,
the myth, as well as other evidence from cult life, puts emphasis upon
eboka as a plant of the deep forest—a plant *par excellence* of the
Pygmies, who are the denizens of the forest. Bwiti, both in its original
form among the Mitsogo of Southern Gabon and among the Fang,
emphasizes by ritual sequences the integration of village and forest.
In this sense *eboka* is a plant grown in the villages, yet of the deep
forest, which mediates between village and forest. It is an agent of
transition. It enables men to pass from the familiar village to the
mysterious forest, which harbors the secrets of the dead. This passage
from clearing to deep forest is, moreover, a traumatic one in Fang
culture history. For the Fang, as celebrated in the Adzap Mboga legends,
themselves have had to move from savannah to equatorial forest.

Secondly, we note that the crucial events of this legend take place
in a cave. And although it is far-fetched to suggest a Platonic image of
the cave here, the Bwiti cult house is treated as an arena (particularly
during initiation) in which greater realities take shape and are manifest.
The membership is brought by *eboka* and the rituals to a vision of
the greater realities of the realm of the dead. During initiation in
MBiri the members involved sit in the middle of the chapel staring
without and consuming *eboka*. In time they "see" their ancestors come
to them from without through a mirror placed at the entrance! In
Bwiti, initiates generally sit with their backs to the entrance, waiting
and watching for manifestations at the back of the chapel.

* This is a white mushroom with a very large cap, often used in herbalist concoctions. In powdered form it is sometimes eaten in Bwiti but never in my experience,
despite the legend. I know of no special psychedelic effect to be attributed to it.
Walker and Sillans (1961:457) list it without mention of any special psychoreactive
quality. But I would urge further ethnobotanic inquiry here.

† When this small sweat fly flies into the eye it is said to be for the purpose of
warning a person that he has taken or is about to take the wrong path. The inter-
jection of the *Olarazen* at this moment is reminiscent of the brushing of the eyeball
with the latex of *ayañ beyem*. The purpose of this action, as well, was to place the
initiate on the proper path to the dead.

‡ The originating branch of Fang Bwiti is sometimes called Disoumba.

We note, thirdly, the importance of the wife in the discovery of *eboka* and in establishing effective communication with the dead. Bwiti, unlike most traditional cults, has a functionally integral and virtually equal place for men and women (in MBiri women are dominant). Moreover, the cult directs itself, in respect to the great gods and in distinction from the ancestors, to Nyingwan Mebege, the female principle of the universe. She is the author of procreation and the guarantor of a prosperous life. If one wishes to go into some of the more subtle symbolic elements, it is of interest that *eboka* is the left-hand plant—left is the female side of the chapel—while the phallic-form mushroom stands to the right, the male side of the chapel.

Finally we may note the eucharistic implication of the planting of the parts of the Pygmy to germinate the *eboka* plant. This makes the consumption of the roots an act of communion with the Pygmy—originator of the cult who had been chosen by Zame and brought to heavenly abode. The Pygmies are in some sense saviors of the Fang, as the Adzap Mboga legends imply. Hence we have in the eating of *eboka* a eucharistic experience with similarities to Christian communion. How much of this is a syncretism with Christianity and how much is original with the Fang it is difficult to say. One can suspect more of the former. For not only do members of Bwiti practice communion, employing *eboka* instead of bread, but they also boast of the efficacy of *eboka* over bread in its power to give visions of the dead. Some of the more Christian branches of Bwiti, not fully cognizant of the origin legend, even speak of *eboka* as a more perfect and God-given representation of the body of Christ!

The Nature of the Drug

The *eboka* plant itself is an apocynaceous shrub growing to about four feet in height. The main alkaloid—ibogaine—is largely contained in the roots, particularly in the root bark, so that the mode of consumption in Bwiti maximizes access to this alkaloid. This root bark is rasped and eaten directly as raspings, ground as a powder and eaten, or soaked in water and drunk as an infusion. There appear to be, as we have mentioned, several plant members of the genus *Tabernanthe* with similar psychotropic properties (*T. iboga* and *T. manii*), but *T. iboga* is the plant of choice. Isolation of the crystalline ibogaine from the dried roots shows a chemical structure typical of many alkaloids. Ibogaine, although the major, is not the only alkaloid in *T. iboga*, and it may be the work of several alkaloids in combination rather than ibogaine alone that accounts for the effect of the drug. The reader may consult the most recent compilation of information on *iboga* in Pope (1969).

A good deal has been written on the pharmacological properties of the hallucinogenic drugs which is hard to interpret in terms of central-nervous-system or peripheral-nervous-system events. In respect to *eboka,* it is sometimes said that it is accompanied by "intense and unpleasant central stimulation and peripheral relaxation and depression" (Pope, 1969:178). But it would be as helpful to consider the experiences articulated by people who take the drug on a regular basis.

It must be kept in mind that *eboka* is consumed in two ways: (1) It is taken regularly in small doses (two to three teaspoonsful for women and three to five for men) before and in the early hours of the ceremonies. An additional several grams may be eaten at mid-course after midnight. This represents a total ingestion of up to 20 grams of powdered *eboka.* (2) Once or twice in the career of a banzie a massive dose of *eboka* is taken for purposes of initiation and to "break open the head" in order to effect contact with the ancestors through collapse and hallucination. One to three small basketsful may be consumed at this time over an 8- to 24-hour period. This represents an ingestion of between 300 and 1000 grams.

Research has indicated that the main alkaloid (ibogaine) constitutes about 5 per cent of the bark. This would mean that between 75 and 125 mg. of the psychoactive agent are consumed per regular dose, which is a threshold dose as noticeable effects are experienced. The initiation dose of 15 grams of ibogaine per basket can run as high as 40 to 60 times the threshold dose. In the upper reaches, the dosage approaches toxicity. Of course, the psychotropic drugs show a wide range from threshold to toxic effect—some tranquilizers, in contrast to aspirin, for example, run up to a factor of 100—but it is not surprising that the death of initiates is commented upon in all cults. And even more deaths would be experienced if the initiates were not occasionally allowed to move around and evacuate! In mid-course they are sometimes taken to a stream to be ritually cleansed. In the last forty years there have been perhaps a dozen cases of murder or manslaughter brought against Bwiti cult leaders who lost initiates through overdosage.* Most

---

* The late-evening death of a young boy at Mitzik in November, 1950, after heavy ingestion of *eboka* provoked accusations from non-Bwiti villagers and local priests that deliberate poisoning had taken place (there was also a question of panther whiskers mixed in the *eboka*) in order to obtain a cadaver. The heads of the cult were brought to trial, and the original judgment was seven years at hard labor. There were appeals to Libreville, where testimony on Bwiti was sought from a representative of the Church, Père Gilles Sillard, and the Gabonese politician and Mayor of Libre-ville—later the first president of Gabon—Leon Mba. Père Sillard testified that ritual murders were reputed to be common in Bwiti and the heavy ingestion of *eboka* was integral to that intent. Leon Mba, who throughout his career was accused of being a member of Bwiti and having used it for political purposes, said that Bwiti was simply a cult of the ancestors, like Fang Bieri, and that *eboka* was an excitant and

Fig. 36. Women initiates to *Mbiri* begin their initiation in the morning. Between their legs lies the skin of the civet cat upon which the powdered *eboka* (*Tabernanthe iboga*) is piled. Behind them the sacred harp—*ngombi*—is played, as it is throughout the initiation ceremonies.

of these cases involved women or young people of small body size. The folklore of death in initiation is that Bwiti or *Eboka*—the drug, as we have said, is often anthropomorphized as a supernatural in its own right, a kind of generic ancestor—so valued the individual or so rejected him that it took him away to the other side.

In view of the massive doses taken at initiation, it is not surprising that initiates display a gross reduction in their ability to moderate or program motor activity. Since they sit in initiation gazing expectantly out of the cult house (or to the rear) and into the mirror propped upon

not a poison. He, as Conseiller Territorial, was against Bwiti because it was secretive and because those who entered it refused to do any further work (Cour d'Appel de l'A.E.F. Tribunal d'Oyem No. 5558. Année 1952, juillet 21; and Tribunal de Libreville; Notes d'audience criminelle du mercredi 2 décembre 1953).

the ground, they eventually fall over and have to be carried from the chapel, either to a special chamber within the cult house or to a special arena in the forest behind the cult house. There the soul of the initiate (the soul shade or shadow [*nsisim*]) is said to have left him and in the company of the ancestors is wending its way to a final and confirming revelation in the land beyond—the land of the dead.

The lighter regular dosage—two to five teaspoons—does not produce hallucinations, although adepts of the cult claim that once a man has "met *eboka*" and been taken by "him" to the "otherside," any subsequent amount will raise up in his mind many of his former experiences. The regular dosage, therefore, may have that associative power, but it is taken primarily to enable the adepts to engage in the arduous all-night ceremonies without falter or fatigue. Members often say that *eboka* taken in this way also lightens their body so that they can float through their ritual dances. It thus enables them to mingle more effectively with the ancestors at the roof of the chapel. They do not report visions under the influence of such amounts then—only modest changes in body perception and some dissociation.

We might stress here that in Bwiti most cult leaders do not look kindly on heavy ingestion of *eboka* by members except during initiation, when they are engaged in the search for deep contacts with Bwiti. The taking of too much *eboka* regularly, it is felt, confuses the flow of ritual action and the imitation of heavenly activity. Possession that takes place in the midst of ceremonial action is felt to be nonsensical action *(eboéboé)*, although it occurs from time to time, particularly in women, under the influence of small amounts of *eboka*. Some Bwiti leaders, playing on words, call such possession *ebogan* and regard it as a result of an individual's imperfections rather than a desirable thing. The curing cult of MBiri takes just the opposite view and regards any instance of possession as having positive value.

Initiation: Reasons and Visions

In my work with various branches of the cult for more than a year, I interviewed some sixty *banzie* (angels). Fifty of these interviews, conducted in very open-ended fashion, produced reliable information on the initiation experience. Some of the interviews elicited extensive accounts of the visions *eboka* produced. There is some variability as well as some stereotyping in this experience, and we may usefully tabulate both the reasons given for eating *eboka* and the content of the vision.

Reasons	*N. = 50*	*Per Cent*
1. A dead relative came to me in my sleep and told me to eat it.	20	40

Reasons	N. = 50	Per Cent
2. I was sick (impotent, sterile, sleepless, in pain, etc.) and was counseled to eat *eboka* to cure myself.	12	24
3. Catholicism (or Protestantism) is not our religion. I am not happy in the mission churches.	8	16
4. I wanted to know God—to know things of the dead and the land beyond.	5	10
5. Other: I liked to play the Cult Harp. I had nothing else to do. A friend persuaded me.	5	10

It seems clear that men eat *eboka* for a variety of reasons, of which the one given to the ethnographer may—or may not—have been the most salient.

I also inquired about what was seen in initiation. That is a trickier question and is subject, no doubt, to much secondary elaboration —if there is no reticence. But the high percentage who saw and heard nothing out of the ordinary (23 per cent) is of interest.

Content	N. = 38	Per Cent
1. Saw nothing and heard nothing.	9	23
2. Heard many voices, a great tumult, and recognized the voices of ancestors.	8	21
3. Heard and saw various of my ancestors. They walked with me and instructed me on my life in Bwiti and elsewhere.	13	34
4. I walked or flew over a long, multicolored road or over many rivers which led me to my ancestors who then took me to the great gods.	8	21

It is not clear in my interviews whether those who claimed to have no significant experience are also those who became so bilious as to vomit repeatedly and finally withdraw from the initiation. In any case the high percentage of insignificant experiences accounts for the fact that many members have undergone initiation more than once.

There is in Bwiti a remarkable stereotyping of the vision experience in the last category (#4) although as the following examples demonstrate, the stereotyping tends to be true only within the various local traditions.

The Vision (ndem eboka) *of Ndong Asseko*
(Age 22; clan Essabam; unmarried)

When I ate *eboka* I found myself taken by it up a long road in a deep forest until I came to a barrier of black iron. At that barrier, unable to pass, I saw a crowd of black persons also unable to pass. In the distance beyond the barrier it was very bright. I could see many colors in the air but the crowd of black people could not pass. Suddenly my father descended from above in the form of a bird. He gave to me then my *eboka* name, Onwan Misengue, and enabled me to fly up after him over the barrier of iron. As we proceeded the bird who was my father changed from black to white—first his tail feathers, then all his plumage. We came then to a river the color of blood in the midst of which was a great snake of three colors—blue, black, and red. It closed its gaping mouth so that we were able to pass over it. On the other side there was a crowd of people all in white. We passed through them and they shouted at us words of recognition until we arrived at another river—all white. This we crossed by means of a giant chain of gold. On the other side there were no trees but only a grassy upland. On the top of the hill was a round house made entirely of glass and built upon one post only. Within I saw a man, the hair on his head piled up in the form of a Bishop's hat. He had a star on his breast but on coming closer I saw that it was his heart in his chest beating. We moved around him and on the back of his neck there was a red cross tattooed. He had a long beard. Just then I looked up and saw a woman in the moon—a bayonet was piercing her heart from which a bright white fire was pouring forth. Then I felt a pain on my shoulder. My father told me to return to earth. I had gone far enough. If I went further I would not return.

The Vision of Eman Ela
(Age 30; clan Essamenyang; married with one wife)

When I ate *eboka* very quickly my grandfather came to me. First he had black skin. Then he returned and he had white skin. It was he that gave me my *eboka* name. My grandmother then appeared in the same way. Because my grandfather was dead before I was born he asked me if I knew how I recognized him. It was through *eboka*. He then seized me by the hand and we found ourselves embarked on a grand route. I didn't have the sense of walking but just of floating along. We came to a table in that road. There we sat and my grandfather asked me all the reasons I had eaten *eboka*. He gave me others. Then my grandfather disappeared and suddenly a white spirit appeared before me. He grasped me by the arm and we floated along. Then we came to a crossroads. The road on which we were traveling was red. The other two routes were black and white. We passed over. Finally we arrived at a large house on a hill. It was built on one post. Within I found the wife of my mother's father. She gave me my *eboka* name a second time and also gave me the talent to play the *ngombi* harp. We passed on and finally arrived after passing over more crossroads at a great desert. There I saw descend from the sky—from the moon—a giant circle which came down and encircled the earth, as a rainbow of three colors—blue, red, and white. I began playing the *ngombi* under the rainbow and I heard the applause of men. I returned. All the *banzie* thought I had gone too far and was dead. Since then I have seen nothing in *eboka*. But each time I take it I hear the spirits who give the power to play the *ngombi*. I play what I hear from them. Only if I come into the chapel in a bad heart does *eboka* fail me.

These visions are fantasies that weave together experiences in several realms. I will clarify only a few of these elements. It is very common in these visions to be met by a relative who guides one over the obstacles in the visionary landscape. Often these relatives are white, clothed in white, or change to white, for white is the color of the dead. The crowd of black men that is seen at first is always composed of those who have not eaten *eboka* and are, therefore, unable to pass to the beyond. The reference in the first vision to river crossings and a great snake in the water is a motif taken directly from Fang migration legends, which involve difficulties in crossing various water courses and the use of various giant chthonic animals as aides: crocodiles, snakes, hippopotami, lizards. It is of interest that in crossing these rivers the visionary comes finally to a grassy upland. This reverses the migration experience of the Fang, which began in a grassy upland, the savannah, and descended into the rain forest. We frequently note a correlation *in reverse* between the visions and the events of Fang migration legends as shown in various collections and particularly in the literary version of Ondoua Enguta, *Dulu Bon be Afri Kara* (1951). The visionary experience is very often represented as a journey down a long road that eventually leads to great powers. As the initiate pursues this route, other, older ancestors are presented to him. Various obstacles are encountered, including rivers of various colors, until finally the initiate passes out of the forest onto a bare hill, where he makes his final confirming encounter with the great gods. Since the Bwiti cult itself is, in part, a ritual celebration of primordial Fang experience, and since a key technique of worship in the cult is the recitation of long genealogies in which men mount back up to their origins, ancestor by ancestor, and to the founding gods of their clans and people, it is not surprising that the *eboka* visions themselves follow a legendary genealogical framework, albeit in reverse.

Two other elements may be clarified. The Bishop with the piled hair in the first vision may be Jesus, while the woman in the moon is Nyingwan Mebege. Their pierced and streaming hearts can probably be traced to Christian iconography, which features the sacred heart of Mary in intrathoracic display. The reference to the glass house built on one post, which appears in a number of these visions, is, I believe, elaborated out of Fang experience with a world globe, which they have seen in schools or in colonial dwellings. Such an entire representation of the earth is more metaphysically impressive than we might suspect.

There is similarity between the two visions reported here in respect to the coming of ancestors as guides and namegivers, the many-colored routes, and the one-stanchioned house. No rivers appear in the second vision, however; the grassy upland becomes a desert, which may be more precise in respect to the actual migration experience, and the river crossings become crossroads. None of the great gods is seen, but the initiate does arrive at the center of the rainbow, that blessed spot from which he can see the entire circle of the rainbow. This is a sign of the success of his vision even though he saw none of the great gods.

The stereotyping of the visions reminds us of the fact, well recognized in the study of hallucinogens, that the content of the physiological experience is much more a function of the attitude set of the individual himself, of the social situation in which he takes the drug, and of the cultural setting of beliefs and values than of anything in the drug itself. The various cult chapels of Bwiti and the various branches of the cult differ in the sets they provoke in their initiates, the situation of initiation, and the Fang and Christian cultural setting they invoke.

When heavy doses of *eboka* are being taken, some chapels modify the ritual. Sometimes the initiate is surrounded by a vertiginous circle of members dancing, singing, and shouting. Drums may be beaten incessantly even in the initiate's ear, in representation of the sufferings of life pounding upon the spirit within the body until it is finally enabled to break through and fly. So fierce and insistent is the ritual turmoil that it seems that no drug would be needed at all for the initiate to be astounded, mesmerized, and carried away in enthusiasm or ecstasis. Some cults provide very careful supervision of the initiate. He is given *eboka* parentage: a mother of *eboka (nyiaboka)* and a father of *eboka* (*esaboka*), who watch over him solicitously and encourage him against anxiety while protecting him against overdosage. Initiates often begin to mumble or even shout incoherently under high dosage; the *eboka* mother and father listen intently to see if they can make out any message from *Eboka*. It is their own soft voices whispering in the initiate's ear that he may take as the voices of the dead, while the turmoil of dancing and drumming is easily interpreted as the turbulent crowds of the dead. Some cult houses provide none of this careful construction of set and situation, and these tend to be the houses afflicted with bad trips (*ndem abe,* literally bad dreams).

Relevance of the Pharmacological Properties of Iboga to the Purposes of the Bwiti Cult

Differences in set, setting, and situation account for the considerable differences in the *iboga* experience itself from cult house to cult house and from one branch of Bwiti to another. Nevertheless, there are certain physiological reactions common to most hallucinogens, whether tetrahydrocannabinol, mescalin, LSD, or ibogaine. I would like to list these as they are commonly put forth in the literature * and then offer an indication of how the cult of Bwiti turns these to its own uses, giving

* As for example in Hoffer and Osmond, *The Hallucinogens* (1967).

them an interpretation suitable to its purposes and its members' needs and expectations.

1. Somatic changes
2. Body perception
3. Visual changes
4. Time perception
5. Dissociation-detachment
6. Hearing, smell, and taste synesthesia
7. Task performance
8. Moods and emotions

Somatic Changes. The apparent suppression obtained by *eboka,* even in mild dosage, of tissue-deprivation impulses, as well as its depressive effect upon certain autonomic processes, cardiac output, etc., enables the members to maintain a high level of engagement in the ritual development over a long period of time without complaint or fatigue. There is a puritan element in this cult that denigrates the physical body and regards the soul *(nsisim)* as englutted by corporeality. It is a clear objective of cult life to escape to higher and better things. The extracorporeal floating feeling obtained by *eboka* serves this ecstatic objective very well. *Eboka* is often said to be an aphrodisiac (Walker and Sillans, 1961:90), but there is no evidence in Bwiti that this is the case. The set and situation of the cult emphasize chastity, and the cultural setting sublimates sexual impulses into symbolic statements. To the degree that *eboka* is an aphrodisiac (probably only in the relaxed endurance it gives), it would work against cult purposes. It cannot be, in any case, a sufficient aphrodisiac to break through the Bwiti set, situation, and setting.

Body Perception. In regular dosage, there is little change in body perception other than that subsumed under somatic change. The body feels lighter. Heavier dosages produce a feeling of elongation accompanied by feelings of floating. In the very heavy dosages of initiation, the perception of one's own figure and face in a mirror (employed primarily in MBiri) or of one's fellow worshipers is so drastically altered as to convince the initiate that he has seen the ancestor. It is of interest to note that mirrors have been used in the measurement of body perception in laboratory experimentation on hallucinogens (Masters and Houston, 1966).

Visual Changes. The spectrums on the margins of perceived objects that are often produced by hallucinogens do not become evident with *eboka* until high dosage. But in initiation doses spectrums, or rainbows, are often reported in objects, roads, rivers, and animals. These spectrums are taken by the banzie as indications that the user is approaching the precincts of the dead and the great gods.

Time Perception. The timing of ritual activity is highly important, for the cult succeeds only insofar as it approximates the ritual of the other world. Alarm clocks are kept in most chapels to ensure that timings are exact. Hallucinogens tend to increase the sense of elapsed time as compared to "real" time. This effect is most apparent under initiation dosage; it is the impression of the initiates that they are involved in their spiritual journeys for many hours, if not days.

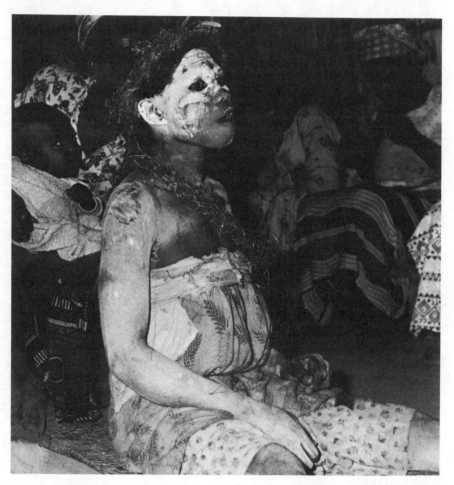

Fig. 37. Toward the end of her initiation and under the influence of a full dose of *eboka* (*Tabernanthe iboga*), the initiate stares intently out of the chapel, waiting for her ancestors to "arrive." Because white is the color of the ancestors, she has been painted all over with kaolin. Behind her sits the *nyia-eboka*, her "mother of *eboka*," who gives her encouragement.

Dissociation-Detachment. Even under light doses, he who takes *eboka* experiences some dissociation and sense of detachment. The feeling of "here I am and there is my body going through its actions" is reported by members as a happy indication that the soul will shortly mingle with the ancestors at the roof of the chapel—one of the declared objectives of Bwiti. The sense of dissociation directly moves toward that objective. There is a feeling of escape from burdensome individuality in such dissociation. This fits in with the desire of the cult to achieve *nlem mvore* (one-heartedness) in the membership. The consequences of the drug in this area thus serve the communal objectives of Bwiti and enable it, in the members' view, to combat more effectively what they regard as the excessive economic and organizational individualism of transition from traditional tribal culture to membership in a modern state on the Western model.

Hearing, Smell, and Taste Synesthesia. I have little data on sharpened or synesthetic perceptions of smells and tastes. Hearing seems to be affected with large doses, which produce a loud buzzing. Tumult is often reported. With regular doses banzie claim that they can hear the cult harp more clearly and more beautifully. They say that the strings are the voice of Nyingwam Mebege, the female principle of the Universe, who speaks to them. Synesthesia, the effect when one sense mode seems to harmonize or integrate with another, is not reported. However, it would seem to accord with the effort of many cult leaders to convince the membership that Bwiti proves all things are one rather than many (Fernandez, 1965:909).

Task Performance. There is high emphasis in Bwiti on performing the ritual task in such manner as to achieve a sense of wholeness, which we might call logico-aesthetic integration. Heavy doses of *eboka* are therefore discouraged as a general practice. But light regular doses, by suppressing fatigue and excessive autonomic claims, would seem to add to the capacity to concentrate upon the ritual work at hand.

Moods and Emotions. All the possible physiological effects are meaningless unless we understand the context in which they appear. In respect to moods and emotions, the context of taking *eboka* is especially important. We have indicated that some cult houses are so careful in regulating context—providing solicitous mothers and fathers of *eboka*—that there is hardly a bad trip. In others, more neglectful, initiates often abandon their initiation in mid-flight through sickness or terror. But there is always some somber apprehension and anxiety involved in taking massive doses of *eboka* in any cult house, because of its reputation for causing deaths. For the rest of the membership, however, the mood is generally euphoric, especially in the last hours before sun-up. Members look forward with a fine appetite to the communal meal after the rituals. However, the beauty and integration achieved in this cult by dance and song are virtually sufficient in themselves to achieve euphoric results, even without *eboka*.

CONCLUSION

A certain regret underlies this account of Bwiti *eboka*. I worked for many, many months with the Fang and in Bwiti—a people and an institution I esteem. But I ate only modest amounts of *eboka,* and I never experienced any soaring ecstasy, any weighty meaning, any visions of my own awesome dead or theirs. *Eboka* had a very bitter taste to me. It made me slightly nauseated. And I was never inspired to go on and follow that road it opens up with large doses.

Why was this? First of all, the richness of Bwiti liturgy and cosmology was standing before me to be described and worked out. This challenge alone lifted me on every cult night to a plane of very intense experience of other cultural realities in which my emotions and my intellect were sharply stepped up, so that I felt no need for any narcotic excursions. But, further, it is now clear to me that my attitude set was inappropriate to the drug. Although my wife and I tried to establish participation with the Fang in every respect—living their village life as we could and dancing in the cult—nevertheless, in the end, our communion with them was conditioned by the fact that I was the agent of a Western scientific culture. This is an inescapable form of separation that operates in the work of an anthropologist. I suppose my resistance to the drug was the result of a commitment to objective observation. The subjective revelations promised me at the time by the drug seemed irrelevant to my task. I failed to appreciate *eboka*'s usefulness in stimulating all-night inquiry.*

It now strikes me with all the force of the obvious that science itself surely required that I explore the properties of this plant in every possible way. Of course, from the Bwiti point of view, one is not being honest with *eboka* if one takes it only in the chaste spirit of inquiry. One takes *eboka* because one needs to see, to know, and to communicate with greater powers that are hidden in it and known through it. As, in the end, an agent of science, I felt no such needs. Because of significant differences in set, situation, and setting, taking the drug in the spirit of professional inquiry can never produce the same experience as a banzie achieves.

Of course such considerations as these are very far from the Bwiti point of view. Members of this cult take *eboka* because they believe it to be a very powerful instrument of their intentions. We may argue from our view that taking the drug is an expressive form of com-

---

* See above for similar observations by Sharon.

munion achieved by exteriorizing interior states. It really, after all, does
not change much in the object world, and surely Africans in this mod-
ernizing period are challenged with the necessity of making changes in
that world. In fact the Gabonese elite generally deprecate Bwiti because
banzie "work no more" and are no longer of use to the national enterprise. The banzie, on the other hand, cannot agree with this criticism,
for they are seriously engaged in the "work of the ancestors," which they
do not regard as self-indulgent. As for the taking of the drug itself,
which is also excoriated by the elite, the banzie would have support from
the pre-World War I colonial Germans, who found it a useful drug at
certain levels of ingestion.

In view of the widespread drug abuse in this country—by no means
only in the hallucinogens—it may be salutary to emphasize again that
the Bwiti cult in most of its branches carefully controls members' uses
of *eboka*. The "work of the ancestors" can easily be harmed by an over-
dose. Only initiates are free to pursue the potentialities of *eboka* virtually to the limit of their powers. For another kind of ecstasis, perhaps
more satisfying and enduring, is to be achieved in the cult, and that is
the ecstatic satisfaction of a logically and aesthetically whole performance
of the ritual task. One qualifies for participation in that ecstasis by a
staggering dose of *eboka*. But one achieves it periodically only by very
modest amounts.

All this would seem to launch us, as anthropological presentation so
often does, upon the high seas of ontological relativism, for we have
two definitions of work and two definitions of ecstasis. One man's work
seems to be another man's play. And there seems to be an ecstasis of
interiorization and an ecstasis of exteriorization. I propose two axioms
to put us at ease and prepare us for the future:

1. Since any drug, including the hallucinogens, can be used or abused,
we may, in the end, judge the difference between use and abuse only in
relation to a culture's definition of work or pleasure. Hence, although
there is a bit of a tautology involved: a drug is abused when it ceases
to facilitate work as a culture defines that work.

2. Men universally try to manifest in themselves, and to work with,
the optimal mix of instrumental and expressive tendencies. Cultures
differ from one to another in their notion of the optimal mix, and
over periods of time change that mix. One source of change, the essence
of revitalization, arises when the hard facts of reality, developing either
out of the culture's own processes or by imposition from without, prove
intractable in men's attempts to work with them or within them. The
colonial reality proved especially intractable to the Fang, just as for
many Americans today the harried, highly organized industrial jugger-
naut of our culture proves intractable in their attempts to work within

it to any satisfaction. Some Fang and some Americans, therefore, turn away to search for and express a new reality. They have found drugs very useful to that task—although in the end ceremonial events, song and dance, may have as great a power. Hence: the mix of instrumental and expressive modes of being in any culture is dependent upon the satisfactions of the work of that culture and the ecstatic possibilities found in that work.

10

WESTON LA BARRE

Hallucinogens and the Shamanic Origins of Religion

This study proposes that all our knowledge of the supernatural derives *de facto* from the statements made by religious visionaries or ecstatics (i.e., prophets and shamans)—the priests only administrate the ecclesia established on this supernatural basis—and that the nature of the shamanic ecstasy may be illuminated by attention to ancient hallucinogens. The use of some psychotropic substances can be traced certainly to the Bronze Age, and others, with some clear evidence, at least to Mesolithic times. This paper first delineates the psychological and cultural matrix of shamanistic religious innovation and then presents evidence of the large part hallucinogens have played in shamanistic ecstasy.

Throughout history, extravagant attention has been paid to the nature of the gods, whose nature it is to be quite inaccessible to examination. The result of this preoccupation is that there is absolutely no consensus concerning the sacred. At the same time, we have paid relatively little attention to the impresarios of gods, the prophets and shamans, who in fact are available for scrutiny. Indeed, each contemporary crisis cult shows a new "origin" of religion in a living visionary's revelation. Thus, in this secular world, we need only examine the peculiar vatic personality of the visionary in order to understand religion psychologically, and we have only to scrutinize its function in groups in order to understand it anthropologically.

We have too long supposed that the Unknown *mysterium tremendum et fascinosum* of religion was outside us, when in fact that Unknown, although ego-alien or unconscious, was all the while within us: the alleged "supernatural" is the human "subconscious." Doubtless, a whole

261

universe full of mystery still lies outside. But insofar as religion is a subjective experience, we have been looking in the wrong direction for understanding. We have neglected to explore this inner world.* If the Cosmic Environment is never convincingly manlike, or moral, or parental-nurturant, it may only be that we project the species-specific childhood experience of our inner humanity onto the blank screen of that outside Unknown.

Man has two worlds, the sacred and the secular. The secular world is one that we can all see and point to and talk about. In material culture, this secular world is not merely intersubjective but even intertribal, with the consequence that any material-culture adaptation of one society is potentially borrowable by the whole human species and with relative ease, whereas societies battle to the death over differences in sacred culture. It might even be argued that this material kind of secular adaptation to the environment accumulates and evolves like any other animal adaptation. By contrast, sacred culture is mere psychological adaptation to inner anxieties. Some of these inner anxieties (e.g., those concerning death) perhaps exist in all human beings; hence faith in an animistic, separable, and indestructible soul is well-nigh panhuman. But some inner anxieties are created by variable and changing pressures in cultures themselves, or by idiosyncratic vicissitudes in enculturation. Thus, whereas secular material culture is highly communicable and diffusible, sacred culture is often ineffable, inexpressible, and uncommunicable, whether intertribally, tribally, or personally. Furthermore, sacred culture does not manifest cumulative evolution ecologically for the species, but only cultural difference and psychological change.

The secular world is that of the *ob-ject*—literally, the thing that is "thrown across" the path of our animal wish. The sacred world is that of the *sub-ject*—that is, the experience that is "thrown under" us, the ground of our conscious being, the basis of our apperception, our specific humanity, and each learned personality. The secular world is perforce convincing—if only because the ob-ject very commonly frustrates raw animal wish; hence we must adapt to it if we would stay in business as an animal. But the subjective world is impressively convincing too: we *trust* subjective personality because every last shred of it is based either on inherited animal adaptations or on individual life-experience

---

* The "separate reality" that Carlos Castaneda postulates is very close to my concept of the "inner world" of sacred, subjective, and ineffable feeling, as opposed to the communicable secular world of jointly experienced objects. Freud has also made a dichotomy between the Pleasure Principle of subjective feeling and gratification (early mediated by the nurturant mother and nonincestuously returned to in the wife), as opposed to the Reality Principle of sternly obdurate objects (of which the first paradigm is the father, frustrator like the real world, and surrogate of society in the growth of conscience or dominating superego).

of the world. One's personality has been—all of it—honestly, if sometimes painfully, learned.

The secular world of objects presents itself to our senses persistently, unasked for and obdurately, while we are awake. By contrast, we are closest to the subjective world of the self when we are divested of sensory input from the outside. That is to say, the subjective self emerges most purely in states of sensory deprivation, when the blank screen of consciousness has projected upon it only the individual hallucinatory subjective self, without sensory correction or editing, without reality testing or any such objective "noise." This hallucinatory projection can be demonstrated in sensory-deprivation experiments, with the subject suspended in a warm, soundless, sightless tank like a synthetic womb. The same hallucinatory projection comes to us spontaneously at night in dreams, in the REM state of sleep,* when the mind is cut off from the sensory body-ego and is furiously "in business for itself" cognitively. Schizophrenia, indeed, seems to be basically a chronic wide-awake dream state, accessible perhaps to sensory input, but by emotional preference attentive mainly to "primary process" internal rumination or daydream fantasy. Both the sacred and the secular world are therefore as real to us as are sensory experience and dreaming, and as sleeping and waking.

Nevertheless, our sacred and secular worlds are quite commonly in conflict, just as wish and perception often are. It is the twin experiences of waking and dreaming that first made man an epistemologist. What can a man believe? This is his dilemma. An organism that gave up all subjective insistence on its essential organic homeostasis would soon cease to be an organism: it would be uncontained dead matter, undisturbed by life or consciousness. On the other hand, no open system like an organism can maintain its improbable existence unless it adapts to and constantly borrows its energies from the outside. In complex organisms like ourselves, perhaps sleeping and waking are themselves ultimately responses to the ecological fact of night and day on this revolving earth, for all warm-blooded species on earth are alternately wide awake and sleeping, and all of them have discernible REM states and are thus able to dream. It may even be that the possibility of sleep is the enabling factor behind complex waking life itself.

Among human institutions, science is closest to a pure type of conscious animal adaptation. Science is the cognitive state of mind we strive most strenuously to base on our secular experience of objects and to divest of the subjective and the wished-for. Science is the state in which

---

* REM is the "Rapid Eye Movement" dream state in humans and animals which investigators of sleep and dreams have found to be, not deep unconsciousness, but a state of inward concentration in which the sleeper is insensitive to external or peripheral stimulation.—ED.

we try most earnestly to communicate about the nature of what we sense and see. But in order to see and to communicate, scientists must have both hypotheses and symbolic languages—both of these being subjective human artifacts—so that it is quite unclear whether science is cumulative adaptive knowledge, like genes and snowballing material culture, or a succession of disjunctive cognitive maps, no more real than the group dreams we call languages or cultures. Certainly scientific thinking does change through time; hence we must suspect that it may never have salt on the tail of that cosmic bird Truth, contaminated as science must always be by group-hypotheses and culturally given symbol-systems.

Among human institutions, in turn, religions of the supernatural perhaps represent the purest form of subjective wish, for in the supernatural we deny the natural world, and in religion we willingly ignore the mundane in our yearning for the idea(l). A religion is a kind of group dream—the subjective poetry in which, supporting one another's faith or need to believe, we strive desperately to believe. That a large component of every religion is *willful belief* is shown in the fact that adherents to such crisis cults as the nineteenth-century Ghost Dance religion of the Plains Indians (see fn., p. 14) or the twentieth-century Cargo Cult of Melanesia believe in what "common sense" already knows to be untrue— what never does and never will come to pass. Crisis cults, like group schizophrenias, are constantly dereistic and, for all their emotional seductiveness, ultimately nonadaptive. The Xosa Millennium, for example, has never arrived in South Africa, in spite of the unilateral bargain with fate by men who dutifully destroyed all their crops and killed all their animals to make the millennium come and the hated white man depart. As to the personal wish for immortality, we still await the return of the man who died but did not die, the man who really was God, and a god who was himself sacrificed to Himself for others' sins toward himself/ Himself—all of which propositions would seem to contain a sufficient modicum of the inconsistent and the improbable. Plainly, religion is a way men have of bearing one another's emotional burdens and of trying to cope with their unresolved and perhaps unresolvable fears in an inhuman and absurd universe—that is, an environment not pre-edited in the individual's special interest, as was the womb-Eden and the tendentiously protective family of the human child, neither of which states of grace can we ever really unlearn.

The *mysterium tremendum et fascinosum* in religion is human, not divine, love though it be. Every religion, in the last analysis, is the beliefs and behaviors of identifiable men; hence every sacred cult can be studied in secular terms—group-cults, by anthropology and sociology; the individual originator or communicant, by psychology and psychiatry. In secular terms, every single item of religious "information" comes from the words of some individual vatic personality, shaman, prophet, or visionary, since it is information about himself. Since, in his trance state, the alleged Cosmic Unknown remains totally and studiously unknown to his sleeping senses, the real Unknown (unknown to himself) is the unconscious self of the visionary. Like the paranoid schizophrenic, the vatic personality pretends to be talking about the grandiose outside cosmic world, but he is really talking grandiosely in symbolic ways only about his narcissistic self and his inner world. The mystic pretends to discard his sensory self in order to meld with the cosmic Self; but in discarding his senses he abjures his only connection with the cosmos and re-encounters only himself. The realities he expounds are inside him, not outside in the world. He reveals only inner space, not outer space, in his revelation.

The REM dream of the shaman is therefore a fragment of his autobiography; a cult is the Rorschach protocol of the society. Any meaning seen is a function of the seer, not of the meaningless (since unknown) Unknown. Thus, the diffusion of a cult is in all ways precisely like the diffusion of a culture, from individual to individuals; and if we understood the function of cults we should probably understand the function of cultures. Every established ecclesia of the majority began in a minority crisis cult of one, in real historic, not supernatural, time; and the cult spread and diffused historically, sometimes until it became the Established Religion, whose priests (as opposed to visionary shamans) are merely the non-ecstatic journeyman officiants of routinized established cults. Every religion, in historic fact, began in one man's "revelation"— his dream or fugue or ecstatic trance. Indeed, the crisis cult is *characteristically* dereistic, autistic, and dreamlike precisely *because* it had its origin in the dream, trance, "spirit" possession, epileptic "seizure," REM sleep, sensory deprivation, or other visionary state of the shaman-originator. All religions are necessarily "revealed" in this sense, inasmuch as they are certainly not revealed consensually in secular experience.

A neurosis or psychosis is the pathological operation of the defense mechanisms of a confused and troubled individual under stress. A religion is in origin the defense mechanism of a society in confused and crisis-torn times. In states of crisis-cult helplessness, the prophet provides the omniscience, the shaman the omnipotence, that the people need. "God" is often clinically paranoiac because the shaman's "supernatural helper" is the projection of the shaman himself. The personality of Yahweh, so to speak, exactly fits the irascible personality of the sheikh-shaman Moses; the voices of Yahweh and Moses are indistinguishable. Of course, shamans do not always have an easy time of it. If the dereistic dreamer arouses too much anxiety, people call him crazy, just as people must put themselves at a psychological distance from the frightening and uncanny schizophrenic. But if the dreamer largely allays anxiety in the society, then he is the shaman-savior. Thus it is that outsiders to the society cannot tell the difference between a psychotic and a vatic personality. Only the society itself can discriminate between its psychotics and its shaman-saviors.

All the allegedly supernatural phenomena of religion can be seen in completely naturalistic terms. Charisma, that "supernatural" animal magnetism that seems to stream compellingly from the sacred vatic personage or religious innovator, is really a quite secular phenomenon psychologically. The "compelling force" comes not from the great man as he voices new supernatural Truth; he speaks only to the powerful anti-commonsensical fantasy already present in the unconscious wish of each communicant, commonly Let Time's Arrow Reverse Its Flight, or Let Onerous Actuality Be Undone. The voice of the vatic has an "uncanny" consistency with each one's private wish; his phatic "message" is psychic actuality already, in a sense, *déjà vu* to his communicants: they are now overwhelmed by the supernatural authority of the wished-for. The charismatic leader is the "liberator" who unlocks hidden wish; hence some psychopathic leaders can release psychopathic behavior in mobs that is usually repressed in the individuals composing the mob. When individuals emotionally abdicate the ego functions of reality testing in favor of wishful belief, they sometimes also abandon superego repressions in their behavior. The leader of the mob and the mob itself mutually sanction each one's mob behavior.

The psychological voltage of the leader's "charisma" is the exact measure of his emotional appeal. Any uninvolved bystander, either one alien to the tribe or a tribesman with his own reality testing intact, can clearly perceive the dubious reality status of the group dream, whether new or old. But he may express insight only at his peril. With incredibly savage and nobly justified wrath, True Believers turn and rend the skeptic for his sin of unbelief. Fanatic faith obscurely realizes that it is mistaken in its fantasies, for denied common sense tells it so. But just as the psychoanalyst who exposes the defense mechanisms of his neurotic patient must expect an annihilating blast of anger in return, so also the unwary free-thinker who naively offers reality testing to the cult-mob, when this is the last thing it wants, must expect his own human sacrifice in order to verify their Truth.

True Believers are authoritarian personalities, for they are infantile dependents on the divine authority of the shaman, not mature assessors of their own judgments. Fundamentalists depend abjectly on past tribal culture, not on their own contemporary common sense; every Fundamentalism is an intellectual lobotomy. "God" is only the infantile shaman's-eye view of a father one has not grown emotionally into, a child's psychic recreation of his Creator. The "omnipotence" of the paranoid shaman, possessing or being possessed by the father-power, serves a similar function for the True Believer. The unreal omnipotence of the shaman is the reciprocal of the unreal helplessness of the cultist; the omnipotence of charismatics only feeds on the supposed impotence of men.

We are so accustomed to belief in gods, or at least in our own True God, that we forget Durkheim's insight that supernatural projections can derive only from the secular historic reality-states of societies. Anthropologically speaking, the post-Alexandrian High God as "Emperor of the Universe" could not possibly be present in the Paleolithic cave of Trois Frères because these ancient Magdalenian hunters had never known the secular political structures first created in the Alexandrian world. The so-called High God that some scholars of the Viennese *Kulturkreislehre* thought to find in the Old Stone Age cave is merely a projection backward in time of their own Catholic theology.

In such ethnographic situations, one authentic Stone Age painting serves us better than even the contemporary theological truth of the matter. The "Dancing Sorcerer" of Trois Frères (and similar masked figures in other Old Stone Age caves) is simply the animal-masked dancing shaman of prehistoric hunting peoples. Any subsequent "Master of Animals" supernaturalized to his model is exactly the sacred projection we would expect, given the secular anxieties, ecological relevancies, and social organization of small bands of ancient hunters. The Dancing Sorcerer himself is only a man dressed up in animal skins, shamanizing in the hunter's small world. He is the group shield from anxiety. He pretends (but not with any intent to deceive) to be able to do what they need to believe he can do: he has the power to dance success in the uncertain hunt, and he controls the fertility of the animals hunted so that they will always be abundant.* He simply "controls" what people cannot. Nothing more. He is not a High God, Creator of the Cosmos, because the concept of cosmos did not exist until late Hellenistic times. Besides, the shamanistic world view takes the world for granted; the

---

* Perhaps the naively wished-for reincarnation or re-embodiment of the life of animals—since human lives seem to continue indefinitely as long as they feed on the lives of animals, hence Paleolithic cave art is mainly concerned with the fertility and accessibility of the animals hunted—actually preceded the notion of human immortality. Our earliest clear notion of the latter is in the shamanist Orphic religion, probably of central European inspiration, revived in the Eleusinian and Dionysian Mysteries. In any case, European prehistorians argue convincingly for the antiquity of the "animal-bone cult" or hunter's ritual at the site of the kill, to bring back the animal incarnate; certainly it is intercontinental in spread.

shaman merely manages the changing elements in it, the life and death of men and animals, the weather, and the like.

The Dancing Sorcerer is at most a shamanic trickster-transformer: the cave artist at Lascaux perceives an unevenness in the rock wall, and on this he paints the animal into existence deep in the womb of the earth. He literally creates what he "conceives"—out of a half-reality he has perceived. His wish apperceives and magically transforms into reality the animals needed by his group. The Dancing Sorcerer is only the artist-creator, like the mythological trickster-transformer of the California Indians. He is like the Oceanic *tuhunga,* the shaman-craftsman who sings his canoe into existence and builds a new structure into the structure of the world with the aid of his creative magic formulas. Even the Indic Shiva merely dances the world into shape with his transformer's magic. Classic "great religion" deities still bear many marks of their shamanic origins. Manlike Zeus, for example, the majestic Cloud Compeller and cosmic rain maker of classic Athens, was once only a man, a shaman who could make rain with the help of his spirit familiar, the eagle—the great Thunderbird so ancient that he is found intercontinentally in the northern hemisphere on Mesolithic horizons.

That the ancient shamanic hunters' religion is not a projective fantasy of our own is indicated in the fact that the religion of all hunting peoples known in early modern times has remained this same simple shamanism, consistent with both the hunter's world horizons and his life anxieties. Eliade (1964) has massively demonstrated that shamanism is still found among the ethnographically conservative peoples of Oceania and on all the continents except Africa, he thinks; * but Nadel (1946) has found true possession shamanism in Africa as well. In Africa, indeed, ancient weather shamans have grown into the rain kings of the Sudan, and divine kings like the Pharaohs in Egypt; in South America and elsewhere in the New World, man-god shamans still grandiosely control the cosmic weather. In the Paleolithic Ur-culture that Kluckhohn (1965) discerned in the whole world, it is quite plain that there were shamans before there were gods. For gods are only charismatic power-wielding shamans, hypostatized after death and grown in stature with the increased world horizons.

Greek Zeus the fire-juggler still has the many animal metamorphoses of the ancient shamanic fertility daemon. His brother Poseidon, Owner of the Sea Animals, still carries the antique trident of the old Eurasiatic

---

* Eliade tends to concentrate on the "supernatural" experience of the *mysterium tremendum et fascinosum* and ignores entirely any secular-minded notion of real psychotropic substances that might inspire shamanic ecstasy. A fuller development of the present paper's thoroughly naturalistic approach to religion (including discussion of the role of drugs in religion) may be found in Weston La Barre, *The Ghost Dance: The Origins of Religion* (New York: Doubleday, 1970).

shaman, still found in the eighteenth century among various Paleo-Siberian tribes. The Greek nature gods are manlike for the simple reason that they were once men, human shamans. And, like other shamans, Greek gods still had their old animal familiars, Zeus the eagle, Apollo the wolf, Athena the owl and serpent, Artemis the bear, Hermes the snake, Proteus the seal, and so forth. In Greece, dead shamans became the Immortals. In India, the Indo-European cognates of these shamans stayed human, or, more exactly, the old Brahmanic shaman-bards persisted as human man-gods or living deities, and the whole thrust of Indic religion is for the self to merge into the Self and man to become god.

In old Judaic tradition, Abraham's wife, Sarah, was given fertility late in old age by a mysterious manlike daemon visitor; and Jacob wrestled physically at the Ford of Jabbok with just such a daemon and extorted from him the gift of countless progeny for Israel. This old Semitic place-deity of the deep Jabbok gorge as "husband of the land" is not unlike the artist-inseminator of the earth-womb in European caves or the Greek fertility daemon, the snake found so abundantly in pre-Olympian religion by Jane Ellen Harrison (1908).

In the Pentateuch, Moses and Aaron were still represented as shamans at the court of the Pharaonic rain king, in shamanistic rivalry with his magicians. Moses turned his shaman's staff into a snake and back again, he afflicted Egypt with pestilence and other magic plagues, he parted the Red Sea with his shaman-staff, he set up in the desert a brazen Nehush-tam, or serpent image, of his Familiar, he struck water from a rock in the wilderness—all like the magic shaman he was, or perhaps compound of several traditional shamans, since one Moses served the volcano-spirit adopted from the Kenites. Judaism, in fact, is ultimately the revelation of the shamanic Moses, and the composite Mosaic snake-bull-volcano god grew into the Most High, as Israel grew into a united kingdom under the Saul-David-Solomon line—initially with the aid of the shaman Samuel and a local Canaanite shamaness, "a woman that hath a familiar spirit" and "saw gods ascending out of the earth" (I Samuel 28: 7 and 13), the Witch of Endor. The growth of Yahweh into Jehovah was all in good Durkheimian fashion, with the magnitude of projected gods exactly commensurate in scale with each new contemporary political structure.

All sacred truths came originally from the revelations of inspired shaman-seers, in historic and ethnographic fact even the Hellenistic Paul's One God we have inherited. Jesus the Charismed himself was once as much a human savior-messiah as was Moses, first shaman-messiah of the Hebrews, in an earlier crisis time. The secular fact remains that all religions begin with either a paranoid shamanic self-impresario or a shaman-priest impresario of his supernatural Spirit-Helper or animal familiar. All gods are at least as real as shaman's visions, although perhaps not provably any more so. For the secular reality of shamans we need postulate only a human ability to dream, to fall subject to trance or epileptic seizure (like Paul), or to experience sensory-deprivation hallucinations.

Now, very possibly the vast majority of supernatural experiences can be traced to such autonomous psychological states. But in the whole shamanic visionary complex of the Paleolithic Ur-religion, there is one very powerful impetus to vision as yet unmentioned: the proven ability of some psychotropic drugs to produce convincing hallucinatory experience. Some individuals, "spiritually" quite ungifted in spontaneous visionary skill, are nevertheless capable of authentic hallucinations, given pharmacodynamic help. With some other anthropologists, I believe that the use of powerful botanical hallucinogens has been a real and important vehicle of shamanistic ecstasy, not only in modern ethnographic time but also in prehistoric antiquity.

For a demonstration of this, one need only turn to the most recent work of a number of scholars in the field of shamanism—not only ethnologists but prehistorians, ethnobotanists, and students of "primitive" or tribal arts. Indeed, the basic theme of the symposium of which this volume is a result is the many ethnological uses of psychotropic drugs as an ecstatic bridge to the "supernatural" world of shamanic religion. Here I wish to single out only one especially memorable achievement, that of R. Gordon Wasson on narcotic mushrooms in both the Old World and the New, because it bears so directly on my own hypothesis of the very great antiquity of man's ritual utilization of plants with psychotomimetic properties. Wasson's data demonstrate (I think) a Mesolithic age for the use of narcotic mushrooms, a remote enough date to make proto-Indo-European, Uralic, Paleo-Siberian, and American Indian use of narcotic mushrooms all ethnographically related (cf. La Barre, 1970b). His work also shows, in my opinion, that the nectar and ambrosia that made the Greek gods divine were probably fermented honey-mead and a narcotic mushroom, both of which would be psychotropic if taken by a human shaman.

There is another reason to suggest Mesolithic (even Paleolithic) antiquity, since the base culture of the American Indian, as shown in culture traits shared from Alaska to Patagonia, is essentially Paleo-Mesolithic in horizon; and Boas long ago noted that the base religion everywhere in the New World was shamanism. In this respect, aboriginal religion in the whole New World represents a kind of Mesolithic fossil, little changed except in high cultures founded on agriculture, and the religion even in these cultures still shows shamanic origins. For example,

Mexican gods—often dressed in the skins of their animal and bird spirit familiars, the shaman's human head encased in an animal or bird head—have to be fed continually on the souls of sacrificial victims in order to maintain their spirit power. This is not unlike the head-hunting of the Jívaro, done in order to keep up the individual's stock of medicine power. The only difference is that gods are spirits and shamans are men.

There exists a very striking statistical anomaly with respect to psychotropic drugs, which a pooling of botanical and ethnographic knowledge may serve to explain. This anomaly is that whereas New World natives knew eighty to a hundred such drugs, the Old World had only about a half-dozen. There is good reason to expect the reverse to be true: (1) The Old World has a far greater land mass than the New; hence we might suppose that it could support a proportionately greater variety of psychotropic plants. (2) Surely the Old World contains as great a variety of climates as the New World, and since the psychotropic elements in plants (some genera of which are metropolitan) are contained as alkaloids, glucosides, resins, and essential oils in the bark, leaves, stem, sap, flowers, roots, and other parts of plants, it is difficult to explain the discrepancy on grounds of botanical distribution or ecology. (3) Men and protomen who might have discovered the psychotropic properties. of plants have existed for an incomparably longer period in the Old World than in the New, Australopithecines and *Homo habilis* several millions of years ago as opposed to mere tens of thousands of years for late Paleolithic and Mesolithic men in the Americas. (4) Of perhaps 800,000 plant species, among the 200,000–500,000 Angiosperms only about 3000 are known ever to have been used directly as human food, and only about 150 of these are important enough to have entered world commerce; in fact, only about 12 or 13, all of them cultivated, really stand between man and starvation. Small as this number is, the provenance of major food plants is nevertheless reasonably balanced between the Old and New Worlds. Since ingested plants are in each case at issue, *why should not psychotropic plants be as balanced in their hemispheric provenance as are food plants?* (5) Again, despite the brilliant researches of Spruce and Schultes and others, it can hardly be maintained that New World plants are better known to science than those of the long-researched Old World—in fact, the many new species discovered by Schultes alone would contradict this supposition. (6) Further, the critical point is that not only are more narcotics *known* from the New World, but also *they were already known to the American Indians.**

* In one of those notes that panel members, anxious not to disturb the main discussion, pass back and forth at conferences, I wrote Schultes (in San Juan), "Do you think there are any major psychoactive drugs that American Indians did *not* use?" His reply: "Yes. They may have *discovered* them but they are not employed, possibly

Although I originally (1964) postulated an aboriginal "narcotic complex" in the New World on purely ethnographic grounds, it seems to me that these additional botanical and ethnobotanical considerations further support the hypothesis. The striking discrepancy between the Old and New Worlds in the numbers of known psychotropic plants must rest on ethnographic rather than botanical grounds. It is, in fact, the ubiquitous persistence of shamanism in aboriginal hunting peoples of the New World that provides the solution. The evidence is consistent. On the one hand, many anthropologists have shown that simple shamanism is everywhere the religion of hunting peoples, whether ancient or surviving hunters. On the other hand, we know that Old World religions (although still discernibly derived in part from prior shamanism) have been massively modified by the "Neolithic Revolution," and the same has been true of the religions of agricultural peoples in the Americas. It is simply that in the Americas the hunting base of shamanism has been better preserved to "ethnographic present" times. Although the very Neolithic parallels in both hemispheres themselves prove our point about change, otherwise the Americas represent ethnographically a kind of Paleo-Mesolithic "fossil" of the Old World. We shall demonstrate this in a moment. Meanwhile, it should be noted that ecstatic-visionary shamanism is, so to speak, *culturally programmed for an interest in hallucinogens and other psychotropic drugs.*

Although essentially Asiatic Paleo-Siberians (the Akmak people) * early hunted in interior Alaska and on the tundra of "Beringia" at the height of the last glaciation—when so much water was tied up in glacial ice that Asia and North America were connected by a 1300-mile-wide, dry-land corridor—the rest of the New World was blocked to man by an all-Canada glacier that gapped only about 14,000 years ago. Americanists now date the first considerable invasion by proto-Indians to the Late Paleolithic big-game hunters of the interior North American plains. Their culture can be traced through the "Magdalenian" of Lake Baikal sites in Siberia westward to the classic Magdalenian of western Eurasia. Most authorities hesitate to go beyond this evidence. Baby mammoth bones in California, charred whether by man-made or natural fires, imply in date a

---

because they are too toxic or otherwise dangerous. Especially: a number of the Solanaceae. The Apocynaceae (the family richest in alkaloids or at least the best studied [since] *Rauwolfia* [is] a member) *must* have a number with psychoactive principles, but I know of none that are used except *iboga*."

* Cf., D. D. Anderson, "A Stone Age Campsite at the Gateway of America," *Scientific American*, 218, No. 6 (June 1968) 24–33, p. 29. Standard contemporary opinion on proto-Indians: J. B. Griffin, "Some Prehistoric Connections Between Siberia and America," in J. R. Caldwell, ed., *New Roads to Yesterday, Essays in Archaeology* (New York: Basic Books, 1966). G. R. Willey, "New World Prehistory," in Caldwell, *op. cit.*, pp. 302–32, and "New World Archeology in 1965," *Proceedings of the American Philosophical Association*, 110, No. 2 (22 April 1966) 140–45.

Neanderthal phase of man in America that has never been found paleontologically and that few believe in. Certainly in physical type the American Indian is only a standard paleo-Mongoloid version of modern *Homo sapiens*.

On the evidence of cultural traits universal or near-universal, from Alaska to Patagonia (e.g., the bow and arrow, which is merely Upper Paleolithic in Eurasia, the spear thrower, the dog), it is evident that the southward trickle of paleo-Siberian hunting bands continued on into the Mesolithic, a conclusion based on the sporadic and widely scattered occurrence of Mesolithic-type remains in Middle and South America. At this time, some authorities believe, the late-comer Eskimo somewhat blocked further incursions of Asiatic cultures and peoples. This picture is fully confirmed: archaeologically, by Asiatic-American semi-subter-ranean houses from Siberia to Alaska and the American Southwest; lin-guistically, by tone languages like Navaho and Apache, linked, through proto-Athapaskan and proto-Sinitic, to the Tibeto-Chinese tone languages of Asia; culturally, by the conical tipi-wigwam extending from western Asia across Siberia to the Central Algonkians of the Great Lakes, snow vehicles from Finland to Maine, the circumboreal bear ceremonialism, the Tungus olonism and American vision-quest complex, with many other cognates in ancient Eurasia; folkloristically, in the Eurasiatic-American lightning-eagle, the magic flight motif, the Orpheus legend, and other mythic themes; and even botanically, in the absence of aborigi-nally shared cultigens. Even latitudinarians who grant later influences (the close-to-Asia late and limited diffusion of body armor, the similarity of Northwest Coast and other New World art motifs to those on the earliest Chinese Shang Dynasty bronzes, the very probable sporadic Oceanic influences on the west-coastal New World) all hold to this basic consensus. Archaeological, linguistic, cultural, folkloristic, and all other kinds of evidence agree with the physical-anthropological: the American Indians were unspecialized Mongoloids bearing a late-Paleolithic and Mesolithic paleo-Siberian hunting culture and religion.

All the invaders from Siberia were simple hunters and gatherers. All American agriculture and animal domestication (except the Mesolithic dog) were later local developments wholly independent of Asia. No later animal domesticates and no cultivated plants were intercontinentally shared in pre-Columbian times, although they diffused with astonishing speed in post-contact times, especially food plants such as maize and the potato, as well as tobacco. Significantly, however, the use of wild narcotic mushrooms in shamanistic religion is found both in aboriginal Siberia and America and also in very ancient (perhaps even Mesolithic) Eurasia. The ethos of American Indians was and essentially remained that of hunters (La Barre, 1970c: 121–60).

For one basic example, economic organization and social status every-where—even to the potlatch giveaway feasts of the wealthy Northwest Coast fishermen, the economic take-and-give of thé "great-house" chiefs of Amazonia, and the stored tax hoards of the royal Inca communal state—all were ultimately based on the invidious ability of hunters to provide shared largesse for their dependents (La Barre, 1970d: 128, 154–55). In this male-centered hunting society, curiously a boy's manhood and manly prowess in hunting and war and sexuality *all came as gifts from the outside*—that is, as "medicine power" imbibed from the outside, generalized, impersonal, mana-like, supernatural: the Siouan *wakan*, Algonkian *manitou,* Iroquoian *orenda,* etc. All aspects of male potency or "power" came not from any endogenous endocrine entelechy unfolding from within. At adolescence this power was acquired, or struck in like lightning (phallus-shaped, sometimes additionally ithyphallic, Zuñi "war-god" fetishes must be made of lightning-struck wood), or incorporated into the individual,* whether in the individual vision quest, the shamanic spirit-possessed ecstasy, or the therefore invariably *sacred* eating, drinking, snuffing, or smoking of psychotropic plants.

Even in the developed hierarchic agricultural societies of the Aztec of Mexico and the Chibcha of Colombia—with the generalized or impersonal supernatural now become personalized gods (e.g., the Aztec god of war whom, before sacrifice, the bravest war captive impersonated for a year: they "worshiped" not the enemy but the soon-to-be-incorporated "power" in him)—these gods still needed to be fed spirit-power like food, from human-sacrificial victims. The Aztec captured these victims; the Chibcha bought them in a lively trade with their neighbors. Quite as Andeans brought tribute to the Inca man-god, and as young Amazonian hunters perforce brought their game to the great-house chief to distribute, so also in religion hierarchic Aztec and Chibcha brought (appropriately) human-spirit food to their gods. The *hunting* of these victims was the chief motive of Aztec war; farther north scalping and farther south head-hunting had the same motive, the acquisition of spirit-power from scalp or skull, whether for the individual or for the tribe, a *collecting* of supernatural male "power." *Mos saecula, mos religiosa:* men need "power" for success in all male activities, gods need power to remain gods.

On the basic shamanic level it strikes us as strange that in the whole

---

* The Huichol assimilation of Elder Brother *deer* to *peyote* (actually hunted as if it were deer), to the nectar-and-ambrosia of *parched corn in sugar-water,* to the *peyote-footprint* of the supernatural deer, and to the male-ancestor Grandfather Fire (see Furst, above) is profoundly consistent in ideology with the symbolism of head-taking by the Jívaros. Both are quintessentially American Indian, and both expound what I consider to be the very core of New World religion, including that of Plains power-incorporation in the vision quest, down to and including peyotism.

area of the American narcotic complex, the "doctor," rather than just the sick patient, takes the "medicine." But we should not foist our pharmacodynamic category of secular medicine upon the American aborigines. The medicine man's taking of the *supernatural* "medicine" is entirely logical in native terms, since it is the shaman who needs the supernatural "power" to effect a cure—i.e., to diagnose the human or physical cause (often a crystal, a feather, a claw to be sucked out), to contest a rival's malevolent magic causing the illness, to prognosticate, for clairvoyance, to control the weather, etc.

Even more widely than in the narcotic-complex area proper, the shaman-visionary has power over an illness, manifestly, because with supernatural power, characteristically, he has himself recovered once from the illness. Therefore, any patient whom he cures naturally joins the "medicine society" of the shaman. Cure is much like initiation into a secret ritual one witnesses and learns. Thus, all the members of the Bear Society, for example, share "bear power" taught them by the shaman and ultimately originating in the shaman's supernatural "vision." Shaman and clients form a psychic sodality, like Alcoholics Anonymous.

For the American Indian, the presence in a plant of any psychotropic effect whatever was plain evidence of its containing supernatural "medicine" or spirit-shaking "power." One introjected the power exactly as he ate food. This principle was true even of so mildly psychedelic a drug as tobacco. Aboriginally, tobacco was *always* used in a sacred magico-religious context, and never for mere secular enjoyment or indulgence. Thus when the post-adolescent Amazonian boy dipped his spatula into the thick tobacco infusion in the men's palaver-pot and licked it off,* this act signified and sealed his yea-vote under sanction of supernatural punishment by the potent "power" in the tobacco were he to contravene what was really an oath; in usual Indian fashion all votes were by convention unanimous. And when, in the Woodlands or Plains, Indian chiefs in grave intertribal pow-wow smoked the sacred calumet or peace pipe, the rite similarly meant invoking the power of tobacco upon their sacred oath.

An Iroquois visionary made the appropriate gift to a "tobacco-begging supernatural" he was lucky enough to encounter in the woods and thereupon carved the face of the supernatural on a living basswood tree trunk; subsequently, in any dance of the False Face Society, he possessed the "power" of that supernatural when he wore the cut-off mask. In Plains peyotism, the participant censes himself in the smoke of the shavings the Cedar Chief casts into the ritual fire and rubs the sweet smell of *Artemisia* on his joints to preserve his body from aches and

---

* Some Amazonian tobaccos, it should be noted, are far more potent in nicotine than are the mild North American commercial cigarette tobaccos.

pains—but he is specifically "praying" when he smokes a blackjack oak-leaf- or cornhusk-wrapped cigarette in a peyote meeting. The abundant evidence from both continents would suggest, in fact, that tobacco is *the* supernatural plant *par excellence* of the American Indian, for tobacco was used aboriginally everywhere it would grow in the New World—that is, from middle Canada southward to Patagonia.

In similar fashion, no Andean communicant would dream of approaching the supernatural without being intoxicated with the chewed coca leaf, *Erythroxylon;* more precisely, the psychedelic effect *is* the presence of the supernatural. In Mexico, even into historic times, ritual intoxication on alcohol occurred in a sacred religious context; and the same was true in tribal drinking fiestas from the non-Pueblo Southwest to the Andean plateau and Amazonia.*

The Virginian "huskinawing" with the *Ilex* (*yaupon, cassine,* or *vomitoria*) "black drink" was a puberty ritual; the use of *Ilex paraguayensis,* of course, recurs in South America. *Datura* intoxication was variously part of a puberty ordeal or of shamanistic possession in southern California; sacrificial victims in Mexico appear to have been stupefied (more properly "possessed" from an Aztec point of view) by quantities of *Datura;* and in any other use of *Daturas* in South America, a similar magico-religious context should be sought. The same should be done with respect to the *Virola* snuffs and *cohoba,* hallucinogenic mints, etc.

Aboriginal Aztecan and modern Mazatecan use of the *teonanacatl* (*Psilocybe,* etc.) mushrooms (literally, eating the "flesh of the god") has very ancient cognates in the paleo-Siberian use of *Amanita* fly agaric in shaman-led group intoxications; the alleged "mushroom stones" in southern Mesoamerican archaeology represent probably just that. The Red Bean *Sophora secundiflora* had supernatural power whether laced on a moccasin fringe, hidden in a medicine bundle, or worn as a necklace, since it obviously had "medicine power" when eaten in a puberty ordeal. *Sophora* was used in the aboriginal Red Bean Cult spreading from prehistoric Texas (the evidence is archaeological) to the southern Siouans; it was probably the red bean used by some of the Ghost Dance cultists of 1890; and if the bean was used in mescal pulque, this may account for the egregious misnomer "mescal bean" for the peyote cactus (La Barre, 1938a, 1969).

With all specific tribal cultures now largely gone, Indians bearing residual generic Plains culture still regard the hallucinations produced by eating *peyotl* (an Aztec term for *Lophophora Williamsii*) as visionary proof of the presence of the supernatural. In fact, one might argue that

---

* See especially Bunzel, 1940:361–87; Carpenter, 1959:148–51; Daily, 1968:45–59; and La Barre, 1938b:224–34.

peyotism spread so rapidly in the Plains after 1890 because these vision-seeking cultures—even into southern Saskatchewan and California-Nevada tribes—were in a sense aboriginally "pre-adapted" to peyotism.* Whether shaman alone, or shaman and communicants, or communicants alone imbibe or ingest *Ilex* drinks, *Datura* infusions, tobacco in whatever form, native beers and wines, peyote cactus, ololiuqui or morning-glory seeds, mushrooms, narcotic mint leaves or coca, the ayahuasca "vine of the dead spirits" (*Banisteriopsis Caapi*), or any of the vast array of Amerindian psychotropic plants, the ethnographic principle is the same. *These plants contain spirit power.*

Although the earlier Indian use of psychotropic drugs in shamanistic hunting societies is still thoroughly visible in the Aztec use of many such drugs in their more codified seasonal rites to gods (*peyotl*, *Sophora* beans, *Agave* pulque, *teonanacatl* mushrooms, *yauhtli*, *toloache* [*Datura*], *ololiuqui* morning-glory seeds, narcotic mints, tobacco, etc.)—and to a degree also in the use of coca and other psychotropic plants in advanced agricultural-herding states of the Andes, such as the Aymara and the Inca—ethnologists have repeatedly remarked that the intensively agricultural Pueblos, with their more tightly organized politico-religious theocracies, manifest almost a positive repugnance to the use of alcohol and, with certain significant exceptions, other psychotropic substances. Nearer geographically than Plains Indians to the natural area of *Lophophora Williamsii,* the Pueblo Indians nevertheless are not peyotists. Historically, they have been longer exposed to Mexican-Southwestern peyotism than have Plains tribes; but only Taos, interestingly enough the most Plains-like of the Pueblos, has become even partly peyotist, and that only after a centuries-long battle. In the midst of Athapaskan and Yuman tribes, with their typical ritual use of many beers and wines, the Pueblos yet shun alcohol. They also lack any red bean cult, although again the plant is more accessible to them than it is to the northern Siouans; and although they border on Mexican tribes that use narcotic mushrooms, ololiuqui, psychotropic mints, etc., the Pueblos use none of these agents. Among Pueblo agriculturalists, erstwhile shamans have become primarily rain-priests, emphasizing almost exclusively the old ability of shamans to control the weather and to cure. Nevertheless, even here there are strong echoes still of the shaman's ancient relationship to psychotropic plants, especially among the Zuñi, where *A'neglakya, Datura stramonium,* is sacred and "belongs" to the rain priests and the directors of certain religious fraternities. Only they are allowed to collect it. The priests ingest *Datura* to achieve trance states, to "listen to the voices of the

---

* Ruth Shonle (1925:53–75) predicted that peyotism would spread as far as the aboriginal vision quest in the Plains. This is precisely what subsequently happened.

birds," to cure and divine—in other words, in the traditional shamanistic manner. *Datura* is also employed by Zuñi curers as an external medicine for wounds and bruises.

It would seem that although shamanism is strongly associated with a general hunting ecology, a considerably changed priestly religion is to be expected among settled Neolithic societies, as though their whole anxiety structure had changed with their ecology. If so, this would account for the masking over of shamanic origins and change from the earlier religion among advanced agricultural peoples, including Europeans. Evidently the "aleatic" anxiety of agriculturalists and pastoralists is the weather, not the contingencies of the hunt. In ethos essentially still hunters, American Indians (to some degree even the high agricultural centers) kept in their religion the characteristic shamanism of hunters. American Indians still actively sought the mystic visionary experience. Their epistemological touchstone for reality was direct personal psychic experience of the forces in nature; their shamanism fits the individualism of hunters, as priestly hierarchies fit agricultural societies. Under the religio-cultural inspiration of shamanism, they still sought the actively psychotropic drugs that ensure this state. Their cognitive map was that of mystics, perhaps, but it was also pharmacodynamically pragmatic: *some plants house spirits and psychedelic forces.*

Because the Americas in contact times still gave domicile to primarily hunting peoples, and because in great part the New World contained more of the little-changed hunting cultures than was the case in much of the Neolithic Old World, the generally Mesolithic drug-using shamanisms in America developed, over time, the distinctive "narcotic complex" we encounter ethnographically. In our medico-psychiatric search for psychotropic substances, perhaps the ethnobotanist and paleoethnologist need only learn again what earlier men already knew.

Bibliography

AARONSON, BERNARD, and HARVEY OSMOND, 1970. *Psychedelics: The Uses and Implications of Hallucinogenic Drugs.* Garden City, N.Y.: Doubleday.

ABERLE, DAVID F., 1966. *The Peyote Religion Among the Navaho.* Chicago: Aldine.

AGURELL, S., BO HOLMSTEDT, and J.-E. LINDGREN, 1968a. "Alkaloid content of *Banisteriopsis Rusbyana,*" *American Journal of Pharmacy,* CXL, 148–51.

———, 1968b. "Alkaloids in certain species of *Virola* and other South American plants of ethnopharmacologic interest," *Acta Chemica Scandinavica,* XXIII, 903–16.

———, R. E. SCHULTES, 1968. "Identification of two new B-carboline alkaloids in South American hallucinogenic plants," *Biochemical Pharmacology,* XVII, 2487–88.

ALBARRACIN, LEOPOLDO, 1925. *Contribución al Estudio de los Alcaloides del Yagé.* Bogotá.

ALLEGRO, JOHN, 1970. *The Sacred Mushroom and the Cross.* Garden City, N.Y.: Doubleday.

ALTSCHUL, SIRI VON REIS, 1964. "A taxonomic study of the genus *Anadenanthera,*" *Contributions of the Gray Herbarium, Harvard University,* No. 193, 3–65.

———, 1967. "Vilca and Its Use," in D. Efron, ed., *Ethnopharmacologic Search for Psychoactive Drugs.* Public Health Service Pub. No. 1645. Washington, D.C.: U.S. Government Printing Office, pp. 307–14.

ANDERSON, EDWARD F., 1961. "A Taxonomic Revision of Ariocarpus, Lophophora, Pelecyphora, and Obregonia." Unpublished Ph.D. thesis, Claremont Graduate School, Claremont, Calif.

———, 1969. "The biogeography, ecology, and taxonomy of Lophophora (Cactacea)," *Brittonia,* XXI, 4, 299–310.

ANDREWS, G., and S. VINKENOOG, 1969. *The Book of Grass: An Anthology of Indian Hemp.* New York: Grove Press.

BACKEBERG, CURT, 1959. *Die Cactaceae. Handbuch der Kakteenkunde,* Vol. II. Jena: Gustav Fischer Verlag.

BADASZ, J., 1968. "The Hungarian Shaman's Technique of Trance Induction," in V. Dioszegi, ed., *Popular Reliefs and Folklore Tradition in Siberia.* Bloomington, Ind.: Indiana University Press, pp. 53–75.

279

BARRIGA VILLALBA, A. M., 1925. "Un nuevo alcaloide," *Boletín de la Sociedad Colombiana de Ciencias Naturales* (Bogotá), pp. 31–36.

BARRON, FRANK, MURRAY E. JARVIK, and STERLING BUNNELL, JR., 1964. "The hallucinogenic drugs," *Scientific American*, CCX, 4, 29–37.

BARTHEL, THOMAS, 1966. "Mesoamerikanische Fledermausdämonen," *Tribus* (Stuttgart), XV, 101–24.

BECHER, HANS, 1960. "Die Surará und Pakidái, zwei Yanananii Stämme in Nordwestbrasilien," *Mitteilungen aus dem Museum für Völkerkunde in Hamburg*, XXVI, 1–138.

BENITEZ, FERNANDO, 1968a. *En la Tierra Mágica del Peyote*. México: Biblioteca Era.

——, 1968b. *Los Indios de México*. Vol. II. México: Biblioteca Era.

——, 1970 *Los Indios de México*. Vol. III. México: Biblioteca Era.

BENNETT, WENDELL C., and ROBERT M. ZINGG, 1935. *The Tarahumara, an Indian Tribe of Northern Mexico*. Chicago: University of Chicago Press.

BENTOWA, S., 1936. *Le Chanvre dans les Croyances et les Coutumes Populaires*. Warsaw, Poland: Institute of Anthropological Sciences.

BERG, C. C., 1969. "New taxa and combinations in the neotropical Olmedieae," *Acta Botanica Neerlandica*, XVIII, 462–65.

BEVERLY, R., 1705. *History and Present State of Virginia*, II. London: R. Parker.

BIBRA, ERNST VON, 1855. *Die Narkotischen Genussmittel und der Mensch*. Nürnberg, Germany: Verlag von Wilhelm Schmid.

BIOCCA, ETTORE, 1965–66. *Viaggi tra gli Indi. Alto Rio Negro–Alto Orinoco. Appunti di un Biologo*, 4 vols. Rome: Consiglio Nazionale delle Ricerche.

BLOOMQUIST, E. R., 1968. *Marihuana*. Los Angeles: Glencoe Press.

BOKE, NORMAN H., and EDWARD F. ANDERSON, 1970. "Structure, development, and taxonomy in the genus Lophophora," *American Journal of Botany*, LVII, 5, 569–78.

BORHEGYI, S. A. DE, 1961. "Miniature mushroom stones from Guatemala," *American Antiquity*, XXVI, 498–504.

BOWDICH, T. EDWARD, 1819. *Mission from Cape Coast Castle to Ashantee and Geographical Notices of Other Parts of the Interior of Africa*. London.

BOWLES, P., 1962. *A Hundred Camels in the Courtyard*. San Francisco: City Lights Bookshop.

BOYCE, S. S., 1900. *Hemp (Cannabis Sativa)*. New York: Orange Judd Co.

BRAGA, D. L., and J. L. MCLAUGHLIN, 1969. "Cactus alkaloids V. Isolation of hordenine and N-methyltyramine from *Ariocarpus retusus*," *Planta Medica* (Stuttgart), XVII, 1, 87–94.

BRAVO, H., 1967. "Una revisión del género *Lophophora*," *Cactaceas y Succulentas Mexicanas*, XII, 8–17.

BRETSCHNEIDER, C., 1870. *On the Study and Value of Chinese Botanical Works with Notes on the History of Plants and Geographical Botany from Chinese Sources*. Fouchow.

BRISTOL, MELVIN L., 1965. "Sibundoy Ethnobotany." Unpublished Ph.D. thesis, Harvard University, Cambridge, Mass.

——, 1966a. "Notes on the species of tree Daturas," *Botanical Museum Leaflets*, Harvard University, XXI, 229–48.

——, 1966b. "The psychotropic *Banisteriopsis* among the Sibundoy of Colombia," *Botanical Museum Leaflets*, Harvard University, XXI, 113–40.

——, 1968. "Sibundoy agricultural vegetation," *Proceedings of the XXXVII International Congress of Americanists*, II, 575–602.

————, 1969. "Tree Datura drugs of the Colombian Sibundoy," *Botanical Museum Leaflets,* Harvard University, XXII, 165–227.

BRITTON, N. L., and J. N. ROSE, 1920. *The Cactaceae: Descriptions and Illustrations of Plants of the Cactus Family.* Publication No. 248, Vol. II. Washington, D.C.: Carnegie Institute.

BRUZZI ALVES DA SILVA, ALCIONILIO, 1962. *A Civilizacão Indígena do Uaupés.* São Paulo, Brazil: Linográfica Editôra, Ltda.

BUNZEL, RUTH, 1940. "The role of alcohol in two Central American cultures," *Psychiatry,* III, 361–87.

CAMPBELL, T. N., 1958. "Origin of the mescal bean cult," *American Anthropologist,* LX, 156–60.

CANDOLLE, A. DE, 1869 (1882). *The Origin of Cultivated Plants.* Paris.

CARPENTER, E. S., 1959. "Alcohol in the Iroquois dream quest," *American Journal of Psychiatry,* CXVI, 148–51.

CASTANEDA, CARLOS, 1969. *The Teachings of Don Juan: A Yaqui Way of Knowledge.* New York: Ballantine Books.

————, 1971. *A Separate Reality: Further Conversations with Don Juan.* New York: Simon & Schuster.

CASTILLO, GABRIEL DEL, 1963. "La ayahuasca, planta mágica de la Amazona," *Perú Indígena,* X, 88–98.

CHAGNON, NAPOLEON A., PHILIP LE QUESNE, and JAMES M. COOK, 1971. "Yanomamö hallucinogens: anthropological, botanical, and chemical findings," *Current Anthropology,* XII, 1, 72–74.

CHEN, A. L., and K. K. CHEN, 1939. "Harmine, the alkaloid of caapi," *Quarterly Journal of Pharmacy and Pharmacology,* XII, 30–38.

CHIAPPE, MARIO, 1968. "Psiquiatría Folklórica Peruana: El Curanderismo en la Costa Norte del Perú." MS. partially published in *Anales, VIII Congreso Boliviano (V Congreso Latinoamericano), Sobre Psiquiatría en América Latina,* pp. 530–48.

CLARK, WALTER HOUSTON, 1969. *Chemical Ecstasy—Psychedelic Drugs and Religion.* New York: Sheed and Ward.

COE, MICHAEL D., 1966. *The Maya.* New York: Praeger Publishers.

COHEN, SIDNEY, 1970. "The Hallucinogens," in W. G. Clark and J. del Giudice, eds., *Principles of Psychopharmacology.* New York: Academic Press, pp. 489–503.

CREVAUX, J., 1883. *Voyages dans l'Amérique du Sud.* Paris.

CRUZ SANCHEZ, G., 1948a. "Aplicaciones populares de la cimora en el norte del Perú," *Revista de Farmacología y Medicina Experimental* (Lima), I, 253 ff.

————, 1948b. "Farmacología de *Opuntia cylindrica,*" *Revista de Farmacología y Medicina Experimental* (Lima), I, 143 ff.

CUATRECASAS, JOSÉ, 1958. *Prima Flora Colombiana 2—Malpighiaceae. Webbia,* XIII, Florence, 343–664.

DAILEY, R. C., 1968. "The role of alcohol among North American Indians as reported in the Jesuit relations," *Antropológica,* X, 1, 45–59.

DER MARDEROSIAN, ARA H., 1965. "Nomenclatural history of the morning glory *Ipomoea violacea* (L.)," *Taxon,* XIV, 234–40.

————, 1966. "Current status of hallucinogens in the Cactaceae," *American Journal of Pharmacy,* CXXXVIII, 204–12.

————, 1967. "Hallucinogenic indole compounds from higher plants," *Lloydia,* XXX, 23–38.

————, KENNETH M. KENSINGER, JEW-MING CHAO, and FREDERICK I. GOLDSTEIN,

1970. "The use and hallucinatory principles of a psychoactive beverage of the Cashinahua tribe (Amazon basin)," *Drug Dependence,* No. 5, 7–14.

——, HOMER V. PINKLEY, and MURREL F. DOBBINS, 1968. "Native use and occurrence of N, N-dimethyltryptamine in the leaves of *Banisteriopsis Rusbyana," American Journal of Pharmacy,* CXL, 137–47.

——, and H. W. YOUNGKEN, JR., 1966. "The distribution of indole alkaloids among certain species and varieties of *Ipomoea, Rivea* and *Convolvulus (Convolvulaceae)," Lloydia,* XXIX, 35–42.

DEULOFEU, V., 1967. "Chemical Compounds Isolated from Banisteriopsis and Related Species," in D. Efron, ed., *Ethnopharmacologic Search for Psychoactive Drugs.* Public Health Service Pub. No. 1645. Washington, D.C.: U.S. Govt. Printing Office, pp. 393–402.

DIOSZEGI, VILMOS, 1968. *Tracing Shamans in Siberia.* Oosterhout, the Netherlands: Anthropological Publications.

DOBKIN (DE RIOS), MARLENE, 1968. "Trichocereus pachanoi: a mescaline cactus used in folk healing in Peru," *Economic Botany,* XXII, 2 (April–June), 191–94.

——, 1969a. "Folk healing with a psychedelic cactus in north coastal Peru," *International Journal of Social Psychiatry,* XV, 1 (Fall–Winter), 23–32.

——, 1969b. "Curanderismo psicodélico en el Perú: continuidad y cambio," *Mesa Redonda de Ciencias Prehistóricas y Antropológicas* (Lima), Ier tomo, Publicaciones del Instituto Riva-Aguero, No. 58A, 139–49.

——, 1969c. "Fortune's malice: divination, psychotherapy, and folk medicine in Peru," *Journal of American Folklore,* LXXXII, 324 (April–June), 132–41.

——, 1970. "A note on the use of ayahuasca among urban Mestizo populations in the Peruvian Amazon," *American Anthropologist,* LXXII, 1419–22.

DOBRIZHOFFER, P. MARTIN, 1822. *An Account of the Abipones, an Equestrian People of Paraguay.* Transl., Sara Coleridge from the Latin edition of 1784. 3 vols. London.

DOWNING, D. F., 1962. "The chemistry of the psychotomimetic substances," *Quarterly Review,* XVI, 133–62.

DRAGUNSKY, LUIS, 1968. "El Curanderismo en la Costa Norte Peruana." Unpublished MS. On file at Latin American Center, University of California at Los Angeles.

DUCHAILLU, PAUL, 1903. *Adventures in the Great Equatorial Forest and in the Country of the Dwarfs.* New York.

DUCKE, ADOLPHO, 1939. *As Leguminosas da Amazônia Brasileira.* Rio de Janeiro: Servicio de Publicidade Agricula.

DURÁN, FRAY DIEGO, 1971. *Book of the Gods and Rites and the Ancient Calendar.* Transl. and ed., Fernando Horcasitas and Doris Heyden. Norman: University of Oklahoma Press.

EFRON, DANIEL, ed., 1967. *Ethnopharmacologic Search for Psychoactive Drugs.* U.S. Public Health Service Pub. No. 1645. Washington, D.C.: U.S. Govt. Printing Office.

ELGER, F., 1928. "Ueber das Vorkommen von Harmin in einer südamerikanischen Liane (Yagé)," *Helv. Chim. Acta,* XI, 162–66.

ELIADE, MIRCEA, 1961. *Images and Symbols.* New York: Sheed & Ward.

——, 1964. *Shamanism: Archaic Techniques of Ecstasy,* Bollingen Series LXXVI. New York: Pantheon Books.

ENGUTU, ONDOUA, 1954. *Dulu Bon be Afrikare.* Ebolowa, Cameroun.

EPLING, C., and C. D. JAVITA-M., 1962. "A new species of Salvia from Mexico," *Botanical Museum Leaflets,* Harvard University, XX, 75–76.

EUGSTER, C. H., 1967. "Isolation, Structure and Syntheses of Central-Active Compounds from *Amanita Muscaria* (L. ex Fr.) Hooker," in D. Efron, ed., *Ethnopharmacologic Search for Psychoactive Drugs.* Public Health Service Pub. No. 1645. Washington, D.C.: U.S. Govt. Printing Office, pp. 416–18.

FADIMAN, JAMES, 1965. "Psychedelic properties of *Genista canariensis,*" *Economic Botany,* XIX, 383–84; also C. Tait, ed., in *Altered States of Consciousness.* New York: Wiley & Sons, 1969.

FARNSWORTH, NORMAN R., 1968. "Hallucinogenic plants," *Science,* CLXII, 1086–92.

FERNANDEZ, JAMES W., 1964. "African religious movements, types and dynamics," *The Journal of Modern African Studies,* II, 4, 531–49.

———, 1965. "Symbolic consensus in a Fang reformative cult," *American Anthropologist,* LXVII, 4, 902–27.

———, 1969. "Contemporary African religion: confluents of inquiry," in G. M. Carter, ed., *Expanding Horizons in African Studies.* Evanston, Ill.: Northwestern University Press.

FIELDS, F. HERBERT, 1969. "*Rivea corymbosa:* notes on some Zapotecan customs," *Economic Botany,* XXIII, 206–09.

FISCHER CARDENAS, G., 1923. "Estudio Sobre el Principio Activo del *Yagé.*" Tesis inédita, Universidad Nacional, Bogotá.

FRIEDBERG, CLAUDINE, 1959. "Rapport sommaire sur une mission au Pérou," *Journal d'Agriculture Tropicale et de Botanique Appliquée,* VI, 8–9, 439–50.

———, 1963. "Mission au Pérou: mai 1961–mars 1962," *Journal d'Agriculture Tropicale et de Botanique Appliquée,* X, 1–9, 33–52, 245–58, 344–86.

———, 1964. "Utilisation d'un cactus à mescaline au nord du Pérou (*Trichocereus Pachanoi* Brit. et Rose)," *Proceedings, VI International Congress of Anthropological and Ethnological Sciences,* II, pt. 2, pp. 21–26.

———, 1965. "Des Banisteriopsis utilisés comme drogue en Amérique du Sud," *Journal d'Agriculture Tropicale et de Botanique Appliquée,* XII, 403–37, 550–94, 729–80.

FRIEKEL, PROTÁSIO, 1961. "Mori—a festa do rapé (Indios kachiryana, rio Trombetas)," *Boletim, Museu Paraense Emílio Goeldi,* n.s., Anthrop. 12, 1 ff.

FURST, PETER T., 1967. "Huichol conceptions of the soul," *Folklore Americas,* XXVII, 2, 39–106.

———, 1970. "The *Tsité* (*Erythrina* spp.) of the Popol Vuh and other psychotropic plants in pre-Columbian art," *Annual Meeting of the Society for American Archaeology,* April 29–May 2, Mexico.

———, 1971a. "*Ariocarpus retusus,* the 'false peyote' of Huichol tradition," *Economic Botany,* XXV, 182–87.

———, 1971b. "Concepto huichol del alma," in *Coras, Huicholes y Tepehuanos.* Estudios etnográficos, Colección de Antropología Social del Instituto Nacional Indigenista, Mexico.

———, 1971c. "Psychotropic Flora and Fauna in Pre-Columbian Art." Symposium on The Prehistoric Arts of Arid America, October 29, 1971. The International Center for Arid and Semi-Arid Land Studies and the Museum of Texas Tech University, Lubbock (in press).

———, and BARBARA G. MYERHOFF, 1971. "El mito como historia: ciclo del peyote y del datura entre los Huicholes de México," in *Coras, Huicholes y Tepehuanos.* Estudios etnográficos, Colección de Antropología Social del Instituto Nacional Indigenista. Mexico.

GALLEY, SAMUEL, n.d. *Dictionnaire Fang-Français et Français-Fang.* Neuchâtel.

GAMAGE, J. R., and E. L. ZERKIN, 1969. *A Comprehensive Guide to the English-*

language Literature on Cannabis (Marihuana). Beloit, Wis.: STASH Press.

GARCIA-BARRIGA, HERNANDO, 1958. "El yajé, caapi o ayahuasca—un alucinógeno amazónico," *Universidad Nacional de Colombia,* 23, 59–76.

GENEST, K., W. B. RICE, and C. G. FARMILO, 1965. "Psychotomimetic substances in morning glory seeds," *Proceedings of the Canadian Society of Forensic Studies,* 4, 167–86.

GILLIN, JOHN, 1936. *The Barama River Caribs.* Papers of the Peabody Museum of American Archaeology and Ethnology of Harvard University, XIV, No. 2, Cambridge, Mass.

———, 1945. *Moche: A Peruvian Coastal Community.* Washington, D.C.: Smithsonian Institution.

GIRAL, F., and S. LADABAUM, 1959. "Principio amargo del zacatechichi," *Ciencia,* XIX, 243.

GOLDMAN, IRVING, 1963. *The Cubeo—Indians of the Northwest Amazon.* Illinois Studies in Anthropology, No. 2. Urbana: University of Illinois Press.

GONCALVES DE LIMA, OSWALDO, 1946. "Observações sobre o 'vinho de jurema' utilizado pelos indios Pancarú de Tacaratú (Pernambuco)," *Arquivos do Instituto de Pesquisas Agronómicas,* IV, 45–80. Recife.

GONZALEZ HUERTA, INES, 1960. "Identificación de la Mescalina Contenida en el *Trichocereus Pachanoi* (San Pedro)," *Revista del Viernes Médico* (Lima), XI, 1, 133–37.

GRANIER-DOYEUX, M., 1965. "Native hallucinogenic drugs: Piptadenias," *Bulletin of Narcotics,* XVII, 29–38.

GROF, STANISLAV, 1970a. "Beyond Psychoanalysis: I. Implications of LSD Research for Understanding Dimensions of Human Personality." Paper presented as preprint at the Second Interdisciplinary Conference on Voluntary Control of Internal States, Council Grove, Kansas, April 13–17. Published in *Darshana International,* X, 3 (July, 1970), 55–73.

———, 1970b. "Beyond Psychoanalysis: II. A Conceptual Model of Human Personality Encompassing the Psychedelic Phenomena." Second ICVCIS, Council Grove, Kansas, April 13–17.

GUERRA, FRANCISCO, and H. OLIVERA, 1954. *Las plantas fantásticas de México.* México, D.F., México: Imprenta del Diario Español.

GUNN, J. A., 1937. "The Harmine Group of Alkaloids," in B. Hefter, ed., *Handbuch der Experimentellen Pharmakologie.* Berlin.

GUTIÉRREZ-NORIEGA, CARLOS, 1950. "Area de mescalinismo en el Perú," *América Indígena,* X, 215.

———, and G. CRUZ SÁNCHEZ, 1947. "Alteraciones mentales producidas por la *Opuntia cylindrica,*" *Revista de Neuropsiquiatría* (Lima), X, 422 ff.

GUZMÁN-HUERTA, GASTÓN, 1959a. "Estudio Taxonómico y Ecológico de los Hongo Neurotrópicos Mexicanos." Tesis Profesional, Instituto Politécnico Nacional, Ciencias Biológicas, Mexico.

———, 1959b. "Sinopsis de los conocimientos sobre los hongos alucinogénicos mexicanos," *Boletín de la Sociedad Botánica de México,* No. 24, 14–34.

HAMMERMAN, A. F., 1930. "Le yagé en Amazonie," *Rev. Bot. Appl. Agric. Colon,* X, 600 ff.

HARNER, M. J., 1968. "The sound of rushing water," *Natural History,* LXXVII, 28–33, 60–61.

HARRISON, JANE ELLEN, 1908. *Prolegomena to the Study of Greek Religion.* 2nd ed. Cambridge: Cambridge University Press, Meridian paperback.

HARTWICH, C., 1911. *Die Menschlichen Genussmittel.* Leipzig: Chr. Herm. Tauchnitz.

HEIM, ROGER, 1956a. "Les champignons divinatoires utilisés dans les rites des Indiens mazatèques. . . ." *Comptes Rendus Hebdomadaires des Séances de l'Académie des Sciences*, Paris, 242, 965–68.

——, 1956b. "Les champignons divinatoires recueillis. . . ." *Comptes Rendus*, Paris, 242, 1389–95.

——, 1957a. "Les agarics hallucinogènes du genre *Psilocybe* recueillis. . . ." *Comptes Rendus*, Paris, 244, 659–700.

——, 1957b. "Notes préliminaires sur les agarics hallucinogènes du Mexique," *Revue de Mycologie*, XXII, 58–79; 183–98.

——, 1963. *Les Champignons Toxiques et Hallucinogènes*. Paris: N. Boubée & Cie.

——, 1965. "Les substances indoliques produites par les champignons toxiques et hallucinogènes," *Bulletin de Médicine Légale*, VIII, 122–41.

——, 1967. *Nouvelles Investigations sur les Champignons Hallucinogènes*. Paris: Editions du Muséum National d'Histoire Naturelle.

——, and R. GORDON WASSON, 1962. "Une investigation sur les champignons sacrés des Mixtèques," *Comptes Rendus*, 254, 788–91.

HERNÁNDEZ, FRANCISCO, 1651. *Nova Plantarum, Animalium et Mineralium Mexicanorum Historia*. . . . Rome: B. Deuersini et Z. Masotti.

HISSINK, KARIN, and ALBERT HAHN, 1961. *Die Tacana: Ergebnisse der Frobenius-Expedition nach Bolivien, 1952 bis 1954*. Vol. I: Erzählungsgut. Stuttgart: W. Kohlhammer.

HOCHSTEIN, F. A., and A. M. PARADIES, 1957. "Alkaloids of *Banisteria Caapi* and *Prestonia amazonicum*," *Journal of the American Chemical Society*, LXXIX, 5735–36.

HOFFER, A., and H. OSMOND, 1967. *The Hallucinogens*. New York: Academic Press.

HOFFMANN, R. M., 1968. "Datura: Its Use Among Indian Tribes of Southwestern North America." Unpublished MS., Botanical Museum, Harvard University, Cambridge, Mass.

HOFMANN, ALBERT, 1961. "Chemical, pharmacological and medical aspects of psychotomimetics," *Journal of Experimental Medical Sciences*, V, 31–51.

——, 1963. "Psychotomimetic substances," *Indian Journal of Pharmacy*, XXV, 245–56.

——, 1963. "The active principles of the seeds of *Rivea corymbosa* and *Ipomoea violacea*," *Botanical Museum Leaflets*, Harvard University, XX, 194–212.

——, 1966. "The Active Principles of the Seeds of *Rivea Corymbosa* (L.) Hall F. (Ololiuhqui, Badoh) and *Ipomoea Tricolor* Cav. (Badoh Negro)." In: *Summa Antropológica en Homena je a Roberto J. Weitlaner*, Instituto Nacional de Antropología e Historia, México, pp. 349–57.

——, 1968. "Psychotomimetic Agents," in A. Burger, ed., *Chemical Constitution and Pharmacodynamic Action*. New York: M. Dekker, II, pp. 169–235.

——, and H. TSCHERTER, 1960. "Isolierung von Lysergsäure-Alkaloiden aus der mexikanischen Zauberdroge Ololiuqui (*Rivea corymbosa* (L.) Hall, f.)," *Experientia*, XVI, 414–16.

HOLLISTER, LEO E., 1968. *Chemical Psychoses: LSD and Related Drugs*. Springfield, Ill.: Charles C. Thomas.

HOLMSTEDT, BO, 1965. "Tryptamine derivatives in Epená, an intoxicating snuff used by some South American tribes," *Archives Internationales de Pharmacodynamie et de Thérapie*, CLVI, 285–305.

———, 1967. "Historical Survey," in D. Efron, ed., *Ethnopharmacologic Search for Psychoactive Drugs.* Public Health Service Pub. No. 1645. Washington, D.C.: U.S. Govt. Printing Office, pp. 3–32.

———, and JAN-ERIK LINDGREN, 1967. "Chemical Constituents and Pharmacology of South American Snuffs," in D. Efron, ed., *Ethnopharmacologic Search for Psychoactive Drugs.* Public Health Service Pub. No. 1645. Washington, D.C.: U.S. Govt. Printing Office, pp. 339–73.

HOWARD, JAMES H., 1957. "The mescal bean cult of the Central and Southern Plains: an ancestor of the peyote cult?" *American Anthropologist,* LIX, 75–87.

HUERTA, INES GONZALEZ, 1960. "Identificación de la Mescalina Contenida en el Trichocereus pachanoi (San Pedro)," *Revista del Viernes Médico* (Lima), XI, 1, 133–37.

JOHNSTON, J. B., 1939. "Elements of Mazatec witchcraft," *Ethnological Studies,* IX, 119–50.

KARSTEN, R., 1920. "Berauschende und narkotische Getränke unter den Indianern Südamerikas. Beiträge zur Sittengeschichte der südamerikanischen Indianer," *Acta Academiae Aboensis Humaniora,* I, 28–72.

KLINEBERG, OTTO, 1934. "Notes on the Huichol," *American Anthropologist,* n.s., XXXVI, 446–60.

KLUCKHOHN, CLYDE, 1965. "Recurrent Themes in Myths and Mythmaking," in Alan Dundes, ed., *The Study of Folklore.* Englewood Cliffs, N.J.: Prentice-Hall.

KLUVER, HEINRICH, 1966. *Mescal and Mechanisms of Hallucinations.* Chicago: University of Chicago Press.

KNOBLOCH, FRANCISCO, 1967. "Die Aharabu-Indianer in Nordwest-Brasilien," *Collect. Inst. Anthropos,* I.

KOCH-GRUNBERG, THEODOR, 1909. *Zwei Jahre Unter den Indianern.* Berlin: Ernst Wasmuth A.-G.

———, 1917–28. *Vom Roroima zum Orinoco.* 4 vols. Berlin: D. Reimer.

LA BARRE, WESTON, 1938a. *The Peyote Cult.* New Haven, Conn.: Yale University Publications in Anthropology, No. 19.

———, 1938b. "Native American beers," *American Anthropologist,* XL, 224–34.

———, 1960. "Twenty years of peyote studies," *Current Anthropology,* I, 45–60.

———, 1964. "Le complexe narcotique de l'Amérique autochtone," *Diogène,* XLVIII. 120–34.

———, 1969. *The Peyote Cult.* Revised and augmented edition. New York: Schocken Books.

———, 1970a. "Old and new world narcotics: a statistical question and an ethnological reply," *Economic Botany,* XXIV, 73–80.

———, 1970b. Book Review: *Soma: divine mushroom of immortality,* by R. Gordon Wasson, *American Anthropologist,* LXXII, 368–73.

———, 1970c. Film Review: "To find our life: the peyote hunt of the Huichols of Mexico," *American Anthropologist,* LXXII, 5, 1201.

———, 1970d. *The Ghost Dance: The Origins of Religion.* New York: Doubleday.

LECOMTE, AUBREY, 1864. "Notes sur quelques poisons de la côte occidentale d'Afrique," *Archives Médicaux Navales,* II, 260–64.

LEETE, E., 1959. "The Alkaloids of *Datura*," in A. G. Avery, S. Satina, and J. Rietsema, eds., *Blakeslee: The Genus Datura.* New York: Ronald Press, pp. 48–56.

LEMBERGER, LOUIS, *et al.*, 1970. "Marihuana: studies on the disposition and metabolism of delta-9-tetrahydrocannabinol in man," *Science*, CLXX, 1320–22.

LEWIN, LOUIS, 1929. Banisteria Caapi, *ein neues Rauschgift und Heilmittel.* Berlin: George Stilke.

——, 1964. *Phantastica: Narcotic and Stimulating Drugs* (Transl., P. H. A. Wirth, foreword by B. Holmstedt). London: Routledge & Kegan Paul.

LÓPEZ AUSTIN, ALFREDO, 1967. "Terminos del nahuallatolli," *Historia Mexicana* (El Colegio de México), XVII, 1, 1–36.

LUMHOLTZ, CARL, 1900. "Symbolism of the Huichol Indians," *American Museum of Natural History, Memoirs*, I, No. 2, New York.

——, 1902. *Unknown Mexico.* II, New York: C. Scribner's & Sons.

LUNDSTRÖM, JAN, and STIG AGURELL, 1967. "Thin-layer chromatography of the peyote alkaloids," *Journal of Chromatography*, XXX, 271-72.

McCLEARY, JAMES A., PAUL S. SYPHERD, and DAVID L. WALKINGTON, 1960. "Antibiotic activity of an extract of peyote *Lophophora Williamsii (Lemaire) Coulter*," *Economic Botany* XIV, 247–49.

MacDOUGALL, THOMAS, 1960. *"Ipomoea tricolor:* a hallucinogenic plant of the Zapotecs," *Boletín del Centro de Investigaciones Antropológicas de México*, No. 6, 6–8.

MALLOL DE RECASENS, M. R., 1963. "Cuatro representaciones de las imágenes alucinatorias originadas por la toma de yajé," *Revista Colombiana de Folklore* (Bogotá), VIII, 61–81.

MASTERS, R. E. L., and J. HOUSTON, 1966. *The Varieties of Psychedelic Experience.* New York: Holt, Rinehart & Winston.

MAURER, DAVID W., and VICTOR H. VOGEL, 1946. "The Pancararú," in J. H. Steward, ed., *Handbook of South American Indians.* Bureau of American Ethnology Bulletin 143, 1. Washington, D.C.: U.S. Govt. Printing Office, p. 561.

——, 1969. *Narcotics and Narcotics Addiction*, 3rd ed. Springfield, Ill.: Charles C. Thomas.

MECHOULAM, RAPHAEL, 1970. "Marihuana chemistry," *Science*, CLXVIII, 3936, 1159–66.

MEULI, K., 1935. "Scythia," *Hermes*, LXX, 2, 121–76.

MILLER, WALTER S., 1966. "El Tonalamatl Mixe y los Hongos Sagrados," in *Summa Antropológica en Homenaje a Roberto J. Weitlaner.* Mexico: Instituto Nacional de Antropología e Historia, pp. 317–28.

MORS, WALTER B., and C. T. RIZZINI, 1966. *Useful Plants of Brazil.* San Francisco: Holden-Day.

MORTON, C. V., 1931. "Notes on yagé, a drug plant of southeastern Colombia," *Journal of the Washington Academy of Sciences*, XXI, 485–88.

MURILLO, A., 1889. *Plantes Médicinales du Chili.* Paris: A. Roger et F. Chernoviz, Imprimerie de Lagny, pp. 152–55.

MYERHOFF, BARBARA G., 1968. "The Deer-Maize-Peyote Complex Among the Huichol Indians of Mexico." Unpublished Ph.D. dissertation, University of California, Los Angeles. University Microfilms, Ann Arbor.

——, 1972. *The Peyote Hunt.* Ithaca, N.Y.: Cornell University Press (in press).

NADEL, S. F., 1946. "A study of shamanism in the Nuba Mountains," *Journal of the Royal Anthropological Institute*, VII, 25–37.

NARANJO, CLAUDIO, 1965. "Psychological Aspects of *Yajé* Experience in an Experimental Setting." Paper presented at the 64th annual meeting, American Anthropological Association, Denver. Mimeo.

———, 1967. "Psychotropic Properties of the Harmala Alkaloids," in D. Efron, ed., *Ethnopharmacologic Search for Psychoactive Drugs.* Washington, D.C.: U.S. Govt. Printing Office, pp. 389–91.

NARANJO, PLUTARCO, 1958. "Drogas psicotomiméticas," *Archivos de Criminología, Neuropsiquiatría y Disciplinas Conexas,* VI, 23, 358–79.

———, 1969. "Etnofarmacología de las plantas psicotrópicas de América," *Terapia,* XXIV, 5–63.

———, 1970. *Ayahuasca, Religión y Medicina.* Quito, Ecuador: Editorial Universitaria.

NEAL, J. M., and J. L. McLAUGHLIN, 1970. "Cactus alkaloids. IX. Isolation of N-methyl-3,4-dimethoxy-phenethylamine and N-methyl-4methoxy-phenethylamine from *Ariocarpus retusus,*" *Lloydia,* XXXIII, 3, 395–96.

NEWCOMB, W. W., JR., 1967. *The Rock Art of Texas.* Paintings by Forrest Kirkland. Austin: The University of Texas Press.

O'CONNELL, F. D., and E. V. LYNN, 1953. "The alkaloids of *Banisteriopsis inebrians* Morton," *Journal of the American Pharmaceutical Association,* XLII, 753–54.

OPLER, MARVIN K., 1970. "Cross-cultural Uses of Psychoactive Drugs (Ethnopsychopharmacology)," in W. G. Clark and J. del Giudice, eds., *Principles of Psychopharmacology.* New York: Academic Press, pp. 31–47.

ORTEGA, JOSÉ, 1887. *Historia del Nayarit.* Mexico (originally published under the title *Apostólicos Afanes de la Compañia de Jesús, en la América Septentrional,* Barcelona, 1754).

OSMOND, HUMPHREY, 1955. "Ololiuqui: the ancient Aztec narcotic," *Journal of Mental Science,* CI, 526–27.

———, 1957. "A review of the clinical effects of psychotomimetic agents," *Annals of the New York Academy of Science,* LXVI, 418.

OSTER, GERALD, 1970. "Phosphenes," *Scientific American,* CCXXII, 2, 83–87.

PAHNKE, WALTER N., *et al,* 1970. "The experimental use of psychedelic (LSD) psychotherapy," *The Journal of the American Medical Association,* CCXII, No. 11, 1856–63.

PARDAL, R., 1937. "Medicina aborigen americana," *Humanior,* Sección C, 3.

PENNES, H. H., and P. H. HOCH, 1957. "Psychotomimetics, clinical and theoretical considerations: harmine, Win-2299 and naline," *American Journal of Psychiatry,* CXIII, 887–92.

PENNINGTON, CAMPBELL W., 1963. *The Tarahumar of Mexico—Their Environment and Material Culture.* Salt Lake City: University of Utah Press.

———, 1969. *The Tepehuan of Chihuahua—Their Material Culture.* Salt Lake City: University of Utah Press.

PÉREZ ARBELÁEZ, ENRIQUE, 1956. *Plantas Utiles de Colombia.* Tercera edición. Bogotá.

PÉREZ DE BARRADAS, JOSÉ, 1950. "Drogas ilusionogenas de los indios americanos," *Antropología y Etnología,* No. 3, 9–107. Consejo Superior de Investigaciones Científicas, Madrid.

PÉREZ DE RIBAS, ANDRÉS, 1944. *Historia de los Triunfos de N.S. Fe Entre Gentes Mas Barbaras y Fieras del Nuevo Orbe* (Madrid, 1645), México: Editorial Layac.

PERROT, E., and R. HAMET, 1927a. "Le yagé, plante sensorielle des Indiens de la région amazonienne de l'Equateur et de la Colombie," *Compte Rendu de l'Académie des Sciences,* CLXXXIV, 1266.

————, 1927b. "Yagé, ayahuasca, caapi et leur alcaloïde: télépathine ou yagéine," *Bulletin des Sciences Pharmalogiques*, XXXIV, 337–47, 417–26, 500–14.

PHILIPPI, R. A., 1858. *"Latua Ph.,* ein neues Genus der Solanaceen," *Botanische Zeitung*, XVI, 33, 241–42.

POISSON, J., 1960. "The presence of mescaline in a Peruvian cactus," *Annales Pharmaceutiques Françaises*, XVIII, 764–65.

————, 1965. "Note sur le 'natem,' boisson toxique peruvienne et ses alcaloides," *Annales Pharmaceutiques Françaises*, XXIII, 241–44.

POPE, H., 1969. "Tabernanthe iboga: an African narcotic plant of social importance," *Economic Botany*, XXIII, 2 (April–June), 174–84.

POYNTER, F. N. L., and H. LEI, 1969. Cited in Frederic Rosengarten, Jr., *The Book of Spices*. Wynnewood, Pa.: Livingstone Publishing Co., p. 19.

PRANCE, GHILLEAN, 1970. "Notes on the use of plant hallucinogens in Amazonian Brazil," *Economic Botany*, XXIV, 62–68.

————, and ANNE E. PRANCE, 1970. "Hallucinations in Amazonia," *The Garden Journal*, XX, 102–07.

PREUSS, K. TH., 1908. "Die religiösen Gesänge und Mythen einiger Stämme der mexikanischen Sierra Madre," *Archiv für Religionswissenschaft*, XI. Leipzig: B. G. Teubner, pp. 369–98.

RAVICZ, ROBERT, 1961. "La Mixteca en el estudio comparativo del hongo alucinante," *Annales del Instituto Nacional de Antropología e Historia, 1960,* XIII, 73–92.

REICHEL-DOLMATOFF, GERARDO, 1960. "Notas etnográficas sobre los indios del Chocó," *Revista Colombiana de Antropología,* IX, 75–158.

————, 1967. "Rock paintings of the Vaupés: an essay of interpretation," *Folklore Americas*, XXVII, 2, 107–13.

————, 1968. *Desana: Simbolismo de los Indios Tukano del Vaupés*. Bogotá, Colombia: Universidad de los Andes.

————, 1969. "El contexto cultural de un alucinógeno aborigen: *Banisteriopsis Caapi*," *Revista de la Academia Colombiana de Ciencias Exactas, Físicas y Naturales*, XIII, 327–45.

————, 1971. *Amazonian Cosmos. The Sexual and Religious Symbolism of the Tukano Indians*. Chicago: University of Chicago Press.

REINBERG, P., 1921. "Contribution à l'étude des boissons toxiques des Indiens du nord-ouest de l'Amazone, l'ayahuasca, le yajé, le huanto," *Journal de la Société des Américanistes de Paris*, n.s., XIII, 25–54, 197–216.

REKO, B. P., 1934. "Das mexikanische Rauschgift Ololiuqui," *El México Antiguo*, III, 3–4, 1–7.

REKO, V. A., 1949. *Magische Gifte: Rausch- und Betäubungsmittel der Neuen Welt*. Stuttgart: F. Enke.

RIOS, OSCAR, 1962. "Aspectos preliminares al estudio fármaco-psiquiátrico del ayahuasca y su principio activo," *Anales de la Facultad de Medicina*, Universidad Nacional Mayor de San Marcos, XLV, 22–66.

ROBICHAUD, R. C., M. H. MALONE, and A. E. SCHWARTING. 1964. "Pharmacodynamics of cryogenine, an alkaloid isolated from *Heimia salicifolia* Link and Otto, part I," *Archives Internationales de Pharmaco-dynamie et de Thérapie*, CL, 220–32.

ROCHA, JOAQUIN, 1905. *Memorandum de Viaje: Regiones Amazónicas*. Bogotá.

RODRIGUEZ SUY SUY, VICTOR ANTONIO, 1970. La medicina tradicional en la costa norte del Perú actual," *XXXIX Congreso de Americanistas*, Lima (in press).

ROSZAK, THEODORE, 1969. *The Making of a Counter Culture.* New York: Doubleday.

ROUHIER, ALEXANDRE, 1926. "Les plantes divinatoires," *Revue Métapsychique,* pp. 325–31.

———, 1927. *La Plante Qui Fait les Yeux Émerveillés—le Peyote.* Paris: Gaston Doin et Cie.

RUIZ DE ALARCÓN, HERNANDO, 1892. "Tratado de las Supersticiones y Costumbres Gentílicas Que oy Viuen Entre los Indios Naturales Desta Nueua España (1629)." Francisco del Paso y Troncoso, ed., *Anales del Museo Nacional de México,* ep. I, VI, 123–223.

RUSBY, H. H., 1923. "The aboriginal uses of *caapi*," *Journal of the American Pharmaceutical Association,* XII, 1123 ff.

SAFFORD, WILLIAM EDWIN, 1916. "Identity of Cohoba, the narcotic snuff of ancient Haiti," *Journal of the Washington Academy of Sciences,* VI, 548–62.

———, 1917. "Narcotic plants and stimulants of the ancient Americans," in *Annual Report of the Smithsonian Institution for 1916.* Washington, D.C.: U.S. Govt. Printing Office, pp. 387–424.

———, 1920. "Daturas of the Old World and New," *ibid., 1920.* pp. 537–67.

———, 1921. "Peyote, the narcotic mescal button of the Indians," *Journal of the American Medical Association,* LXXVII, 1278–79.

SAHAGUN, FRAY BERNADINO DE, 1950–63. *The Florentine Codex.* General History of the Things of New Spain. Transl., Arthur J. O. Anderson and Charles E. Dibble, Santa Fé, New Mexico: The School of American Research and the University of Utah.

SALMAN, D. H., and R. H. PRINCE, eds., 1967. "Do psychedelics have religious implications?" *Proceedings of the 3rd Annual Conference, R. M. Bucke Memorial Society for the Study of Religious Experience.*

SANTESSON, C. G., 1937a. "Notiz über Piule, eine mexikanische Rauschdroge," *Ethnologische Studien,* IV.

———, 1937b. "Piule, eine mexikanische Rauschdroge," *Archiv der Pharmazie und Berichte der Deutschen Pharmazeutischen Gesellschaft,* pp. 532–37.

———, 1938. "Noch eine mexikanische 'Piule'—Droge—*Semina Rhynchosiae phaseoloides D.C,*" *Ethnologische Studien,* VI, 179–83.

SANTOSCOY, ALBERTO, 1899. *Nayarit. Colección de Documentos Inéditos, Históricos y Etnográficos, Acerca de la Sierra de Ese Nombre.* Guadalajara.

SATINA, S., and A. G. AVERY, 1959, in Avery, A. G., S. Satina and J. Rietsema, eds., "A Review of the Taxonomic History of Datura." In: *Blakeslee: The genus Datura,* pp. 16–47. New York: Ronald Press.

SCHULTES, RICHARD EVANS, 1937. "Peyote (*Lophophora Williamsii* [Lemaire] Coulter) and Its Uses." Unpublished Ph.D. thesis, Harvard University, Cambridge, Mass.

———, 1938. "The appeal of peyote (*Lophophora Williamsii*) as a medicine," *American Anthropologist,* XL, 698–715.

———, 1939. "Plantae Mexicanae II. The identification of teonanacatl, the narcotic Basidiomycete of the Aztecs," *Botanical Museum Leaflets,* Harvard University, VII, 37–54.

———, 1940a. "Teonanacatl—the narcotic mushroom of the Aztecs," *American Anthropologist,* XLII, 429–43.

———, 1940b. "The aboriginal therapeutic use of *Lophophora Williamsii,*" *Cactus and Succulent Journal,* XII, 177–81.

———, 1941. *A Contribution to Our Knowledge of Rivea Corymbosa, the*

Narcotic Ololiuqui of the Aztecs, Botanical Museum of Harvard University, Cambridge, Mass.

———, 1954a. "Plantae Austro-Americanae IX," *Botanical Museum Leaflets,* Harvard University, XVI, 202–03.

———, 1954b. "A new narcotic snuff from the northwest Amazon," *ibid.,* XVI, 241–60.

———, 1955. "A new narcotic genus from the Amazon slope of the Colombian Andes," *ibid.,* XVII, 1–11.

———, 1957. "The identity of the malpighiaceous narcotics of South America," *ibid.,* XVIII, 1–56.

———, 1960. "Tapping our heritage of ethnobotanical lore," *Economic Botany,* XIV, 257–62.

———, 1961a. "Native narcotics of the New World," *Texas Journal of Pharmacy,* I, 141–67.

———, 1961b. "Botany attacks the hallucinogens," *ibid.,* pp. 168–85.

———, 1962. "The role of the ethnobotanist in the search for new medicinal plants," *Lloydia,* XXV, 257–66.

———, 1963a. "Botanical sources of the New World narcotics," *Psychedelic Review,* I, 145–66.

———, 1963b. "Hallucinogenic plants of the New World," *Harvard Review,* I, 18–32.

———, 1965. "Ein halbes Jahrhundert Ethnobotanik amerikanischer Hallucinogene," *Planta Medica,* XIII, 126–57.

———, 1966. "The search for new natural hallucinogens," *Lloydia,* XXIX, 293–308.

———, 1967a. "The Botanical Origin of South American Snuffs," in D. Efron, ed., *Ethnopharmacologic Search for Psychoactive Drugs.* U.S. Public Health Service Pub. No. 1645. Washington, D.C.: U.S. Govt. Printing Office, pp. 291–306.

———, 1967b. "The Place of Ethnobotany in the Ethnopharmacologic Search for Psychotomimetic Drugs," *ibid.,* pp. 33–57.

———, 1968. "Some impacts of Spruce's Amazon explorations on modern phytochemical research," *Rhodora,* LXX, 313–39.

———, 1969a. "Hallucinogens of plant origin," *Science,* CLXIII, 245–54.

———, 1969b. "De plantis toxicariis e Mundo Novo tropicale commentationes V. *Virola* as an orally administered hallucinogen," *Botanical Museum Leaflets,* Harvard University, XI, 229–40.

———, 1969c. "The plant kingdom and hallucinogens," *Bulletin on Narcotics,* XXI, 3, 3–16; 4, 15–27; XXII (1970), 25–53.

———, 1969d. "The Unfolding Panorama of the New World Hallucinogens," in J. E. Gunckel, ed., *Current Topics in Plant Science.* New York: Academic Press, pp. 336–54.

———, 1970a. "The botanical and chemical distribution of hallucinogens," *Annual Review of Plant Physiology,* XXI, 571–98.

———, 1970b. "The New World Indians and their hallucinogens," *Bull. Morris Arb.,* XXI, 3–14.

———, and ALBERT HOFMANN, 1972. *The Botany and Chemistry of Hallucinogens.* Springfield, Ill.: Charles C. Thomas (in press).

———, and BO HOLMSTEDT, 1968. "De plantis toxicariis e Mundo Novo tropicale commentationes II," *Rhodora,* LXX, 113–60.

———, BO HOLMSTEDT, and JAN-ERIK LINDGREN, 1969. "De plantis toxicariis e

Mundo Novo tropicale commentationes III. Phytochemical examination of Spruce's original collection of *Banisteriopsis Caapi,*" *Botanical Museum Leaflets,* Harvard University, XXII, 121–32.

———, and ROBERT F. RAFFAUF, 1960. *"Prestonia:* an Amazon narcotic or not?" *ibid.,* XII, 109–22.

SEITZ, GEORG, 1965. "Einige Bemerkungen zur Anwendung und Wirkungsweise des *Epena*-Schnupfpulvers der *Waika*-Indianer," *Etnologiska Studier,* No. 28, 117–32.

———, 1967. "Epéná, the intoxicating snuff powder of the Waika Indians and the Tukano medicine man, Agostino," in D. Efron, ed., *Ethnopharmacologic Search for New Psychoactive Drugs.* U.S. Public Health Service Pub. No. 1645. Washington, D.C.: U.S. Govt. Printing Office, pp. 315–38.

SHONLE, RUTH, 1925. "Peyote, the giver of visions," *American Anthropologist,* XXVII, 53–75.

SINGER, ROLF, 1958. "Mycological investigations on teonanácatl, the Mexican hallucinogenic mushroom. Part I. The history of teonanácatl, field work and culture work," *Mycologia,* L, 239–61.

———, and ALEXANDER H. SMITH, 1958. "Mycological investigations on teonanácatl, the Mexican hallucinogenic mushroom. Part II. A taxonomic monograph of *Psilocybe,* section *Caerulescentes,*" *ibid.,* 262–303.

SLOTKIN, JAMES S., 1955–56. "The peyote way," *Tomorrow,* IV, 3, 64–70.

———, 1956. *The Peyote Religion.* Glencoe, Ill.: The Free Press.

SÖDERBLOM, NATHAN, 1968. *Rus och Religion.* Uppsala, Sweden: Bokfenix.

SOLOMON, D., 1966. *The Marihuana Papers.* Indianapolis: Bobbs-Merrill.

SPRUCE, RICHARD, 1908. *Notes of a Botanist on the Amazon and Andes,* 2 vols. London: The Macmillan Co.

STRADELLI, E., 1890. "L'Uaupés e gli Uaupés," *Bollettino della Società Geografica Italiana,* serie III, 3, 425–53.

TAYLOR, NORMAN, 1949. *Flight from Reality.* New York: Duell, Sloan and Pearce.

THOMPSON, J. ERIC S., 1970. "Tobacco Among the Maya and Their Neighbors," in his *Maya History and Religion.* Norman, Calif.: University of California Press, pp. 103–23.

TOZZER, ALFRED M., 1907. *A Comparative Study of the Mayas and Lacandones.* Archaeological Institute of America. New York: Macmillan.

TURNER, WILLIAM J., 1963. "Experiences with primary process thinking," *The Psychiatric Quarterly* (July), pp. 1–13.

———, and JACK J. HEYMAN, 1961. "The presence of mescaline in *Opuntia cylindrica (Trichocereus pachanoi),*" *Journal of Organic Chemistry,* XXV, 2250.

TYLER, VARRO E., JR., 1966. "The physiological properties and chemical constituents of some habit-forming plants," *Lloydia,* XXIX, 275–92

UNDERHILL, RUTH M., 1965. *Red Man's Religion.* Chicago: University of Chicago Press.

URBINA, MANUEL, 1903. "El peyote y el ololiuqui," *Anales del Museo Nacional* (Mexico), VII, 25–38.

USCÁTEGUI M., NESTOR, 1959. "The present distribution of narcotics and stimulants amongst the Indian tribes of Colombia," *Botanical Museum Leaflets,* Harvard University, XVIII, 273–304.

———, 1960. "Distribución actual de las plantas narcóticas y estimulantes usadas por las tribus indígenas de Colombia," *Revista de la Academia Colombiana de Ciencias Exactas, Físicas y Naturales,* XI, 215–28.

VESTAL, PAUL A., and RICHARD EVANS SCHULTES, 1939. *The Economic Botany of the Kiowa Indians as It Relates to the History of the Tribe,* Botanical Museum of Harvard University, Cambridge, Mass.

VILLAVICENCIO, MANUEL, 1858. *Geografía de la República del Ecuador.* New York.

WAGLEY, CHARLES, and EDUARDO GALVAO, 1949. *The Tenetehara Indians of Brazil.* New York: Columbia University Press.

WAGNER, G., 1932. "Entwicklung und Verbreitung des Peyote-Kultes," *Baessler Archiv,* Völkerkunde 15, pp. 59–144.

WALKER, A. RAPONDA, and ROGER SILLANS, 1961. *Les Plantes Utiles du Gabon.* Paris.

WASSÉN, S. HENRY, 1964. "Some general viewpoints in the study of native drugs especially from the West Indies and South America," *Ethnos,* Nos. 1–2, 97–120.

——, 1965. "The use of some specific kinds of South American Indian snuff and related paraphernalia," *Etnologiska Studier,* No. 28.

——, and BO HOLMSTEDT, 1963. "The use of parica in ethnological and pharmacological review," *Ethnos,* No. 1, 5–45.

WASSON, R. GORDON, 1956. "Lightning-bolt and mushrooms: an essay in early cultural exploration," in *Festschrift for Roman Jakobson.* The Hague: Mouton, pp. 605–12.

——, 1958. "The divine mushroom: primitive religion and hallucinatory agents," *Proceedings of the American Philosophical Society,* CII, 221–23.

——, 1961. "The hallucinogenic fungi of Mexico: an inquiry into the origin of religious ideas among primitive peoples," *Botanical Museum Leaflets,* Harvard University, XIX, 7, 137–62.

——, 1962. "A new Mexican psychotropic drug from the mint family," *ibid.,* XX, 77–84.

——, 1963a. "The hallucinogenic mushrooms of Mexico and psilocybin: a bibliography" (2nd printing, with corrections and addenda), *ibid.,* 25–73.

——, 1963b. "Notes on the present status of *Ololiuqui* and the other hallucinogens of Mexico," *Botanical Museum Leaflets,* Harvard University, XX, 161–93.

——, 1966. "Ololiuhqui and the other hallucinogens of Mexico," in *Summa Antropológica en Homenaje a Roberto J. Weitlaner.* Mexico: Instituto Nacional de Antropología e Historia, pp. 329–48.

——, 1968. *SOMA, Divine Mushroom of Immortality.* Ethno-Mycological Studies, No. 1. New York: Harcourt, Brace & World. New edition, 1971, by Harcourt, Brace Jovanovich.

——, and VALENTINA P. WASSON, 1957. *Mushrooms, Russia and History.* New York: Pantheon Books.

WEIL, ANDREW T., 1972. *The Natural Mind.* Boston: Houghton, Mifflin (in press).

——, and N. E. ZINBERG, 1969. "Acute effects of marihuana on speech," *Nature,* CCXXII, pp. 434–37.

——, N. E. ZINBERG, and J. M. NELSEN, 1968. "Clinical and psychological effects of marihuana in man," *Science,* CLXII, 1234–42.

WILBERT, JOHANNES, 1957. "Rasgos culturales circuncaribes entre los Warrau y sus inferencias," *Memoria de la Sociedad de Ciencias Naturales La Salle* (Caracas), XVI, 45, 237–57.

——, 1963. *Indios de la Región Orinoco-Ventuari.* Monografía No. 8. Caracas: Fundación La Salle de Ciencias Naturales.

——, 1970. *Folk Literature of the Warao Indians.* Latin American Studies

Series, Vol. 15. Los Angeles: Latin American Center, University of California.

———, 1972. *Survivors of Eldorado*. New York: Praeger Publishers, Inc.

WILLIAMS GARCIA, ROBERTO, 1963. *Los Tepehuas*. Jalapa, Mexico: Universidad Veracruzana, Instituto de Antropología.

WITTMACK, L., n.d. See Reininger, W., "Remnants from prehistoric times," in *Ciba Symposia*.

WURDACK, JOHN, 1958. "Indian narcotics in southern Venezuela," *Garden Journal*, VIII, 116–18.

ZERRIES, OTTO, 1964. *Waiká. Die Kulturgeschichtliche Stellung der Waiká-Indianer des Oberen Orinoko in Rahmen der Völkerkunde Südamerikas.* Munich: Klaus Renner Verlag.

———, 1969. "Primitive South America and the West Indies," in E. O. James, ed., *Pre-Columbian American Religions*. History of Religion Series. New York: Holt, Rinehart & Winston, pp. 230–358.

ZINGG, ROBERT, 1938. *The Huichols: Primitive Artists*. New York: G. E. Stechert.

Index

The Contributors

William A. Emboden, Jr., is Professor of Biology, San Fernando Valley State College, Northridge, California, and Consultant in Botany to the Museum of Natural History of Los Angeles County. A specialist in narcotic plants and author of many scientific articles, Dr. Emboden has served as a consultant in legal cases involving hallucinogens. His most recent book is *Narcotic Plants* (1972).

James W. Fernandez is Professor of Anthropology at Dartmouth College and consultant and lecturer at the Foreign Service Institute, Washington, D.C. Dr. Fernandez has done extensive field research in Africa and on the Iberian Peninsula and is a frequent contributor to professional journals.

Peter T. Furst is Professor of Anthropology and Chairman of the Department of Anthropology at the State University of New York at Albany. He has written extensively on contemporary Mexican Indian religion and symbolism and on pre-Columbian art. Author of a forthcoming book on the pre-Columbian art and civilization of Mexico, Dr. Furst was formerly Associate Director of the University of California at Los Angeles Latin American Center.

Weston La Barre is well known for his work on the anthropology and psychology of religion. Among his best-known books are *The Peyote Cult* (1938), *They Shall Take Up Serpents: Psychology of the Southern Snake-handling Cult* (1962), and, most recently, *The Ghost Dance: The Origins of Religion* (1970). A long-time member of the anthropology faculty at

Duke University, Dr. La Barre was recently appointed James B. Duke Professor of Anthropology.

Gerardo Reichel-Dolmatoff, a distinguished Colombian anthropologist and formerly Chairman of Anthropology at the Universidad de los Andes in Bogotá, is the author of numerous books in Spanish and English on the ethnology and archaeology of Colombia. His most recent book is *Amazonian Cosmos: The Sexual and Religious Symbolism of the Tukano Indians* (1971).

Richard Evans Schultes is Director of the Botanical Museum and Professor of Botany, Harvard University. One of the world's leading authorities on hallucinogenic plants, Dr. Schultes is author of numerous scientific papers. His books include *Botany and Chemistry of Hallucinogens* (1944), written with Dr. Albert Hofmann, the discoverer of LSD.

Douglas Sharon, after several years of archaeological and ethnological field research in Peru and Mexico, is preparing for his doctoral degree in anthropology at the University of California at Los Angeles.

R. Gordon Wasson is a distinguished amateur ethnomycologist whose researches into the historical and cultural roles of hallucinogenic mushrooms in Mexico and the Old World have brought him international scholarly recognition. A former vice-president of J. P. Morgan and Company, he began his studies as an avocation in 1927. They culminated in such well-known works as *Mushrooms, Russia and History* (1957), written with his wife, the late Valentina P. Wasson, and, most recently, *Soma: Divine Mushroom of Immortality* (1968, 1971).

Johannes Wilbert is Professor of Anthropology and Director of the Latin American Center, University of California at Los Angeles. Recognized as one of the leading ethnologists of South American Indians, Dr. Wilbert is the author of many scientific articles, monographs, and books on the Indian cultures of northern South America. Among his most recent books are *Folk Literature of the Warao Indians* (1970) and *Survivors of Eldorado: Four Indian Cultures of South America* (1972).